THE
SCIENCE EDUCATION
OF
American Girls

THE
SCIENCE
EDUCATION
OF
American Girls

A Historical Perspective

Kim Tolley

RoutledgeFalmer
NEW YORK AND LONDON

Published in 2003 by

RoutledgeFalmer
29 West 35th Street
New York, New York 10001

Published in Great Britain by

RoutledgeFalmer
11 New Fetter Lane
London EC4P 4EE

RoutledgeFalmer is an imprint of the Taylor & Francis Group.
Copyright © 2003 by RoutledgeFalmer

Printed in the United States of America on acid-free paper.

Chapter Two, "Science for Ladies, Classics for Gentlemen," first appeared as Kimberly Tolley, "Science for Ladies, Classics for Gentlemen: A Comparative Analysis of Scientific Subjects in the Curricula of Boys' and Girls' Secondary Schools in the United States, 1794–1850," History of Education Quarterly, 36 (summer 1996): 129–153. © History of Education Society. Reprinted by permission.

Frontispiece, cover illustration:
"Astronomy," in Thomas Smith's *The Scientific Library* 1815, © American Antiquarian Society.

Cover illustrations:
"Girl Performing a Science Experiment," in Richard G. Parker's *Juvenile Philosophy: or, Philosophy in Familiar Conversations* (1857 [1850]), courtesy of Cubberley Library, Stanford University.

"The Botanist," in (ed.) Charles Peters's *The Girl's Own Outdoor Book* (1889), courtesy of The Ohio State University Libraries, Columbus.

10 9 8 7 6 5 4 3 2 1

Library of Congress Cataloging-in-Publication Data
Tolley, Kimberley.
    The science education of American girls : a historical perspective /
Kim Tolley.
        p. cm. — (Studies in the history of education)
Includes bibliographical references and index.
    ISBN 0-415-93472-9 (hardcover : alk. paper) — ISBN 0-415-93473-7
(pbk. : alk. paper)
    1. Science—Study and teaching—United States—History. 2.
Women—Education—United States—History. I. Title. II. Studies in the
history of education (RoutledgeFalmer (Firm))
    Q183.3.A1 T66 2002
    507.1'073—dc21

                                                    2002010793

To Emma and Nathan,
my daughter and son

Series Preface

The RoutledgeFalmer Studies in the History of Education series includes not only volumes on the history of American and Western education, but also on the history of the development of education in non-Western societies. A major goal of this series is to provide new interpretations of educational history that are based on the best recent scholarship; each volume will provide an original analysis and interpretation of the topic under consideration. A wide variety of methodological approaches from the traditional to the innovative are used. In addition, this series especially welcomes studies that focus not only on schools but also on education as defined by Harvard historian Bernard Bailyn: "the transmission of culture across generations."

The major criteria for inclusion are (a) a manuscript of the highest quality, and (b) a topic of importance to understanding the field. The editor is open to readers' suggestions and looks forward to a long-term dialogue with them on the future direction of the series.

Edward R. Beauchamp

Studies in the History of Education
Edward R. Beauchamp, Series Editor

Contents

Illustrations

Tables

Acknowledgments

This book has come to fruition with the support and assistance of many individuals and institutions. I am particularly indebted to those at the University of California at Berkeley who first introduced me to the pleasures of historical research: Roger Hahn and Geraldine Jonçich Clifford. Geraldine Clifford served as my dissertation advisor at Berkeley and will always remain an important role model for my work as a historian. Because key primary sources for this study are scattered in special collections across the country, much of the initial research for this project would not have been possible without a grant from the Vice Chancellor for Research at Berkeley, for which I am very grateful.

A number of scholars provided sound advice and encouragement along the way, including Nancy Beadie, Barbara Beatty, Lawrence Lowery, and John David Miller. For their careful reading of the manuscript and suggestions for improvement, I would like to thank Joan Burstyn, Linda Eisenmann, and Patricia Ann Palmieri. Over the past several years, this study has been waylaid by the requirements of teaching, administration, family, and my attention to other projects, including a book on American academies. In the long run, this delay has been beneficial, because interactions with other scholars working on the antebellum period has helped to clarify my thinking in regards to the issues addressed in this book. In particular, I would like to acknowledge a debt to James Albisetti, Roger Geiger, Bruce Leslie, and Margaret A. Nash. Several scholars generously shared their expertise, suggesting sources or further avenues for research. Among this group, I would like to thank Victoria-Maria MacDonald and Jana Nidiffer. In particular, I am grateful to the late Paul Hurd at Stanford for suggesting that I dig deeper into the nature-study movement.

Librarians and archivists were unfailingly helpful in my research, which led to university libraries and state historical societies in California, Illinois, Massachusetts, New York, North Carolina, Ohio, and Wisconsin. The reference librarians at Cornell University and Ohio State University, Columbus, deserve special praise for their ability to locate seemingly obscure documents among unprocessed additions. The staff of Cubberley Library at Stanford University unfailingly complied with my unending requests for eighteenth- and nineteenth-century textbooks locked behind glass cabinet doors and journals stored deep in the basement. I would like to thank Barbara Celone and Kelly Roll for their assistance with the process of creating reproductions from some of the texts in Cubberley's collection. John Frederick deserves my unending gratitude for sharing his thorough documentation of the unprocessed science textbooks in the Emanual Rudolph Collection at Ohio State University Special Collections.

Finally, I would like to thank those individuals whose support and encouragement has helped me throughout various stages of this project. Carole Swain and my former colleagues at Saint Mary's College, California, constituted an important support group for the early phases of this research. Diane Guay of Notre Dame de Namur University expressed strong support and encouragement during my years at that institution, and when I resigned a tenure-track position there to devote more time to family and research, she provided astute insight and advice to help me make the transition. Kathleen Murphy and Kathleen Cruikshank's optimistic faith and continual prompts to "send the manuscript to a publisher tomorrow" helped enormously. Ron Davies converted my original thesis, originally composed in Wordstar, to Microsoft Word and, without his help, I might have been permanently stalled in an obsolete word-processing program.

Various members of the History of Education Society have been extremely helpful, either in offering suggestions for improving my writing or in providing ideas for possible publishers. In particular, I would like to thank B. Edward McClellan, William J. Reese, Robert A. Levin, and Richard Altenbaugh. I would also like to thank the members of the History of Education Society's Henry Barnard Prize Committee for honoring the second chapter with the Henry Barnard Prize.

For encouragement and confidence in this project, I thank Joe Miranda, education editor at Routledge/Falmer, and his assistant, Paul Foster Johnson. Richard Rothschild adroitly shepherded this volume through production, and Kathleen Achor's thoughtful and meticulous copyedits improved the final manuscript.

One of the greatest pleasures of working on this project has been the opportunity to discuss and share ideas with a historian very close to me: my husband, Bruce Tolley. His support and encouragement were key factors in the successful completion of this study. He read every chapter, showed compassion and caring during the occasional moments of frustration, and thankfully reminded me to keep a good sense of humor throughout.

Introduction

"Females, in particular, are not expected to enter into the recesses of the temple of science," wrote the female educator Almira Phelps in 1846. "[I]t is but of late that they have been encouraged to approach even to its portals, and to venture a glance upon the mysteries therein."[1] More than a hundred years after Phelps wrote these words, young women appeared to have made little—if any—progress. In 1959, after surveying the attitudes of American high school students toward science, the anthropologist Margaret Mead concluded that the student most often identified by teachers and fellow students as a future scientist was "almost always a boy."[2]

Over the past several decades, a number of scholars have drawn attention to continuing inequities in the science and mathematics achievement of adolescents. Recent research in the field of science education suggests that girls in particular feel alienated from science and develop low self-esteem and a lack of confidence in science beginning as early as elementary school. Once they reach high school or college, most admit that they take science courses only to fulfill requirements for college admission, not because they view science as a worthwhile field of study.[3] Many educators and policy makers appear to believe that this state of affairs has always been present in American education. According to one author, "Boys have historically outscored girls in math." Similarly, the American Association for the Advancement of Science reports in a recent document, "In the past, [girls] have largely been bypassed in science and mathematics education."[4] As pervasive as this belief appears to be among modern science educators, the research undertaken for this study reveals a surprisingly different picture.

Proportionally more girls than boys studied science in many early nineteenth-century academies. Such historical sources as school catalogs, newspaper advertisements, textbooks, and contemporary accounts indicate that by the midnineteenth century, a greater percentage of girls' higher schools offered natural philosophy (physics), astronomy, and chemistry than did comparable institutions for boys. Of course, we know that this situation did not persist throughout the century. As historians have noted, by the 1930s boys outnumbered girls in most science and mathematics courses in private and public secondary schools across the country.[5] How and why this shift occurred is the focus of the following chapters.

It is a central conclusion of this study that women and men alike played active roles in discouraging girls from pursuing the advanced study of science and mathematics in the early twentieth century. Discrimination and barriers to access established by leading men in the scientific and education communities played an important part. Still, documentary sources indicate that such obstacles accounted for only half of the story. On their own initiative, seeking access to higher education, aiming to create a broad coalition among women to fight for suffrage, and desiring to elevate the status of "women's work," many women turned their backs on science, a field in which women had once placed great hopes for occupational and personal fulfillment. The choices made by both sexes in the first decades of the twentieth century, strengthened and institutionalized in school policy and curriculum during later periods of economic and political upheaval, ultimately resulted in long-range negative effects on the enrollments of girls in advanced science and mathematics courses at the secondary level. The institutional legacies of that era endured for decades.

The following chapters cast an extensive net in order to capture and analyze three related curricular transformations. The first is the cultural construction of the physical sciences, from subjects that postcolonial parents and educators construed as particularly suited to females, to predominantly male domains a century and a half later. The second is a parallel 180-degree shift, from the eighteenth-century view that women were incapable of studying the classics to the commonly expressed twentieth-century opinion that the study of Latin was inherently more appealing to girls than to boys. The third, occurring within the context of women's growing occupational opportunities and increased political activism, is the eventual inclusion of homemaking and other vocational subjects in the secondary school curriculum, additions that ultimately contributed to declining female enrollments in advanced science and mathematics courses. All three transformations occurred in response to economic, demographic, political, and cultural changes, as well as to wide-ranging debates among men and women over the presumed differences between the sexes, debates that centered on women's inherent abilities, economic opportunities, and growing political power.

Why focus on the historical experiences of adolescents? After having made significant progress at the turn of the century, the proportion of women earning advanced academic degrees in the sciences declined significantly from 1920 to 1960. Currently, scholars are unsure of the reasons underlying this trend. Explanations for the reduction in the proportion of women earning doctorates in the sciences during this period include a diminishment of feminist activism following the suffrage victory in 1920, greater restrictions on job opportunities for women during the Great Depression, continuing job discrimination against women in the 1940s and 1950s, or the sudden rise in births after World War II.[6] To date, researchers have given little attention to factors influencing student enrollments in high schools during these years.

There are compelling reasons to include secondary institutions in historical analyses of women and science. From the time that colleges and universities first opened their doors to women, secondary schools have always been an important part of the so-called pipeline that leads ultimately to careers in science. A decline in the numbers of students entering colleges and universities with sufficient background, aptitude, or interest in science would inevitably affect the pool of students available to enter science majors as freshmen. Recently, scholars studying factors influencing women to take up careers in science have concluded that positive experiences and success in high school serve as the most consistent and important predictors of students' future interest in science. Thus, experiences at the secondary level, including grades and scores on college entrance examinations, "have a significant effect on both men's and women's decision to enter science majors as freshmen, as well as on their ultimate choice of a science career."[7]

Today, a developing body of critical literature on women and science attests to an ongoing discussion over the extent to which the interests of science may be antithetical to feminist concerns. Because current historical explanations of girls' relative lack of interest or achievement in science are primarily based on analyses of the experiences of women in the sciences, many of the explanations regarding the performance of girls at the secondary level mirror the theories about why women at the college and professional level do not attain similar levels of achievement as do their male counterparts. Feminist scholars have identified both structural and cultural obstacles that hinder women's progress in science. The reasons given for women's relative lack of success in science fall into two general categories: *deficit theories* and *difference theories*.[8] Deficit theories focus on the ways that women and girls experience discriminatory treatment in science, and difference theories emphasize presumed cultural, biological, or philosophical distinctions between the two sexes.

Researchers working within the framework of deficit theories have identified both formal and informal structural obstacles that contribute to the discrimination faced by women. Formal structural obstacles include the differential admission rules of colleges and universities; admission policies in scientific associations; and gender discrimination that denies women access to good entry-level jobs, promotions, tenure, and research funding.[9] Federal and state legislation passed in the last decades of the twentieth century eliminated any legal basis for the maintenance of formal structural obstacles, and yet full gender equity remains elusive within the scientific professions. Therefore, recent scholarship has focused on the informal barriers that women face within the social system of science. These may include reduced access to such strategic resources as social networks and mentors. Compared with male scientists, women may be more socially isolated from mentors, who are usually male. Thus, women tend to remain in the "outer circle," remote from the influential clique of key researchers, administrators, and scientific power brokers.[10] Both formal and informal structural obstacles may not only affect the careers of women already in the scientific professions, but may also indirectly affect women by dissuading them from a science career. If women perceive that structural obstacles in the sciences may prevent their attaining meaningful career goals, they may select instead a career with potential benefits that appear to outweigh potential costs.

Scholars working within the framework of difference theories have explored a variety of cultural obstacles to women's participation in science. Some scholars have argued that gender-specific socialization throughout society can deter women from viewing science as a worthwhile occupation. Women may be more likely than men to be socialized with general orientations and attitudes that reduce the drive toward professional success in any given field. In the larger society, general cultural attitudes about science may define it as a male field and, as a result, encourage men and discourage women from participation. Numerous studies have identified educational curricula and instructional practices that reinforce the notion that science is a thoroughly male domain. For example, researchers have identified scientific textbooks that mention and picture men almost exclusively or that depict women in gender-stereotypical roles. Young female students may lack role models of successful women scientists. Additionally, family members may socialize girls away from science by portraying scientific fields as better suited to boys.[11]

Looking to the experiences of women in the professional fields of science, some researchers have argued that the history of discriminatory practices against women in science has resulted in a masculine construction of science as a field of endeavor.[12] Going further, many feminist scholars have theorized that science also has been culturally constructed around white, middle- and upper-class work and family values. According to this view, the political and social development of structural and cultural obstacles to limit the representation of women and minorities in Western science has resulted in a modern scientific culture that is infused with norms and values that conform to white, middle-class, heterosexual, and masculine world views.[13] Some historians have pointed to the monastic culture of the medieval Christian era as an important influence on the evolution of Western science as a "world without women."[14]

Examining the theme of difference from a philosophical perspective, a number of scholars have argued that historically developed epistemological gender differences may make science itself fundamentally incompatible with women's ways of thinking. According to this view, science embodies a masculine type of objectivity and rationality, whereas women's epistemological style—whether inherent or culturally constructed—differs in being more intuitive, synthetic, and holistic.[15] Some researchers have claimed that women's declining participation in the sciences can be explained by contemporary methods of science education that emphasize the kinds of rules and experimental controls that presumably appeal to men. Women may be uncomfortable with science "presented as a strict set of rules" and may view such representations of scientific methodology as incompatible with feminine culture.[16]

In an approach antithetical to that of feminism, a few scholars have argued that differences in achievement between men and women are due to inherent biological differences between the sexes. Among these arguments is the claim that a gender-related genetic factor provides males with superior mathematical abilities.[17] This theory has been challenged by scholars who see early socialization as the cause of the gender difference in mathematics achievement. Very recently, the gap in mathematics achievement between males and females has narrowed to the point that some scholars argue there no longer exists a statistically significant difference between the sexes. Currently, there is no general consensus among scientists about the existence of genetically determined advantages or disadvantages affecting male and female achievement in mathematics or science, although arguments of genetic difference have resurfaced during the last decade as part of an emerging societal concern over the academic achievement of boys.[18]

Structural and cultural obstacles can interweave into a chronology of barriers dissuading women from science, beginning with early family influence, informal and formal elementary and secondary education, college and graduate school training, professional experiences, and the perceived responsibilities of parenthood, marriage, or family. Some researchers refer to this as the career pipeline, arguing that at various segments of the pipeline, females may drop out but rarely drop in.

From childhood through the later stages of scientific professional development, gender deficits and differences can shape both opportunities and obstacles and influence the way that individuals respond to both. At the earliest stage, important processes of gender-role socialization occur in the family and influence women's later career and life choices.[19] Schools promote cultural gender roles that affect the attitudes of girls toward achievement in science. Both teachers and peers contribute to the socialization process, and school counselors may participate in the maintenance of structural barriers by directing girls away from advanced-placement mathematics courses.[20] Cultural and structural obstacles persist throughout college, influencing women away from careers in science.[21] In graduate school, women encounter insufficient financial support relative to men, fewer opportunities to become research assistants, and fewer chances for contact with male mentors and advisors.[22] During the course of their professional careers, female scientists most clearly experience structural obstacles, primarily in the form of job discrimination, differential treatment in promotion, tenure awards, or research funding. Women scientists tend to be marginalized from the inner circle of the scientific establishment.[23] Finally, although researchers have drawn varied conclusions when examining the effect of marriage and motherhood on scientific productivity, cultural stereotypes may lead men to view women as lacking commitment and prone to leave science in favor of raising a family.[24]

By investigating the access of both sexes to the sciences within the context of the historical evolution of the overall secondary curriculum, this study reveals a complex web of social and cultural influences that have facilitated and hindered the participation of girls in science. Although the vast majority of the studies on women and science have focused on obstacles to achievement, a large portion of this book takes a different perspective, focusing on both structural and cultural factors that encouraged young girls and women to take up the study of the sciences after the American Revolution.

What can we learn from a historical study of the formal schooling available to girls at the precollege level? Colleges and universities did not open their doors to women until the third decade of the nineteenth century, and even then, relatively few women attended such institutions until the century's end. Opportunities for females to take up the formal study of the sciences therefore occurred in nineteenth-century academies, seminaries, and selected venture schools and their later public secondary school counterparts, institutions designated in this study as *higher schools*. By focusing on the experiences of women at the college level or in the professional fields of science, historians not only have neglected the great majority of women who studied science in the nineteenth century, but also have overlooked the most widely traveled science-related career path available to women during that era: that of science teacher. Some scholars have investigated the roles played by nineteenth-century women as amateur scientists and popularizers of science.[25] Although such studies illuminate our understanding of the acceptable niches available to women in science during that era, it is important to analyze the development of science education in private and public schools in order to understand the formal and deliberate choices American society made for the education of its young men and women.

To date, no published historical study has undertaken a comparative analysis of the science education of adolescent boys and girls; nor has any analyzed the evolution of girls' scientific interests from the antebellum era to the twentieth century. As a result, some critical questions have been left unanswered: Why did the various sciences first enter the school curricula available to females? To what extent were the science studies of girls comparable to those of boys during the early nineteenth century? How can we explain the cultural construction of science as a boys' subject in the twentieth century? What were the social, cultural, and economic contexts in which this shift occurred?

To address such questions, the following chapters examine the experiences of students and teachers in educational institutions serving adolescents: private venture schools, incorporated seminaries and academies, boarding schools, the preparatory departments of colleges and universities, publicly funded high schools, and, in some cases, the higher classes of graded common schools. In the following chapters, the term *higher schooling* denotes any advanced variety of formal education beyond the common school level apart from that offered in colleges and universities. Such modern terms as *elementary, secondary*, and *higher education* are not particularly useful for the historian of education, because although the colonial and antebellum academies most closely fit the middle category, in practice they overlapped all three. For the most part, higher schools enrolled students from the ages of twelve to eighteen during the nineteenth century, although many took in pupils as young as eight.[26] During much of the century, classrooms were not age-graded. Students proceeded through various "classes" according to their mastery of the subject matter; as a result, very young students could occasionally be found studying alongside far more mature classmates. The vast majority of these students, male and female, did not go on to college. As late as 1900, only four percent of the eighteen- to twenty-one-year-old age group entered institutions of higher learning, and fewer still completed a full college course.[27]

Because of the multiple and evolving nature of the educational institutions open to females from 1784 to 1960, this study examines the mathematics and science curricula available to adolescent girls and boys in a variety of settings. The first portion of the book focuses largely on education as it occurred in the most common form of institutions open to girls during the antebellum period: day schools, boarding schools, female seminaries, common schools, lyceums, and so on. Such institutions generally catered to children of the upper and middle classes, although scholarships and town grants for poor children of high aptitude slightly broadened their student populations in some cases. As the movement to establish free public high schools gained ground after the Civil War, the attention of the following chapters concentrates on these institutions as well and on the somewhat more socioeconomically diverse population of students attending them.

This book also looks beyond schoolrooms to developments in popular culture and in the workplace. There have existed many influences on children's learning apart from formal educational institutions. Throughout the nineteenth century, educators debated how schooling should best fit girls. Contemporary Americans included this within the broader "woman question." It could not be answered without first addressing the larger issue of women's proper role in society. Any inquiry into the schooling of females must therefore also explore this larger political, social, and economic context. Thus, the reader will find that the following discussion looks beyond schooling in formal institutional contexts to explore growing opportunities for women in the workplace, examine evolving depictions of women and science in the media of popular culture, and analyze the reactions of leading male educators through such sources as personal correspondence and the records of professional associations. In order to probe the extent to which women viewed science as a fruitful area of endeavor during any given period, this study also investigates the changing nature and degree of women's participation in science, not only as students, but also as science writers, amateur investigators, and science educators.

Understanding the relation of social class and science education in the United States is central to comprehending not only why females embraced the sciences in the first place after the Revolution, but why some abandoned it so readily during the later nineteenth century. The following chapters explore the changing relations between social class and girls' interests and opportunities in science education. Additionally, this study builds on the work of other scholars who have begun to document the ways in which some of the educational reforms implemented to better align schooling with women's presumed vocation in the home reflected an impulse to differentiate the secondary course of study, not only along gender lines, but along ethnic and racial lines as well.[28]

The first four chapters explore the origins and evolution of the sciences and mathematics in the formal curricula available to females from the American Revolution to the midnineteenth century. The chapters included in this section highlight the role of social, economic, and political contexts in shaping the views of Americans about gender roles and the value, purpose, and meaning of a scientific education.

How and why science initially entered the curriculum of female schools is the focus of the opening chapter. Geography was the first science to appear in girls' schoolbooks after the American Revolution. Why did Americans consider geography an appropriate subject for females? Although some scholars have argued that contemporaries supported some scientific study for young women in order to prepare them for "republican motherhood," documentary sources suggest that during the period from 1784 to 1840, arguments related to motherhood just as often supported the opinion that a young girl's education should center on the topics of hearth and home. Many historians have argued that the introduction of the sciences into postcolonial American educational institutions resulted from the reforming ideas of Enlightenment thinkers. However, different rates of development and diverse outcomes in female education among various countries that served as important sites of Enlightenment philosophy cast doubt on the premise that a causal relationship between philosophy and practice existed in nineteenth-century female education. While acknowledging the prominent role Enlightenment ideas played in contemporary educational rhetoric, this chapter identifies the social, cultural, and economic motives that impelled Americans to introduce some study of the sciences into the curricula available to their daughters.

Toward the middle decades of the nineteenth century, the schooling of young middle-class women increasingly included some study of the sciences. School examinations, published courses of study, and selected enrollment data indicate that female higher schools placed a greater emphasis on scientific subjects than did similar, contemporary institutions for males. The second and third chapters undertake a comparative investigation of the scientific studies of girls and boys in private secondary schools during the antebellum period. These schools educated the majority of the nation's secondary students before 1880, and many were single-sex rather than coeducational schools. Chapter 2 analyzes the courses of study and examinations of boys' and girls' schools in order to evaluate the degree to which they emphasized scientific subjects. To compare the content and level of difficulty of the sciences available to girls with those offered boys, Chapter 3 examines samples of textbooks used in male and female institutions. Before 1840, the textbooks used in female schools generally emphasized a conceptual, rather than a mathematical, understanding of scientific principles and usually conveyed content through the medium of a conversational format. After 1840, the most advanced science textbooks offered in female schools were comparable to the most advanced texts in male academies, a development that coincided with a revolution in the mathematics education of American girls.

Why did females largely abandon the study of the physical sciences during the later nineteenth century? Some historians of science have suggested that nineteenth-century American girls turned away from the physical sciences because of their increasing mathematical complexity. In order to test this theory, Chapter 4 investigates the evolving mathematics education of American girls from the antebellum period to the end of the nineteenth century and compares the curricula available to girls with that offered their male counterparts. An analysis of the textbooks used in female institutions indicates that by the midnineteenth century, the mathematical complexity of the most advanced physics texts used in female schools did not differ from those used in male schools.

Chapters 5 and 6 investigate the rise of natural history in the courses of study available to girls during the period from 1840 to 1880. They focus on the experiences of women in a range of settings: as amateurs within the growing community of nineteenth-century naturalists; as nature writers, teachers, and educational leaders; and as students in both higher and elementary schools. Taken as a whole, the chapters highlight issues of gender ideology, the role of informal networks and personal friendships in developing a culture of science perceived as welcoming to women, and the impact of women's increased political power on female roles in science education.

Although several scholars have theorized that young women turned to the nonmathematical science of natural history because they did not receive advanced training in mathematics during the antebellum period, documentary evidence suggests that although natural history increased in female schools, this increase did not accompany a corresponding decline in natural philosophy or physics. Chapter 5 demonstrates that the turn to natural history occurred during the same period that the level of mathematics in female institutions achieved parity with that in comparable male institutions. Although natural history entered the curriculum relatively late in the nineteenth century, this highly popular science had long been the province of amateur naturalists, male and female alike. The subject appeared near midcentury and increased thereafter in the published courses of study of female schools, coinciding with a period in which employment opportunities for women increased in such related fields as botany, horticulture, entomology, scientific illustration, museum work, and natural history teaching. Among all the sciences appearing in female schools during the nineteenth century, none afforded more employment opportunities for women than natural history.

The role of women in science education during the late nineteenth and twentieth centuries is the subject of Chapter 6. The spotlight shifts from girls to women because during the late nineteenth and early twentieth centuries, the vast majority of young women who studied science in secondary schools and higher institutions did so in order to become teachers. This chapter analyzes women's growing participation and leadership in a form of natural-history education known as nature study.

Chapters 7 and 8 analyze several factors that contributed to a decline in female enrollments in advanced science and mathematics courses at the secondary level from 1890 to 1960. They emphasize the emergence of both structural and cultural obstacles to female participation in science as a result not only of a strong male backlash against women's increasing political power and growing presence in the professions, but also of educational policy initiatives advanced and supported by women themselves.

The strategies of nineteenth-century female educators to gain greater status and power for women contributed to the demise of science as a girls' subject. Chapter 7 documents this phenomenon through an analysis of two important educational movements. The first of these, which originated earlier in the nineteenth century, was the trend among elite girls' schools to emphasize the classics in their curricula as part of an effort to elevate the status of their institutions. The second was a national movement at the century's end to include vocational and commercial subjects in secondary schools as part of a larger effort to adjust schooling to the presumed future destinies of boys and girls, especially those of the working classes. During an era when women sought to attain greater political power, broader occupational opportunities, and increased access to higher education, female educators themselves initiated a number of educational reforms that ultimately resulted in declining female enrollments in advanced science and mathematics courses. The creation of alternative educational pathways in the liberal arts, home economics, and commercial courses attracted female enrollments at a cost to the sciences.

The backlash of the male education community against the increasing influence of women in the nature-study movement constituted a third factor in the decline of science as a girls' subject, and shifting attitudes toward science itself constituted a fourth. Chapter 8 details the creation of institutional barriers to women's employment and advancement in science education, roadblocks erected by a number of newly formed professional organizations in the science education community. Within the context of a societal backlash against women, this chapter focuses on issues of professionalization within the field of science education, the influence of wartime policies on peacetime institutions, and the emergence of structural and cultural obstacles to female participation in science. Additionally, this chapter investigates the changing attitudes of Americans toward science in the aftermath of the Second World War, attitudes that may have contributed to the self-selection of female students away from high school courses in the physical sciences.

The evolution of precollege science education in America left a number of cultural and institutional legacies that today continue both to influence practices in secondary educational institutions and shape social perceptions concerning women and science. These legacies are the focus of the Conclusion. They include (1) a widespread cultural association of women with the presumably more "feminine" qualities of the natural, rather than the physical sciences; (2) institutionalized methods and practices in textbook publishing, classroom instruction, and secondary school counseling that may continue to guide girls away from higher mathematics and science courses; (3) an infrastructure of secondary schooling that retains the life sciences as a foundation to the subsequent study of chemistry and physics; and (4) an ongoing body of empirical data for the study of the varied processes that contribute to gender stereotyping of the curriculum.

This study suggests that the experiences of women in science should not be generalized across all scientific fields. Uncoupling the sciences allows us to see that historically women have been relatively successful in the life sciences, from the time girls initially undertook the formal study of natural history in the nineteenth century to the present. The concluding essay includes an analysis of the factors that have contributed to female success and persistence in the life sciences, along with some discussion of implications for current policy and practice in science education.

The story recounted in the following chapters contributes to the existing body of literature on women and science by expanding our understanding of the structural and cultural obstacles that emerged to dissuade young women from advanced study of the sciences in the early twentieth century. It also documents the strategic choices women made to advance political rights for women, broaden employment opportunities, and increase access to institutions of higher education, choices that resulted in declining enrollments among girls in advanced science and mathematics courses at the secondary level. In preceding efforts to recount the history of precollege science education in the United States, some historians have completely ignored developments in female education. This leaves their readers to conclude that the activities of girls and women had little bearing on the historical course of events.[29] In an attempt to redress such omissions, other scholars have erred by focusing on females to the exclusion of males. This strategy leaves unanswered a number of important questions about the extent to which the science education available to girls was comparable to that offered boys. The research undertaken for this study reveals that both of these limited approaches obscure an important interaction. The form and content of precollege science education developed, in part, as a result of the greater social interaction and often the direct competition of the two sexes.

1

Geography Opens the Door

"The revolution has been favorable to science in general, particularly to that of the geography of our own country," wrote the Reverend Jedidiah Morse.[1] In 1784, when Morse published his first geography textbook, he dedicated it "To the Young Masters and Misses Throughout the United States," signaling its appropriateness for females.[2] Highly popular among boys and girls alike, Morse's *Geography Made Easy* ran through numerous editions at least until 1820, when the twenty-third edition appeared.[3] Geography was the first science to appear widely in girls' schoolbooks after the American Revolution.

Why did postcolonial Americans consider geography an appropriate subject for females? Some historians have identified the eighteenth-century rhetoric of "republican motherhood" as the most significant factor in encouraging young women to take up the study of science. According to this view, females gained access to popular scientific topics because they were responsible for the early education of future citizens.[4] However, documentary sources suggest that during the period from 1784 to 1840, rhetoric related to motherhood did not always justify the study of science. In fact, some Americans used the same rhetoric to support their position that a young girl's education should center on the topics of hearth and home.[5] Other scholars have looked to the reforming ideas of Enlightenment thinkers as an important influence on female education.[6] Nevertheless, the introduction of scientific subjects to young women cannot solely be explained by the long-accepted theory that Enlightenment philosophy created support in America for the introduction of scientific study, because in such countries as France and Germany, important sites of Enlightenment ideas, the education of girls did not follow a similar path.[7]

This chapter explores the political and societal forces that led Americans to introduce their daughters to the study of geography. The increasing presence of this science in the curriculum of female schools occurred during an expansion of higher schooling opportunities in general for women after the Revolution. Textbook authors and founders of academies and seminaries during the antebellum era cited a number of rationales for providing a useful and meaningful education for females. Of these, some bore directly on women's relationships to others—as wives, daughters, or mothers—and others related to issues of self-improvement.

Although some of the late-eighteenth-century rationales for teaching geography to girls mirrored the justifications used by promoters of women's education generally, there were differences arising from the specific character of the subject. For instance, contemporaries believed that geography could instill habits of good citizenship, develop national pride, and create public support for surveys and scientific expeditions, pedagogical goals not necessarily achievable through the study of such subjects as French or arithmetic. Within each of the three broad categories of utility, nationalism, and self-improvement, advocates espoused a number of reasons why the nation would benefit from encouraging females to study the subject. This rhetoric proved to be enormously successful, because the justifications advanced at the end of the eighteenth century for teaching geography to girls established the groundwork for young women's further inroads into the study of the individual sciences in the early nineteenth century.

The geography as it appears today in American schoolrooms bears only a feeble resemblance to the subject that entered the curriculum after the Revolution. Currently, the topic has largely constricted to political geography and is almost wholly subsumed within the social studies.[8] In contrast, at the end of the eighteenth century, schoolroom geography comprised the branches of physical, political, and astronomical geography. The earliest geographies published in the United States often included some discussion of such related subjects as natural history, astronomy, geology, mineralogy, and natural philosophy.[9] At the end of the Enlightenment, natural philosophy (delimited and later called physics) was an enormous category that included both living and nonliving phenomena. Medicine and physiology—as well as the study of heat, magnetism, optics, and mechanics—formed part of natural philosophy. Natural history embraced the entire range of observable forms, from limestone formations to plants, incorporating what are now the distinct sciences of zoology, botany, geology, and meteorology.[10] In the words of one contemporary, a geography text served as a useful and "judicious compendium, which collects knowledge widely scattered, and disseminates through every class of society, the illuminating rays of science."[11] In order to discover the means by which this subject first entered the curriculum available to girls, the discussion begins with the status of schooling available to females just before the Revolutionary War.

THE EDUCATION OF DAUGHTERS

Diverse groups inhabited the thirteen colonies in the eighteenth century, from the Moravians in the Allegheny regions to the Congregationalists in the Northeast and the Anglicans all along the coast. Here and there existed a few Catholic settlements scattered among the Protestant majority, and beyond the colonies, Catholic Spain and France claimed most of the land to the west. As for the proper form that schooling should take, colonists like Benjamin Franklin advocated a practical education along the lines developed earlier by such Enlightenment reformers as John Locke, whereas others argued in favor of the traditional classical education offered in many institutions of higher learning. By and large, the inhabitants of the colonies expressed a wide range of opinion on virtually any topic offered for debate. Still, it is possible to draw some conclusions about general trends in female education.

Traditional views of appropriate gender roles and social status influenced the choices colonial parents made concerning the schooling of their children. Although such communities as the Quakers espoused a relatively radical egalitarianism, the largest Protestant groups—the Congregationalists, Presbyterians, and Anglicans—generally distinguished between men and women's proper spheres of action, assigning men the public arena and women the private realm of hearth and home. As a number of scholars have noted, contemporary rhetoric did not always reflect actual practice. Most colonists lived in rural areas where the lines between public and private activity overlapped. For instance, the men and women who lived on farms and homesteads physically shared the spaces of home and work, and they often engaged in many of the same routines and chores. Even in small towns and villages, some colonial women worked outside the home as innkeepers, seamstresses, herbalists, midwives, shopkeepers, or printers. Colonial religious beliefs condoned the teaching of reading to women as well as men, because Puritan reformers argued that unmediated access to Scripture was essential to gaining knowledge of God. Nevertheless, studies of colonial literacy indicate that relatively few girls learned how to write. For example, in New England, only one-third of the women in the first generation of settlers could sign their names, and only fifty percent could do so at the end of the colonial period, as opposed to eighty percent of the men.[12]

Generally, the colonists believed that females should acquire abilities and skills appropriate to the social standing of their fathers or husbands. Thus, the wife or daughter of a small farmer might benefit from learning to read and write a little or perform some simple calculations, but the present or future wife of a prosperous landowner should be sufficiently educated to engage her husband and his guests in polite conversation about some of the literature, science, or arts of the day, and she should be able to provide entertainment to family members and visitors by performing a little music or displaying some expertise in drawing, painting, or embroidery. What a female needed to know, in other words, was tied not only to traditional views of gender roles, but also to perceptions of her current and future social status.

The educational opportunities available to the sexes differed, both in the nature of the institutions available for schooling and in the range of subjects offered for study. Colonial females received a rudimentary but not advanced education unless they came from wealthy families able to hire private tutors or pay the tuition at selected private academies or venture schools that catered to young women. In contrast, males had access to more advanced forms of schooling through local town schools, venture schools, and academies. Entrepreneurial venture schools, characterized by market supply and demand, offered fee-based instruction in a wide range of subjects, in some instances providing advanced classical training and in other cases offering a range of mathematical, scientific, or commercial subjects.[13] Males also could study in town schools that appeared in northern and southern communities during the eighteenth century. Governed by an elected group, these schools received varying degrees of financial support from local grants. Like church schools, these institutions offered a basic education in literacy and numeracy. Perceptions about social status also affected the educational choices colonial parents made on behalf of their male children. Middle- and upper-class parents desirous of providing a classical training for their sons enrolled them in local Latin grammar schools, where boys studied such additional texts as the *Anabasis* and the *Iliad*, either in preparation for college or to attain the gentlemanly polish necessary to maintain or improve their social standing.[14]

Although elite females may have had opportunities for higher schooling outside the home in some private academies and venture schools, the curricula offered in institutions catering to elite colonial girls differed from that of elite boys. Because classical education played a large role in preparing men for the ministry, women very rarely studied the classics unless their families arranged for private tutoring at home. Even the provision of advanced private instruction did not necessarily entail the inclusion of Latin in the curriculum. Some families considered by contemporaries to be extremely liberal for their views on female education omitted the classics from their daughters' private studies. For example, when Jane Colden (1724–1766) learned Linnaeus's new binomial system for categorizing plants from her father, the well-known botanist Cadwallader Colden, he translated the Latin terms for her, because he thought that women were incapable of learning Latin.[15] Because contemporaries believed instruction in higher mathematics to be inextricably linked to male careers in surveying, navigation, or the military, virtually no female institutions provided instruction in mathematics beyond basic arithmetic. Although few extant sources remain to allow us a clear picture of the curricula available to young women studying in colonial higher schools, the course of study offered by the Ursulines in the convent academy established in New Orleans in 1727 may have been fairly typical. Girls enrolled at the academy during the early years learned reading, writing, arithmetic, catechism, religion, and industrial training.[16] Mideighteenth-century venture schools conducted by women ranged from day schools offering instruction in just a few subjects such as French and needlework to boarding schools advertising a wide range of subjects, including reading, grammar, history, arithmetic, and occasionally geography. For example, in 1734, the school of the Widow Varnod in Charleston, South Carolina, specialized in French and embroidery. In 1770, Mrs. Duneau's school for girls advertised instruction in reading, grammar, arithmetic, needlework, history, geography, and dancing, drawing, and music.[17]

By and large, colonists in both the north and south appear to have believed that education for females was essentially a private matter, a concern of the family rather than the state. In many communities, long after the establishment of public free schools, it was common for only boys to attend them. According to Horace Mann, referring to early developments in Massachusetts, "[T]he first improvement in this respect consisted in smuggling in the girls, perhaps for an hour a day, after the boys had recited their lessons and gone home."[18] By the mideighteenth century, increasing numbers of Massachusetts towns began to open "women's schools," employing female teachers to provide instruction to girls and young boys. When girls desired instruction more advanced than basic reading or writing, their parents sometimes arranged for them to enroll in the town schools where they received instruction from the master at odd hours, before the boys arrived or after they left. Here and there, venture schools originally serving boys began to offer instruction to girls in separate departments. For example, Robert Leeth's school placed an advertisement in the *New York Gazette–Weekly Post Boy* in 1751, offering instruction to both sexes in "two handsome Rooms, with Fire-places, the one for Boys and the other for Girls."[19] Gradually, at different times and within varying political contexts, the educational opportunities of girls expanded in town after town.[20]

REVOLUTION AND REFORM

After the Revolutionary War, Americans faced the enormous task of building a new, independent country. Such leaders as Benjamin Franklin, Thomas Jefferson, Noah Webster, and Benjamin Rush (professor of chemistry at the University of Pennsylvania) conceived of a complete reformation of American life, a reform based on the Enlightenment ideals of reason and progress. "The American War is over," pronounced Rush, "but this is far from being the case with the American revolution." Rush argued that the United States required a new educational program particularly suited to the development of an enlightened citizenry in a democracy. Whereas training in the classics constituted the traditional higher education of the Old World, the new Republic required an innovative educational program, one that included such sciences as geography, natural philosophy, astronomy, natural history, and chemistry. The criteria by which Rush claimed to select his subjects were the degree to which they were "accommodated to the present state of society, manners and government of the United States."[21]

Americans required new textbooks reflective of their independent status and social goals. The first author to fill this need was the Reverend Jedidiah Morse, a graduate of Yale University. In the preface to his hugely popular *Geography Made Easy,* Morse proclaimed, "We have humbly received from Great Britain our laws, our manners, our books, and our modes of thinking, and our youth have been educated rather as subjects of the British Kings, than as citizens of a free and independent nation. But the scene is now changed."[22] As Morse rather sharply put it, "We are independent of Great Britain and are no longer to look up to her for a description of our own country."[23]

Initially, the subject was accessible only to a relatively elite portion of the American population, because the study of geography required a solid foundation of literacy. Few Americans attended school at the end of the eighteenth century. In 1800, the average citizen spent only four months and two days in schools during his or her lifetime—long enough to read and write a little and calculate the simplest sums. By 1840, the amount of time spent in schoolrooms had expanded to a mere ten months and eight days.[24] Two years later, the Massachusetts educator Horace Mann reported that of the forty thousand poor children in his state, "only one-half [are] attending schools."[25] Perhaps in recognition of this state of affairs, in the 1795 edition of *Elements of Geography*, Jedidiah Morse claimed that his book served not only as a reading book in common schools but as a "useful Winter Evening's Entertainment to Young People in Private Families."[26]

Geography first entered the curricula available to middle- and upper-class boys in private venture schools, town schools, and incorporated academies and seminaries. During the eighteenth century, boys pursued advanced study with private schoolmasters and in local Latin grammar schools that had been established in some of the larger towns following the colonial General Court's injunction for publicly funded schools to prepare young men for the university. However, as the century progressed, the growth of scattered villages, the division of towns into school districts, and the expansion of district schools accompanied a gradual decline in the number of Latin grammar schools. Well before the Revolution, it was clear that such institutions primarily served the privileged and the few destined for college, and increasing numbers of communities began to support the construction of English grammar schools with the goal of offering instruction in such basic subjects as reading, writing, spelling, and arithmetic to a wider range of students. Those parents seeking a higher schooling for their sons found increasing numbers of private venture schools ready to fill the void. Additionally, the numbers of incorporated private academies proliferated during the decades following the Revolution, founded by local communities, religious groups, counties, fraternal and educational societies, and private individuals. Academies provided a relatively advanced form of schooling that was legally incorporated to ensure financial support beyond that available through tuition alone. The courses of study in the early boys' academies often listed the traditional subjects of English, Latin, Greek, declamation, writing, and arithmetic, and some portion of the newer subjects of geography, French, logic, geometry, and natural philosophy or astronomy.[27]

Newspaper advertisements published in both northern and southern states after the Revolution reveal a growing number of higher schools claiming to provide a relatively advanced form of schooling for girls. For example, Sarah Pierce began her school for girls in the dining room of her home in Litchfield, Connecticut, in 1791. Two pupils from her school,

Table 1.1 Percentage of Pennsylvania Higher Schools Offering Geography, 1750–1889

	1750–1829	*1750–1889*
Female schools	67% (n=36)	83% (n=90)
Male and coeducational schools	74% (n=47)	77% (n=116)

Source: Compiled from James Mulhern, *A History of Secondary Education in Pennsylvania* (New York: Arno Press, 1969), 328 and 428. Mulhern's data are based on the courses of study offered in school catalogs. Sample sizes are indicated in parentheses.

Catharine and Mary Beecher, started a small venture school in 1823 over a harness shop on Main Street in Hartford that eventually evolved into the Hartford Female Seminary. Such institutions described themselves variously as female academies or seminaries, day schools, boarding schools, or ladies' select schools. Because of the diversity of the educational institutions established for girls, this study refers to schools—apart from colleges and universities—that provided instruction beyond the common school level as *higher schools.* Such modern terms as *elementary, secondary,* and *higher education* are not particularly useful terms for describing these schools, because although most closely fit the middle category, they often overlapped all three. Some institutions enrolled girls from the ages of eight to sixteen or eighteen; others admitted students at age twelve. Some schools, perhaps needing the tuition gained by enrolling additional students, took in any students that applied, even those younger than eight.[28] During the antebellum period before 1810, the standard studies in girls' higher schools generally included geography, English, writing, arithmetic, needlework, and several so-called ornamental subjects offered as electives—usually drawing, painting, or music.[29]

During the first decade of the nineteenth century, both male and coeducational higher schools in northern and southern states included geography in their courses of study.[30] For example, in 1801, a local newspaper published a report of the examinations in the female department of North Carolina's Fayetteville Academy, noting that the young ladies answered questions in "geography, reading, spelling, arithmetic, writing [and] needlework."[31] In 1815, Harvard College added knowledge of geography to its

Table 1.2 Percentage of North Carolina Male and Female Higher Schools Offering Geography, 1794–1839

Female schools	94% (n=47)
Male schools	86% (n=56)

Source: Data compiled from newspaper advertisements included in Charles L. Coon's *North Carolina Schools and Academies 1790–1840: A Documentary History* (Raleigh, N.C.: Edwards & Broughton, 1915).

Table 1.3 Percentage of Connecticut and Massachusetts Towns Reporting
Geography Texts Used in Their Common Schools

	Date	Percentage
Massachusetts	1837 (n=30)	100
Connecticut	1846 (n=30)	97

Source: First Abstract of the Massachusetts School Returns for 1837 (Boston: Dutton and
Wentworth, 1838). Annual Report of the Superintendent of Common Schools of Connecticut
(Hartford, Conn.: Case, Tiffany, and Burnham, 1846). The data are based on a random sam-
pling of thirty towns each in the Massachusetts and Connecticut school returns.

list of admission requirements. By the 1830s, the majority of academies
and seminaries in such states as Pennsylvania and North Carolina offered
the subject to both sexes, as shown in Tables 1.1 and 1.2. By the third decade of the century, students in common schools encountered a curriculum
that almost universally included geography (Table 1.3).

Contemporaries used the term *common school* to refer to an institution
under governmental control established for the education of the children
of American citizens; increasingly, such schools were also free. At different
times during the nineteenth century, each state established its own system
of common schools. Massachusetts set up a free school system in 1827.
Delaware followed suit in 1829, as did Pennsylvania in 1834, Vermont in
1850, Indiana in 1851, Ohio in 1853, and Iowa in 1858. In 1833, the textbook author Jesse Olney claimed confidently in his preface, "[T]he introduction of Geography into common schools, as a regular branch of
education, has of late years become nearly universal."[32]

RATIONALES FOR THE STUDY OF GEOGRAPHY

During the postcolonial period, educators came to associate geography
with a broad range of republican values. In order to understand why
American citizens wanted the subject taught to their daughters as well as
their sons, it is necessary to consider the underlying issues that structured
this curricular debate. As described by contemporaries, the principal advantages offered by the study of geography fell into three general categories: utility, nationalism, and self-improvement.

The study of geography was important to Americans for reasons of economic and national utility. During the opening decades of the nineteenth
century, the economic expansion of the country; the opening of the West;
and the development of industry, navigation, transportation, mining, and
agriculture all increased the perceived and practical needs for a greater
knowledge of the nature and resources of this still largely unexplored nation. How did the country look on the map? What treasures lay beneath its
mountains and plains, under its lakes and rivers, hidden in its great forests?

The postrevolutionary period was a time of intense interest in geography and other scientific and technological subjects. New organizations such as lyceums, societies, and research institutions sprang up to investigate these various fields. Wealthy patrons contributed time and money for the promotion of expeditions and surveys of rivers, coasts, mountains, and plains.[33]

Reflecting national priorities, early nineteenth-century popular magazines published for children often included articles on geography and natural history. For example, *The Youth's Companion*, first issued in the United States in 1827, claimed "to be instructive as well as entertaining"; within its pages, readers encountered natural history subjects along with moralistic tales and religious poetry.[34] Magazines created to improve and instruct the young had long been popular in Great Britain, where such periodicals as *The Juvenile Magazine*, first published in 1788, and the *Youth's Monthly Visitor*, published briefly in 1822, often combined an assortment of morally uplifting fiction with samples of botany, metallurgy, astronomy, and geography. Popular in the United States, the British periodical *Children's Friend, or Sunday Scholar's Reward* regularly included articles on geography and botany.[35] According to the historian Kristen Drotner, the expansion of secular periodicals for British children in the 1830s and 1840s was the direct result of the North American influence for the pursuit of useful knowledge. In 1833, the American geography author Samuel Goodrich launched the *Peter Parley* magazine in the United States, a periodical that featured articles on geography, natural history, geology, and astronomy. Goodrich's magazine far surpassed its competitors in the wealth of detail it provided about the height, duration, distance, or weight of natural phenomena. Imitations and spin-offs of Goodrich's magazine quickly appeared in Great Britain, and at one time there existed at least six different *Peter Parleys*.[36]

The popularization of geography may have served to enhance public support for the financing of local expeditions and surveys and for scientific activity in general. During the first decades of the nineteenth century, Americans eagerly sought mineral resources. Public support for financing discovery was crucial to the success of geological surveys. In 1823, North Carolina sponsored the first geological survey in America financed at public expense. Other states soon followed suit: South Carolina sponsored a survey in 1824; Massachusetts in 1830; Tennessee in 1831; New Jersey in 1835; and Georgia, Maine, and New York each launched a survey in 1836.[37] Contemporaries argued that the study of geology and mineralogy potentially benefited the nation. According to one writer, "Their pockets, shelves, and chambers, which are soon loaded with specimens, afford the most satisfactory proof of [children's] industry, as well as of their interest and knowledge in this practical science. The researchers of these young explorers have not unfrequently [*sic*] been rewarded with valuable discoveries, not merely to enrich their collections, but to increase the wealth of the country, and to advance the useful arts."[38] The earliest geographies also introduced young students in a rudimentary way to the subjects of geology and mineralogy. Beginning with the first geography published in 1784, every textbook provided American schoolchildren with some accounts of the "mineral treasures of North America."

Knowledge of astronomy was indispensable to the geographer, and many of the geographies published between 1784 and 1850 included a short section on this science.[39] The earliest textbooks were published in New England, whose coastal towns and villages depended largely on the sea for their livelihood. Astronomy was central to navigation, a skill highly valued in coastal communities. Besides navigation, astronomy was utilitarian for another reason: Town lots could be surveyed by those with a knowledge of elementary mathematics, but the marking of provincial boundaries and the laying out of large blocks of land required astronomy.[40] Geography texts introduced students to the structure of the solar system and the orbits of its planets and comets, the relation of the earth's orbit to seasonal change, and the methods of reckoning latitude and longitude.[41] Some texts included more advanced topics, such as the use of a quadrant of altitude to calculate the distance of any two places on the globe; the reckoning of the latitude and longitude of any given star;[42] or the calculation of the time, from conjunction to conjunction, of any two planets.[43]

Of great concern to early American scientists and educators was the need to develop national expertise in the sciences and mechanical arts. During the first decades after the Revolution, geography textbooks introduced American schoolchildren to the subjects of astronomy, natural history, physical geography, and natural philosophy, subjects deemed necessary to the promotion of the young nation's "flourishing and improving condition."[44] According to Horace Mann, education was the means by which a new generation of inventors and scientists would thrive. "If among ten well-educated children, the chance is that at least one of them will originate some new and useful process in the arts, or will discover some new scientific principle, or some new application of one," wrote Mann, "then, among a hundred such well-educated children, there is a moral certainty that there will be more than ten such originators or discoverers of new utilities; for the action of the mind is like the action of fire."[45] To this end, Jedidiah Morse provided his readers with an overview of the history of science. In his *Elements of Geography*, Morse introduced Americans to the discoveries of the great men of science, from Thales, Pythagoras, and Democritus to Copernicus, Kepler, Galileo, and Newton, and finally to the relatively recent contributions of such scientists as Herschel and Boyle. In an attempt to develop American pride in American products, Morse was scrupulous to bring to the attention of his readers the accomplishments of local scientists as well. For instance, during a discussion of the air pump, he noted, "The air pump is a machine . . . improved by Boyle and others, in England, and lately by the Rev. Dr. Prince, of Salem, Massachusetts."[46]

Although antebellum Americans did not expect their daughters to become practicing geographers, mechanics, navigators, or surveyors, preparation for marriage and motherhood figured as one of many recurring themes in the arguments of those who promoted the study of geography among females. Some educational reformers argued that knowledge of the sciences rendered women more interesting conversationalists and companions for their husbands. According to the well-known female educator Almira Hart Lincoln Phelps, scientific study would result "in enlarging [women's] sphere of thought, rendering them more interesting companions to men of science, and better capable of instructing the young."[47] In general terms, educators often stressed the value of education in assisting women to bring up their children as virtuous and intelligent citizens. Many postcolonial Americans were acutely aware of women's important social role as teachers of the young. During the early nineteenth century, Americans of high and low estate expressed the view, through private letters, speeches, sermons, and periodicals, that women must be better educated to fill their domestic role. In a "letter from a father to his daughter," published in the *Charleston Observer*, one writer echoed the prevailing opinion of that era: "The mother is ever before the mind, and when the pride of intellect has transported the man in maturity beyond the influence of even sound argument and rational conviction, he remembers the lessons of that mother and feels their truth."[48] As regards the specific subject of geography, Americans promoted its study among girls because some contemporaries perceived women as playing a key role in developing scientific interests among children. In contrast to such countries as England or France, which had well-established—if still largely amateur—scientific traditions, the fledgling United States faced the daunting task of building a scientific community largely from scratch. Potential scientific talent lay among children, the majority of whom received their schooling from family members at home.

In addition to promoting useful knowledge and developing a public supportive of scientific enterprise, the study of geography met the political needs of the new country as well. The attention of students to the geographical features of the United States, particularly when described by its own citizens, could instill national pride. Like the authors of reading and spelling books, authors of geography schoolbooks aimed to develop the child's loyalty to the state. Every geography contrasted monarchy with republicanism, seen as the perfect vehicle of liberty in the United States. In the words of one author, "This Constitution, principally from the pen of *Thomas Jefferson*, more happily embraces the equal rights and liberties of man, than any other system on the globe."[49]

The authors of geography schoolbooks sought to develop the child's loyalty to the state by generating national ideals and defining those attitudes and behavior deemed proper for American youth. One means of doing so was to contrast the national character of the allegedly more virtuous United States with that of foreign countries. Children learned from their schoolbooks that each nation evidenced its own peculiar and inherited traits of personality and intellect. A significant proportion of geography authors hailed from the ranks of Protestant ministers, and many presented unfavorable portraits of Catholic countries, including Spain, Italy, and France.[50] "In the Protestant countries," wrote one author, "and in those favored with a mild and liberal form of government, the mass of the people are more enlightened and better informed, than in those where the Roman Catholic is the prevailing religion."[51] In contrast, the same books always presented an optimistic view of American citizens and their institutions. Americans were "generally industrious, intelligent, and enterprising."[52] Americans "[knew] how, at proper times to be liberal, and [were] ever ready to assist the unfortunate."[53] One geography author posed this typical question and answer: "Q. What is the national character of the United States? A. More elevated and refined than that of any nation on earth."[54]

By such means, postcolonial geographies aimed to promote a strong sense of nationalism, a presumably worthy trait that mothers could develop in their children. Thomas Jefferson expressed a point of view common among American elites of this period, claiming it was essential to provide females "a solid education which would enable them to become mothers to educate their own daughters & even to direct the course of sons should their fathers be lost or incapable or inattentive." Jefferson believed the chief aim of a woman's education was to train future generations to be effective citizens of the young Republic.[55]

In addition to arguments of utility and citizenship, contemporaries promoted geography as a subject contributing to the self-improvement of men and women alike. Although some historians have emphasized the role of "republican motherhood" as a rhetorical concept useful to advocates of female education, documentary sources indicate that contemporaries just as frequently used justifications related to the self-improvement of young women.[56] Arguments falling under the heading of "self-improvement" can be categorized into three distinct groups: (1) moral improvement, comprising both general virtues and spiritual or religious growth; (2) mental improvement, construed as the strengthening of the muscles of the mind, leading to improved intellectual prowess; and (3) psychological improvement, defined as the enhancement of personal well-being, increased fortitude, and the ability to provide oneself with intellectual resources leading to pleasure and happiness.[57]

Since the early colonial period, American educators had believed in the necessity of moral education. Schoolbook authors filled their primers and spelling books with moral homilies calculated to lead young minds along the paths of virtue.[58] During the eighteenth century, Americans came to view geography as a subject particularly capable of promoting moral and religious development.

The rise of natural theology in the United States made the study of the natural world morally uplifting. Natural theology, which gained popularity at the beginning of the eighteenth century in Great Britain, was founded on the premise that God could be known by consulting either Scripture or nature itself, both of which led to the same truths. Central to natural theology was the argument of design, in which the mechanism, instrumentality, or design in nature attested to the existence of an intelligent and benevolent Creator. From the beginning of the eighteenth century, English natural philosophers published a stream of books aiming to reveal the wonders of God's creation through the natural sciences. In newspapers published just after the American Revolution, popular titles in natural theology can be found alongside the titles of the latest novels in the advertisements of local booksellers.[59] Arguably the best known was *Natural Theology* (1802) by William Paley, who claimed that the more humans learned to understand and appreciate God's design in nature, the more they would grow in knowledge of God.[60]

Americans readily embraced natural theology because traditional Puritan religious beliefs supported the study of the natural world. The dominant theological ideology of the American colonies was derived from the work of the Protestant reformer John Calvin (1509–1564). Calvin had taught that the subjective awareness of God and God's will could be supplemented by reflecting on the structure of the external world: "[God has] . . . revealed himself and daily discloses himself in the whole workmanship of the universe. As a consequence, men cannot open their eyes without being compelled to see him."[61] Calvin's thinking dovetailed with the ideas of other Enlightenment thinkers who emphasized the importance of studying nature to learn about "nature's God." For many Puritan reformers of the eighteenth century, living a "godly life" required not only time spent devoted to prayer, acts of charity, self-reflection, and the study of Scripture, but also the careful examination of the natural world. For example, the American revivalist preacher Jonathan Edwards (1703–1758) supplemented acts of prayer and contemplation of the Bible with the study of atoms, rainbows, and the lives of spiders.[62]

Imported from abroad, natural theology found fertile soil in the United States in the early nineteenth century, a period when religious movements swept the nation. The religious fervor of the Second Great Awakening contributed to a popular enthusiasm for the study of nature. Historians apply the phrase "Second Great Awakening" to the period running roughly from 1795 to 1837. During this era, a variety of Protestant groups—Methodists, Presbyterians, and Baptists—presided over revivals in such southern states as Kentucky and Tennessee; the Congregationalists conducted revivals in New England. Evangelicals believed in a literal interpretation of the Bible and the need for spiritual rebirth through conversion.[63] Some church groups promoted the study of the natural world for its presumed theological benefits.[64] In the 1830s, when the American Sunday School Union began offering Sunday school libraries for sale to common schools, its collections included maps and volumes on natural history and travel.[65]

The rhetoric of natural theology portrayed as highly desirable the inclusion of the sciences into the curriculum. "The analysis of science and revealed religion," proclaimed John Ludlow in his 1834 address at the opening of Albany Female Academy, "will ultimately terminate in the same point . . . the invisible God."[66] As did many members of the British and American scientific communities during this period, textbook authors frequently invoked natural theology as they extolled the benefits of studying the sciences. Jedidiah Morse prefaced his *Elements of Geography* with a statement of natural theology fairly typical of the geographies during this period: "The *first* branch of this Science, viz *Astronomical Geography,* as treated in this little book, furnishes the young Pupil with such a general knowledge of the heavenly bodies, as will facilitate his acquaintance with Geography, and elevate and enlarge his views of the wisdom, power, and greatness of the CREATOR."[67]

Female educators strongly promoted geography as a vehicle for the moral and spiritual improvement of girls and women. For example, in her influential *Structures on Female Education* (1799), writer Hannah More suggested geography as a subject for moral instruction. Emma Willard, the founder of Troy Female Seminary, recommended the study of geography as a means of gaining knowledge of God. "The study of geography may lead your mind to pious reflections bringing to your view the power, wisdom, and goodness of God," wrote Willard. ". . . [A]ll these are the workmanship of His Hands, whose creatures we are . . . while we contemplate *them,* we shall learn to adore him."[68]

Focusing on the natural theology of many geography schoolbooks, some historians have concluded that textbook writers were woefully out of touch with the scientific issues of the day. Such a portrayal is anachronistic, however, because science was not in conflict with natural theology in the early nineteenth century. In any case, the doctrine of natural theology occupied only an incidental place in the content of geography schoolbooks published after the Revolution. William Paley's argument of design in *Natural Theology* was so familiar that most authors simply invoked it, rather than expounding at length. An occasional reference to *Design* and *the Creator,* usually located in the preface, but occasionally sprinkled here and there throughout the text, was enough to cast a reverent aura over any geography. When such expressions of natural theology occurred in the texts of geographies, they usually directed the student's attention to incidents of design. For example, it was not uncommon for authors of geographies to present the natural world as having been created for humans, thus standing as evidence of the benevolence of God.[69]

The natural theology in most geography texts functioned to preserve traditional beliefs and values, but some authors introduced geological evidence that may have tended to undermine tradition. Consistent with the philosophy of natural theology, many textbook authors upheld the belief that the true history of the earth came from the book of Genesis. For example, Samuel G. Goodrich upheld the biblical account of the creation of the world, an approach fairly typical of the geography textbooks of this period. In discussing the earth's origin, Goodrich wrote, "This wonderful event took place about six thousand years ago. The story of it is beautifully told in the first chapter of Genesis."[70] This view was also not uncommon among members of the geological community. Many geologists hotly debated theories of the earth's origin well after the publication of Charles Lyell's *Principles of Geology* in 1830. Lyell theorized that all of the features of the earth could be explained by geological processes observable today, a position that was anathema to those intent on upholding Bishop Ussher's date of creation at 4004 B.C.[71]

Even as they preserved the Genesis account of the creation of the world, the same schoolbooks taught American children that the earth had existed for many ages and that its features had undergone many changes. At least two prominent and widely read authors introduced American girls and boys to the notion that some of the earth's species had become extinct. An 1806 edition of Morse's *Geography Made Easy* describes the woolly mammoth as an "unknown animal, whose bones are found in the northern parts of both the old and new world" and whose "bones prove them to have been 5 or 6 times as large [as an elephant]."[72] Going even further, Samuel Goodrich's 1832 *Malte-brun Geography* informed students that "whole races of animals" had become extinct. "The bones of still larger animals have also been discovered," wrote Goodrich. "It appears probable that, at a very remote period, whole races of animals, different from any existing in any part of the world, and far surpassing the elephant and rhinoceroos [*sic*] in magnitude, once roamed the forests of North America."[73]

The concept of extinction, introduced to schoolchildren by Morse and Goodrich, may have been potentially disruptive of the short history of humankind promoted by Bishop Ussher and others. One might even argue, whether intended by its authors or not, that the concept of extinction, along with depictions of the stratified appearance of the earth, served to undermine, rather than support, conservative ideas. Later in the century, some social commentators found such ideas exceedingly dangerous. From 1852 to 1854, more than fifty years after Morse introduced the concept of extinction in *Geography Made Easy*, the editor of the *Theological and Literary Journal* wrote and published a series of articles against contemporary geology, arguing, "[T]he theory generally entertained by geologists respecting the great age of the earth would, if founded on just grounds, disprove the inspiration of the Bible."[74] Nevertheless, although the tensions between scientific theory and religious interpretation would grow more acute for scientists and educators later in the century, Americans of the antebellum period generally were untroubled by potential conflicts between science and religion.

In addition to its moral and spiritual benefits, textbook authors claimed that the study of geography also strengthened the mental discipline of American schoolchildren. As citizens of a new political experiment, there were new requirements for young Americans. Faced with the task of building a nation on democratic principles, educational leaders argued that the development of an enlightened, rational citizenry was the key to a successful republic. The task of creating an educational system and a curriculum capable of molding children into enlightened citizens became a political imperative. The ability of a particular subject to promote mental discipline, to strengthen the faculties of the mind, was of utmost importance to educators. According to its advocates, to a greater degree than any other subject in the school curriculum, geography developed the student's reasoning ability. Drawing maps could "fix the wayward attention of children." Altering the scale in drawings would "exercise the power of judgment to a degree of which few studies are capable," and learning geographical facts could "exercise the memory."[75]

Early textbook authors extolled the virtues of geography as a rigorous study for both sexes, often contrasting it with such trivial pursuits as top spinning or hair curling. In the preface to their geography published in 1818, Vinson and Mann warned parents of the dangers of encouraging their girls to decorate dolls and of allowing their boys too much time for idle play: "The parent, who is contented merely with emulating a son by the spinning of a top . . . or, a daughter by learning her to decorate a doll, to curl her hair . . . must not be surprised nor disappointed if he discovers no higher, no purer emotions in their bosoms, and ideas in their minds . . ."[76] In contrasting the study of geography with such frivolous pursuits as doll play, Americans evidenced the beginnings of an educational agenda quite distinct from that of France, a country that served as an important source of Enlightenment ideas. With few exceptions, the content of girls' education in France from the Revolution until the latter half of the nineteenth century stressed religion, reading, writing, and such ornamental subjects as music and drawing. Although French society encouraged women's amateur scientific interests, Jean-Jacques Rousseau's *Emile* (1762) largely shaped French views of female education, stressing women's need for an essentially domestic education in which young girls learned to please men and become good mothers.[77]

Another compelling rationale for increasing the mental discipline of American youth stemmed from the belief that men and women's increased mental faculties passed to their offspring through inheritance. This view may have originated from the theories of eighteenth-century naturalist Jean Baptiste Antoine de Monet, Chevalier de Lamarck. The evolutionary theory of Lamarck proposed a predetermined path by which life progressed from simpler to more complex forms. According to Lamarck and his followers, the natural environment created a variety of needs that each animal used its body to fulfill. Over time, the effect of exercise, of use or disuse, caused some body parts to develop and others to degenerate. Lamarck assumed that the characteristics acquired as the result of effort passed to the animal's offspring, thereby enabling the effect to become cumulative.[78] Early nineteenth-century educators conceived the human mind as composed of a carefully detailed hierarchy of faculties capable of improvement through "mental discipline." According to this view, properly directed mental exercise could strengthen the mental faculties, just as rigorous and repeated use strengthened the muscles of the body. Such American Lamarckians as paleontologist Edward Drinker Cope argued that Lamarckism allowed living things to be in charge of their own destiny. Through an ideal educational program, one that developed and strengthened the mental faculties, humans could artificially direct the characteristics of future generations, thereby accelerating progress toward the Creator's ultimate goal.[79]

In his efforts to build popular support for the common-school movement in New England during the 1840s, the eminent educator Horace Mann occasionally expressed views similar to those of Lamarck and his followers. According to Mann, the American experiment of offering children free public education would result in enormous social benefits because of the resulting improved mental faculties of the population. "In the whole of the past history of the world," he claimed, "no generation has yet existed, whose faculties have not, to a very great extent, lain dormant,"—a state of affairs that the new experiment in mass education was soon to reverse.[80] Through his public speeches and annual reports as secretary of the Massachusetts board of education during the 1840s, Mann espoused a glorious vision in which each succeeding generation of Americans, through education, progressed to greater heights of intellect and achievement. "The greater the proportion of minds in any community which are educated, and the more thorough and complete the education which is given them," stated Mann, "the more rapidly, through these sublime stages of progress, will that community advance in all the means of enjoyment and elevation, and the more will it outstrip and outshine its less educated neighbors."[81] During her visit to the United States during the 1840s, Swedish commentator Fredrika Bremer conversed with Mann about his belief that the mental gains achieved by one generation could be passed to the next through inheritance. According to Bremer, "Horace Mann talks on this subject with a faith which might move mountains."[82] As a subject presumed to contribute significantly to children's mental discipline, geography would have appealed strongly to those educators who ascribed to Lamarkian views.

Another important dimension of the concept of mental self-improvement was an attitude toward study and learning that was educational in the classical sense, aimed at the development of knowledge and virtue rather than at the attainment of practical or potentially vocational skills. Recently, using such sources as student diaries and letters, scholars have noted the emphasis placed by middle-class young antebellum women themselves on "the necessity of improving every leisure movement" through serious study.[83] Letters from parents to their daughters also indicate that for some families, the purpose of higher schooling for young women was not solely to provide training for motherhood or marriage. For example, after Bessie Lacy arrived at Edgeworth Seminary in Greensborough, North Carolina, her mother wrote, "we who love you so much & study to find out what is for your good think it is best to send you [where you can] endeavor to improve yourself."[84]

In addition to justifications based on moral or mental improvement, advocates of higher schooling for women often touted what today might be called the psychological benefits of learning geography. Writers praised the pleasures of learning in general terms for women, portraying knowledge as a beneficial resource during trying times. Whereas men had access to various forms of public activity and vocations outside the home, some viewed women, presumably more secluded, as needing additional rewards to mitigate the sufferings of unhappy marriages or reversals in fortune. Echoing this view, a female student writing in 1794 claimed that women required an education more than did men, because women "lead a more solitary life, and must, unavoidably, sometimes fall into melancholy and dejection if not supported by a good education, which would enable us to pass those pensive hours in contemplation and writing, which would . . . sweeten adversity, and soften the cares of life."[85]

Certainly some of the earliest geography authors aimed to provide not only scientific content but also reading pleasure to young students. Jedidiah Morse's books described exciting views of far-off lands, such exotic animals as the woolly mammoth, and news of thrilling scientific discoveries. From Morse, Americans learned about the vast and still unexplored areas of the North American continent. He beckoned young explorers with intriguing descriptions of such geographical features as the *Shining Mountains* lying away west of the Mississippi, but little known."[86] Such later authors as Jesse Olney and Samuel Goodrich also added spice to their descriptions of natural phenomena. Goodrich undoubtedly captivated young audiences with his description of glaciers, vast icy expanses in which "a thousand spires glitter in the sunshine . . . [and] vast pyramids and obelisks are presented to the astonished beholder."[87] At least one contemporary writer assumed that the impact of these fascinating passages on schoolchildren was enormous. Fifty years after the publication of Olney's geography, a writer in *The Youth's Companion* reminded his readers of an illustration that had appeared in Olney's text, confident that everyone of a certain age would remember it: "Those who studied Olney's geography fifty years ago, can doubtless recall the picture that illustrated the description of Brazil. It depicted a white man riding on the back of an alligator, which a dozen natives were hauling on shore."[88] By making geography an entertaining subject, schoolbook authors assisted in the promotion of a popular enthusiasm for science, helping to develop an image of science not only as a useful but also highly pleasurable subject.

PEDAGOGICAL DEBATES

Understanding the contemporary rationales for the study of geography helps to explain why the subject came to have a place in the core curriculum for both sexes, but such rhetoric reveals nothing about the learning that occurred in actual schoolrooms. How did students learn geography? Did they simply read and recite from the texts, or did instructors provide opportunities for investigation and discussion? Did the instruction of girls differ from that of boys?

Although few sources remain to give a clear picture of how students studied geography in their schoolrooms, we can draw some general conclusions about the nature of teaching and learning during this period. The prefaces of early geography textbooks provide a glimpse into contemporary American debates over the best methods for teaching scientific subjects. During this era, such texts represented one of the means by which teachers gained access to new pedagogical skills. The first popular American pedagogical textbook, Samuel Read Hall's *Lectures on Schoolkeeping*, did not appear in print until 1829. In their prefaces, many authors included a section devoted to the procedures and merits of the teaching methods they deemed most appropriate. Some believed that learning should be based on the direct, firsthand observation of the environment; others stressed the importance of reading and recitation to gain knowledge and mental discipline.

Several popular authors, particularly those writing for a younger or less literate audience, followed traditional methods by modeling their books on the catechismal format of the *New England Primer.* In many cases, entire textbooks were written as a series of short questions and answers.[89] The following passage from Roswell Smith's 1845 text serves as a typical example of the catechismal method: "Q. What are these divisions called? A. Natural divisions. Q. Why are they so called? A. Because they are not made by man but exist in nature."[90] Opponents such as Jedidiah Morse, Emma Willard, and William C. Woodbridge argued that such methods led to an overemphasis on memorization and recitation at the expense of higher reflection. William C. Woodbridge, a well-known educator and later editor of the *American Annals of Education and Instruction* from 1831 to 1837, scathingly described catechismal teaching as comprised of "stultifying methods . . . which impair, instead of improving, those habits of observation and reflection on which the success of the pupil in study, and in future life, depends."[91] However, despite spirited opposition, catechismal texts by such authors as Jesse Olney and Peter Parley (aka Samuel Goodrich) were widely used in the 1830s and 1840s in the common schools of Massachusetts and Connecticut, as shown in Table 1.4. In 1831, one teacher reported that many instructors relied on Nathaniel Dwight's catechismal text as a reader in common schools, perhaps because of the brevity of its sentence structure.[92]

Among those who stressed the importance of firsthand observation in the teaching of geography, contemporaries generally credited Emma Willard (1787–1879) and William C. Woodbridge with introducing the inductive method of teaching into geography textbooks. Willard, the founder and principal of Troy Female Seminary in New York, collaborated with Woodbridge on several geography texts. Their first book, *Rudiments of Geography,* appeared on the American market in 1821, and subsequent revisions were also published in France.[93]

Table 1.4 Geography Texts Most Commonly Reported in the Common School Returns of Massachusetts and Connecticut

Massachusetts (1837)		Connecticut (1846)	
Olney	79%	Smith	57%
Parley	45%	Olney	43%
Maltebrun	27%	Parley	30%
Smith	14%	Mitchell	27%
Morse	1%	Morse	23%

Source: First Abstract of the Massachusetts School Returns for 1837 (Boston: Dutton and Wentworth, 1838); *Annual Report of the Superintendent of Common Schools of Connecticut, 1846* (Hartford, Conn.: Case, Tiffany, and Burnham, 1846). The data are based on a random sampling of thirty towns each in the Massachusetts and Connecticut school returns.

The inductive method of teaching geography began with the study of the student's hometown. Woodbridge advised teachers to begin by leading the child to observe and describe the surrounding environment, thereby providing "a sort of geographical account of the place in which he lives, and the objects around him."[94] This reversed the deductive procedure used by a number of early authors, who began their texts with celestial geography or the geography of Europe. Emma Willard described the method very simply: "Instead of commencing the study of maps with the map of the world, which is the most difficult to understand, the pupil here begins, in the most simple manner imaginable, to draw the map of his own town."[95]

The books of Willard and Woodbridge, like the other most commonly used geographies, were marketed to a general audience and appeared in segregated male and female schools alike. Among the geographies that comprised the sample for this study, none included any recommendations in the preface concerning modifications of the curriculum or instruction to accommodate presumed gender differences. Although teachers may well have varied their instruction when teaching boys or girls, the authors of geography texts—unlike some of the authors of natural philosophy, chemistry, or natural history texts published specifically for a female audience—appear to have operated on the assumption that Americans would accept geography as a subject suitable for both sexes.

Many of the most popular authors of geographies who published for the growing common school market during and after the 1820s embraced the innovative inductive method of Willard and Woodbridge. Nevertheless, rather than incorporate questions designed to stimulate observation or discussion, most writers targeting younger or less literate students simply grafted this approach onto the traditional catechismal method. Advocates of the inductive method argued that "the learner must make himself master of simple things, before he can understand those which are complex."[96] Rather than recommending outdoor excursions in which children might learn geography at first hand, many schoolbooks simply began the study of the subject with a list of questions about the students' hometown. For example, Samuel G. Goodrich began his first lesson by asking, "What place do you live in? Is it a town or a city you live in?"[97] As it appeared in the texts of most early geography authors, even those writing for higher schools, the inductive method was a far cry from the direct observation of nature advocated by Woodbridge and Willard.

Although some firsthand observation of the environment, as recommended by Woodbridge and Willard, may not have been widespread in early nineteenth-century schools, their work may have paved the way for the later reception of object teaching and nature study, pedagogical methods attributed to the famous Swiss educator, Johann Pestalozzi (1746–1827). Pestalozzi emphasized the importance of sense perception, verification, and original research in learning. It is difficult to evaluate the extent to which Pestalozzi may have influenced the early geographies of Woodbridge and Willard, particularly in light of the fact that each author claimed to have originated his or her method independently of any outside influences. However, Pestalozzi's methods were not entirely unknown in the United States at the time. The Swiss reformer's influence had appeared in America through the work of such educators as William Maclure and Joseph Neef. The Scottish geologist Maclure, who had visited Pestalozzi in 1804 and 1805, promoted Pestalozzi's methods of direct observation, not only in an article published in the *National Intelligencer* in 1806, but through the educational programs in his experimental colony at New Harmony, Indiana, during the 1820s. Joseph Neef, a former colleague of Pestalozzi's, opened a short-lived school in 1809 on the outskirts of Philadelphia. According to an account by a former student, Neef regularly took students outdoors on "long tramps through the adjacent country" to obtain firsthand knowledge of geography and natural history, ". . . pointing out their practical illustration in the grain fields, the gardens, the rocks and streams along our route."[98] Whether directly influenced by Pestalozzi or not, the inductive method developed by Woodbridge and Willard and embraced to some degree by subsequent generations of textbook authors may have facilitated the later reception of object teaching and nature study. Woodbridge regularly included articles on Pestalozzi's methods during his tenure as editor of the *American Annals of Education* during the 1830s, and Willard trained generations of future schoolteachers at Troy Seminary, a highly influential female school.[99] Some scholars have argued that object teaching, which involved using items from the child's environment in instruction, became highly popular with classroom teachers across the country during the second half of the nineteenth century. If so, this may be due in part to the efforts of earlier geography educators, who long since had argued that the child's natural environment was the logical starting place for learning.[100]

CONCLUSION

The publication of the first American geography in 1784 marked the beginning of an educational era that would last well into the nineteenth century. Its hallmarks included a fervent belief in the utilitarian and political benefits of reason and science and a faith that the moral character of young Americans could be improved by the study of the natural world.

In spite of ideological differences among diverse communities, Americans appear to have united rather quickly in support of geography as a suitable subject for their children. A broad coalition of groups promoted the subject in private and common schools after the Revolution. Those who thought that a new, enlightened republic could only be created through the efforts of men and women on an equal basis supported the study of geography for both sexes. Others, believing that a woman's proper site of activity was the domestic sphere, supported the study of this science in order to better prepare women for motherhood. Educators desiring to elevate the intellect of the American populace over successive generations promoted the inclusion of so-called higher studies in order to increase the mental discipline of both sexes. Late eighteenth- and early nineteenth-century Protestant evangelical reformers served as an important constituency for promoting the study of science among young women. The marriage of Enlightenment ideas with Puritan theology had an enormous impact on female education in the United States and Great Britain. Many evangelical communities embraced the Enlightenment emphasis on science, nature, and human progress as entirely compatible with a literal belief in Scripture and faith in personal salvation.

The rhetoric advanced in support of geography gained impetus from the unique social, economic, and political context of the young republic. The relatively limited impact of institutionalized schooling and the rudimentary nature of America's scientific community—coupled with the expanding political, economic, and technological needs of the growing nation—induced Americans to promote the study of geography among their daughters as well as their sons. To ensure the success of their new political experiment, Americans required the assistance of both sexes. As mothers and teachers, women played an important role in providing the moral and intellectual training required of young citizens in a new republic. By educating women, Americans thought that they guaranteed the transmission of important mental improvements to subsequent generations. By encouraging both sexes to study the natural world, educators believed they could develop future generations with an elevated sense of morals and increased knowledge of God. Finally, by providing a pleasurable and self-improving source of reading, the study of geography served not only national interests but women's personal interests as well.

The introduction of geography into postcolonial schoolrooms marked an important shift in the way Americans began to think about the education of their daughters. Through geography, science became an acceptable part of the education of American girls. As the nineteenth century progressed, textbooks devoted exclusively to such subjects as botany, astronomy, and natural philosophy appeared in higher schools and diminished in geography textbooks, where they became redundant. Although scientific content declined in later geography texts, it did not disappear from the curriculum available to females. In the decades to come, increasing numbers of girls and young women would take up the study of science in their educational institutions.

2

Science for Ladies,
Classics for Gentlemen

In the spring of 1815, when twenty-four-year-old Susan Nye traveled south from New York to North Carolina to assume her duties as head of the female department in Raleigh Academy, she apparently brought with her knowledge of chemistry. At the time of her arrival in Raleigh, the published course of study in the female department included such subjects as reading, arithmetic, grammar, geography, astronomy, natural philosophy, and rhetoric.[1] Six months later, her students presented a demonstration of chemistry experiments during the public school examinations conducted in the fall. In preparation for this nerve-wracking event, Nye and her students assembled at the academy and marched in style to the statehouse. There, the girls took their places on an elegantly decorated stage before the institution's board of trustees, parents, representatives of the two local newspapers, and a room crowded with spectators.[2] To everyone's undoubted relief, the chemistry experiments were an unqualified success. "The experiments made by the Students in Chemistry did honor to Miss Nye," reported a local newspaper.[3]

Susan Nye was one of a growing number of teachers in higher schools interested in showcasing the scientific knowledge of female students. By the early nineteenth century, many female educators viewed knowledge of scientific subjects as a mark of a rigorous education. From the close of the eighteenth century until just after the Civil War, natural philosophy, astronomy, chemistry, and botany were among the ten subjects most frequently listed in the published courses of study of female academies and seminaries.[4]

Documentary evidence indicating that some girls not only studied the sciences in their textbooks, but also conducted demonstrations and experiments during the first decades of the nineteenth century raises a number of questions. Were scientific subjects available only to a very few girls in elite schools? How can we compare the relative emphasis placed on the sciences in male and female institutions? Such questions cannot be answered without considering a diverse sample of schools from various regions of the country, a sample comprising institutions ranging from relatively large to small, from elite to nondescript. Based on data compiled from newspaper advertisements, published accounts of school examinations, and state superintendents' reports, this chapter compares the emphasis placed on scientific subjects in boys' and girls' private, proprietary, and endowed schools on both northern and southern states.

THE PROPER COURSE OF STUDY FOR GIRLS

What was to be the proper course of study for young women? The same arguments that earlier had justified the teaching of geography to girls supported the introduction of astronomy, natural philosophy (physics), chemistry, and botany as separate subjects. Some of the individual sciences had their own particular set of justifications. For example, concerned about the physical strength of young American girls, both educators and doctors recommended botany, a subject viewed as particularly suited to females because "its pursuits, leading to exercise in the open air, are conducive to health and cheerfulness."[5] The arguments of natural theology applied to every branch of science. For instance, the popular textbook author J. L. Comstock assured his readers that chemistry was a suitable vehicle for moral instruction, because "this subject teaches, that nothing has been formed by the fortuitous concurrence of atoms, but that even the 'stocks and stones' bear the impress of creative agency and design."[6] Proponents of mental discipline portrayed the sciences as among the most rigorous subjects a young woman could study. Because the mind of a woman, like that of a man, needed intellectual exercise, some educators argued that girls should be given additional instruction in the "solid" branches of science rather than in the merely "ornamental" branches of drawing, painting, and needlework.[7] Although classical studies had traditionally played the role of training the mind, many educators argued that the sciences could serve the same function by training students to observe critically and think logically.[8]

While such influential Americans as Thomas Jefferson felt that the subjects of study most useful for American boys included both the classics and the sciences, relatively few reformers before 1830 claimed that girls should study the classics.[9] Traditionally, a classical education had been the prerogative of middle-class boys and men, and it remained so until the mid-nineteenth century. Many educators looked to find rigor in a program for girls not to the classics at first, but to the sciences.[10]

Six years after Susan Nye's students performed chemistry experiments at Raleigh Academy, Troy Female Seminary opened in 1821 under the leadership of Emma Willard, one of a number of institutions that would become important centers for the diffusion of new educational ideas in the early nineteenth century. At the close of the eighteenth century, the standard curricula in girls' higher schools generally had included such subjects as geography, English, writing, arithmetic, and plain needlework, along with several ornamental subjects offered on an elective basis. In contrast, the curriculum at

Troy emphasized mathematics, science, modern languages, history, philosophy, geography, and literature. Such gifted speakers and prolific writers as Emma Willard and her sister Almira Hart Lincoln Phelps; Catharine Beecher, head of Hartford Seminary; Zilpah Grant, head of Ipswich Female Seminary; and Mary Lyon, head of Mount Holyoke Seminary were highly influential in spreading the new views of female education through the work of teachers trained at their institutions. Many of their graduates eventually taught in distant states, bringing these ideas to different parts of the country.[11]

Newly founded higher schools advertised their courses of study in local newspapers in order to attract students. During the period from 1800 to 1845, such advertisements often provided a complete list of the subjects offered in schools, sometimes accompanied with the titles of the textbooks used in various courses. Catharine and Mary Beecher's 1824 advertisement is representative in its degree of detail (see Plate 2.1).

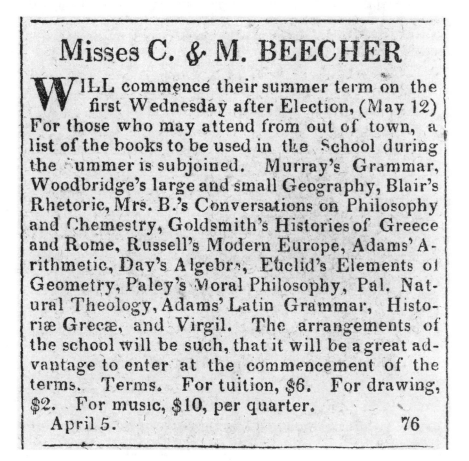

Plate 2.1 "Misses C & M Beecher," in *American Mercury*, Hartford, Connecticut, 20 April 1824. (*Courtesy of the Department of Special Collections, Stanford University Libraries.*)

Although advertisements are unreliable as a means of evaluating either the content or method of the actual instruction delivered in educational institutions, as marketing tools these sources illuminate the degree to which educational institutions differentiated their curricula according to the gender of their desired clientele.

During the first half of the nineteenth century, the curricula of academies and seminaries expanded enormously. Amid a rising belief that girls were indeed endowed by nature with minds to be trained by discipline, many schools began to include such presumably solid subjects as natural philosophy, astronomy, chemistry, and (more rarely) botany during the 1820s and 1830s.[12] In order to remain competitive in attracting students, schools advertised when they added new subjects to their courses of study, or when they added new teachers, textbooks, or scientific apparatus to their programs. A fairly typical example of the curriculum expansion in girls' schools can be seen in the growing number of subjects advertised by North Carolina Shocco Female Academy from 1818 to 1830 (Table 2.1[13]).

The tuition rates in newspaper advertisements indicate that although the sciences never attained the core status of such basic subjects as reading, writing, or arithmetic, more girls' schools included scientific subjects than the so-called ornamental subjects in the basic course of studies, referred to as the English course. It has been a fairly common misconception among historians of education that the ornamental subjects were a staple in the schooling of early nineteenth-century American girls. Thomas Woody first

Table 2.1 Expansion of the Curriculum of Shocco Female Academy, North Carolina, 1818–1830

1818	1823	1826	1830
Reading	Reading	Reading	Reading
Writing	Writing	Writing	Writing
Arithmetic	Arithmetic	Arithmetic	Arithmetic
Grammar	Grammar	Grammar	Grammar
Geography	Geography	Geography	Geography
Needlework	Needlework	Needlework	Needlework
Drawing	Drawing	Drawing	Drawing
Painting	Painting	Painting	Painting
	Spelling	Spelling	Spelling
	Astronomy	Astronomy	Astronomy
	Natural philosophy	Natural philosophy	Natural philosophy
		Chemistry	Chemistry
		Botany	Botany
		History	History
		Music	Music
			Mythology
			Lacework

Source: Data compiled from newspaper advertisements included in *North Carolina Schools and Academies 1790–1840: A Documentary History,* ed. Charles L. Coon (Raleigh, N.C.: Edwards & Broughton, 1915), 604–612.

advanced this interpretation of the place of ornamentals in his 1929 study of female education, claiming that "the [female] seminary continued to offer the fripperies of filigree, painting, music, and drawing in far greater profusion" during the antebellum period.[14] Nevertheless, an examination of advertised tuition rates suggests that the ornamental subjects rarely appeared in the core course of study. For instance, in a sample of thirty-one girls' schools in North Carolina, forty-two percent included the sciences under the basic tuition, while fifty-eight percent charged extra. In contrast, the so-called ornamental subjects, comprising music, painting, drawing, embroidery, and so on, were almost universally offered on a supplemental basis and were sometimes taught by adjunct faculty. In fact, the additional tuition charged for the ornamental subjects was often as much as or even greater than the tuition for the entire English course, which frequently included the sciences. In 1831, a girl seeking to study the subjects of drawing, painting, and music in the Wake Forest Female School had to pay twice the tuition of the English course: "The course of instruction will be that usually pursued, viz; Reading, Writing, Arithmetic, History, Natural Philosophy and Astronomy, Composition, Plain Needle Work and Embroidery, Drawing and Painting, and Music on the Piano. The prices of Tuition for the Session of five months, will be; for the ordinary branches of an English Education $10–Needle Work and Embroidery $5–Drawing and Painting, $5–Music on the Piano $15, payable always in advance."[15]

SCIENCE FOR YOUNG LADIES

Although some of the most prominent female seminaries included such traditionally male subjects as Latin and Greek in their courses of study, a minority of schools followed this pattern until later in the century, choosing instead to offer students an educational program deemed more suitable for females.[16] During the second and third decades of the nineteenth century, an increasing percentage of institutions advertised a curriculum that included such subjects as astronomy, natural philosophy, chemistry, and, to a lesser extent, natural history. So prevalent was the addition of science to a girl's course of studies in North Carolina in 1826 that the female department of Tarborough Academy described its program as being "as extensive as at other Female Seminaries, including Chemistry, Astronomy, Natural Philosophy, Rhetoric and History." The Academy's advertisement added, "such as desire it may be taught plain and ornamental Needle Work, Painting on Paper and Velvet, and Music."[17] Similarly, the 1830 prospectus of Connecticut's New Haven Female Seminary claimed that its course of study embraced "all the scientific and ornamental branches necessary to complete the female education."[18]

Visitors from abroad were struck by the relatively rigorous education of American girls. De Toqueville contrasted the cloistered schooling of girls in France with the practice in America, where "unable and unwilling to keep a girl in perpetual and complete ignorance, [Americans] are in a hurry to give her precocious knowledge of everything."[19] The Englishwoman

Frances Trollope, who lived in the United States for several years during the late 1820s, recounted her experience at the annual public exhibition of a New England girls' school, where she "perceived, with some surprise, that the higher branches of science were among the studies of the pretty creatures I saw assembled there."[20] In 1850, the Swedish writer Fredrika Bremer concluded that American girls advanced as far in their scientific studies as did American boys, "[o]pportunity is afforded [girls] to advance as far as the young men in study and the sciences, which have hitherto been considered as too difficult for them, are as easy for them to acquire as that superficial knowledge and accomplishment to which hitherto their education has been confined."[21]

In actuality, the opportunity to study the sciences was largely confined to females from wealthy families. Relatively few American girls had either the leisure or financial means to study the sciences during the antebellum era. Some of the textbooks published during the antebellum period reveal the assumptions of contemporaries about the social status of females who engaged in scientific investigation. For example, Richard G. Parker's *Juvenile Philosophy*, a popular elementary text, conveys scientific principles through the medium of a mother's conversation with her daughter. The elite status of this pair is implied in their surroundings and apparatus. One illustration depicts the two of them in a well-appointed drawing room, using a gold coin to perform a science experiment (see Plate 2.2).[22]

Although the study of the sciences was largely the prerogative of the middle and upper classes, it was not restricted to the children of Anglo-Saxon, Protestant families. Indications of the movement to bring science into girls' courses of study can be found in some Catholic schools and in several academies serving Native Americans. Some of the academies run by various orders of the Catholic Church adapted to the newer American views of female education by offering scientific subjects to middle-class girls. For example, in 1842, the Maryland Carmelite Sister's Academy advertised natural philosophy, botany, and astronomy in its course of study, along with such other subjects as sacred history.[23]

In frontier St. Louis, the Society of the Sacred Heart reserved most scientific subjects for the daughters of well-to-do families. In her discussion of the Society of the Sacred Heart schools in St. Louis, Nikola Baumgarten describes both the curriculum offered to indigent girls in the free school and that offered to girls in the order's more prestigious academy. In the free school, girls studied reading, writing, spelling, arithmetic, and religion. Advanced studies, offered in the 1830s for a small fee, included grammar, geography, and sewing. In contrast, girls in the academy studied natural philosophy, astronomy, chemistry, and geography, along with the other usual branches of a presumably solid education. Baumgarten attributes the inclusion of scientific subjects in the Catholic curriculum to the influence of such female educators as Emma Willard and Catharine Beecher.[24]

Scientific subjects were also offered to the daughters of elites in the Cherokee Nation. Since 1839, wealthier mixed-blood Cherokees had sent their daughters to the Fayetteville Female Academy in Arkansas, where they were instructed in geography and ancient history, logic, natural phi-

you to understand.   But I will try to make it easy for you to understand.   There is a basin of water on the table.   Take this gold coin and put it into the basin, and tell me where it goes to.

CHILD.—It has gone down to the bottom of the basin, mother.

MOTHER.—Now take the cork from that bottle, and put that into the basin.

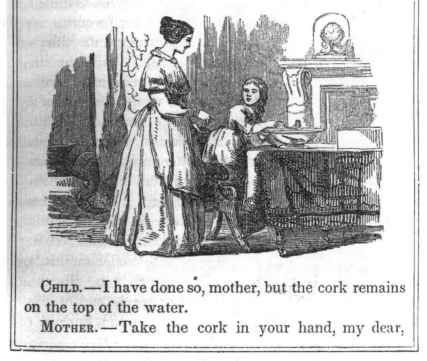

CHILD.—I have done so, mother, but the cork remains on the top of the water.

MOTHER.—Take the cork in your hand, my dear,

Plate 2.2   "Conversation on Rain," a mother and daughter conduct an experiment to determine which objects sink or float. In Richard G. Parker's *Juvenile Philosophy*, 1850. *(Courtesy of Cubberley Library, Stanford University.)*

losophy, literature, astronomy, and other subjects conducive to elevating the "female character in the Nation." Established in Tahlequah in 1843, another option for young Cherokee women was the Cherokee Female Seminary, where pupils were instructed in a curriculum that included the natural sciences.[25]

In 1847, the Cherokee National Council enacted a law requiring the teachers of the Female Seminary to teach "all the branches of literature and science commonly taught in the academies of the United States." As a source of faculty for the seminary, Cherokees looked to Mary Lyon's Mount Holyoke Female Seminary. Between 1839 and 1856, twenty-four Mount Holyoke alumnae taught among North American tribes.[26]

Modeled on the curriculum at Mount Holyoke Female Seminary, the course of study at Cherokee Female Seminary was distinguished from that in the Nation's common schools by its emphasis on literature and the sciences. In 1852, students in Cherokee common schools studied a basic course of reading, spelling, geography, and arithmetic. During the same period, the daughters of wealthier Cherokee families were instructed in such additional subjects as botany, natural philosophy, and astronomy.[27]

Documentary evidence suggests that in some communities, the daughters of free African-Americans studied science in town schools and private academies during the antebellum period. Such an individual was Charlotte Forten Grimké, who came of a free elite Philadelphia family. In the 1850s, she attended school with white students in Salem, Massachusetts. Her journal entries reveal that while a student at Higginson Grammar School, she studied geography, geology, natural philosophy, and entomology.[28] Some private institutions serving free African-Americans included the sciences in their courses of study. For example, it is likely that Rebecca J. Cole (1846–1922) studied science when she was a student at Philadelphia's Institute for Colored Youth. The institute derived support from the bequest of Richard Humphreys, a Quaker goldsmith who directed the establishment of a school for "The benevolent design of instructing the descendants of the African Race" in 1832. Humphreys had originally conceived of a school that would offer instruction in practical subjects such as mechanics, trades, and agriculture. However, after a failed experiment with a farm school, the board of managers met in 1848 to consider apprenticing students to black mechanics in the city. As a result of these discussions, the Quaker board eventually gave a group of black tradesmen the authority to establish a board of education auxiliary to develop a new school that would apprentice students by day and provide instruction at night. When they met to determine the course of study, the board proposed to offer higher schooling comparable to that available to white students in Philadelphia. The institute opened its doors in 1849 with a class of thirty students. After Rebecca Cole graduated from this school in 1863, she went on to receive her medical degree from Woman's Medical College in 1867, becoming the second African-American woman physician in the United States.[29]

SCIENCE FOR GIRLS, CLASSICS FOR BOYS

A variety of contemporary sources indicate that while the sciences maintained a marginal presence in boys' academies, they were highly visible in girls' schools. Newspaper advertisements published in both northern and

Table 2.2 Percentage of North Carolina and Virginia Higher Schools Advertising Various Sciences, 1800–1840

	Natural philosophy	Astronomy	Chemistry	Botany	Mineralogy	Natural history
Girls' schools (n=78)	74	47	54	35	5	13
Boys' schools (n=86)	47	22	21	2	3	1

Source: Data compiled from newspaper advertisements for sixty-one Virginia schools published in the *Richmond Enquirer* (Virginia, 1835–38) and 103 schools included in *North Carolina Schools and Academies 1790–1840: A Documentary History,* ed. Charles L. Coon (Raleigh, N.C.: 1915).

southern states reveal that a larger percentage of female institutions advertised scientific subjects than did male institutions during the same period. Natural philosophy, astronomy, and chemistry were the most commonly advertised sciences in both male and female institutions. Botany appeared in a majority of girls' schools only after 1840 (see Tables 2.2, 2.3, and 2.4).

In comparing the results for northern and southern states, there appears to be little regional variation in the percentage of girls' schools advertising scientific subjects; the higher figures reported for Pennsylvania are attributable to the later time period (1830–1889) represented by the schools in Mulhern's sample. However, although evidence is sketchy, the newspapers examined for this study indicate that a larger percentage of boys' schools in northern states advertised the sciences than did their southern counter-

Table 2.3 Percentage of Higher Schools in Selected Northern States Advertising Various Sciences, 1820–1842

	Natural philosophy	Astronomy	Chemistry	Botany	Mineralogy	Natural history
Girls' schools (n=24)	63	50	58	25	0	4
Boys' schools (n=15)	53	33	53	27	20	0

Source: Data compiled from newspaper advertisements for thirty-nine schools published in *American Mercury* (Connecticut, 1820–29 [incomplete]); *Columbian Centinel* (Massachusetts, 1827–31); *Baltimore Sun* (Maryland, 1841–42); *New York Evening Post* (1 August 1835–31 May 1836); *The Globe* (Washington D.C., 1831); *Daily National Intelligencer* (Washington D.C., 1825).

Table 2.4 Percentage of Pennsylvania Higher Schools Offering Various Sciences, 1830–1889

	Natural philosophy	Astronomy	Chemistry	Botany	Mineralogy	Natural history
Girls' schools (n=90)	88	67	72	77	33	—
Boys' and coed schools (n=116)	54	47	56	33	28	—

Source: Data compiled from tables in James Mulhern, *A History of Secondary Education in Pennsylvania*, 328–29; 428–429. Mulhern's data are based on an analysis of school catalogs.

parts, a trend that may have developed in response to the growing industrialization of the North.

CLASSICS FOR YOUNG GENTLEMEN

While a girl's education commonly included doses of scientific subjects, a boy's education more often centered on Latin and Greek, particularly in the South. For example, in Virginia and North Carolina, Latin was the most frequently advertised subject in boys' academies and private schools from 1790 to 1840; ninety-one percent of boys' schools advertised Latin, and eighty-five percent advertised Greek. In contrast, only eighteen percent of girls' schools advertised Latin, and a very meager five percent advertised Greek. In the North, only a slightly larger percentage of boys' schools than girls' schools advertised Latin, although female institutions usually offered the subject on an elective basis only.[30]

Another way to compare the curricula offered to the two sexes is to examine the courses of study in schools with both male and female departments. Of the 103 schools represented in the North Carolina sample, seven placed advertisements describing curricula for the male and female departments of the same institution.[31] Six of the seven institutions advertised a different science curriculum for their male and female departments. As shown in Table 2.5, the curriculum of Vine Hill Academy exemplifies variations in the subjects available to middle-class males and females; the classics, higher mathematics, navigation, and surveying were offered to males; whereas natural philosophy, astronomy, chemistry, botany, and several other subjects were offered to females.

In New York's Genesee Wesleyan Seminary, which offered the same number of scientific subjects to both sexes in separate departments, girls predominated in the science courses. Despite the fact that boys composed sixty-two percent of the student body in 1834, enrollment data reveal that

Table 2.5 Comparison of the Male and Female Courses of Study Advertised by Vine Hill Academy, North Carolina, 1837

Male department	Female department
Spelling	Spelling
Reading	Reading
Writing	Writing
Grammar	Grammar
Geography	Geography
History	History
Arithmetic	Arithmetic
Rhetoric	Rhetoric
Logic	Logic
French	French
Latin	—
Greek	—
Algebra	—
Geometry	—
Navigation	—
Surveying	—
—	Natural philosophy
—	Chemistry
—	Astronomy
—	Botany
—	Moral and intellectual philosophy
—	Natural theology
—	Elements of criticism
—	Drawing and painting

Source: Data compiled from the *Raleigh Star* (17 May 1837), in *North Carolina Schools: A Documentary History,* ed. Charles L. Coon (Raleigh, N.C.: 1915), 176–177.

a significantly larger percentage of girls than boys studied the sciences (Table 2.6). According to historian Nancy Beadie, "males, by contrast, dominated in Latin, algebra, Greek, Hebrew, bookkeeping, trigonometry, various branches of applied geometry (for surveying and navigation.)"[32]

School examinations provide another source of information about the relative importance of scientific subjects in the curriculum. Newspapers

Table 2.6 Number and Percentage of Each Sex Enrolled in Science Courses at Genesee Wesleyan Seminary, New York, 1834

	Total enrollment	Natural philosophy	Astronomy	Chemistry	Botany
Girls	144	85 (59%)	7 (5%)	33 (23%)	11 (8%)
Boys	232	64 (28%)	0	20 (9%)	0

Source: Nancy Beadie, "Emma Willard's Idea Put to the Test: The Consequences of State Support of Female Education in New York, 1819–67," *History of Education Quarterly* 33 (winter 1993): 559–560n.

occasionally published accounts of the examinations of the larger and more prestigious local academies and seminaries, often including the names of examinees and the subjects on which they were examined. Although institutions may have included scientific subjects in their advertised courses of study in order to appeal to a broad market of parents and guardians, the published reports of examinations indicate to a far greater degree the subjects that students actually studied.

Because the success or failure of its students reflected on the quality of instruction at each institution, it is unlikely that subjects taught incidentally were included in examinations. Public examinations were high-stakes performances. They were conducted orally, often in the presence of a large audience of relatives, ministers, trustees, and visiting preceptors from other schools. In an era when few forms of public entertainment were available, the examinations in some cases assumed the form of a spectacle. When Mary Lyon was teaching at Ipswich Female Seminary with Zilpah Grant, "public examination carryalls from Andover rolled over to Ipswich to help swell the audience."[33] The examinations sometimes lasted for several days, no doubt creating an atmosphere of terror and excitement for students. Depending on the procedures outlined in a school's charter, examinations might be held at the end of each term or more frequently. At Salisbury Academy in North Carolina, students endured both private and public examinations. Each year was divided into two sessions, each session consisting of two quarters. At the end of each quarter, a committee appointed by the board of trustees privately examined students on their various studies over a period of two days. Twice a year, the committee conducted a public examination and reported the results in local newspapers.[34]

In their academies, boys were almost always examined on the classics and on such core subjects as geography, arithmetic, and grammar. For example, at North Carolina's Raleigh Academy in 1807, while the rest of his classmates endured questions on such topics as Horace, Virgil, Caesar, Selectae Veterii, Erasmus, Aesop's Fables, the Greek Testament, and Latin grammar, Thomas Gales was the sole student examined on natural philosophy and astronomy, evidencing "by his ready and unembarrassed answers, his perfect acquaintance with them."[35] It was not uncommon for a boys' academy to include natural philosophy or astronomy in its advertised course of study but to exclude these subjects from its examinations.[36]

Published accounts of examinations in North Carolina reveal that a greater percentage of girls' schools included scientific subjects in their exams than did boys' schools of the same period (Table 2.7). Although the majority of girls were examined on such core subjects as geography, reading, spelling, and grammar, and on such ornamentals as fancy needlework and painting, it was not uncommon also to find classes of girls examined in natural philosophy, astronomy, or chemistry. Female students generally impressed their examiners with their knowledge of various scientific subjects. For instance, in 1826, the examiners of Charlotte Female Academy noted with admiration, "the abstruse principles of Natural Philosophy and Astronomy were fully comprehended and understood by those who are yet but children."[37]

Table 2.7   Percentage of Selected North Carolina Schools Including Scientific Subjects in Their Examinations, 1800–1840

Girls' schools (n=9)	Boys' schools (n=14)
78	14

Source: Data compiled from newspaper advertisements in *North Carolina Schools and Academies: A Documentary History,* ed. Charles L. Coon (Raleigh, N.C.: 1915).

In New England, the examinations given in the common schools of Boston, Massachusetts, under the leadership of Horace Mann reveal a similar situation. The Boston common schools of this period offered free instruction to the children of Boston's citizens. Each school was really two schools in one: a writing school and a grammar school. Older children were generally divided from younger children in four recitation groups called classes, corresponding somewhat to present-day grades. Students could not be admitted from the primary to the grammar and writing schools until they were seven years old, at which point they could enter the fourth class. The master of the writing school taught the subjects of writing, arithmetic, algebra, geometry, and bookkeeping, and the master of the grammar school taught the subjects of grammar, reading, geography, history, and sometimes natural philosophy and astronomy.[38]

The School Committee of the City of Boston appointed a subcommittee in 1845 to examine the highest—or first—class in each of the nineteen grammar schools in Boston. Five schools catered exclusively to girls, five to boys, and the remaining schools were coeducational.[39] The students in the first classes were about to graduate, being on average fourteen years old. Among the tests created for this purpose were those in natural philosophy and astronomy. The subcommittee examined each of the schools in the city and published the results.[40]

Thirteen of the nineteen common schools in Boston reportedly offered natural philosophy as an elective, and four offered astronomy on the same basis. Because taking the examinations in these subjects was optional, schools that did not provide instruction in astronomy or natural philosophy declined to submit scholars for questioning.[41] Although the city offered scientific subjects on an elective basis in its common schools, the subject still retained something of its elite character. For example, it is likely that Smith School, an institution serving African-American children, did not offer instruction in astronomy or natural philosophy, because although Smith examined students in other subjects, the school declined to produce scholars for examination in the sciences.[42] All five of the girls' schools produced scholars for the natural philosophy examination, and two of these schools, Franklin and Johnson, produced scholars for the astronomy examination as well. In contrast, only two boys' schools produced scholars for the natural philosophy examination, and no boys' school consented to be examined on astronomy (Table 2.8).

Table 2.8   Students in Boston Common Schools Examined in Natural Philosophy and Astronomy, 1845

Girls' schools	Enrollment	Number examined in natural philosophy	Number examined in astronomy
Bowdoin	508	45	0
Wells	307	27	0
Franklin	418	14	19
Hancock	509	20	0
Johnson	547	44	50
Total	2,289	150	69

Boys' schools	Enrollment	Number examined in natural philosophy	Number examined in astronomy
Brimmer	513	35	0
Eliot	456	0	0
Adams	418	0	0
Mayhew	368	19	0
New South	136	0	0
Total	1,891	54	0

Source: Data compiled from Otis W. Caldwell and Stuart A. Courtis, *Then & Now in Education 1845–1923* (Yonkers-on-Hudson, N.Y.: World Book Co., 1925), 342, 344.

Because students from both the top-ranked girls' and boys' schools took the examination in natural philosophy, it is possible to compare the relative performance of boys and girls. According to the examining committee, Bowdoin was the top-ranked girls' school, and Brimmer was the top-ranked boys' school.[43] Although the scores overall were rather disappointing to the citizens of Boston, the girls scored much higher than the boys. The girls from Bowdoin correctly answered thirty-six percent of the questions on the natural philosophy examination, whereas the boys from Brimmer correctly answered only nineteen percent.[44] Ironically, although the examiners ranked Brimmer as the highest-quality boys' school, in all of the examinations scholars from other schools consistently outperformed its scholars. The examiners, perhaps unable to see beyond the social status of Brimmer's students, nevertheless held unfailingly to a belief in the intelligence of the school's scholars: "The boys of the first class have . . . a general intelligence, which was perfectly obvious to the committee, but of which no record can appear in our tables."[45]

The evidence provided by newspaper advertisements, tuition rates, and reports of school examinations reveals a distinctly greater emphasis on scientific subjects in schools for middle-class girls than in similar institutions for boys. At first offered to the children of elites in academies and seminaries, the sciences began to appear more frequently in common schools in the late 1830s. A sampling of the school returns in Massachusetts reveals a substantial increase in the percentage of towns reporting the use of sci-

Table 2.9 Massachusetts Towns Reporting Science Textbooks in Their Common Schools, 1837 and 1841

	1837	*1841*
Natural philosophy	17%	73%
Astronomy	7%	23%
Chemistry	10%	20%
Natural history	0	3%

Source: Data compiled from a random sampling of thirty towns each in *Abstract of the Massachusetts School Returns for 1837* (Boston, Mass.: Dutton and Wentworth, 1838) and *Abstract of the Massachusetts School Returns for 1840–41* (Boston, Mass.: Dutton and Wentworth, 1841).

ence textbooks in the common schools during a brief four-year period beginning in 1837 (Table 2.9).

SOCIAL AND CULTURAL INFLUENCES

Why did the sciences become more prevalent in middle-class girls' schools than in comparable institutions for boys before the Civil War? In formulating an answer to this question, it is important to consider some of the social and cultural context influencing these institutions in the early nineteenth century.

One explanation for the dominance of the traditional classical curriculum in boys' academies lies in the entrance requirements of local colleges. In 1810, the University of Pennsylvania required candidates to translate Caesar's *Commentaries* and Virgil, to translate English exercises into Latin, and to translate the gospels from Greek. Thirty years later, admission requirements of male colleges generally covered parts of Caesar, Virgil, Cicero, the *Anabasis*, and the *Iliad*.[46] Many college presidents were ministers serving under predominantly clerical boards of trustees. Trained in the classics themselves, such leaders valued a classical education as the best preparation for college.[47] For students who were college bound, the years of study necessary to achieve mastery in the classics must have left little time for other studies. Nathaniel True, a student at Maine's North Yarmouth Academy during the 1820s, recalled his classical studies as being all-consuming: "I sat up one night a week during the term without retiring and studied every night until midnight. I averaged more than eighteen hours a day in getting my two Latin lessons each day for recitation."[48]

A second reason for the durability of the classical curriculum was the social prestige of classical study in American nineteenth-century culture. Although the majority of academy students may not have gone on to college,[49] the attainment of classical knowledge conferred a gentlemanly polish on boys who eventually planned to manage their fathers' plantations or pursue a career in business. In their interviews with British middle-class parents in the 1860s, inspectors for the Taunton Commission discovered that parents simply did not wish to experiment with the education of their sons. Instead, parents expressed the belief that "to learn the classics was a definite mark of an upper class and clearly separated the education of their sons from that of a merely commercial school."[50] Americans were equally anxious to maintain or elevate the social status of their children. The curriculum in some nineteenth-century mechanics institutes illustrates this trend. For example, during the 1820s, the founders of the Franklin Institute in Philadelphia, viewing the classics as the traditional prerogative of "children of the rich," deliberately included classical subjects in the institute's high school department in order to promote the upward social mobility of their pupils.[51] Impelled by the same motive, the trustees of Philadelphia's Institute for Colored Youth added Latin and Greek to the curriculum by 1857.[52]

The schoolmasters in boys' academies constitute a third factor in the resistance of these institutions to offer scientific instruction. Having been trained in the classics themselves, many instructors were probably reluctant to add new subjects to the curriculum. Often, those who defended Latin as the ideal educational instrument for mental training had vested interests in maintaining the status quo, being either schoolmasters or professors of Latin in college classics departments.[53]

A fourth influence on the curricula in male academies was the existing job market. Because there were relatively few profitable career opportunities for young men as physicists, astronomers, geologists, or botanists in the early nineteenth century, there was little incentive to promote these subjects in the academies on the basis of their vocational value. As one educator concluded in 1825, "A large proportion of the sciences, taught in our Colleges, has no other use than as a discipline of the mind."[54] By the third decade of the century, the era of the great surveys was just beginning. In 1830, a writer noted that the science of geology was virtually unknown in the smaller communities of the United States: "A geologist in a retired town, engaged in his examination of rocks, is often surrounded by a collection of individuals, eyeing him with contempt; pity, or suspicion."[55] Even forty years later, the appearance of a scientist in a small town was a novelty.[56] Although entrance to the medical profession required scientific study, those aspiring to become doctors traditionally studied the sciences in college after a rigorous classical training at the academy. A similar path, in which classical training preceded scientific study, lay ahead of those seeking to become professional scientists.

In fact, what might be termed vocational subjects remained relatively scarce in academies before 1840. For example, while some forms of employment required knowledge of navigation, mensuration, or surveying, fewer than one-third of academies in Pennsylvania and North Carolina provided instruction in these subjects before 1840.[57] This state of affairs can be explained by the existence of competing institutions. Such institutions as mechanics' institutes and other evening schools offered vocational training to young men needing to work during the day.[58] The following advertisement for an evening school in North Carolina is fairly representative: "The subscriber will open an Evening School . . . [where] will be taught Reading, Writing, English Grammar, Geography, Arithmetic, Trigonometry, Mensuration of Surfaces and Solids, Navigation and Surveying."[59]

We can infer that many upper- and middle-class American parents considered the study of the sciences an unnecessary frill in the education of their sons. Marketing their programs to this audience through local newspapers, male academies advertised the classics far more frequently than the sciences. It is likely that parents disdained the sciences because such subjects were not needed to gain entrance to college, had little value in imparting the gentlemanly polish of liberal culture, and afforded relatively few career opportunities. When he visited America in the 1850s, Swedish commentator Per Siljestrom noted with surprise that Americans appeared to hold the natural sciences in relatively low esteem.[60]

Although parents may not have considered the sciences quite good enough for their sons, they viewed them as acceptable for their daughters. The most important factor in the rise of scientific subjects in girls' schools is the novelty of the institutions themselves. Unlike boys' academies, which were preceded by the Latin grammar schools, there was no precedent for the curriculum in female seminaries. As a result, educational reformers seeking to bring the sciences into secondary schools were far more likely to succeed in girls' schools.

College entrance requirements, so influential in the male academies, held little sway over educational institutions for girls. Because colleges were generally not open to women before 1850, girls' schools were free of the burden of preparing students for entrance requirements in the classics.[61] In addition, the study of the classics was traditionally the prerogative of males. In 1803, one writer who supported the education of girls nevertheless cautioned against allowing them to study the classics, advising parents to "Let your girls go in hand with your boys, as far as reading, writing, and accounts; there draw a line, for girls have nothing to do with Latin and Greek."[62]

The influence of trends from Europe undoubtedly played a part in the development of women's scientific interests in the United States. The eighteenth century witnessed an increase in the production of popular science in both Great Britain and France, and the numbers of science books written for a female audience gradually increased. These publications were primarily elementary textbooks for women and children, in which concepts of natural philosophy, chemistry, or natural history were conveyed through the medium of female characters, a format that effectively emphasized the appropriateness of women's scientific interests. Since the seventeenth century, there had been a steady flow of ideas from Great Britain and Europe to North America, and the same sources of transmission increased in the eighteenth century. Newspapers, books, pamphlets, and periodicals published reprints of European and British articles and stories. In addition, personal contact by travel and correspondence guaranteed an exchange of ideas between countries. Soon, Americans published their own popular science books for women, and their texts quickly appeared on bookstore shelves next to European imports.[63]

The almost complete lack of public opposition to the study of science in girls' schools can be attributed to the tacit acceptance of this movement among many American scientists. For America's fledgling scientific community, there were benefits to be gained by encouraging girls and women to study the sciences. First, as popularizers of science, women helped to create a supportive public. In an era when few public funds were available for scientific enterprises, the popularization of science ensured a public receptive to the necessary financing of experiments, surveys, and expeditions. Second, as consumers of popular science, women's numbers swelled the audiences at lyceum lectures, helping to pay the salaries of male scientists who traveled the lecture circuit. Also, such scientists as Benjamin Silliman, Denison Olmsted, Asa Gray, and others wrote science textbooks and developed scientific apparatus for the use of academies and seminaries, and the royalties from the sales of these texts in girls' schools must have produced handsome profits. Third, as collectors of mineral and botanical specimens, women amateurs served as unpaid assistants aiding the research efforts of professional male scientists in herbaria, museums, and colleges.

The social and cultural influences briefly outlined here helped to create an educational climate in which scientific subjects easily gained entry into the curricula of educational institutions for middle- and upper-class girls. Although science was initially included in the courses of study of academies and seminaries, by the midnineteenth century its presence was also beginning to be felt in common schools.

Ironically, the same elites who studied scientific subjects in seminaries and academies helped to dismantle science's privileged status by introducing it into common schools. The graduates of female seminaries often became schoolteachers. Having studied some natural philosophy, astronomy, or chemistry themselves, convinced of the utility and moral worth of such subjects, and supported in their purpose by like-minded contemporaries who advocated science in common schools, seminary graduates undoubtedly felt it only natural to introduce science to the older students in their classrooms.[64]

CONCLUSION

Increasingly toward the middle decades of the nineteenth century, a young woman's schooling included the study of the sciences. The reported courses of study of early female schools, seminaries, and academies evidences a greater emphasis on scientific subjects than the curricula of similar, contemporary institutions for boys.

Historians of science have frequently noted the rapid entry of women into scientific fields in the United States in the latter half of the nineteenth century. Until now, explanations of this phenomenon have centered either on the extracurricular scientific literature increasingly aimed at a female audience during the late eighteenth and early nineteenth centuries or on the opening of colleges and universities to women during the latter decades of the nineteenth century.[65] The research in this study reports a consistent body of evidence to support the conclusion that a scientific curriculum was widely implemented in higher female schools from the first decades of the nineteenth century. The science education of American girls in the antebellum period thus constitutes a likely and hitherto overlooked factor in the rise of science as a female interest after the Civil War.

Long after the Revolution, Americans continued to take social class into consideration when selecting the subjects their children should study. Although such reformers as Benjamin Franklin, Noah Webster, and Benjamin Rush had claimed that the Revolution would serve as a catalyst for a thorough reform of society, Americans' awareness of social distinctions did not change. Like the colonists, antebellum parents believed their daughters should acquire abilities and skills appropriate to the family's social standing. As the subject of geography entered the lower classes of common schools, the more advanced study of the individual sciences, attainable at the higher levels in private schools, not only provided the presumed benefits of scientific study generally, but also conveyed the social distinction of culture and the perceived attributes of a higher-class status. Eventually, the gradual introduction of the individual sciences into publicly funded common schools would bring some form of scientific study to students from a much broader range of ethnic and socioeconomic backgrounds. Nevertheless, the impulse to distinguish among students along class lines would persist, with consequences for the scientific study of young women near the end of the century, a development discussed later in this volume.

By the 1840s, the young women who read Almira Hart Lincoln Phelps's botany text undoubtedly would have agreed with her assessment that females "have been encouraged to approach even to [science's] portals." Some educators of that era believed that young women would progress even further. In his 1845 address on female education, William Johnston asked, "Where shall ladies leave off while gentlemen press forward? Into what profound mystery of science shall man be permitted to enter where woman may not follow?"[66]

3

"What Will Be the Use of This Study?"

In 1837, Virginia's Bedford Female Academy published a blistering indictment of the science education offered in rival institutions. "Women are not destined to be Navigators, nor Opticians, nor Almanac-makers, nor Practical Mechanics, nor Miners, nor Engineers, nor Doctors of Medicine;" instead, ". . . [they] should understand . . . much more of Cookery than of Chemistry."[1] According to Bedford, the science commonly taught in female seminaries was a "pretended science taught only in name," a subject incapable of strengthening or adorning the female mind. A conservative female school that took pride in offering a so-called ornamental rather than a scientific education for girls, Bedford claimed that scientific study misled young women from their true vocation in the home.[2] The claims made by Bedford Academy raise two interesting questions about the science education of girls in the early nineteenth century. First, did girls indeed study science "only in name," a science best characterized as rudimentary? Second, to what extent did the science in girls' schools include topics related to such traditionally male vocations as navigation, mining, mechanics, or engineering?

To date, no published study has undertaken a comparative analysis of the science studied in nineteenth-century higher schools. As a result, historians have either speculated, with understandable caution, that science offered in female schools may have been quite elementary, or have boldly claimed, on the basis of the subject listings in selected girls' courses of study, that the sciences studied in female institutions were comparable to those offered in male institutions. Over the last several decades, a number of scholars working in different fields have contributed to our understanding of girls' scientific interests in the nineteenth century.[3] As yet, an important question remains unanswered: How did the method, content, and level of difficulty of the sciences offered to girls compare with those offered to boys?

One means of evaluating the sciences offered the two sexes is to compare the textbooks used by each in their respective educational institutions. As a means of assessing actual classroom instruction, of course, this method is quite limited. For a number of imaginable reasons, the science girls learned in their schoolrooms may in fact have borne little resemblance to the content of their schoolbooks. In some cases, well-trained instructors may have set aside the texts altogether, preferring to teach by demonstration and discussion, and their less-prepared colleagues may have omitted entire sections of the texts in order to avoid potentially difficult or unfamiliar material. On the other hand, the students themselves may have been idly daydreaming or preoccupied with extracurricular matters during their science lessons, and thus retained little of the textbook content at the end of the course. Nevertheless, because most contemporary accounts of nineteenth-century schooling indicate that instruction and examination was based largely on recitation from texts, these sources bring us as close as we are likely to get to assessing the scientific content imparted in nineteenth-century classrooms.[4]

Using textbooks as a source can illuminate two issues that are central to the study of gender and science. Because mathematics is a prerequisite to the advanced study of the sciences, some scholars today argue that girls avoid scientific subjects because of their mathematical complexity. An examination of the textbooks used in nineteenth-century girls' schools yields information about the level of mathematics included in the sciences then available to females. Textbooks can also reveal the extent to which precollege science content was differentiated by gender. Some late eighteenth- and nineteenth-century advocates of women's education argued that rather than learn so-called pure science, girls should attend to a domestic science focused on the activities of hearth and home. Examining science textbooks written specifically for a female audience can reveal the extent to which they successfully implemented their rhetoric in practice.

Another means of evaluating the sciences in girls' schools is to examine the apparatus available to females. Of course, the mere existence of laboratory equipment in a school does not guarantee that students ever used it, because chemicals, minerals, and telescopes may have remained locked away in closets throughout most of the school year. Nevertheless, an investigation of the resources available to girls can at least help to reveal the extent to which such resources appear to have been equitable with those available to boys.

In order to shed light on these and other issues, this chapter compares the content, method, and level of difficulty of natural philosophy, astronomy, and chemistry offered to boys and girls in their separate secondary schools before 1850. Because natural history occurred less frequently in the curricula during this period, it is considered separately in Chapter 5.

DEBATES OVER PURE OR DOMESTIC SCIENCE

What kind of scientific content did nineteenth-century Americans offer their daughters? Since the mideighteenth century, colonial and later American bookstores had carried self-help texts aimed to instruct women on everything from "the choice of a Husband," to gardening, baking, and preserving foods.[5] Seeking to institutionalize a distinctively female science curriculum, from an early period such educational reformers as Benjamin Rush, Catharine Beecher, Almira Hart Lincoln Phelps, and others advocated a curriculum for girls centered on the applications of science to the tasks of the household.[6] Contemporaries used the term *domestic science* to indicate the specific application of scientific principles to domestic activities. Thus it was distinguished from the term *domestic arts,* which denoted the activities of the household.

Professor of chemistry at the University of Pennsylvania, Benjamin Rush had suggested a curriculum for girls that included a "general acquaintance with the first principles of chemistry, and natural philosophy, particularly with such parts of them as are applicable to domestic and culinary purposes." As early as 1787, Rush actually taught such a chemistry course at the Young Ladies' Academy in Philadelphia. In this twelve-lecture course, Rush devoted the first seven lectures to general chemistry and the last five to the applications of chemistry to cooking and housekeeping, speaking on such topics as "the means of preserving female beauty," "the means of preparing vegetables for food," and "of rendering a house clean and wholesome."[7]

Given the prominence of those individuals who advanced the rhetoric of domestic science, it is not surprising that some historians have taken the rhetoric at face value, assuming that the concept of domestic science gained widespread acceptance through the work of such educators as Emma Willard and Catharine Beecher. However, an examination of the textbooks used in girls' schools reveals that this was far from being the case.[8]

The first, certainly the most widely used science text appearing in girls' schools from 1810 to 1830 focused on so-called pure rather than domestic science. This was Jane Marcet's *Conversations on Chemistry, intended more especially for the Female Sex.* Marcet's text appeared in England in 1805, achieving enormous popularity. The first American edition came on the market in 1806, and a sixteenth edition appeared in 1853. She wrote other *Conversations*: on vegetable physiology, on natural philosophy, and on political economy. According to Deborah Jean Warner, Marcet's *Conversations on Natural Philosophy* went through three dozen American printings before the Civil War, and her *Conversations on Vegetable Physiology* achieved a similar success.[9] In her texts, Marcet wrote about the principles of science rather than its applications to the activities of the household.

Although Marcet was not the first to write science books specifically for a female audience, in the opinion of many of her contemporaries, she stood head and shoulders above the rest. In her *Biographical Sketches*, the well-known author Harriet Martineau wrote, "Mrs. Barbauld's *Early Lessons* were good; Miss Edgeworth's were better, but Mrs. Marcet's are transcendent as far as they go."[10] The British scientist Michael Faraday reportedly took up chemistry because of reading Mrs. Marcet's books as a youth.[11]

The topics covered in Marcet's books were similar to those presented in elementary textbooks written primarily for a male audience. For instance,

Conversations on Natural Philosophy included chapters on the properties of matter, mechanics, hydrostatics, hydraulics, pneumatics, acoustics, and optics. *Conversations on Chemistry* included chapters on light, heat, metals, alkalis, compound bodies, and muriatic and oxygenated muriatic acids. Although *Conversations on Chemistry* also contained several chapters on vegetables and animals, these dealt with such topics as the various processes of fermentation, plant structure, animal physiology, and so on.[12]

Marcet's books were not unique in their coverage of scientific topics, for the lack of attention to so-called domestic science characterized almost every American science textbook used in girls' secondary schools before midcentury. Only two textbooks in the sample used for this study come close to what might be called domestic science. The first is Almira Hart Lincoln Phelps's *Chemistry for Beginners*, first published in 1834. Herself an advocate of domestic science, Phelps occasionally inserted examples of the practical applications of chemistry into her text. For example, she included advice on how to make ice cream and discussed the use of charcoal as an antiseptic, the uses of muriatic acid, and the effects of gypsum as a fertilizer.[13] Nevertheless, even Phelps recognized the limited extent of her efforts to apply chemistry to women's sphere. Taken as a whole, the content of her book is similar to that of many other elementary texts used in male and female academies, with the notable exception that some illustrations depict girls performing various experiments, as shown in the example provided by Plate 3.1. In her introduction, Phelps acknowledged the scarcity of domestic science in her text and advised female readers to attend to chemical principles in general, explaining, "As chemists are not housekeepers, nor housekeepers chemists, there has been little opportunity for the study of domestic economy in its relation to chemistry."[14]

The second is Richard G. Parker's *Juvenile Philosophy: or Philosophy in Familiar Conversations* (1850).[15] Intended for the youngest readers in common schools, Parker wrote his text as a series of conversations between a mother and her daughter about rain, color, vision, the eye, light, fire, heat, and wind. It is domestic not in its content, but in its context; set within the environs of the kitchen and farmyard, the mother demonstrates the principles of science to her daughter.

In order to understand the lack of attention to domestic science in school lectures and experiments and in the texts of Marcet and other schoolbook authors, it is necessary to consider the social and cultural context of the period. Marcet, like other writers of science textbooks, derived her information from the public lectures and treatises of well-known scientists, men who geared their presentations to a primarily male audience. As a result, textbook writers seeking to develop a specifically domestic science curriculum had no authoritative model to follow. Benjamin Rush, the only practicing scientist known to have developed such a curriculum, produced only a brief syllabus on which he based his lectures. Additionally, Rush taught his domestic science course only once, and his syllabus was never reprinted in America.[16]

In the first half of the nineteenth century, educators who wished to offer girls domestic science found no available textbooks. This was a serious im-

Properties of Iodine.

Plate 3.1 A Girl Performing an Experiment with Iodine, in Almira Hart Lincoln Phelps's *Chemistry for Beginners,* 1838 [1834], 134. (*Courtesy of Cubberley Library, Stanford University.*)

pediment, given the common practice of basing instruction on recitation from texts. How could one talk about the applications of chemistry to cookery, without knowing the chemical processes involved? Few instructors in secondary schools had the knowledge or background to develop such a course.

Another likely factor in the lack of domestic science in girls' courses of study was the vocational nature of the subject as then conceived. The topics Rush included in his 1787 course—such as preserving vegetables, preparing soups, and providing home remedies for warts—were similar to the sorts of topics some educators recommended in a curriculum geared to children of the lower and farming classes.[17] Presumably, few middle- and upper-class parents would have found such study attractive in providing their daughters with the refined polish necessary to attain a higher status in society.

Although the domestic arts may have seemed exceedingly utilitarian and common, contemporaries viewed science as fashionable and genteel. Many of the women who developed scientific interests in Great Britain or France during the eighteenth century hailed from the upper classes. Some discussion of scientific subjects was *de rigeur* for ladies seeking to establish themselves in society. In her salon, the well-bred lady could easily discourse on meteor showers, hydrostatics, or recent developments in pneumatic pumps.[18] Aping the fashions of the higher classes was undoubtedly common among those seeking increased social status in the United States. For many wealthy Americans, some of the urge to give their daughters a traditional scientific education may have been due to this desire for upward social mobility.

Another explanation for the fact that girls' schools preferred to offer experimental demonstrations of steam engines rather than lessons on bread making lies in the nature of the public scientific lectures in the early nineteenth century. Exhibitions of technology had long formed a part of public lectures in natural philosophy. Since the eighteenth century, the American, British, and European public, male and female, enjoyed demonstrations of experiments with magnetism, electricity, and steam. So prevalent were these demonstrations in America that in the 1840s, the physicist Joseph Henry complained that "every man who can . . . exhibit a few experiments to a class of young ladies is called a man of science."[19] It is therefore likely that many educators viewed the technology included in natural philosophy textbooks as a desirable extension of this popular form of scientific entertainment.

Finally, from the Early Republican period until the midnineteenth century, the traditional scientific disciplines served the rhetoric supporting female education far better than did domestic science. As discussed above, many early advocates of education for women cited factors related to self-improvement when arguing for their cause. Learning about the natural world could lead to greater knowledge of God, increase intellectual ability, provide solace during difficult times, and develop qualities of self-discipline and morality. Recently, historians have noted that some of the arguments advanced by women reformers during the Early Republican period stressed women's intellectual equality with men rather than their cognitive differences. Margaret Nash argues that during the first decades after the Revolution, many educators in female institutions held virtually the same pedagogical goals as educators in comparable male institutions, promoting mental discipline, self-improvement, and academic competition among their students. As an example of this point of view, she cites Elizabeth Hamilton, author of the popular *Letters on Education* (1801), who, when asked whether a "triumph of reason over the passions" might be unattractive in a woman, retorted, "I beg your pardon; I thought we were speaking of the best method of cultivating the powers of *human beings*. . . . In this I can make no distinction of sex."[20] Where was the intellectual rigor in learning to preserve fruits and vegetables? Even those who supported the higher education of women so that they could better train their children had difficulty understanding why they should pay tuition at a private academy so that their daughters could better learn to cook and sew. How could a woman put such knowledge to use in training her sons? Why couldn't she simply learn these things at home, for free? On the other hand, a traditional science education presumably provided grist for mental discipline, gave women the intellectual background to interest their sons in the useful arts of science and technology, and provided husbands with stimulating companions capable of discussing recent scientific developments.

Although the notion of a domestic science curriculum for girls had a small but consistent appeal to some educators, the subject would not become widespread in higher schools until the final decades of the nineteenth century.[21] When the renowned women's educator Catharine Beecher authored a textbook on domestic economy in 1840, many of her contemporaries still questioned the value of a field of study that dealt with the common concerns of home and hearth. George B. Emerson, a well-known Boston teacher who endorsed Beecher's text, described the widespread criticism as a "constantly-recurring inquiry, 'What will be the use of this study?'"[22] The social and cultural context of the early nineteenth century led middle- and upper-class Americans to prefer a pure rather than an applied science for their daughters. Nevertheless, Beecher's views continued to find an audience, not only among parents and educators, but among schoolgirls, where her opinions could be found in a school reader published for use in female institutions. In an essay titled "The Profession of a Woman," she argued that female educators had erred in neglecting those topics most related to a woman's profession. "Is it not the business, the profession of a woman, to guard the health and form the physical habits of the young?" Addressing her young female readers, Beecher asked, "Were you ever taught to understand the operation of diet, air, exercise, and modes of dress upon the human frame?" In a pointed critique of the so-called pure science taught in female academies, she concluded, "No. We have attended to almost every thing more than to this. We have been taught more concerning the structure of the earth, the laws of the heavenly bodies, the habits and formation of plants . . . than concerning the structure of the human frame, and the laws of health and reason."[23]

In spite of such occasional criticism, newspaper advertisements indicate that girls' schools continued to purchase equipment more useful in demonstrating the principles of electricity than those of cookery. According to historian Deborah Jean Warner, aside from buildings and furnishings, scientific apparatus often represented the largest single investment made by a girls' school; as a result, the possession of apparatus was often treated as a prime attraction. In New York City, Rutgers Female Institute stated that few colleges could "boast of greater facilities for instruction."[24] Schools equipped with the latest apparatus were quick to advertise the fact as a means of attracting potential students. For example, in 1837, F. G. Smith's girls' boarding school in Lynchburg, Virginia, boasted of its new equipment: "The apparatus is very new, and contains all the leading and important instruments in the circle of Physical Sciences . . . A full Chemical apparatus, one of the largest electrical machines, with batteries, etc., models of all the varieties of Pumps, a superior Air Pump and Pneumatic apparatus, a series of working models illustrating the history of the steam engine, a large Solar Microscope . . . a splendid four-foot Gregorian telescope."[25]

Nor did scientific apparatus sit idly in school closets; documentary sources provide evidence that in some schools, students used apparatus to conduct demonstrations and experiments. As discussed earlier, students in the department of Raleigh Academy, North Carolina, performed chemistry experiments during their school examinations in 1815. According to an 1823 advertisement in Andrews and Jones' North Carolina Female Academy, "the truths of Natural Philosophy, Chymistry and Astronomy, are experimentally illustrated." Three years later, North Carolina's Oxford Female Seminary went even further in declaring that every lecture in "Chymistry, Natural Philosophy, Astronomy and Mineralogy will be . . . illustrated by appropriate experiments." In its 1832–1833 Plan of Education, the Greenfield High School for Young Ladies in Greenfield, Massachusetts, emphasized the importance of its chemical apparatus in providing demonstrations of recent scientific discoveries: "In Chemistry we are as well furnished. In connection with this branch, we design not only to afford experimental illustrations of the great principles and facts embraced in our manual, but likewise to communicate later discoveries, exhibiting always the actual state of the science."[26] Institutions enrolling both sexes advertised the use of experimental lectures in both male and female departments. For example, in an 1827 advertisement, Groton Academy of Massachusetts claimed to offer experimental lectures in natural philosophy and chemistry to both its male and female students.[27]

THE LEVEL OF DIFFICULTY OF SCIENCE TEXTS APPEARING IN FEMALE SCHOOLS

How did the level of difficulty of the science offered to girls compare with that offered to boys? Comparing texts poses a challenge, because the determination of whether or not a text is difficult can be made on the basis of a variety of such categories as vocabulary level, sentence length, number of pages or topics, format, or mathematical complexity. In the ensuing discussion, a textbook's level of difficulty is determined solely on the basis of two categories: format and mathematical complexity. It is within these two categories that texts available to girls seem to have differed, for a period, from those available to boys.

During the first three decades of the nineteenth century, many of the science texts commonly found in girls' schools used a conversational format. Although she was not the first to organize her content this way, Marcet popularized the conversational style of science writing among those interested in authoring science books for girls. Swiss by birth, Mrs. Jane Marcet

(1769–1858) moved to London with her husband Alexander, a wealthy doctor who had retired to indulge his passion for chemistry. In Britain and Europe, the Marcets numbered some of the best-known scientists among their social circle. Encouraged by her husband, Marcet began to attend public experimental lectures. Because she had no scientific background, she found it difficult at first to follow the rapid pace of the demonstrations. However, by conversing with others on the subjects of natural philosophy and chemistry, and by repeating the experiments at her own leisure, she became increasingly familiar with the principles of these sciences. As she overcame her own difficulties, she endeavored to ease the way for other women whose education was "seldom calculated to prepare their minds for abstract ideas, or scientific language." To this end, she authored several of the most widely used and influential scientific textbooks in the early nineteenth century.[28]

Marcet wrote each of her books as a dialogue between "Mrs. B," a refined lady with scientific interests, and her two young disciples, Emily and Caroline. In the course of their conversation, Mrs. B illustrates a variety of concepts through experiment and demonstration. For example, in *Conversations on Natural Philosophy,* Emily asks, "Would not water, as well as ether, boil with less heat if the pressure of the atmosphere were taken off?" After confirming this hypothesis by describing the experiments of De Sassure on Mt. Blanc, Mrs. B. provides a demonstration, explaining, "But I can show you a pretty experiment, which proves the effect of the pressure of the atmosphere in this respect."[29]

The scientific lady, as conceived by Marcet, was far from being a stereotypical bluestocking. In Marcet's books, Mrs. B represents the ideal woman of the Enlightenment: intelligent, sophisticated, and exquisitely refined. Her scientific interests add to her feminine charms, and her knowledge of experimental methods gives her a fashionable allure.[30] Marcet used the conversational format, in which she conveyed scientific content through the medium of female characters, to effectively underline the naturalness of young women's participation in science.

When Marcet's texts first appeared on the American market, they spawned a host of imitations. Among American authors to use the conversational format was Mary Townsend, sister of the naturalist John Kirk Townsend. In 1844, Townsend published her *Life in the Insect World: or, Conversations Upon Insects Between an Aunt and her Nieces.* In 1879, Elizabeth Cady Agassiz used a somewhat similar approach in her book on marine life. The wife of the Harvard scientist Louis Agassiz, Elizabeth Agassiz published a natural history of marine flora and fauna in a book addressed to a female readership. Agassiz wrote her text in the form of a letter from Aunt Lizzie to her two nieces, Lisa and Connie. Not all conversational texts presented discourses between adults and children. During the nineteenth century, some American readers presented conversations among children about scientific topics. For example, two girls and two boys discuss physics in a reader published in 1852. In one passage, Nancy asks her friend Lucy to explain the meaning of the word *inertia*. In reply, Lucy explains, "It means that those things which have not life, such as stones, sticks, water, etc., have no power to move themselves, and cannot stop of their own accord, when put in motion. If a stone lies still, it will never stir unless some person or thing moves it; and if thrown into the air it would never stop unless caused to, by something beside itself."[31] Through the medium of these and other texts, American authors underscored the appropriateness of girls' scientific interests.

Although she wrote for a general female audience, both male and female seminaries widely used Marcet's texts as schoolbooks. In the United States, plagiarized or near-plagiarized versions of Marcet's books quickly appeared on the market with adaptations calculated to make the books appealing to educators.[32] For instance, the *Conversations on Natural Philosophy* edited by the Reverend J. L. Blake included questions at the foot of each page to facilitate its use in school examinations. Blake's edition was the most commonly reported natural philosophy textbook in the Massachusetts common schools in 1837.[33]

In the 1830s, use of the conversational format came under attack from a new generation of textbook writers, of whom the best known and most successful was John Lee Comstock (1787–1858). A surgeon by profession, Comstock served in the War of 1812, having charge of three hospitals on the northern frontier. At the close of the war, he practiced medicine in Hartford, Connecticut, and began to write schoolbooks.[34] The first chemistry textbook published under Comstock's name was an edited version of Jane Marcet's *Conversations on Chemistry*. In 1831, Comstock published his own *Elements of Chemistry*, written in a straightforward prose style. Comstock's new text, arguably the most popular chemistry text in secondary schools before the Civil War, went through more than fifty editions in America, appearing predominantly in male academies.[35]

In *Elements of Chemistry*, Comstock abandoned the conversational format made popular by Marcet, claiming that it was falling rapidly into disuse abroad: "We learn, that in those parts of Europe where the subject of education has received the most attention, and consequently where the best methods of conveying instruction are supposed to have been adopted, school books in the form of conversations are at present entirely out of use."[36] Other textbook authors targeting the academy market followed suit. For example, in 1840, James Renwick, professor of natural philosophy and chemistry at Columbia College, authored a text in prose format "for the use of schools, academies, and the lower classes of college."[37]

Although Comstock did not discuss the issue of gender, the fact that Marcet's popular chemistry text was written as a series of conversations among females must have rendered its use problematic in boys' schools. It is certainly no coincidence that after the appearance of Comstock's text, increasing numbers of boys' secondary schools began to add chemistry to their courses of study in the 1830s. A survey of male academies in North Carolina illustrates this trend (Table 3.1); James Mulhern found similar results in his survey of secondary schools in Pennsylvania.[38]

As boys' schools turned to the newer textbooks, girls' schools also began to use texts published in the presumably more modern prose format. For instance, Almira Hart Lincoln Phelps, whose chemistry text appeared three

Table 3.1 Number and Percentage of North Carolina Male Higher Schools Advertising Chemistry, 1800–1840

	1800–1809	1810–1819	1820–1829	1830–1840
Number of schools	0	1	1	8
Number in sample	15	11	26	20
Percentage	0	9	4	40

Source: Data compiled from newspaper advertisements included in Charles L. Coon, ed., *North Carolina Schools and Academies 1790–1840: A Documentary History* (Raleigh, N.C.: Edwards and Broughton, 1915).

years after Comstock's, used a prose rather than a conversational format.[39] Although dealt a serious blow in higher schools, the older format lingered throughout the century in materials written for younger children. A few natural history texts, books published for younger children in common schools, and articles written for children's magazines continued to feature the dialogue as a medium of scientific instruction. For example, *The Rose Bud or Youth's Gazette* featured a running series in the 1830s titled "The Young Botanists," in which two small boys and an older brother discuss botany as they ramble through the countryside.[40]

Because relatively few female seminaries provided instruction in advanced mathematics before 1830, the scientific texts used in girls' schools were less advanced mathematically than texts used in boys' schools during the early nineteenth century. This state of affairs began to change during the next two decades, as increasing numbers of girls' schools began to include such subjects as geometry, algebra, and trigonometry in their course offerings.[41]

Although the subject of chemistry was a girls' subject until midcentury,[42] their lack of advanced mathematics caused girls initially to miss the revolution in secondary school chemistry education occurring in the 1830s. This new departure consisted of requiring students to use chemical notation and formulae to calculate the atomic weight of various compounds. John Comstock was the first chemistry author to introduce chemical formulae to a secondary school audience.

Comstock's use of simple formulae represented a radical departure in textbooks designed for secondary schools. Symbolic notation had only begun to gain acceptance among American chemists in the early 1830s. Many chemistry textbooks published in the 1830s continued either to omit symbolic notation altogether or to use it only in headings and notes. For example, in an 1834 edition of a textbook designed for use in medical schools, colleges, and academies, Lewis C. Beck, professor of chemistry and botany in New York University, made only minimal use of chemical formulae. In his preface, he explained: "Symbols have not heretofore found much favor among our chemists . . . I at first intended to carry through the press without introducing [symbols], although I had observed that they were employed by several English chemists."[43] Refraining from using notation in his text, Beck restricted symbols to subject headings so that "their meaning will at once be understood, and cannot occasion the least embarrassment to the subject."[44] The following heading, found in a section on hydrogen and chlorine, is representative of the headings in Beck's text:

Hydrochloric or Muriatic Acid—Atom. Num. 36.45—
Symb. Cl + H—sp. gr. 1.269 air = 1

Although American chemists began to apply algebraic formulae to chemical notation in the 1830s, the underlying mathematics of early nine-teenth-century chemistry was relatively simple. Chemical calculations rarely appeared in textbooks designed for academies and seminaries. According to the historian John Nietz, out of a sample of twelve chemistry texts published between 1784 and 1815, none included chemical calculations; thirty-six texts published between 1816 and 1865 devoted less than one percent of space to calculations.[45] In the few cases in which authors did include calculations, students required prior knowledge of only arithmetic and the simpler rules of algebra.

Comstock's text went far beyond Marcet's and even Beck's in its emphasis on chemical nomenclature and the "laws of definite proportions" discovered by John Dalton (1766–1844) at the beginning of the century. Comstock claimed, "The nomenclature of chemistry, the laws of affinity, and the doctrine of proportions, are far more necessary to a proper knowledge of this science, than is a knowledge of mathematics to the study of astronomy."[46] His readers learned how to calculate the atomic weight of a compound by adding the atomic weights of its elements and to express such simple calculations as formulae. The following example for nitrous acid is fairly representative:

By volume this acid is composed of,

Nitrogen 100	By weight, Nitrogen 14
Oxygen 200	Oxygen 32
300	46

Nitrous Acid—46

1p. Nitrogen 14 + 4 p. Oxygen 32[47]

In spite of its enormous popularity, sources indicate that Comstock's text did not appear in girls' schools until the 1840s.[48] Instead, female seminaries throughout the 1830s appear to have preferred textbooks addressed to a general audience. Such texts omitted symbols, formulae, and calculations, and conveyed the principles of chemistry through description and demonstration.[49] However, although a few female seminaries may have continued to use later editions of Marcet's text after the 1830s, textbook listings in newspaper advertisements and school catalogs reveal that as older texts fell increasingly behind the pace of scientific discovery, some girls' schools turned to new authors who provided more relevant or up-to-date content. The evolving curriculum of Knoxville Female Academy in

Tennessee exemplifies the increased rigor in the sciences offered in girls' schools in the 1840s. In 1831, the academy's course of study for the middle or junior class included arithmetic, geography, history, natural philosophy, rhetoric, and botany. In 1847, the academy became the East Tennessee Female Institute. In that year, sophomores studied, among other things, Comstock's natural philosophy, astronomy, chemistry, and mineralogy texts. Juniors studied mechanics, hydrostatics, hydraulics, pneumatics, acoustics, electricity, magnetism and optics, natural history, evidences of Christianity, and geology, along with languages and literature.[50]

Several introductory chemistry texts designed for use in colleges appeared in female seminaries in the 1840s and 1850s, including those by John Porter, professor of chemistry at Yale College; James Renwick, professor of natural philosophy and chemistry at Columbia College; textbook author John Johnston; and Alonzo Gray, instructor at Brooklyn Female Academy.[51] Of these, Gray's text represents the most advanced use of chemical symbols and notation.[52] He used symbols and chemical formulae to a far greater extent than did Comstock, introducing algebraic formulae to express chemical processes throughout the text: "Notwithstanding the great advantages of the chemical nomenclature, a much greater help is given to the student in the *notation*. By this, as in algebra, long and intricate processes are exhibited to the eye at a glance."[53] Gray's text appeared in numerous editions and was evidently widely used in secondary schools.[54]

By the 1850s, the most advanced chemistry texts used in female seminaries were no more elementary in content than were the most advanced texts used in male academies during the same period. The great majority of chemistry texts published for use in academies appeared in the educational institutions of both sexes. The few textbooks appearing predominantly in boys' schools included chemical symbols and formulae no more complex than those studied by girls. For example, both Lewis C. Beck's *A Manual of Chemistry* and William Henry's *The Elements of Experimental Chemistry* appear to have been used primarily in male academies. In both cases, the authors stressed a conceptual understanding of chemical principles rather than the use of chemical symbols and formulae.

Although girls' schools began to offer their students mathematically advanced chemistry texts in the 1840s, most nevertheless seem to have avoided Comstock's text, which continued to be popular in male academies up to and beyond the Civil War. The absence of Comstock's text in most girls' schools is most likely due to the nature of its applied science. Whereas Marcet's text, like many others of the period, dealt largely with so-called pure science, Comstock's text included various examples of the applications of chemistry to everyday male life. Comstock related chemistry not to the female occupations of hearth and home, but to such traditionally masculine occupations as mining, assaying, and tanning. Given its vocational bent, Comstock's text undoubtedly appeared eminently useful to young men. In their practicality, editions published throughout the 1840s and 1850s might even have appealed to those hardy souls hoping to strike it rich in the western gold and silver fields.

Unlike chemistry schoolbooks, which only began to include relatively simple calculations in the 1830s, the more advanced natural philosophy (physics) and astronomy texts written for academies had long required knowledge of higher mathematics. Until girls' schools began to include such subjects as algebra, geometry, and trigonometry in their courses of study in the 1830s and 1840s, their lack of higher mathematics thus served as a barrier to advanced instruction in these sciences.

Natural philosophy and astronomy textbooks appearing in girls' schools before 1840 were very similar to texts developed for popular audiences in Europe and the United States. By the late seventeenth century, the mathematics of natural philosophy and astronomy was beyond the grasp of all but the most accomplished mathematicians. During this period, the emphasis in these sciences had shifted from geometry to algebra and calculus, largely as a result of efforts to solve problems in mechanics.[55] Textbook authors geared their content to the audience served by their texts. When the intended audience was the general public, most authors jettisoned the mathematics altogether. The natural philosophy author explained physical concepts in a conversational or prose format and may also have referred to experiments to demonstrate scientific principles; the astronomy author referred to illustrations within the text. On the other hand, when the intended audience was a class of college students preparing to become practitioners or teachers of natural philosophy or astronomy, textbook authors introduced some of the mathematical reasoning underlying each science.

Before 1840, the natural philosophy and astronomy texts used in girls' schools were almost entirely conceptual in nature. Students would have required knowledge of arithmetic and elementary geometry in order to understand the examples and illustrations included in these books, but they required no knowledge of algebra or trigonometry.[56]

Some texts listed in the published curricula of boys' schools also avoided higher mathematics. For instance, John S. C. Abbott wrote his astronomy text "for use of schools and the general reader," assuring his audience that his book did not include mathematics: "Most treatises upon Astronomy contain much which is quite unintelligible to those who have not passed through a regular course of mathematical studies."[57] Other authors of texts designed for both male and female academies and seminaries made similar statements in their prefaces.[58] Although their introductory texts may not have included higher mathematics, in some institutions, boys had the opportunity to study the sciences at more advanced levels. For example, in 1823, New Bern Academy in North Carolina offered science in both its male and female departments. One of the texts available to both sexes was Marcet's *Conversations on Natural Philosophy*. However, whereas Marcet's was the only text used in the female department, boys in the male department who desired additional scientific study could proceed to the more mathematically complex texts of William Nicholson and Tiberius Cavallo. Although rather outdated, these books required knowledge of plane and spherical geometry and included algebraic analysis in footnotes.[59]

Before midcentury, a number of textbooks appearing predominantly in male academies included advanced mathematics in their pages. Bartlett's

Elements of Natural Philosophy: Spherical Astronomy, designed for use in West Point Military Academy, required knowledge of plane and spherical geometry, algebra, and trigonometry. This text contained numerous examples of the applications of astronomy to navigation, geography, and chronology. In 1845, William A. Norton published *An Elementary Treatise on Astronomy* for use in colleges and "the higher academies." Norton's aim was to "furnish the practical astronomer with rules, or formulae, and accurate tables for performing the more important astronomical calculations."[60]

One of the earliest natural philosophy textbooks appearing in girls' schools to include algebraic formulae was Alonzo Gray's *Elements of Natural Philosophy* (1850). Although the title page stated that it was "designed as a text-book for academies, high-schools, and colleges," Gray claimed in his preface to have written his text for the young women under his "immediate instruction" at Brooklyn Female Academy. An example of Gray's algebraic treatment of Newton's Law of Gravitational Force is shown below in Plate 3.2.[61]

At the same time that Gray's text first appeared, a more advanced level of astronomy became available to girls in some educational institutions. In 1850, James M'Intire published *New Treatise on Astronomy* for the high school market, a text that required prior knowledge of geometry, algebra, and trigonometry. Although M'Intire's text does not appear in the female seminary catalogs and newspaper advertisements used in this study, his opening remarks indicate that he expected or hoped his book would appeal to both sexes: "Even well educated females are expected to have

If the formula in the note below be applied to the third example in numbers, the loss of weight will be equal to

$$\frac{2000(2 \times 4000 \times 500 + 250,000)}{16,000,000 + 2 \times 4000 \times 500 + 25,000} = \frac{8,500,000,000}{20,250,000} = 419\tfrac{81}{81} \text{ lbs.}$$

If the height is not more than half a mile, x^2 may be neglected, and then the formula will be $W - W' = \dfrac{W \times 2x}{r + 2x}$.

Fig. 17.

* Let A, *Fig.* 17, be the earth, C its center, x the height from the surface, then will the weight at s be to the weight at x as the squares of the distances Cx and Cs. Now, to find the loss of weight, we must subtract the weight at x from the weight at s, and then, if we represent the weight at s by W, and at x by W'; also, Cs by r, and sx by x, we shall have the proportion

$W : W - W' :: (r + x)^2 : 2rx + x^2$, or $W : W - W' :: r^2 + 2rx + x^2 : 2rx + x^2$.

The loss of weight, then, will be $= W - W' = \dfrac{W(2rx + x^2)}{r^2 + 2rx + x^2}$.

Plate 3.2 The Formula for Newton's Law of Gravitational Force, in Alonzo Gray's *Elements of Natural Philosophy*, 1850.

added a competent share of astronomical knowledge to the other accomplishments of their sex."[62]

By 1868, some female academies and public secondary schools offered girls texts comparable in their mathematics to the most advanced astronomy and natural philosophy texts used in male academies: E. S. Snell's editions of Denison Olmsted's *An Introduction to Astronomy* and *An Introduction to Natural Philosophy*. Snell, professor of mathematics and natural philosophy at Amherst College, designed these as textbooks "for the use of students in college." These texts required prior knowledge of algebra, geometry, and trigonometry.[63] Snell's editions of Olmsted's texts, along with those of Comstock, were widely used in secondary schools.[64]

White middle- and upper-class girls had access to relatively advanced scientific texts and laboratory equipment, but the picture for girls from other ethnic groups and classes is less clear. For example, the close of the Civil War afforded newly freed African-Americans the opportunity to study the sciences in schools established for their benefit; however, in spite of some uplifting rhetoric about the benefits of science for African-Americans following the conclusion of the war, documentary evidence suggests that uneven allocations of educational resources in some public school systems may have contributed to the development of inequalities in the science content available to African-American and white students.

After the end of the Civil War, a number of teacher-missionaries from the North came to the South to introduce newly freed African-American children to the wonders of science and technology. Such was Lydia Schofield, whose valedictory address, delivered at the village Church on St. Helena Island in 1868, touted the benefits of technology: "By the knowledge of the power of steam we can sail on the broad ocean in safety—ride swiftly in the Locomotive cars, printing is made easy and thousands of labor saving machines are in daily use for the benefit of the world—all this scientific knowledge has been kept from you my friends—You were kept slaves through ignorance—do not run any risk of your children ever being reduced again to bondage by the same thing—urge them on in the acquisition of learning. 'Knowledge is Power' and every day of schooling lessens the possibility of your ever being enslaved again."[65]

Although many white northern teachers working in missionary and Freedmen's Bureau-sponsored schools may have viewed themselves as benevolently providing useful knowledge to those unable to obtain it for themselves, documentary evidence indicates that in some areas in the South, freed blacks had already established academies to provide higher schooling for the personal and professional self-improvement of their youth by the time northern teachers arrived in their communities. According to Chris Span, freedmen-sponsored schools in Mississippi "taught more than the rudiments of learning to a predominantly non-literate and formerly enslaved people." The pedagogical aims of the instructors in such schools differed markedly from the objectives of the missionary- and Freedmen's Bureau-supported schools, institutions that emphasized morality, conformity, thrift, hard work, and self-control as part of an effort to train freed blacks to become wage laborers in the state's postwar free market economy. Nevertheless, in terms of knowing the extent to which freed blacks may have had access to instruction in science, few documentary sources remain to give a clear picture of the curriculum in independent academies during the Reconstruction Era.[66]

Census data collected during the first decade of the twentieth century indicate that of the African-Americans who remained in school past the age of fourteen, a larger percentage was female, as shown in Table 3.2. During this decade, some southern states passed compulsory education laws requiring all children to attend school, including Kentucky (1896), Tennessee (1905), North Carolina (1907), Virginia (1908), and Arkansas (1909).[67] However, in most cases, such requirements did not apply past the eighth grade. Why did girls stay longer in school? Preparation for school teaching may have been a factor. The possibility of employment in agricultural industry may also have drawn proportionally more boys from school at an earlier age. Whatever the reason, we can hypothesize that because they tended to stay longer in school, girls may have had more opportunities than boys to study advanced subjects, including the sciences.

In the South, African-Americans studied the sciences in segregated public secondary schools, although documentary sources for some areas indicate that students usually learned scientific concepts without the benefit of laboratory work. For example, in the colored high school in Lynchburg, Virginia, the county superintendent noted in 1905 that "text book science" was one of the subjects comprising the more advanced work in the school, along with Latin, algebra, and geometry.[68] Similarly, in the same year the public high school for colored students in Memphis, Tennessee, offered a course of study that included Latin, algebra, geometry, and science, without the benefit of laboratory work.[69] During the same year, the Nashville, Tennessee, high school course for African-Americans included three years of science, including physical geography, physics, and chemistry, but there too, study was undertaken without access to a laboratory, and the superintendent noted that "only $25.00 per year are appropriated for materials in this department."[70] Similar conditions existed that year at the Howard High School in Chattanooga, where "the course of study is practically the same

Table 3.2 Percentage of African-Americans in School, 1900 and 1910

	1900		1910	
Age	Male	Female	Male	Female
5–9	23.2	24.2	40.2	42.3
10–14	50.6	57.0	65.6	71.5
15–20	15.0	19.8	23.8	28.9

Source: Data compiled from U.S. Census Reports, in Negro Population in the United States, 1790–1915 (New York: Arno Press, 1968): 377.

as that for the whites, comprising Latin, English and commercial courses. It has, though, no laboratory for its science."[71] On the other hand, young women undertaking advanced study in preparation to become teachers may have had access to laboratory equipment in teacher-training institutions. For example, Frances Benjamin Johnston's photographs of Native American and African-American students at the Hampton Institute in Virginia show women conducting experiments in physics and chemistry classes at the turn of the century.

The experiences of African-American girls after the Civil War illustrate the dangers of generalizing about the experiences of all females, regardless of ethnicity or socioeconomic background. Nevertheless, the small sample

Plate 3.3   Class in Capillary Physics at Hampton Institute, Hampton, Virginia, 1899. Frances Benjamin Johnston, Photographer (*Courtesy of the Library of Congress*).

of southern school reports surveyed here indicates that girls did have access to the sciences in schools for African-Americans, although in most cases they appear to have undertaken such study without the benefit of laboratory apparatus. The legacy of such early scientific study can be seen in the presence of African-American women among the graduates from some of the first medical schools open to women in the United States. Some of these early pioneers may have come from middle-class families able to afford the tuition at private schools, but others worked to support themselves through study. Such was Eliza Anna Grier, who became the first African-American doctor in the state of Georgia. Grier went north to attend the Woman's Medical College of Pennsylvania, from which she graduated in 1897. It took her fourteen years to complete college and medical school, putting herself through by studying one year and returning home to pick cotton the next. After graduation, she returned to Atlanta and devoted her practice to the poor of that city.[72]

CONCLUSION

Present-day scholars have repeatedly noted the presence of scientific subjects in girls' schools and wondered about the nature of these studies. Taking the rhetoric of domestic science advocates at face value, some historians have claimed that a version of science centered on applications to hearth and home entered the curriculum during the antebellum period as part of an effort to professionalize homemaking. Nevertheless, a closer examination of the contemporary debates over domestic science and an analysis of the schoolbooks used in female schools reveals that domestic science never really caught on in higher schools before the Civil War. Domestic science, also known as homemaking, would not enter the curriculum until the late nineteenth century, a movement discussed later in this volume.

Although they rejected domestic science during the antebellum era, Americans remained solidly convinced of the desirability of differentiating the science curriculum for girls. During the early nineteenth century, attempts at differentiation involved presenting science content within the context of the intellectual pursuits of the upper-middle-class lady. By and large, parents preferred to view science as a means of obtaining intellectual attainment, refined polish, and culture for their daughters. Toward the middle of the century, this approach would prevail in the texts of female authors who sought to promote natural history as a school subject, a trend discussed in Chapter 5.

Despite efforts to provide girls with a differentiated science curriculum, the sources examined for this study indicate that after 1840, the most advanced science textbooks offered in female seminaries were comparable in their level of difficulty to the most advanced texts offered in male academies. As we have seen, the introduction of higher mathematics into girls' schools had an enormous impact on the level of difficulty of the sciences offered to females. Before 1840, textbooks used in girls' schools emphasized a conceptual rather than a mathematical understanding of scientific principles and usually conveyed content through the medium of a conversational format. The shift toward a more advanced study of the sciences was accompanied by a revolution in the mathematics education of American girls. How this revolution occurred, and why, is the subject of the following chapter.

4

From Arithmetic to Higher Mathematics

Pursuing a more advanced study of the sciences required knowledge of higher mathematics, a field that most eighteenth-century Americans did not want their daughters to study. According to the Reverend John Bennett, opening the doors of mathematics to girls "was attempting to make them move in a sphere, for which Nature never gave them talents, nor Providence designed them."[1] Not only did many contemporaries view females as intellectually incapable of mastering such subjects as algebra or geometry, higher mathematics had long been associated with such male vocations as navigation and surveying. "GEOMETRY. The sound of this word in reference to females, is very terrific," noted one educator in 1828. "Parents startle at it as though it possessed some talismanic power of converting their delicate daughters into tempest-beaten rovers of the deep, and sun-burnt surveyors of the forest."[2]

Some scholars have suggested that nineteenth-century girls abandoned the study of natural philosophy and astronomy as these subjects became more mathematically complex. According to Stanley Guralnick, faculty members in boys' academies realized by midcentury that the study of the sciences necessitated a thorough preparation in algebra, geometry, and calculus. Only the study of natural history was exempt from this requirement, which "rendered natural history a subject peculiarly suitable for young women, who received little mathematical training."[3] In recent years, scholars seeking to account for the low numbers of women in such fields as engineering and physics have pointed to girls' lack of interest and achievement in advanced mathematics. Some researchers have used the term *math anxiety* to describe the nervousness with which many girls appear to approach the subject. Many educators and policy makers appear to believe that this state of affairs has always been present in American education. According to one author, "Boys have historically outscored girls in math." Similarly, the American Association for the Advancement of Science reports in a recent document that "In the past, [girls] have largely been by-passed in science and mathematics education."[4]

This chapter investigates young women's access to mathematical subjects from the postcolonial period to the early twentieth century. The discussion focuses on the following questions: (1) How did the mathematics offering in nineteenth-century girls' secondary schools compare with that offered in boys' schools? (2) Did the increasing mathematical complexity of physics indeed induce girls to abandon it as a subject of study? (3) What was the relation between girls' mathematical training and their subsequent choice of scientific study? The chapter begins by tracing the shift from arithmetic to higher mathematics in girls' schools.

TAKING UP ARITHMETIC

Few colonial Americans taught arithmetic to girls, because they assumed that women had no need of it in adult life. William Woodbridge, editor of the *American Annals of Education*, stated that in the Connecticut schools of the 1770s, girls learned "rarely even the first rules of arithmetic . . . I have known boys that could do something in the four first rules of arithmetic. Girls were never taught it."[5] Written arithmetic was necessary for commerce and bookkeeping; no women—and relatively few men—had need of this skill in an era of subsistence agriculture and limited trade. According to Mary Beth Norton, documentary evidence suggests that during the Revolutionary period, women typically could not assess the value of their property or testify precisely about the state of their family finances, whereas men could do so in detail.[6] Women's inability to perform these calculations undoubtedly was due to their lack of training in commercial arithmetic and to the culturally pervasive belief that the oversight and regulation of family finances belonged to the affairs of men.

After the Revolution, however, such prominent Americans as Benjamin Franklin, Benjamin Rush, and Noah Webster argued that Americans could benefit from training girls in arithmetic and bookkeeping so that young women could assist their families in business.[7] As the commercial expansion of the nation at the dawn of the nineteenth century drew more families into business enterprises, it became expedient to allow women the task of keeping the books.[8]

The first educational institution to instruct girls in simple arithmetic was the dame school. The term *dame school* appears in documentary sources either in reference to an entrepreneurial venture school conducted by a woman in her home or to a primary school operating with some form of public support. In either case, the teacher was commonly female. Dame schools provided a rudimentary instruction in English to prepare young boys to enter the town grammar schools. Girls also enrolled in these schools, whose curriculum included the alphabet, some spelling, reading, writing, and numbers. To these basic subjects were added knitting and sewing for the benefit of female students.[9]

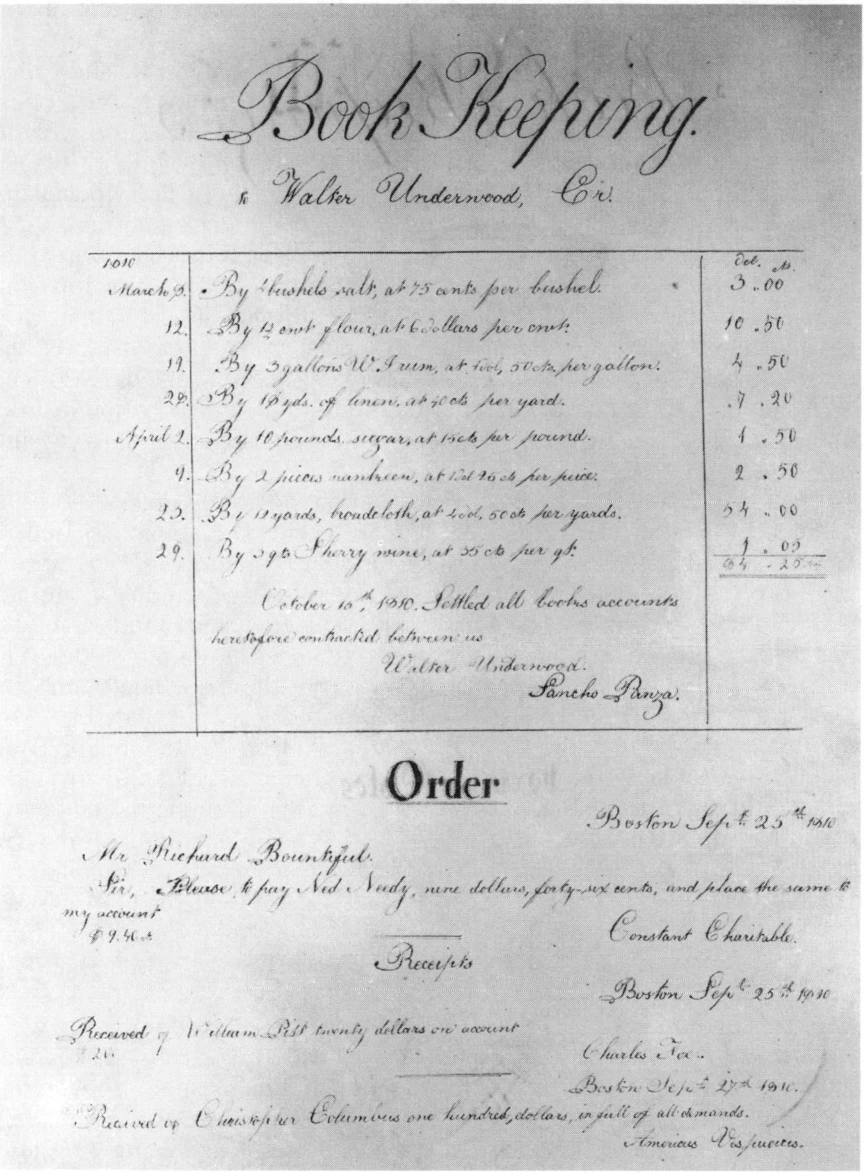

Book Keeping.

Walter Underwood, Cr.

1810		Dol. cts.
March 5.	By 4 bushels salt, at 75 cents per bushel.	3.00
12.	By 1¾ cwt flour, at 6 dollars per cwt.	10.50
19.	By 3 gallons W. I. rum, at 1 dol, 50 cts, per gallon.	4.50
28.	By 18 yds. of linen, at 40 cts per yard.	7.20
April 2.	By 10 pounds sugar, at 15 cts per pound.	1.50
9.	By 2 pieces nankeen, at 1 dol 25 cts per piece.	2.50
25.	By 12 yards, broadcloth, at 4 dol, 50 cts per yards.	54.00
29.	By 3 qts Sherry wine, at 35 cts per qt.	1.05
		84.25

October 10th, 1810. Settled all books accounts heretofore contracted between us

Walter Underwood.

Sancho Panza.

Order

Boston Sept 25th 1810

Mr Richard Bountiful.

Sir, Please to pay Ned Needy, nine dollars, forty-six cents, and place the same to my account

$9.46 cts

Constant Charitable.

Receipts

Boston Sept 25th 1810

Received of William Pitt twenty dollars on account

$20.

Charles Fox.

Boston Sept 27th 1810.

Received of Christopher Columbus one hundred dollars, in full of all demands.

Americus Vespucius.

Plate 4.1 "Book Keeping" in Sarah B. Pollock's Arithmetic Notebook, 1810, Mrs. Rowson's Academy. (*Courtesy of the American Antiquarian Society, Worcester, Massachusetts.*)

Another source of arithmetic instruction for girls was the private school-master, or tutor. Although most such instructors catered to boys, offering such subjects as arithmetic, algebra, geometry, trigonometry, surveying, fortification, and so on, a few marketed their services to girls as well, offering instruction in arithmetic.[10] For instance, in 1766, the *Pennsylvania Gazette* carried the advertisement of a private instructor offering to teach arithmetic to girls, stating that "The rules of [arithmetic] will be peculiarly adapted to the [female] sex, so as to render them concise and familiar."[11]

Although scholars do not know how many received instruction in arithmetic at home, girls also undoubtedly received some such instruction from their mothers or other family relatives; in wealthy families, they may also have received instruction from their brothers' tutors. For instance, the noted female educator Catharine Beecher (1800–1878) recalled that by the time she reached her ninth year, her mother had given her "some instruction in reading, writing, and arithmetic, and a good deal in drawing and painting."[12]

The few private schools open to girls during the last quarter of the eighteenth century also offered instruction in arithmetic. For example, Jedediah Morse's school at New Haven, Connecticut, which opened in 1783, offered instruction in arithmetic, reading, English grammar, geography, composition, and needlework.[13] When Maria Smith opened a school in Winchester in 1788, she offered writing and arithmetic at a special hour, in addition to a regular course of instruction that included "reading, spelling, Tambour, Dresden Embroidery, and all Kinds of plain and colored needlework."[14] By the first decade of the nineteenth century, arithmetic commonly appeared among the subjects listed in the published courses of study of girls' schools. Plate 4.1 (previous page) shows a page from the arithmetic notebook that Sarah B. Pollock kept when she was a student at Mrs. Rowson's Academy in 1810.

PURSUING MATHEMATICS

Whereas the notion of teaching arithmetic to girls received relatively wide support after the Revolution, the idea of teaching girls mathematics was highly controversial. Contemporaries defined arithmetic as the "operations performed by various modes of adding, subtracting, multiplying, or dividing."[15] Mathematics, on the other hand, included such seemingly esoteric subjects as algebra, geometry, trigonometry, and calculus. Almira Hart Lincoln Phelps, a nineteenth-century advocate of higher mathematics education for women, noted that even England's famed Hannah More, in her famous *Strictures on Education* (1799), "did not dare to speak of instructing women in the higher branches of mathematics."[16]

Aside from the fact that contemporaries viewed such study as the prerogative of males, there are a number of other reasons why higher mathematics did not appear in the curricula of girls' schools at the dawn of the nineteenth century. First, the rationales that advocates of women's education often advanced for increasing the rigor of girls' studies could be satisfied by the study of less controversial subjects such as arithmetic or the sciences. By promoting mental discipline, arithmetic and conceptual—or nonmathematical—science presumably developed the female mind. In 1819, the female educator Emma Willard argued, in her address to the members of the New York legislature, that the study of arithmetic and science would produce a more efficient class of wives and mothers.[17] Additionally, although many reformers argued that women needed a solid education in order to better serve as teachers, during the late eighteenth and early nineteenth centuries, the vast majority of female teachers worked in primary schools where the limited curriculum required that they teach arithmetic, not higher mathematics.

Another reason girls did not commonly study mathematics during the late eighteenth and early nineteenth centuries pertained to the vocational nature of the subject. Knowledge of algebra, geometry, trigonometry, and even calculus was necessary to those seeking careers in such fields as surveying, navigation, or the military. Such vocations were traditionally male, whereas most contemporaries identified the home as the occupational center for women. In the eyes of many Americans, knowledge of geometry or algebra bore little relation to women's domestic work. According to one commentator, the subject of geometry was particularly controversial: "An objection has been brought against it as unfit for young ladies, because they are not to be sailors, nor measurers of land."[18]

Although reformers could argue that knowledge of the sciences rendered women interesting conversationalists and companions for their husbands, one could hardly advance the same arguments about higher mathematics. Moreover, unlike the sciences, higher mathematics did not enjoy a popular recreational or cultural appeal among middle-class Americans. Few Americans would have flocked to hear public lectures on algebra or calculus, because the mathematics involved was far beyond the grasp of the average man or woman.

Finally, the study of mathematics conferred a collegiate status on the educational institution offering it. Although many early nineteenth-century American colleges did not require knowledge of geometry or algebra for admission, young gentlemen often encountered such subjects among their collegiate studies. Because colleges were closed to women during this period, it was not considered necessary or desirable for girls to pursue such higher studies in the institutions available to them.

Nevertheless, in spite of opposition, a movement to include higher mathematics in girls' studies began to appear in female seminaries, prompted largely by a desire on the part of some influential educators to elevate the status of women's education. Although she was not the first to teach higher mathematics to girls, her contemporaries generally credited the well-known female educator Emma Willard (1787–1870) with having initiated this movement.[19] Willard's efforts to bring higher mathematics to American girls seems to have arisen from a desire to obtain a collegiate status for girls' secondary schools. Willard herself stated that she developed the idea of "effecting an important change in education by the introduction of a grade of schools for women, higher than any heretofore known."[20]

For the most part, Willard was self-taught in mathematical subjects. After opening her first school for girls in Middlebury, Connecticut, in 1807, she began to teach herself geometry. Having begun Euclid, she requested assistance from her husband's nephew, then a senior in college, stating: "I have gone through twenty-nine propositions of the first book of Euclid. I am delighted with the study, and I see no insurmountable difficulties; but I wish you would take the book and see whether I understand it as you do."[21] After a subsequent examination, Willard received assurance that her understanding was correct and proceeded through Euclid without further help.

In 1818, Willard removed to Waterford, New York, where she opened a girls' school and shocked the local community by teaching geometry to her students. The successful public examination of her first pupil in the subject caused a great deal of excitement, although several of those in attendance claimed that the young woman's accomplishment was due entirely to feats of memory, "for no woman ever did, or could, understand geometry."[22]

While at Waterford, Willard began to study algebra. Initially, she received three or four lessons from a private instructor, but upon discovering that her instructor knew little of the subject, she began to study it independently. Step by step, as she learned higher mathematics herself, she proceeded to teach it to her students. According to a contemporary, "In this manner she learned and afterwards taught her students, one class at a time, through Euclid, including trigonometry . . . algebra, conic sections, and Enfield's Institutes of Natural Philosophy."[23]

Willard laid great emphasis on mathematics, which she was later to view as epoch-making in the history of American women's education.[24] In the spring of 1821, she left her incorporated academy at Waterford and moved to Troy, New York, where she established a female seminary and began to train teachers. At Troy, it was her custom to study a mathematical subject, teach it to a class of students, and then turn the teaching of the subject over to one of her most able students, leaving herself free to develop competency in another subject.[25]

The practice of training female students to be mathematics instructors was motivated in part by financial expediency. It would have cost Willard more than twice as much money to hire educated men to teach the higher branches of algebra and geometry. Still another reason for using women to teach mathematics was that having mastered the subject themselves without having had much formal preparation, Willard believed women to be more sympathetic to female students, more patient, and more innovative in developing teaching methods suited to beginners, girls who were historically presumed to have no mathematical aptitude.[26]

Word soon spread of Willard's work at Troy Female Seminary. According to Catharine Beecher, she and her sister had heard of Willard's innovations when they established a school for young ladies in Hartford, Connecticut, in 1823: "At this time I heard that Mrs. Willard and one or two others were teaching the higher branches, but I knew nothing of their methods."[27] Beecher and her sister were quick to follow suit. The next year, a newspaper advertisement for their school announced that among the books to be used were Day's *Algebra* and Euclid's *Elements of Geometry*.[28]

The books published by Emma Willard's sister, Almira Hart Lincoln Phelps, also helped to build public support for the new curriculum.[29] Phelps became known as an educator around 1830, when she assumed the duties of acting principal at Troy during her sister's visit to Europe. She later took charge of a girls' school at West Chester, Pennsylvania, and in 1841 assumed direction of Patapsco Female Institute at Ellicotts Mills, Maryland. In one of her best-known books, *Lectures to Young Ladies* (1833), Phelps informed her readers that the study of mathematics would improve their mental discipline and thus better qualify them for the discharge of their womanly duties. By the third decade of the nineteenth century, the attitude of many Americans toward mathematics instruction for girls had so changed that Phelps felt confident that the former opposition to such study had melted away: "Our sex . . . have been thought deficient in reasoning powers . . . advantages are now placed before them; they may prove the strength of their reasoning powers, in the study of mathematics, of logic, and even metaphysics, without fear of reproach for attempting to pass the limits, which nature has assigned for the operation of their minds."[30]

New ideas of women's education spread from state to state through the medium of the graduates of Troy Female Seminary.[31] In the 1830s, it was fairly common for girls' schools in North Carolina to announce the arrival of a new faculty member from Troy as a means of enhancing their prestige. The 1837 advertisement of Scotland Neck Female Seminary is representative: "The entire control of this Seminary will hereafter be entrusted to [Miss Eugenia Hanks'] care . . . her qualifications are believed to be of the first order, having finished her education at Mrs. Willard's celebrated school."[32]

Although the addition of a teacher trained at Willard's famed seminary did not guarantee the inclusion of higher mathematics in the curriculum, in some cases girls' schools added courses in algebra or geometry almost immediately after Troy graduates joined their ranks. For example, North Carolina's Northampton Female Academy listed mathematics in its advertised course of study the year that Miss Harriet A. Dellay, a Troy graduate, joined the Academy.[33] As a subject listing, mathematics usually denoted the use of a compendium text that included advanced arithmetic along with such additional subjects as algebra, plane geometry, or conic sections. Phillips' Female Seminary at Chapel Hill, which opened under the superintendency of Mrs. Phillips and her assistant, a graduate of Troy Seminary, offered its students instruction in arithmetic and Euclid in 1836. Two years later, Phillips' Seminary added algebra to its course of studies.[34]

While the notion of teaching mathematics to girls gradually gained acceptance, it was not universally approved. When Illinois's Jacksonville Female Academy opened in 1833, a delegation of women visited its director to advise her that if young ladies "can read and spell, write and count, it is all they need to know."[35] Some educators in girls' schools, opposed to the

Table 4.1 Percentage of Selected Female Higher Schools Offering Mathematical Subjects, 1749–1871

	1749–1829 (55 schools)	1830–1871 (107 schools)
Arithmetic	86	79
Algebra	15	83
Plane geometry	27	79
Plane trigonometry	2	40

Source: Woody, *A History of Women's Education in the United States,* vol. I (N.Y.: Octagon Books, 1980 [1929]), 418.

new trend, argued that "[girls] should understand practical arithmetic, though not mathematics."[36]

In spite of such scattered opposition, growing numbers of girls' schools began to offer higher mathematics after the 1820s (Table 4.1). Based on an examination of the school catalogs of 162 female seminaries from at least twenty states, the historian Thomas Woody concluded that after 1840, arithmetic served as a preparatory subject to more advanced studies. According to Woody, algebra appeared in the 1820s and plane geometry slightly earlier.[37]

By using such sources as school catalogs and newspaper advertisements, it is possible to compare the course offerings in boys' secondary schools with those in girls' schools. During the first two decades of the nineteenth century, the mathematics instruction in Pennsylvania and North Carolina girls' schools consisted primarily of arithmetic (Table 4.2).[38]

Although it is the case that a few of the larger arithmetic textbooks published in America included some algebraic content, such content was usu-

Table 4.2 Percentage of Selected Pennsylvania and North Carolina Male and Female Higher Schools Offering Mathematical Subjects, 1750–1840

	Male schools (91 schools)	Female schools (78 schools)
Arithmetic	63	81
Mathematics	52	3
Algebra	25	4
Geometry	26	8
Trigonometry	9	1
Navigation	11	—
Surveying	20	—

Sources: Data compiled from newspaper advertisements included in Charles L. Coon, ed., *North Carolina Schools and Academies, 1790-1840: A Documentary History* (Raleigh, N.C.: Edwards and Broughton, 1915); James Mulhern, *A History of Secondary Education in Pennsylvania* (N.Y.: Arno Press, 1969) 328–329, 428–429.

Table 4.3 Percentage of Selected Pennsylvania Male and Female Higher Schools Offering Mathematical Subjects, 1830–1889

	Male and coeducational schools (116 schools)	Female schools (90 schools)
Arithmetic	74	90
Mathematics	21	—
Algebra	67	69
Geometry	63	67
Trigonometry	35	22
Navigation	14	—
Surveying	47	—

Source: Data compiled from James Mulhern, *A History of Secondary Education in Pennsylvania,* 328–329, 428–429. Mulhern does not provide data for the subjects of mathematics, navigation, or surveying in the female schools in his sample.

ally restricted to a small section at the end of the book. For example, Nicholas Pike's 512-page compendium, *A New and Complete System of Arithmetic,* published in 1797, included thirty-three pages comprising "An Introduction to Algebra Designed for Use in Academies" and an additional seventy pages devoted to geometry, trigonometry, mensuration, and conic sections.[39] There is no way of knowing how many girls might have studied the introductory algebra contained in such texts. After 1830, while girls' schools still lagged somewhat behind boys' schools in offering trigonometry, the numbers of girls' and boys' schools offering algebra and geometry were roughly equal (Table 4.3).

A shift toward increased offerings in higher mathematics also occurred in boys' schools. Before 1840, only a minority of male academies in Virginia offered instruction in algebra or geometry as separate subjects, although roughly half provided instruction in what was called "mathematics" (Table 4.4). The mathematics texts of this period were omnibus texts that often included sections devoted to arithmetic, algebra, geometry, and sometimes trigonometry, mensuration, or even surveying. For example, John Ward's text, *The Young Mathematician's Guide,* included five parts:

Table 4.4 Percentage of Virginia Male and Female Higher Schools Offering Algebra and Mathematics, 1835–1837

	Male schools (30 schools)	Female schools (27 schools)
Mathematics	57	7
Algebra	17	7

Source: Data compiled from newspaper advertisements in *The Richmond Enquirer,* 1835–1837.

arithmetic, algebra, geometry, conic sections, and "the arithmetic of infinities."[40]

While such mathematical subjects as algebra, geometry, and trigonometry gained acceptance in girls' schools, those associated with male vocations, such as navigation and surveying, did not. Navigation and surveying do not appear in the above sample of Pennsylvania and North Carolina girls' schools before 1840, nor do they appear in the sample of Pennsylvania girls' schools from the later period, 1830–1889. In his study, Thomas Woody noted that surveying and navigation occurred principally in schools for both sexes.[41] We can infer that girls probably rarely, if ever, studied these subjects. Throughout the century, the mathematics included in these vocational subjects provided boys with additional sources of access to advanced mathematics that, by virtue of contemporary beliefs and values, were unavailable to girls.

By 1880, it appears that roughly equal numbers of boys' and girls' academies and seminaries offered algebra and geometry to their students. Similar developments occurred in the nation's few publicly supported high schools at midcentury. Although perhaps initially motivated by a desire to elevate the status of women's education, the movement to instruct girls in mathematics was also advanced by a very practical and pressing need for female teachers and teaching assistants in the publicly supported grammar and high schools.

During the same period that higher mathematics entered the curricula of private schools serving the children of well-to-do families, such subjects as algebra and geometry began to appear in the highest grades of some common schools as well, where they became available to girls from a wider range of class backgrounds. The case of the Boston common schools illustrates some of the financial and administrative concerns that beset a city grappling with the issue of offering advanced studies to girls. In practice, the policy decisions made by Boston's School Committee resulted in greater numbers of girls than boys studying bookkeeping, algebra, and geometry in Boston's grammar (upper-elementary grade) schools in 1845, as shown in Table 4.5. At the time, algebra and geometry were elective subjects. Only the Hancock and Bowdoin schools taught geometry, both of which catered solely to girls: "[Algebra and geometry are] permitted in such cases as thought expedient. For this reason algebra is studied in only about two-thirds of [schools], and geometry in two, viz: the Hancock and Bowdoin."[42]

More girls than boys studied higher mathematics in Boston's grammar schools. School authorities dismissed boys at age fourteen, but allowed girls to remain up to age sixteen. As a result, greater numbers of girls than boys reached the higher grammar school classes in which instruction in algebra and geometry appeared in the curriculum. This arrangement originated seventeen years earlier, when Boston's short-lived High School for Girls closed in 1828. Because the story of the High School for Girls illustrates the difference in the educational aims of the two sexes, it is worth recounting briefly here.

Table 4.5 Percentage of Students in the First Class of the Boston Grammar Schools Studying Bookkeeping, Algebra, and Geometry, 1845

Female schools	*Number in the first class*	*Number studying bookkeeping*	*Number studying algebra*	*Number studying geometry*
Bowdoin	113	60 (53%)	75 (66%)	25 (22%)
Wells	77	35 (46%)	35 (46%)	0
Franklin	40	9 (23%)	11 (28%)	0
Hancock	100	51 (51%)	38 (38%)	38 (38%)
Johnson	113	30 (27%)	27 (24%)	0
Total	443	185 (42%)	186 (42%)	63 (14%)

Male schools	*Number in the first class*	*Number studying bookkeeping*	*Number studying algebra*	*Number studying geometry*
Brimmer	40	19 (48%)	19 (48%)	0
Eliot	80	27 (34%)	0	0
Adams	72	0	0	0
Mayhew	54	0	18 (33%)	0
Total	246	46 (19%)	37 (15%)	0

Source. Data compiled from Otis W. Caldwell and Stuart A. Courtis, *Then and Now in Education, 1845–1923* (N.Y.: Yonkers-on-Hudson: World Book Co., 1925), 222–226.

In 1826, Boston opened a high school for girls, ostensibly to promote their moral and intellectual development, to better prepare them for marriage and motherhood, and to train teachers for the city's primary schools. The experiment was so successful that 130 pupils out of 286 candidates enrolled. The high number of students the first year, and the even larger number of girls who sought entrance the next, stunned members of the city School Committee, who noted that "The High School for boys has been in operation ever since 1821, and in every respect has been successful . . . yet the greatest number of applicants for admission which ever offered was ninety."[43]

Because smaller numbers of boys enrolled in high school, and most left school to seek employment before the end of the full course, the city incurred relatively little expense in providing secondary education to boys. According to a committee report: "The number of those annually admitted into [the High School for boys] is constantly and rapidly diminishing, every successive year, as the parents of scholars are able to find places to put them out as apprentices, or in counting houses. So that the fact is that the greatest number of these who have continued through their whole course is seventeen,—and they belonged to a class consisting originally of about seventy members."[44]

Taken aback by the large numbers of girls who sought admission to the new Girls' High School, and cognizant of the fact that the girls, unlike the boys, would most likely continue throughout the entire high school course, the committee voted to close the school in 1827.[45] With the closing of the Girls' High School, however, the School Committee adopted a series of resolutions by which girls could continue in the city's grammar schools two years longer than the boys. At the same time, the committee recommended introducing the higher branches previously taught in the Girls' High School into the grammar schools.

Although boys had the opportunity to continue their studies in high school, it is unlikely that significantly greater numbers of boys studied higher mathematics than girls in Boston. The reason lies both in the nature of Boston's high schools and in the boys' secondary school attendance. In Boston, boys had the choice of two schools: the Public Latin School or the English High School. The Public Latin School aimed to prepare boys for college. In 1858, the Boston School Committee reported that at this institution, "the greatest part of the time is devoted to the teaching of the Greek and Latin languages." Although the English High School emphasized higher mathematics in its course of study, the committee lamented that "too small a number enter it annually from the Grammar schools, and of this number too many leave before completing the regular course of study." So anxious were boys to enter employment that few were willing to stay and complete the course.[46]

By 1847, Boston's grammar schools offered the same studies to boys and girls, a practice supported by the majority of Bostonians but opposed by a vocal minority. The writer of the report of the examination committee, Joseph M. Wightman, argued that the branches of higher mathematics were unnecessary for girls: "Many portions of arithmetic and the whole of algebra, are as unnecessary to female education in our Grammar Schools, as would be the science of engineering, or a course of law studies."[47] Instead, suggested Wightman, girls should learn habits of industry and economy through instruction in plain sewing. Given sufficient needlework, Wightman believed that in time "the ambition of the pupils will be, to excel in this most legitimate of female avocations."[48]

BECOMING MATHEMATICS TEACHERS

In spite of opposition, Boston continued to offer algebra and geometry to girls in its grammar schools, and in 1852, the city established a Girls' High and Normal School to prepare the teachers who were increasingly needed not just in the primary schools, but in the grammar schools as well. During this period, financially strapped school boards across the country perceived the desirability of hiring female assistants to teach under a male master at their grammar and high schools.[49] Because the salaries paid to female teachers were often less than half that paid to males, it was far less expensive to hire women, a point driven home by the prominent educator Henry Barnard in 1856: "As the compensation of female teachers is less than one half that paid to males, every instance of the employment of a female teacher in place of a male teacher in the district school, will save one half of the wages paid to the latter."[50]

At the time Barnard and other reformers exhorted educators nationwide to consider the benefits of hiring female teachers, several coeducational high schools already boasted female teachers of mathematics, whose classes included boys as well as girls. During his visit to the United States during the 1840s, the Swedish writer Per Siljestrom observed that a female teacher gave the mathematical lessons in Hartford High School in Connecticut. Siljestrom claimed that "[this] is, indeed, frequently the case in the United States."[51]

During the Civil War years, school boards became acutely conscious of the desirability, even the necessity, of hiring female teachers, when men were not only expensive, but scarce. According to the Reverend Fraser, a British commentator, the "effect of the war was not to close the schools, but merely to transfer them to the management of women instead of men."[52] In Richland County, Wisconsin, the state inspector in 1862 witnessed a reduction in the number of male teachers and the disappearance of larger boys from schoolrooms. The older female pupils also withdrew from their studies to "supply the lack of teachers."[53]

Like Emma Willard several decades earlier, some of the first female mathematics teachers in secondary schools had to bring themselves quickly up to scratch in their subjects in order to teach effectively. In 1838, at the age of forty-eight, Susan Nye Hutchison embarked on the study of algebra while she served as principal of a school for girls in Salisbury, North Carolina. Although her primary objective may have been to upgrade her school's curriculum in order to compete more effectively with other institutions that were beginning to offer higher mathematics to females, Hutchison found algebra to be immensely enjoyable. "I find it an absorbing study and my progress in it give [sic] me much gratification,"[54] she wrote. "I am delighted with algebra."[55] Several days later she "got into equations of the 8th degree and felt much rejoiced."[56] Later generations of women who had learned algebra in school still required additional study in order to teach the more advanced subjects that many secondary institutions added to the curriculum at midcentury. For instance, in a letter to her parents in 1854, Connecticut teacher Mary A. Dodge described the preparation required to provide instruction in a variety of subjects at Hartford High School, including algebra and geometry: "I have five classes: three in Latin, one in Algebra, and one in Geometry . . . Algebra is so familiar to me that I do not study it at all out of school . . . [after Latin] comes a class in geometry. This I need to study, but do it when I am not employed, the hour after Algebra."[57]

Young women teachers without the necessary mathematics training often found themselves in less demand than those who could teach geometry and algebra. For example, in 1863, Emma Holmes wrote about her difficulty in obtaining a teaching position in Mrs. McCandless School for Girls in Camden, South Carolina: "We had a very Pleasant conversation, and [Mrs. McCandless] seemed quite pleased with my views of teaching. But I told her I could not teach Algebra; I knew nothing of it, having especially disliked it—a branch in which she wished assistance particularly. So nothing was settled, or will be, till she opens school week after next, when she will organize her classes and let me know if she needs my assistance."[58]

Fueled by the demand for female teachers to teach algebra and geometry in secondary schools, and supported by the rationale of increased mental discipline, increasing numbers of girls' schools began to include higher mathematics in their courses of study. Monticello Female Seminary, which opened in Illinois in 1838, was one of many whose officials justified the study of advanced mathematics as a means of disciplining the female mind. The writer Lucy Larcom, a former student at the seminary, recalled her struggles to attain the discipline that only trigonometry and conic sections could provide: "I had a natural distaste for mathematics, and my recollections of my struggles with trigonometry and conic sections are not altogether those of a conquering heroine. But my teacher told me that my mind had need of just that exact sort of discipline, and I think she was right."[59]

Because many nineteenth-century Americans considered mathematics a male domain, the subject was thought to pose great difficulties for girls, but several contemporary reports indicate otherwise. In 1858, a student of Tuskegee Female Academy wrote enthusiastically about mathematics in her diary, noting the encouragement of her male instructor: "Mr. Price praised us this evening in Geometry. He said that we were able to study any mathematical study, it makes no difference how difficult it is. I told him that mathematics is my favorite study."[60] The principal of the coeducational Woodward High School of Cincinnati wrote in 1859 that visitors often asked "if the girls equal the boys in the severer branches, such as Geometry." Clearly they did, he replied: on the mathematics exam, the eight girls averaged "86 [and] 37/176 percent, whilst that of the ten boys was 85 and 21/23 percent."[61]

In some coeducational secondary schools, girls' reported mathematics achievement exceeded that of boys. For example, in 1854, the principal of the Cleveland High School reported: "the first class of girls permitted to take the full course in mathematics stood considerably higher, on the average, than the boys."[62] In an 1865 report designed to create support for Indiana's practice of hiring increasingly greater numbers of female teachers, Joseph J. Bingham, state superintendent of public instruction, particularly emphasized women's aptitude for mathematics: "Some of the best mathematicians I have ever taught were females. The best algebraist that ever recited to me was a female, who had earned with her needle, in a tailor's shop, the means of paying her expenses, and educating herself . . . the best reciter of geometry I ever saw, was a fair young girl, of beautiful person and delicate sensibilities."[63] More than fifty years later, Walter S. Monroe reported a study of failure rates by sex in Indiana city and rural schools, concluding that "the boys are much less successful than the girls . . . even in mathematics the girls show a slight superiority."[64] And in 1910, the principal of Central High School in Cleveland, Ohio, reported that there were as many girls as boys enrolled in a class set aside "for those who are really stars in mathematics . . . who are eager for all the original investigation and demonstrative work that may be given to them."[65]

In contrast to the sciences, educators never attempted to develop a differentiated mathematics curriculum for females. Instead, educators in female schools appear to have relied on the textbooks published for the academy market in general. Girls who enrolled in early coeducational public high schools studied the same texts as their male classmates.

Because the most advanced natural philosophy and chemistry textbooks in use in secondary schools by the end of the century required prior knowledge of algebra and geometry, the fact that girls now had equal access to such subjects meant that they were equally prepared to undertake the study of the mathematical sciences in their secondary schools as were boys. Enrollment statistics compiled in 1890 confirm this. In coeducational public high schools, roughly equal numbers of boys and girls enrolled in such courses as algebra, geometry, physics, and chemistry, with girls having a slight enrollment advantage (Table 4.6). The historians David Tyack and Elizabeth Hansot note that individual school reports reveal the same pattern of similar course enrollments among boys and girls in coeducational schools.[66]

Because researchers often look at self-selection as an indicator of gender preference, comparing the percentages of men and women who taught algebra or geometry in high schools reveals the extent to which contemporaries construed these subjects as appropriate for males or females. Girls may have enrolled in high school algebra and geometry classes to fulfill graduation requirements, but the numbers of young women who went on to become high school mathematics teachers made this choice freely, unencumbered by similar requirements. Nor were there financial incentives to take up the subject of mathematics; nineteenth- and twentieth-century high school teachers of mathematics were no more highly paid than were teachers of English or history.

A study of the teachers providing instruction in algebra and geometry in Wisconsin public high schools reveals that roughly equal numbers of men and women taught these subjects. From 1915 to 1928, school inspectors visited the high schools, observing classes, noting the instructor's name and the subject taught, and providing a brief evaluation. Thus, the reports of

Table 4.6   Percentage of Boys and Girls Enrolled in Certain High School Subjects, 1890

	Boys	*Girls*
Physics	22.5	23.2
Chemistry	9.9	10.4
Algebra	45.3	46.0
Geometry	21.7	21.3

Source: John Francis Latimer, *What's Happened to Our High Schools?* (Washington, D.C.: Public Affairs Press, 1958), 149.

the inspectors indicate the sex of those teaching various subjects. Unlike physics, a subject that seems to have attracted men almost exclusively, or English, a subject almost always taught by women, both sexes taught mathematics, as shown in Table 4.7.[67]

In California, the demand for mathematics teachers at the secondary level encouraged young women to pursue mathematics both as an undergraduate and graduate study.[68] At Stanford University, although few students graduated each year with a bachelor of arts degree in mathematics, women received a large proportion of the mathematics degrees, as shown in Table 4.8. The percentages are all the more significant when considered in light of the proportion of female enrollment at Stanford. In 1899, women composed forty percent of students, a number that seemed to portend the impending feminization of the university. Wishing to maintain the university's reputation as an institution "primarily for men," Mrs. Leland Stanford established a limit on enrollments, such that "The number of women attending the University as students shall at no time ever exceed 500." Thus, during the years from 1899 to 1932, when the trustees rescinded the enrollment limit, women comprised an increasingly smaller proportion of students.[69] During the academic year 1911–1912, when women received seventy-five percent of the bachelor of arts degrees in mathematics, they composed less than a third of the undergraduate student body. Nor, in later years, did the

Table 4.7 Percentage of Male and Female Wisconsin High School Teachers Responsible for Teaching Selected Subjects, 1915–1928

	Algebra	Geometry	English	Physics
1915–16 (40 schools)				
Male teachers	50	76	4	97
Female teachers	50	24	96	3
1919–20 (32 schools)				
Male teachers	31	66	9	93
Female teachers	69	34	91	7
1923–24 (21 schools)				
Male teachers	55	36	13	100
Female teachers	45	64	87	0
1927–28 (38 schools)				
Male teachers	62	55	0	92
Female teachers	38	45	100	8

Source: Data compiled from *Department of Public Instruction Office of the State Superintendent High School Inspection Reports* [Wisconsin], Wisconsin State Historical Society, boxes 1–4.

Table 4.8 Percentage of Bachelor of Arts Degrees in Mathematics Conferred at Stanford University, 1891–1932

Year	Total number of degrees	Percentage of female students out of total enrollments	Degrees awarded to men	Degrees awarded to women
1892	2	25	100	0
1897	3	37	33	67
1902	3	35	33	67
1907	3	30	33	67
1912	4	28	25	75
1917	7	23	29	71
1922	7	14	29	71
1927	14	11	50	50
1932	10	13	60	40

Source: Data compiled from *The Leland Stanford Junior University First Annual Register, 1891–1892* (Palo Alto, Calif.: Stanford University, 1892), 105–106; *Sixth Annual Register, 1896–1897,* 172; *Eleventh Annual Register, 1901–1902,* 206; *Sixteenth Annual Register, 1906–1907,* 232; *Twenty-first Annual Register, 1911–1912,* 219; *Twenty-sixth Annual Register, 1916–1917,* 271; *Thirty-first Annual Register, 1921–1922,* 327; *Thirty-sixth Annual Register, 1926–1927,* 388; *Forty-firstAnnual Register, 1931–1932,* 478–497,in Special Collections at Green Library, Stanford University.

number of women in mathematics decline in proportion to their enrollment at Stanford; in 1932, the percentage of women receiving degrees in mathematics was three times the percentage of women in the overall student body.[70]

A similar pattern exists in the mathematics degrees awarded at the land-grant University of California in Berkeley and at the University of Wisconsin in Madison. Berkeley awarded bachelor of science degrees in mathematics in the College of Natural Sciences, which described its curriculum in 1902 as distinguished by "the prominence given to the Natural Sciences as elements of culture, and the preparation afforded for a professional career in science." The 1907 *Register* reveals that women received fifteen of the eighteen bachelor of science degrees awarded in mathematics. In 1911, women received all nine of the bachelor of science degrees in mathematics and two of the three master of science degrees in mathematics. The *Commencements* published by the University of Wisconsin reveal a similar trend.[71]

During the early twentieth century, some women pursued mathematics to the doctoral level. The mathematician Evelyn Boyd Granville attended Dunbar High School in Washington, D.C., a segregated school for African-Americans, where she received encouragement from two of her high school teachers: Ulysses Basset, a graduate of Yale University, and Mary Cromwell, a graduate of the University of Pennsylvania. Granville later attended Smith College on a partial scholarship and eventually received her

Ph.D. in mathematics from Yale in 1949, the same year that Marjorie Lee Browne received a Ph.D. in mathematics from the University of Michigan. Granville and Browne were the first African-American women to receive doctorates in mathematics in the United States.[72]

Within the context of their culturally approved vocational career paths, women actively pursued the study of mathematics both at the undergraduate and graduate levels. Of course, men continued to dominate such traditionally male fields as engineering and mining, studies that also required advanced mathematics. Given their interest and aptitude for mathematics, the almost complete absence of women in college engineering classes had probably more to do with cultural views of gender roles than with the underlying mathematics of the discipline. Far from shunning mathematics, women pursued the subject in their preparation for secondary school teaching.

CRITICISM OF THE MATHEMATICAL GIRL

Although increasing numbers of girls studied higher mathematics as the nineteenth century progressed, the controversy surrounding such study never disappeared. Unlike their seventeenth- and eighteenth-century counterparts, who had debated whether women were capable of rational thought, few nineteenth-century American educators upheld the view that girls were incapable of studying mathematics. Instead, fears began to surface that perhaps girls were too capable by far. The presumed mathematical superiority of girls over boys alarmed some schoolmen. In Groveland, Massachusetts, the school committee noted with concern that girls attended the town's common and high schools more regularly than boys, remained longer in the school course, and achieved higher marks in mathematics: "Every register and examination proves it. Our best mathematicians are not those who, if the present order of the world continues, will have occasion to use such knowledge. The fact should awaken serious inquiry."[73]

Critics argued that the advanced study of mathematics was inappropriate for girls because of its limited usefulness in women's sphere. As more women began to enter the workforce later in the century, these kinds of arguments intensified. For example, in 1865, S. S. Randall, city school superintendent of New York, criticized New York's practice of enrolling girls in the same mathematical course as boys. According to Randall, the study of needlework would be far more practical for girls than advanced mathematics: "Except as a mere mental discipline [higher mathematics] is wholly unavailable for any useful purpose in the ordinary transactions and duties pertaining to the sphere of womanhood."[74]

Many Americans did not consider mathematics to be a useful study for young women destined to become homemakers. In a well-publicized criticism of female education, Horace Greeley (1811–1872), editor of the *New York Tribune*, expressed dismay at the sight of girls "studying algebra and trigonometry and logarithms" in public high schools when they could make better use of their time studying subjects that "they will urgently need to know." In Greeley's opinion, girls of all classes would have derived much greater benefit from learning to cook.[75]

By the turn of the century, American concerns about the growing numbers of women entering the workforce prompted many parents and educators to reconsider the advisability of offering girls a differentiated curriculum centered on the topics of hearth and home. During the last decades of the nineteenth century, an intensified debate over the role of higher mathematics in girls' schooling, coupled with the introduction of vocational classes in the curricula of many public high schools, would fuel a series of reforms leading to declining enrollments among girls in advanced mathematics courses. Such reforms are considered within the context of a number of social and cultural developments and discussed in some detail in Chapter 7.

CONCLUSION

In an attempt to explain the absence of women in the mathematical sciences, some scholars have surmised that girls turned to the nonmathematical science of natural history because they did not receive advanced training in mathematics. However, the documentary evidence examined for this study does not support this hypothesis. As demonstrated in the previous chapter, the courses of study and schoolbooks of girls' secondary schools indicate that the natural philosophy and astronomy textbooks available to them included increasing amounts of mathematics after the 1840s. After midcentury, the mathematical complexity of the most advanced texts used in girls' schools did not differ from those used in boys' schools. Although natural history did increase in girls' schools from 1840 through 1880, this increase did not accompany a corresponding decline in natural philosophy, or physics.[76]

Girls not only studied advanced mathematics in their secondary schools, they chose to become mathematics teachers as well. Self-selection remains an important indicator of gender preference. Although female enrollments in high school mathematics courses can be explained by graduation or college admission requirements, the numbers of young women who choose to become secondary school mathematics teachers made this choice freely. Teachers of mathematics were no more highly paid than teachers of English. Why would young women have made such a choice? Only one explanation fully suffices: love of the subject matter.

Although some scholars have surmised that young women took up the study of natural history as other sciences became more mathematically complex, this shift was not motivated by an inability to understand the underlying mathematics of high school chemistry or physics. Nor was it apparently prompted by a widespread dislike of mathematics. The turn to natural history occurred precisely at the time that girls reached parity with boys in the level of mathematics offered their secondary schools. Why, then, did females flock to natural history? Chapter 5 explores a variety of social and cultural factors that contributed to this development. One cannot understand it, however, without grasping the depth, breadth, and almost revivalist nature of the feeling that Americans brought to natural history near midcentury. As Ralph Waldo Emerson wrote in that era, "I am moved by strange sympathies; I say continually, 'I will be a naturalist.'"[77]

5

The Rise of Natural History

In 1822, Amos Eaton, a well-known New York botanist and geologist, declared, "I believe more than half the botanists of New York are ladies."[1] Throughout the eighteenth century, amateur hobbyists had embraced natural history, a field that included such branches as botany, geology, mineralogy, entomology, and ornithology. In spite of its popularity among the American public, however, natural history was slow to enter the curricula of American higher schools. During the early nineteenth century, the science most frequently included in the courses of study of such schools was natural philosophy or physics, closely followed by astronomy and chemistry. Although a general treatment of natural history topics existed in most geography textbooks at this time, it was relatively unusual for a student to receive instruction in natural history as a separate subject. However, during the middle decades of the century, this picture began to change, and by the dawn of the twentieth century, natural history appeared to be the science most preferred among young women.

How can we account for the overwhelming preference among late nineteenth-century girls for the subjects of natural history? To date, historians have explained this development as a result of the extracurricular nature literature aimed at a female audience during the late eighteenth and early nineteenth centuries, the influence of cultural beliefs linking women to nature, or the presumed deficiencies in girls' mathematics schooling.[2] As demonstrated in the previous chapter, this last explanation is without foundation, because girls' mathematics preparation was comparable to that of boys after midcentury. To what extent can scholars justifiably attribute the feminization of natural history to the influence of cultural stereotypes and the marketing of nature literature to a female audience? Did other social, cultural, or economic developments influence this phenomenon as well? To answer these questions, this chapter examines a variety of media, from magazines and nature literature to schoolbooks, and probes the rhetoric natural history promoters used to encourage the participation of young women. To understand the nature of women's participation in natural history, the following discussion investigates the relations between female amateurs and male professionals. Finally, the chapter also explores the long-range impact of the public support given to women's participation in natural history by several well-known and highly respected naturalists and analyzes the importance of friendships and mentoring relationships among male and female naturalists in encouraging women's interest and creating employment opportunities for women in several related fields.

THE POPULARIZATION OF NATURAL HISTORY

Although it entered the curriculum relatively late as a school subject, American men and women had interested themselves in natural history since the Revolutionary period. Inside the schoolroom, geography textbooks brought an array of natural history topics to American children just after the Revolutionary War; outside the schoolroom, vehicles for the popular dissemination of natural history included magazines, public lectures, and a growing cadre of nature books directed to a general audience.

A variety of media conveyed the appeal of natural history to early nineteenth-century Americans, including lyceums, magazines, and nature books. Both men and women learned to appreciate natural history through lyceum lectures in their towns and villages. The lyceum movement began in the 1820s under the leadership of Josiah Holbrook, a graduate of Yale College. In 1826, Holbrook outlined his plan for a lyceum in a paper printed in the new *American Journal of Education*, and two years later, he organized the American "Lyceum or Society for the Improvement of Schools and Diffusion of Useful Knowledge." The first National Lyceum opened in 1831. By 1834, there were already nearly 3,000 lyceums in the United States, and in 1839, Horace Mann counted 137 in Massachusetts alone.[3] In remote villages across the nation, lyceum lecturers held forth on a broad range of subjects. For instance, when Charlotte Forten attended the lyceum lectures in Salem, Massachusetts, she heard abolitionist speakers, such poets as Ralph Waldo Emerson and James Russell Lowell; the zoologist Louis Agassiz and lesser-known science enthusiasts; and a host of others lecturing on such topics as "Success," "Patriotism," and "The Effects of Physical Science upon the Moral World." The movement gained impetus from a popular enthusiasm for personal development and self-improvement. "Where is science now?" asked William Ellery Channing, for many years a prominent Unitarian clergyman of Boston. "Locked up in a few colleges, or royal societies, or inaccessible volumes? No, science, has now left her retreats: . . . There are parts of our country in which lyceums spring up in almost every village for the purpose of mutual aid in the study of natural science."[4]

Magazines catering to children and families often included articles and stories on natural history subjects. Such widely circulated periodicals as the *Youth's Companion* regularly included something for every member of the family, from beginning readers to adults. Issues published from 1850 to

1905 reveal a consistent American interest in the subjects of natural history, joined in the 1870s by increasing numbers of articles on recent inventions, technology, and agriculture. Gardening articles reprinted from the British magazine *Child's Companion* also found their way into the pages of the *Youth's Companion.*[5] According to Elizabeth Keeney, autobiographical and biographical accounts suggest that "botanizing" was becoming a popular pastime among middle-class American children by midcentury. Children frequently wrote letters about botanizing. Typical of such letters was a missive written in 1847 to the magazine *Youth's Cabinet* by female students in Lewisberry, Pennsylvania, who wrote to request more botany: "We like it very well . . . but we think we would like it still better if you would give us more of Natural History and Botany in its pages."[6]

A developing genre of American nature writing brought various topics in natural history and some scientific nomenclature to a general audience. Nineteenth-century narrators of nature often participated in natural history as amateur collectors or scientists: botanists, ornithologists, or geologists. Unlike physics or astronomy, which retained a somewhat elitist character, its advocates argued that natural history was profoundly democratic. In contrast to the amateur physicist or astronomer, the amateur naturalist's requirements were relatively few and inexpensive. A field guide, collection box, magnifying glass, and a few odd bottles were sufficient to equip the collector. Henry David Thoreau collected specimens in his hat.[7] On several occasions, Thoreau collected specimens of fish and reptiles for the zoologist Louis Agassiz when the latter taught at Harvard. As was typically true of such relationships between amateurs and professionals, Agassiz benefited nicely from the arrangement, receiving a variety of fauna he had never before seen, along with an occasional new species. From Agassiz's assistant, Thoreau learned the Latin names of various specimens and, like other American nature writers, applied his knowledge by typically describing his environment in scientific or near-scientific terms. "I have seen at one time lying on the ice pickerel . . . peppered on the sides with small dark brown or black spots, intermixed with a few faint blood-red ones, very much like a trout," wrote Thoreau. "The specific name *reticulatus* would not apply to this; it should be *guttatus* rather."[8]

The tradition of turning toward natural history to compose and delineate the physical environment continued through the century in the writings of such naturalists as John Burroughs and John Muir, who frequently used scientific nomenclature to identify local flora and fauna. According to Peter A. Fritzell, American nature writers characteristically turned toward the scientific disciplines to help them delineate and quantify their natural world. Fritzell argues that as a result, a form of nature writing developed in America quite distinct from that in Great Britain.[9]

After the Civil War, exciting and controversial theoretical developments in the field of natural history fueled much of the more literate American public's fascination with science. The magazine *Popular Science Monthly* opened its first issue in 1872 with an article by Herbert Spencer and regularly devoted issues to debates on evolutionary theory in subsequent years. The debates over the evolution of species, popularized in newspapers and magazines and carried to a general audience from pulpits across the country, soon made the names of Charles Darwin, Herbert Spencer, and Thomas Huxley familiar to the American on the street.[10] For naturalists, the atmosphere of the period brimmed with excitement. Reflecting on this era many years afterward, Cornell University's Liberty Hyde Bailey reflected, "One who was not reared in that epoch cannot comprehend the ardor of it." It was, he recalled, "like a religious revival, when not only were critical subjects explained but the human spirit was liberated. It was an era of cordial and stimulating philosophies."[11]

NATURAL HISTORY SCHOOLBOOKS FOR GIRLS

Although the popularization of natural history played an important role in arousing middle- and upper-class women's interest in the subject, another key factor was the presumed compatibility between this science and contemporary views of acceptable middle-class female activity. Even before natural history textbooks appeared in great numbers in American schoolrooms, some schoolbook authors had encouraged middle-class American girls to take up an interest in natural history because they viewed the subject as particularly appealing to women. For example, Joseph Richardson's 1811 reader, *The Young Ladies' Selection of Elegant Extracts*, recommended the study of natural history as affording "a delightful study."[12]

Schoolbook authors exhorted girls to study natural history and other scientific subjects, but they did not always agree about the nature of a girl's appropriate participation in science. On the one hand, the well-known advocate of female education Hannah More urged a vigorous course of study for girls: "I would recommend a predominance of those more sober studies . . . which will teach her to elicit truth; which will lead her to be intent upon realities; which will give precision to her ideas; will make an exact mind . . ."[13] Richardson included More's writing in *The Young Ladies' Selection,* but he also informed his young readers that "The sphere of the fair sex [is] marked out by the Creator," and that "woman [was] designed as a helper" to man. This same text cautioned young girls that while they might take up the study of natural history, "it is not however expected that you should have a systematic idea of every vegetable, animal, or insect . . ."[14]

Generations of eighteenth- and early nineteenth-century men and women who argued that the ideal woman was a devoted mother and virtuous wife created a rhetorical model of women's sphere. According to this ideology, the proper site of female activities was the home, where women provided for the physical, mental, and moral well-being of their families.[15] Young girls walked a thin line between attaining intellectual rigor and maintaining feminine modesty. One author ominously cautioned girls to "be even cautious of displaying your good sense," and to keep any learning "a profound secret," especially from men, who "generally look with a jealous and malignant eye on a woman of great parts and a cultivated understanding."[16]

Although some early Republican reformers had claimed the right to an advanced education for women on the basis of their presumed intellectual equality with men, this claim faced increasing challenges as greater numbers of women sought various forms of higher schooling. When Alexis de Toqueville visited the United States in the late 1830s, he reported that Americans had created two distinct realms for men and women: "In America, more than anywhere else in the world, care has been taken constantly to trace clearly distinct spheres of action for the two sexes, and both are required to keep in step, but along paths that are never the same." According to de Toqueville, one would never encounter an American woman in charge of the "external relations of the family." Never would a woman manage a business or interfere in politics. The American woman "is never allowed to leave the quiet sphere of domestic duties." He concluded that in the United States, the doctrine of separate spheres did not detract from women's social equality with men, but that the equality of the sexes was based not on claims of similarity or sameness, but on claims of difference.[17]

Although contemporaries often rhetorically assigned public roles to men and domestic roles to middle- and upper-class women, among the working classes and in slave communities during the antebellum period, the so-called spheres were never that separate. Even among the middle classes, some researchers have highlighted arenas of female political activism and community building in the efforts of educators such as Emma Willard and Mary Lyon to establish higher schools for women,[18] or have illuminated individual cases of married women and widows who worked as educators outside the home out of necessity in order to support their families.[19]

A number of scholars have argued that the ideology of domesticity arose in response to women's greater activity in public affairs and to their entry into urban labor markets. For example, Linda Kerber claims that when de Tocqueville reported two distinct realms of action for American men and women, he described the public *discourse* of separate spheres rather than an actual social practice. Kerber theorizes that the existence of such discourse indicates a renegotiation of gender relations during the nineteenth century and that the enthusiasm with which advocates of domesticity sought to restrict women to their proper place at home was directly related to the increasing numbers of women who sought wider fields of opportunity.[20] Similarly, Alice Kessler-Harris portrays the ideology of domesticity as a response to the growth of industry and urbanization during the 1830s and changing patterns of women's work.[21] However, a closer look at some of the individuals who actively disseminated the doctrine of separate spheres among women complicates this picture.

Higher schools for females served as important centers for the dissemination of the nineteenth-century ideology of separate spheres, institutions commonly located in small towns and in rural, rather than urban, areas. This ideology prevailed in antebellum southern institutions serving elite girls who never expected to work for wages outside the home, in northern schools that explicitly sought to prepare teachers for the nation's growing common schools, and in Catholic academies on the western frontier. In other words, linking the promotion of this ideology to urban, wage-earning populations remains problematic.

In education, some of the same women who sought wider fields of opportunity were among the staunchest supporters of domesticity and advocates of a differentiated curriculum for girls. Among those who developed science textbooks for girls during the antebellum period, many of the most avid proponents of the ideology of separate spheres were leading female educators. In order to understand why these individuals adhered so strongly to what we would today characterize as restrictive roles for women, it is important to examine the beliefs of those who played the greatest role in the expansion of women's higher schooling during the antebellum period. By and large, these were members of religious groups, including Catholics, Quakers, Moravians, and the largest coalition: the Protestant evangelicals.

The growing emphasis on the ideology of separate spheres coincided with the period of the Second Great Awakening. Historians apply this term to the period running roughly from 1795 to 1837, an era characterized by evangelical revivalist fervor. Evangelicals believed in personal salvation, a literal interpretation of the Bible, and the necessity of self-improvement and social reform. The expansion of higher schools for females was made possible, in many cases, through the competitive efforts of both Catholic and evangelical crusaders.[22]

Evangelical Christians promoted advanced education for women based on the conviction that education would better prepare women for their important work as mothers, as benevolent agents in society at large, and as teachers of the young. Prominent female educators like Catharine Beecher[23] and Zilpah Grant[24] portrayed the work of female teachers as equally necessary to the spiritual development of the nation as was the work of male ministers. In their efforts to promote women's education, evangelicals realized the benefits of pooling resources to collaborate in Christian benevolent activity, and many such ventures resulted in the development of nonsectarian higher schools for women. For example, when Mary Lyon chartered Mount Holyoke Seminary as a nonsectarian but Protestant school, the 1835 prospectus stated that the school would "raise among the female part of the community a higher standard of science and literature, of economy and of refinement, of benevolence and religion."[25] Such claims could potentially draw students from a variety of religious backgrounds and still alleviate the concerns of parents who desired a Protestant version of moral and religious schooling for their children. Catholic academies for girls also began spreading to major cities on the western frontier, justifying schooling for girls on the basis of domestic ideology and the need to save souls in the church. In an address to the Protestant clergy in 1846, Catharine Beecher reported that the number of Catholic schools for girls exceeded the number of available Protestant academies.[26]

Clearly, many of the leading women founders of academies in the early nineteenth century espoused the ideology of separate spheres because the doctrine fit so well with contemporary evangelical and Catholic beliefs. In fact, the term *separate sphere* predates the nineteenth century in literature published for a female American audience, where it surfaces in the writings on female education by eighteenth-century Protestant ministers.[27] Few—if any—of the antebellum evangelical nineteenth-century female educators who ascribed to this doctrine of a natural order among men and women would have characterized themselves as feminists; they usually avoided the political issue of slavery and rarely supported women's suffrage. Instead, they promoted traditional gender roles among their female students, even as they advocated the study of such advanced subjects as mathematics and science. Evangelicals embraced the natural sciences for their presumed ability to lead individuals to a closer relationship with God through the study of nature, for their status as subjects promoting mental discipline and mental rigor, and for their utility.

The women evangelicals who authored natural history books for a female audience emphasized women's roles as helpers to male scientists, as collectors, or as popularizers, rather than as producers of scientific knowledge. Although both sexes read the natural history literature published in popular magazines and general readers, the rise of natural history subjects in middle- and upper-class girls' schools may have occurred partly in response to the development of gender-differentiated natural history schoolbooks aimed primarily at a female audience. Among the most influential were those of Almira Hart Lincoln Phelps, who authored textbooks in a number of fields, including botany and geology. Phelps had studied botany under Amos Eaton, the director of the Rensselaer Institute and an ardent promoter of science. Later an instructor at Troy Female Seminary, where her sister Emma Hart Willard was principal, Phelps taught botany to a class of about forty pupils. Finding a dearth of suitable books for beginners, she published her own *Lectures on Botany* in 1829. As noted in Chapter 3, both Phelps and Catharine Beecher advocated a form of science for girls focused specifically on the activities of hearth and home.

Some of the rhetoric Phelps used to advance botany was clearly gender specific. Her portrayal of botany as an admirable vehicle for attaining a variety of pedagogical goals—including the development of moral character, physical strength, observation skills, logical thinking, and orderly habits—probably would have appealed to the parents of both boys and girls. So would her emphasis of botany's utilitarian value.[28] Yet she often referred to the ideology of women's separate sphere to advance natural history among her female readership. For instance, she argued that the beauty and delicacy of flowering plants made botany "peculiarly adapted to females" and that it "provided a source of refined enjoyment." She assured her readers that the vegetable world offered many evidences of the Creator's design, leading "to greater love and reverence for the Deity."[29]

The conversational textbooks written for women by Jane Marcet served as an important precedent for the gender differentiation of later American schoolbooks, but Phelps went one step further. In contrast to some earlier female educators who had emphasized no distinction of sex in the intellectual powers of men and women, Phelps occasionally stressed the presumed cognitive differences between the sexes. According to Phelps, botany was a subject more suited to the intellectual capacities of women than astronomy. Women's "feeble minds" might be overwhelmed by the contemplation of the distant and immense heavenly bodies, but the plant world offered a more modest field of inquiry, one "which may be explored with the most pure and delightful emotions. [In the vegetable world] the Almighty seems to manifest himself to us with less of that dazzling sublimity which it is almost painful to behold in His more magnificent creations; and it might almost appear, that accommodating the vegetable world to our capacities, He had especially designed it for our investigation and amusement."[30]

While highlighting the congruity of natural history and women's sphere, Phelps and other authors were occasionally quite explicit about the limits of girls' appropriate participation in botany. Existing social mores required girls and boys to develop different approaches to botanizing. Although she recommended frequent botanical excursions to her readers so that they might experience the "pleasure from the science, by seeing the flowers in their own homes,"[31] Phelps cautioned that some areas of nature were inaccessible to girls because of their sex: "To the hardier sex, who can climb mountains, and penetrate marshes, many strange and interesting plants will present themselves, which cannot be found except in their peculiar situations; of these you must be content to obtain specimens, without seeing them in their native wilds."[32] At Emma Hart Willard's Troy Female Seminary, young ladies neither ventured deep into the woods nor scaled steep banks in search of botanical specimens; rather, a pattern developed in which boys collected for girls. According to Phelps, "The young gentlemen students of the Rensselaer School were chivalric and indefatigable in their efforts to produce specimens for the ladies' herbaria and so Botany became the fashion of the day."[33] Following the examples set by Phelps and other writers, many textbook authors maintained these kinds of gender distinctions in botanizing throughout the nineteenth century. For instance, in an 1881 book titled *Underfoot, or What Harry and Nelly Learned of the Earth's Treasures*, author Laura D. Nichols distinguished between the children's methods of outdoor exploration: "If Nelly went alone, she did not wander very far, for she was a timid child, and liked to be within easy distance of home and familiar faces; but if Harry were with her they would explore all sorts of places and get twice as many flowers, because he did not mind scratches or tumbles, mud or briars, in securing anything to which he took a fancy."[34]

Whether Phelps and later female educators desired true equality for women but cloaked their reforming efforts in the conservative language of separate spheres to ensure the acceptance and approval of contemporary Americans will never be known. Whatever their motives may have been, such educators effectively linked their students' pursuit of a more advanced knowledge of natural history to traditional mainstream values. By including several women in her overview of the history of botany, Phelps stressed the appropriateness and naturalness of women's botanical interests. She pointed to France, where "Josephine, the first wife of Napoleon, was distinguished for her fondness for this study," along with "other ladies of distinction, stimulated by her example." In England, "Mrs. Wakefield,

IF HARRY WENT WITH HER.

Plate 5.1   "If Harry went with her . . ." from Laura D. Nichols, *Underfoot, or What Harry and Nelly Learned of the Earth's Treasures* (Boston: D. Lothrop & Company, 1881), 29. (*Courtesy of Rare Books and Manuscripts, The Ohio State University Libraries, Columbus.*)

"FIRST CLASS IN BOTANY.—PLEASE RISE!"

Plate 5.2 "First Class in Botany—Please Rise!" in *St. Nicholas Magazine*, 15 (November 1887), 31. (*Courtesy of the Green Library, Stanford University.*)

and the industrious and talented Mrs. Marcet . . . have distinguished themselves as the authors of useful treatises on Botany."[35] Exhorting her readers to popularize natural history by making it fashionable, she encouraged ladies to "frequently exhibit specimens of their own scientific taste" in their parlors.[36] On the other hand, it must also be acknowledged that by characterizing botany as a more suitable science for girls than the physical sciences, and by portraying the latter as too intellectually challenging for women, Phelps and other natural history writers also may have influenced what would ultimately become a strong preference among girls for the sciences of natural history.

Many students from Troy, Amos Eaton's nearby Rensselaer Institute, and Phelps's Patapsco Female Institute in Maryland became teachers, spreading the teaching of botany in institutions across the country. William Kennedy Blake, professor of mathematics in a female college in North Carolina, described the classes of nature study there in 1851: "Never can I forget the delightful strolls through the woods and to the mineral spring with troops of girls making the woods resound with their merry laughter. These walks were not merely for recreation, but for the study of the trees, rocks, insects and other objects of nature."[37] So popular was botany among middle- and upper-class American women, and so common was the belief that mothers should teach it to their children, that magazine illustrations spoofing the trend appeared near the end of the century (Plate 5.2.)

The natural history subjects of botany and geology evidenced an astonishing growth during the nineteenth century. In North Carolina, the compendium subject of natural history and its related subjects of botany, mineralogy, and geology entered the curriculum of middle-class girls' schools during the second and third decades of the nineteenth century. At the same time, these topics attained a visible although proportionally smaller presence in boys schools as well, as shown in Table 5.1. A similar trend occurred in Pennsylvania. School catalogs from girls' and coeducational schools in Pennsylvania reveal that the subjects of botany, geology, and natural history more often appeared in girls' schools, although all three subjects also increased in the curriculum of boys' schools during the nineteenth century (Table 5.2). In an advertisement to the 1840 edition of Phelps's *Botany for Beginners*, designed for use in common schools, the publisher noted that since the publication of her text, botany had been introduced as a regular branch of instruction "not only into Colleges and Female Institutions of the first rank, but into many schools of a more humble character."[38]

Although Phelps's texts were arguably among the first widely used botany texts in female schools, not every botany text produced for the use of female students near midcentury evidenced gender differentiation. Mount Holyoke Female Seminary used the botany text published by Lewis C. Beck, professor of chemistry and botany in New York University. In

Table 5.1   Percentage of Selected North Carolina Male and Female Higher Schools Advertising Various Sciences, 1800–1840

Years		Natural philosophy	Astronomy	Chemistry	Geology	Botany	Natural history
1800–1819	Female schools	28	33	11	0	0	0
	Male schools	35	23	4	0	0	0
1820–1840	Female schools	73	62	62	9	38	9
	Male schools	43	30	20	2	4	2

Source: Data compiled from newspaper advertisements included in *North Carolina Schools and Academies 1790–1840: A Documentary History*, ed. Charles L. Coon (Raleigh, N.C.: Edwards and Broughton, 1915). The 1800–1819 data is derived from a sample of eighteen girls' schools and twenty-six boys' schools; the 1820-1840 data include forty-five girls' schools and forty-six boys' schools.

Table 5.2 Percentage of Selected Pennsylvania Female and Coeducational
Schools Offering Botany, Geology, and Natural History, 1750–1819 and 1830–1889

Years		Botany	Geology	Natural history
1750–1819	Female schools	14	0	11
	Coed schools	0	0	0
1830–1889	Female schools	77	33	29
	Coed schools	33	28	12

Source: Adapted from Mulhern, A *History of Secondary Education in Pennsylvania,* 328–329,
428–429, 542–543. Mulhern's 1750–1819 data are derived from the catalogs of thirty-six girls'
schools and forty-seven boys' schools; 1830–1889 data are derived from the catalogs of
ninety girls' schools and 116 coeducational schools.

1858, Harvard botanist Asa Gray published *Botany for Young People and
Common Schools,* an introductory text that went through numerous editions. Both Beck's and Gray's text presented the principles and concepts of
botany without attempting to differentiate the content for a female audience.[39] Nor was botany the only natural history subject experiencing a
heyday during this period. In New York secondary schools from 1830 to
1870, geology experienced a seventeenfold and botany an almost fivefold
increase. By 1870, roughly equal numbers of New York schools offered
botany as offered astronomy or chemistry, although natural philosophy remained prominent in many schools until the last decades of the century
(Table 5.3). By the dawn of the twentieth century, the science of botany
appeared to have become a girls' subject in both American and British
higher schools. In a 1902 report, British educators noted that instructors
taught botany "particularly well in those [schools] for girls." In 1907, an
American school superintendent expressed concern over the science

Table 5.3 Percentage of New York Secondary Schools Offering Various Sciences,
1830–1870

Year	Natural philosophy	Astronomy	Chemistry	Geology	Botany
1830	77	40	50	2	14
1835	100	83	95	5	45
1840	100	87	93	28	74
1845	96	84	90	35	74
1850	95	91	87	31	70
1855	96	93	79	38	82
1860	92	77	79	41	73
1865	95	67	70	42	70
1870	92	65	67	34	68

Source: Miller, *A History of New York Secondary Schools,* 108–109.

courses in his city's secondary schools because not only were enrollments low, but most of the students taking the botany course were girls.[40]

Besides botany, women nature writers popularized several other natural history subjects as suitable for girls. British authors had published texts on entomology for a female audience during earlier decades, creating a precedent for American interest. For instance, *Dialogues on Entomology*, published in 1819, presented a discourse between a girl named Lucy and her mother. During one conversation, Lucy stated, "Mamma, I believe that I remember all you told me yesterday of the vegetable and animal kingdoms, and of their being divided into classes, and the classes into orders, the orders into genera, and the genera into species." Her mother answered, "You have recollected very distinctly what I told you of these divisions; but do you understand the meaning of genera?"[41] Building on this tradition, American women writers characterized entomology, the study of insects, as suitable for females. Phelps noted, "[T]he study of spiders is one of the most elegant and delightful of all pursuits."[42] In 1844, Mary Townsend, sister of the naturalist John Kirk Townsend, published *Life in the Insect World: or, Conversations Upon Insects Between an Aunt and her Nieces*, in which the conversational format borrowed heavily from the earlier texts published by the British writer Jane Marcet.[43] Writing in 1853, the Swedish author Fredrika Bremer heartily approved of both Townsend's science and her natural theology: "The turn for minute detail, acute perception of the lesser world, which is peculiar to woman . . . together with a poetic feeling which allies it to the spiritual . . . these are all natural endowments which seem singularly to befit woman for that portion of science, and should in their pursuit and their application tend to make the searching soil richer in its daily life."[44] Later women authors who popularized entomology included Anna Botsford Comstock (1864–1930), natural history illustrator and teacher of nature study at Cornell University, who published *Ways of the Six-Footed* in 1903.

Unlike botany and entomology, Americans viewed zoology and ornithology as men's subjects until relatively late in the nineteenth century. Until after midcentury, ornithology required the shooting of live birds for study; few middle-class ladies would have felt it proper to venture forth into the fields with a shotgun in search of bird specimens. Similarly, the study of zoology entailed the dissection of animal specimens. In *Familiar Lectures on Botany*, Phelps favorably contrasted the delicate study of plants with the potentially more grisly study of animals, noting that although female students could easily dissect plants, they could not undertake the dissection of animals "without painful emotions."[45] Similarly, cultural views about dissection worked to exclude women from medical training during the early nineteenth century. The idea that young ladies might take their scalpels to cadavers was incomprehensible to some contemporaries. Women could not possibly emerge from such activities with their moral character intact, explained one Boston physician in 1828: "A female could scarce pass through the course of education requisite to prepare her as she ought to be prepared, for the practice of midwifery without destroying those moral qualities of character which are essential to the office."[46]

Table 5.4　Percentage of Bachelor's Degrees in Scientific Fields Conferred on Women at Stanford University, 1892–1917

Year	Entomology	Botany	Physiology	Zoology	Physics	Geology
1892	0	100	50	0	—	0
1897	0	100	13	0	0	0
1902	—	—	40	40	0	0
1907	67	100	10	50	50	0
1912	25	67	20	75	100	0
1917	33	50	14	33	50	0

Source: Data compiled from *The Leland Stanford Junior University First Annual Register, 1891–1892* (Palo Alto, Calif.: University Press, 1892), 105–106; *The Leland Stanford Junior University Sixth Annual Register, 1896–1897* (Palo Alto, Calif.: University Press, 1897), 173; *The Leland Stanford Junior University Eleventh Annual Register, 1901–1902* (Palo Alto, Calif.: University Press, 1902), 206–207; *The Leland Stanford Junior University Sixteenth Annual Register, 1906–1907* (Palo Alto, Calif.: University Press, 1907), 232–233; *The Leland Stanford Junior University Twenty-first Annual Register, 1911–1912* (Palo Alto, Calif.: University Press, 1912), 219–220; *The Leland Stanford Junior University Twenty-sixth Annual Register, 1916–1917* (Palo Alto, Calif.: University Press, 1917), 271–272.

Although young ladies collected such geological specimens as fossils or minerals, their teachers and guardians did not expect them to go on geological surveys or dig geological specimens out of the earth themselves. Additionally, geology's association with the mining industry may have made it an unsuitable subject for girls. Even near the end of the nineteenth century, and for several decades into the twentieth, geology remained a traditionally male subject, unlike such other subjects as botany, entomology, chemistry, physics, or physiology. For example, during its first quarter century, Stanford University conferred bachelor's degrees on women in every scientific subject except geology[47] (Table 5.4).

　　Girls learned from their schoolbooks that there were limits to the extent of their participation in science. "Females, in particular," wrote Phelps, "are not expected to enter into the recesses of the temple of science."[48] Middle-class girls studied science to attain mental discipline, avoid frivolity, and gain a patina of gentility. As popularizers of science, they served the new republic by making science fashionable; by bringing it into their parlors, they carried science into the very heart of civilized American life.[49]

MOVING OUT INTO THE FIELD

Although the publication of Darwin's *The Origin of Species* in 1859 may have had little immediate impact on the popular enthusiasms of natural history collectors, it did shift the arena of interest for amateurs and professionals alike from the individual specimen to the living organism within its environment. In the concluding paragraph of *The Origin*, Darwin's depiction of an "entangled bank" illustrated the naturalist's new sphere of investigation: "clothed with many plants of many kinds, with birds, singing on the bushes, with various insects flitting about, and with worms crawling through the damp earth . . . [all] dependent upon each other in so complex a manner."[50]

Restricted by social mores from killing animals, women benefited from the shift to field studies spurred by Darwin's revolutionary theory. As the historian Lynn Barber points out, the new generation of naturalists turned its attention to the field, previously the disdained arena of amateurs. Followers of Darwin wanted to study living organisms rather than dead ones, and they wanted to study them in their natural habitats.[51]

Advances in technology also assisted study in the field. The first prism binoculars were patented in 1859, and in the next decades, the invention of film, flashlight, and telephoto lens contributed enormously to the study of living birds.[52] Popular bird books such as Florence A. Merriam's *Birds through an Opera Glass* and Olive Thorne Miller's *The Children's Book of Birds* stressed the importance of bird-watching. Such authors argued that the environment of the living creature, not the laboratory, was the proper site for study. As Olive Thorne Miller advised American children, "to see how birds live is much more interesting than to look at dead ones."[53]

From a profusion of nature books in the second half of the nineteenth century, girls learned repeatedly of the benefits of field studies. For example, from Elizabeth Cady Agassiz, they learned how to study at the seashore such living organisms as sea anemones, corals, jellyfish, and sea urchins. Agassiz instructed her readers to capture living specimens for observation. Wife of the Harvard scientist Louis Agassiz, Elizabeth Agassiz published in 1879 a natural history of marine flora and fauna in a book addressed to a female readership. Using the conversational format made famous by Jane Marcet, Agassiz wrote her text in the form of a letter from Aunt Lizzie to her two nieces, Lisa and Connie.[54]

BACK TO NATURE

Another influence on women's interest in natural history was the back-to-nature movement that emerged among urban Americans after midcentury. With it came increased enthusiasm for outdoor sports, landscape gardening, voyages of discovery, conservation, nature poetry, nature study, magazines of outdoor life, and camping. During this time, women played an important role in developing local parks and gardens in urban communities, in popularizing the need for conserving natural resources, and in bringing nature study to students in common schools.[55]

A likely early role model for the attention that middle- and upper-class American women gave to rural nature was Susan Fenimore Cooper, daughter of the novelist James Fenimore Cooper. Susan Cooper based her novel, *Rural Hours*, on her daily nature journal, which became an overnight success when it appeared in print in 1850.[56] With the publication of *Rural Hours*, Susan Fenimore Cooper launched a tradition of observational nature writing taken up by later generations of American women.

Although hers is a name—unlike that of John Muir or Theodore Roosevelt—less well known in conservation circles, Susan Fenimore Cooper was one of the earliest American writers to draw attention to the destruction of the environment. In *Rural Hours*, Americans learned not only of the seasonal changes in nature, but also of the decimation of certain plant and animal species. "All kinds of black-birds are rare here," Cooper noted on 27 April 1848; "they are said to have been very numerous indeed at the settlement of the country, but have very much diminished in numbers of late years."[57] She wrote despairingly, too, about the wanton obliteration of local forests: "It has been calculated that 60,000 acres of pine woods are cut every year in our own State alone; and at this rate, it is said that in twenty years, or about 1870, these trees will have disappeared from our part of the country."[58]

As they emphasized the importance of studying live organisms in their natural environments, later nineteenth-century women naturalists frequently argued for the protection of living things. According to Anna Comstock of Cornell University, "The nature-study teacher, if she does her work well, is a sure aid in inculcating a respect for the rights of all living beings to their own lives." Comstock claimed that, at Cornell, "[T]hose students who turn aside so as not to crush the ant, caterpillar or cricket on the pavement are almost invariably those that are studying entomology." What Comstock did not mention is that those Cornell students interested in entomology were often women. Cornell's Jugatae Club, an entomological club composed of both faculty and student members, included many women, as shown in a photograph taken in 1901 (Plate 5.3).[59]

Near the end of the century, a prevalent stereotype portrayed boys as the destroyers of wildlife and girls as its preservers. Leaflets disseminated by the early agricultural experiment stations often criticized the depredations of local fauna by American boys through egg stealing and shooting. Among the leaflets produced by Purdue University was "Spring Birds," by Mrs. Jeanette D. Ruby, who opened her article with the question, "I wonder why every boy that can borrow a gun goes out into the woods and tries to kill birds." Many school readers published during the last decade of the century included moralistic nature stories in which boys converted from destroying nature to protecting it. For example, in a typical story titled "In the Rabbit's Place," Frank, a boy fond of chasing and terrorizing his uncle's rabbits, dreamed that he transformed into a rabbit himself. As a rabbit, he raced to escape a menacing boy who chased after him "pell-mell, shouting and shaking a cane." After he awoke from this nightmare, Frank never chased a rabbit again.[60]

Schoolbooks often presented a contrasting image of girls as protectors of wildlife. In most moralistic nature stories, boys rarely heeded the strictures of girls; instead, they usually learned their lessons directly from nature. For example, in "The Wren's Nest," although a young girl urged a boy to leave alone the nest of a wren, the boy paid no attention until the wren itself attacked him about the head.[61] In some stories, girls circumvented the destructiveness of boys by offering alternative, presumably more civilized forms of activity. For example, an American text published in 1883

Plate 5.3 Cornell University's Jugatae Club, 1902, Anna Botsford Comstock Papers 21–23–25. (*Courtesy of the Division of Rare and Manuscript Collections, Cornell University Library.*)

included a story about the demise of a boys' woodchuck society. In the story, the girls of a certain school belonged to a tatting club and the boys to a woodchuck society. Bored with tatting and curious about the boys' activities, the girls asked for admission to the society. After the girls promised to learn woodchuck lore and wear veils to avoid freckles, the boys allowed them to join. At the end of the hunt, however, the girls found it impossible to face killing and skinning the hapless woodchuck. To the leader of the girls, the chairman of the woodchuck society complained, "We've let you into the Society, and you wouldn't have the woodchuck killed. You'll never have the woodchucks killed, and then what is the use in chasing woodchucks?" In response, the leader of the girls immediately made a motion to unite the woodchuck and tatting associations into a picnic club. After explaining that there would be refreshments of lemonade and nuts at the picnic, the approving girls and not unwilling boys seconded and carried the motion. Thus, without deliberation or debate, the boys' woodchuck society met its demise.[62]

Authors of children's nature schoolbooks published during the last decade of the nineteenth century frequently highlighted the necessity of studying nature in order to better protect it. For example, a nature reader published in 1896 told the story of a boy who wondered about the brown and yellow powder he found on his hands after catching a butterfly. His teacher, Miss Allen, gave him a dead butterfly's wing to examine under the microscope. When the boy discovered that the powder forms a part of the insect's wing structure, Miss Allen responded, "I am glad you can see this; for now I am sure you will always be careful in handling the butterflies."[63]

In their socially accepted role as nature's protectors, American girls found an additional rationale to study such sciences as botany, entomology, and the field-based subjects of ornithology and zoology. On the one hand, contemporaries viewed some level of scientific expertise in such studies as an elegant accomplishment; on the other hand, advocacy for the preservation of threatened species fit well with the increased awareness of conservation and the nostalgic back-to-nature movement sweeping middle-class America during the second half of the century.

MALE MENTORS, ADVOCATES, AND FRIENDS

Achievements in natural history appeared to dominate the field of American science during the post–Civil War decade. It was primarily in the biological and earth sciences—botany, zoology, geology, topography, and paleontology—that Americans earned the respect of Europeans. At the top of American science was a small internationally esteemed group that included Asa Gray, Louis Agassiz, James Dwight Dana, and other naturalists. In contrast, American scientists in the fields of physics, chemistry, and astronomy lagged their European counterparts, having published only one-third as much work since the Revolution as the French Academy of Sciences and the Royal Society of London. Apart from Benjamin Franklin and Joseph Henry, few American scientists in physics had ever won foreign acclaim. According to Daniel Kevles, in the 1870s, no more than seventy-five Americans called themselves physicists.[64]

A likely factor in the increasing interest among women in the subjects of natural history was the public support expressed by several highly regarded male naturalists for women's participation in science as collectors, teachers, and writers capable of popularizing scientific subjects. Some female amateurs developed important mentor relationships with male professionals. For instance, Graceanna Lewis (1821–1912), a Quaker from Chester County, Pennsylvania, identified a new bird species, *Agelaius cyanopus* with the help of John Cassin, curator of birds at the Academy of Natural Sciences in Philadelphia. A fellow Quaker, Cassin remained a mentor and friend to Lewis until his death in 1869. She described him as one to whom she could always turn for advice during her early years of study: "He had knowledge, I had not; and he rejoiced in imparting it to me." Most importantly, "he never seemed to think it strange a woman should wish to study."[65] She ultimately authored a natural history of birds and articles for various popular journals of natural history.

Mary Treat (1830–1923), the daughter of an itinerant Methodist minister, collected insects and sent specimens and descriptions to the men who knew the fields she studied: Asa Gray in botany and Auguste Forel, Samuel Scudder, Henry C. McCook, and Charles V. Riley in entomology. Through Gray, she became a correspondent of Charles Darwin, who shared her fascination with the specific mechanisms of carnivorous plants. Darwin mentioned her work in his book *Insectivorous Plants*, stating "Mrs. Treat of New Jersey has been more successful than any other observer" in understanding how bladderworts capture insects. The discoverer of numerous species of insects and plants, Mary Treat received recognition for her work from entomologists in America and other countries. Sereno Watson of the Gray Herbarium at Harvard named a species of lily in honor of her, the *Zephranthes treatae*; Auguste Forel of Switzerlalnd named an ant *Aphaenogaster treatae* for her; Gustav Mayr of Vienna named a cynipid oak fig root gall that she had discovered on a Virginia oak tree in Florida after her as well, calling it *Belonocnema treatae*. As with other collectors and amateur scientists, Treat's relationship with professionals served to benefit both sides. Not only did the amateur receive needed assistance and support, the professional gained access to pertinent observations from the field and samples of potentially new species.[66]

In 1873, the Harvard professor of zoology Louis Agassiz set a highly publicized stamp of approval on the role of women as teachers of natural history. According to both contemporary accounts and the reports of later generations of science educators, this was a landmark year for natural history education.[67] It was also a landmark year for women interested in pursuing careers as natural history teachers. That summer, Agassiz invited fifty students to study at the newly founded Anderson School of Natural History on Penikese Island, just off the coast of Massachusetts.[68] The mission of this summer school was to train teachers: "The conditions for admission at the Anderson School of Natural History are simply these—it is intended especially for teachers—the preference being first for those who are already teachers of Nat. History and who want to make themselves familiar with the best methods of teaching from specimens—next to students intending to become teachers."[69] Instruction was free, the prestige of studying with Agassiz was enormous, and the faculty at the school included some of the best-known names in American natural history. As a result, the number of applicants far exceeded the fifty spaces available.[70]

A phenomenal amount of publicity surrounded the opening of this school, and newspaper reporters crowded into the lecture hall and laboratory to report on every activity. This general brouhaha arose because of Agassiz's enormous popularity and influence. It was said of him that on an occasion when he applied to the Massachusetts legislature for funds to support his Museum of Comparative Zoology at Harvard, one of the legislators publicly protested Agassiz's appearing in person, explaining, "I am not opposed to his institution, and am willing to give to it in reason; but if that man talks to us for an hour we shall vote him whatever he asks for."[71] It is hardly possible to overestimate the position Agassiz held in educational circles. So great was his prestige that the journal *Education* once offered as a gift to new subscribers the choice of a portrait of Horace Mann or Louis Agassiz.[72]

When he opened the doors of the Anderson school, Agassiz surprised some of his colleagues by admitting eighteen women—roughly one-third of the student body.[73] A curious American public opened its newspapers to discover illustrations of women students, not only attending lectures and collecting specimens, but dissecting marine fauna (Plate 5.4).[74] Several of Agassiz's male students apparently disapproved of the presence of women among them. One or two nights after the school opened, six students from Harvard and Amherst tossed into the women's quarters a huge doll baby made from a pillow and blanket. Furious, Agassiz expelled the pranksters the next day.[75]

Why did Agassiz admit women to his school? In his opening address, he announced that the decision to admit women was "a question of no small moment . . . In my mind I had no hesitation from the start. There were those about us whose opinion I had to care for but did not know. I thought the best way was not to ask it, but to decide for myself."[76] Curi-

Plate 5.4   1873 newspaper clipping showing "Lady Students Dissecting" at the Anderson School of Natural History, Mary E. Beaman Joralemon Scrapbook QH31.A2.J6 1873. (*Courtesy the Bancroft Library, the University of California at Berkeley.*)

ously, this statement provides few clues as to the reasons for his decision. His public statements and published writings indicate that Agassiz did not approve of coeducation in general.[77] Given the eyewitness accounts published in contemporary newspapers, he clearly did not admit women with the aim of providing them with advanced training in science; instead, he wished to impart a particular pedagogical method: studying from laboratory specimens and from the field. Agassiz himself described this objective in a letter to Burt Green Wilder of Cornell, inviting Wilder to participate in the school: "Among my plans is a course of practical instruction in Natural History . . . chiefly with the view of preparing our teachers to introduce natural history into our schools."[78] It is likely that Agassiz admitted women because, mindful of their social roles as teachers and popularizers of science, he viewed women as a yet untapped resource for natural history education. As shown in Table 5.3 (page 106), the natural history subjects of botany and geology lagged behind natural philosophy in the curriculum of many secondary schools during this period. Who better to spread the gospel of natural history in schools than women, its traditional promoters?

Although not every professional male naturalist was keen to acknowledge the scientific contributions of female amateurs, the collaborative relationships that occasionally developed between men and women with a common interest in natural history sometimes resulted in long-lasting friendships and strongly supportive attitudes among men toward women's participation in science. The case of the friendship between Lucy Millington (1825–1900) and Liberty Hyde Bailey illustrates this phenomenon. At the age of fifteen, Bailey became interested in botany and began to assemble a herbarium. He borrowed a copy of Asa Gray's book, *Field, Forest, and Garden Botany*, and struggled to learn the unfamiliar terms. When Millington and her husband moved from the state of New York to South Haven, Michigan, fellow villagers told Bailey that a lady botanist had arrived in town. Bailey introduced himself, hoping that she might be willing to guide him through the more difficult parts of the book.[79] During the following two years, Millington identified the plants he collected and taught him the pronunciation of the Latin names.[80] Years later, he credited her with instilling in him a long-lasting research interest.[81]

The name of Lucy Millington was well known in botany circles when she first met Bailey in 1876. An amateur, she was self-taught in botany. Although she considered herself hampered by never having studied Latin, she nevertheless attained an admirable level of expertise. She specialized in the varieties of wild ferns, grasses, and the swamp-growth of the Adirondacks and studied the pine barrens near Warrensburg, New York.[82] When she was in her forties, she contributed to the *Bulletin of the Torrey Botanical Club*, a small New England journal that published notes by some of the most eminent botanists of the day.[83]

In 1871 Millington's discovery of the spruce mistletoe, later known as *Arceuthobium pusillum*, created a great deal of interest in the botanical community. This parasitic mistletoe was responsible for damage to black spruce trees in some areas of New England, a phenomenon then unexplained.[84] Having read of the ravages of a parasite on conifers of the far

West, she set out to determine the cause of a similar devastation she had observed among black spruce near Warrensburg, New York.[85] In September 1871, she sent a few specimens of a parasitic plant she had found on black spruce to the editors of the *Bulletin of the Torrey Botanical Club*, explaining that she believed it to be a mistletoe and describing the locations where she had collected specimens. The editors referred the plant to Asa Gray at Harvard.[86] Within weeks, Charles Peck of Albany, the state botanist of New York, claimed to have made the same discovery. Although both Asa Gray and the editors of the *Bulletin* upheld Millington's prior claim,[87] she did not receive official credit for the discovery until years afterward. In his role as state botanist of New York, Charles Peck had the authority to author a new species, and he promptly did so, naming the mistletoe *Arceuthobium pusillum* in a report before the Albany Institute on 6 February 1872.[88]

The story would have ended there, but for the fact that Millington went on to become an important mentor to Liberty Hyde Bailey (1858–1954). During the course of their many conversations, Millington told Bailey about her discovery of the spruce mistletoe, a story he was to remember long afterward. According to Bailey, Millington claimed that Charles Peck received his original specimens from her: "She found the mistletoe in 1871. She told me she took specimens to Charles H. Peck in Albany, and Peck is the author of the species, having described it in a State Museum Report dated 1873."[89] In 1878, Millington returned with her husband to northeastern New York, leaving Bailey her vasculum—a botany case—as a memento of their friendship. Bailey never saw them again. Years later, after graduating from college with a degree in botany, he took a position at Harvard as Asa Gray's botanical assistant for a number of years. From there, he went to Cornell University's department of agriculture as an assistant professor, and eventually became dean of the department of agriculture, a position he held for many years.

Eleven years after Millington's death in 1900, Bailey took steps to set the record straight and ensure that she received public recognition for her discovery of the spruce mistletoe. There are no records to indicate what might have inspired Bailey to contact Charles Peck in 1911. Perhaps he had a nagging interest in finding out whether he could confirm her story, or perhaps he hoped that after so many years, Peck would acknowledge her prior discovery. Whatever the motivation, Bailey wrote to inquire about Millington's discovery of the spruce mistletoe. Peck sent back a courteous but rather bland and uninformative reply: "She sent me many interesting botanical specimens and was a real botanist to the last and an esteemed correspondent. . . . She was one of nature's noble women."[90] Bailey waited until after Peck's death to take up the issue again. In 1934, he wrote to Peck's successor at the New York State Museum, H. D. House, to inquire about records pertaining to the discovery of *Arceuthobium pusillum*. House confirmed Millington's version of events as told to Bailey more than fifty-five years earlier. In spite of Peck's claim to have discovered the species, a note in his own handwriting indicated that the specimens had indeed been discovered previously by Millington.[91]

Spurred on by the confirmation provided by House, in 1939 Bailey published a biographical article about Millington in the journal *Torreya*. He was eighty-one years old at the time. In describing the discovery of *Arceuthobium pusillum*, he stated that "she was the discoverer of that strange plant," emphasizing the physical exertion expended by Millington in obtaining the specimens, as she "walked to the place and back . . . fifteen miles from her home."[92] The case of Lucy Millington and Liberty Hyde Bailey illustrates a rarely glimpsed role played by a female botanist—that of mentor to a young man. The deep and lasting influence of that relationship is clearly evident, not only in Bailey's words, but in his efforts to create a permanent record of her discovery. Today, a biographical reference book, citing Bailey's *Torreya* article, refers to her as the "earliest botanist friend of Liberty Hyde Bailey," and "discoverer [of] *Arceuthobium pusillum* in 1871."[93]

The case of the mentoring relationship between Millington and Bailey highlights the strength and durability of a personal bond formed during the shared experience of botanizing in the field. Whether relationships between male and female amateur botanists fell into the category of mentor or friend, such experiences could well have influenced men in the so-called life sciences to view women as having a natural role to play in their field. Nor should this social development be viewed as pertaining solely to botany; during the nineteenth century, other scientific fields that attracted large numbers of women in amateur clubs included ornithology and entomology. Although such personal relationships are not the only variable accounting for the relatively greater numbers of women in the life sciences, they are an important if hitherto overlooked factor in women's increasing employment opportunities in this area of science.

EMERGING EMPLOYMENT OPPORTUNITIES IN NATURAL HISTORY AND RELATED FIELDS

By 1871, Americans' view of middle-class women's proper sphere had expanded to include several career paths outside the home, and some women eyed opportunities in natural history with keen interest. As was the case earlier in the century, however, for the many women hailing from the working classes, the middle-class doctrine was a myth. In 1870, women constituted fifteen percent of the nation's workforce, laboring not only in such stereotypically female occupations as laundresses, domestic servants, and seamstresses, but in a great variety of other occupations, including box-factory operatives, cotton-mill operatives, and bookbinders.[94] In discussing employment opportunities for women from the higher classes, one author claimed that although "American sentiment revolts against her employment as a common farm laborer, the lighter work of gardening, with ornamental horticulture, seems perfectly adapted to [women]."[95] Ironically, at the time the report appeared in print, thirteen percent of all agricultural laborers in the country were women.[96] In spite of the rhetoric of egalitarianism advanced by some naturalists, natural history primarily appealed to members of the middle and upper classes. Although the scientist Louis Agassiz proclaimed that his work would "be read by operatives, by fishermen, by farmers, quite as extensively as by the students of our colleges,"[97] there is little evidence that the hobbies of natural history were ever extensively embraced by members of the working classes. In fact, letters about natural history topics published in children's magazines were often from children whose families were sufficiently wealthy to have vacationed in Europe.[98]

In their search for forms of employment compatible with their higher social status, elite women turned to the fields of natural history and agriculture. In 1871, the United States Commissioner of Education published a report titled the "Progress of Education for Women," which listed the following occupations as particularly suitable for women: illustration, nursing and medical practice, horticulture, and school teaching. No one doubted that middle- and upper-class women would find the science involved in the study of horticulture appealing. "For women of leisure," claimed the author of the report, "the studies connected with the course—drawing, botany, chemistry, and entomology—are interesting . . ." After all, contemporaries had long viewed such subjects as highly appropriate for young ladies.[99]

The growing professions associated with natural history afforded women a greater variety of employment opportunities than were available in physics or astronomy. Natural history museums and departments in colleges and universities required the services of zoological and botanical assistants to catalog and maintain their burgeoning collections; scientists required illustrators to prepare drawings for exhibits and manuscripts. In 1873, the members of the New England Women's Club expressed gratitude to Harvard scientist Louis Agassiz for employing women as assistants in his museum. They also noted approvingly that Harvard University had opened the doors of its agricultural school to women.

One particularly useful source for understanding the newer views of women's sphere promoted among the middle and upper classes is the report of the Women's Centennial Executive Committee. The committee was responsible for organizing an exhibition of women's work for the Centennial Exhibition to be held in Philadelphia in 1876. In answering the question "What can women do that is worthy of being displayed at the Exposition?," members of the Centennial Executive Committee listed a variety of accomplishments drawn from the fields of natural history and agriculture. Women of the Centennial Executive Committee expressed enthusiasm about scientific illustration as a career for women. "What more interesting specimen of women's work could be exhibited, than a set of Mrs. Wormley's microscopic drawings, illustrated by herself?" The possibility of obtaining a livelihood from illustration was intriguing, because there seemed to be no limit to the work, "at profitable prices," that women might do as illustrators.[100] Reflecting women's culturally accepted role as naturalist and horticulturist, women of the Centennial Executive Committee asked for contributions from the fields of natural history: "[m]any of our women might make contributions; for instance, collections of the different grains,

grasses, fruits, vegetables, wild flowers, ferns, mosses . . . geological specimens, fossils, insects, butterflies, or stuffed birds . . . arranged in compact
form and with skill and taste, would be valuable."[101]

During the next several decades, growing numbers of women found
some employment as botanical assistants and illustrators, first in herbaria
and museums, and later in the newly formed agricultural departments and
experiment stations.[102] As noted by Margaret Rossiter, the development of
scientific employment within the federal government near the close of the
nineteenth century indicates that the emergence and expansion of opportunities for women could develop where there existed a shortage of available men and an employer who specifically wanted to hire women and
actively marketed positions to a female audience. Erwin Frank Smith, the
U.S. Department of Agriculture's plant pathologist-in-charge, hired more
than twenty women assistants from 1887 until his retirement in the 1920s.[103]
Although Smith may have been motivated to hire women because he
could pay them lower wages, another explanation may be that by the
close of the century, the relationships developed among men and women
in natural history, together with expansion of employment opportunities in
the field and the stamp of approval given by some prominent male scientists for women to assume subordinate roles in the field encouraged some
men to hire women. Growing numbers of women also found work in the
last decades of the century in the private sector as gardeners, nursery
workers, and florists (Table 5.5), although, as in all forms of employment
during this period and later, employers consistently paid lower wages to
women than men.[104]

Growing opportunities in nursing afforded employment to women
from a wide range of class and ethnic backgrounds. Knowledge of the
medicinal properties of plants had been important to the practice of midwifery, a time-honored way for a woman to earn a living throughout the
colonial period. As women began to seek employment in medical fields
during the nineteenth century, training in the life sciences served a similar
preparatory function. During the antebellum period, a relatively small
proportion of wage-earning women worked as nurses. According to Alice
Kessler Harris, native-born middle-income Americans viewed nursing as a

Table 5.5   Percentage of Women Employed as Gardeners and Florists, 1870–1890

Date	Gardeners/nursery workers	Florists
1870	1	4
1880	3	5
1890	8	10

Source: Data for the years 1870 and 1880 compiled from *Compendium of the Ninth Census:
1870* (Washington, D.C.: Government Printing Office, 1872), 604 and *Compendium of the
Tenth Census: 1880 Part 2* (Washington, D.C.: Government Printing Office, 1883), 1368. Data
from 1890 compiled from *Compendium of the Eleventh Census: 1890, Part 3* (Washington,
D.C.: Government Printing Office, 1897), 598–599.

form of work comparable to menial service, and even after the Civil War, those choosing to work as nurses came largely from the ranks of the children of immigrants. Nursing offered some African-American women an opportunity to gain entry to higher study in medicine. For example, Rebecca Lee Crumpler, the first African-American female doctor, worked as a nurse in Massachusetts from 1852 to 1860. She was later admitted to the New England Female Medical College, graduated with a Doctress of Medicine in 1864, and eventually authored a book titled *A Book of Medical Discourses in Two Parts*. By the last two decades of the nineteenth century, the great proportion of women entering medicine joined the nursing profession. Between 1900 and 1910, the number of trained nurses increased 700 percent, and teaching and nursing together accounted for roughly seventy-five percent of the professional jobs held by women. Increasing numbers of women also entered the leading medical schools to train as doctors.[105]

Women sought employment as natural history teachers when the opportunity arose, though sometimes with limited success. The 1870s was a period in which intensified discussions of the importance of scientific knowledge led educators in several areas to attempt to introduce more science courses at both the secondary and primary levels in their public schools.[106] In 1872, the state of Illinois took the step of certifying some of its teachers to teach the natural sciences in its public schools. In order to be certified, candidates had to pass an examination. Equal numbers of men and women teachers took the examination, and equal numbers of males and females successfully passed it. Nevertheless, perhaps taken aback by the numbers of women qualified to teach natural sciences in its schools, Illinois issued certificates to only roughly half as many women as men (Table 5.6).

Women who selected science teaching as a career more often chose to specialize in the subjects of natural history than in physics. In the early twentieth century, many high schools created biology courses to replace the compendium subject of natural history and to offer instruction in the previously separate subjects of botany and zoology. In Wisconsin high schools, teachers of biology were more often female, whereas teachers of physics were predominantly male (Table 5.7).

Table 5.6 Results of the Illinois Examination and Certification in Natural Sciences, 1872

	Number examined	Number successful	Number certified
Males	1,989	1,557	1,018
Females	1,984	1,557	566

Source: Data compiled from the *Report of the Commissioner of Education for the Year 1872* (Washington, D.C.: Government Printing Office, 1873), 75.

Table 5.7   Percentage of Male and Female Wisconsin High School Science
Teachers, 1915–1920

	Male	Female
Biology		
1915–16	50	50
1919–20	33	67
Physics		
1915–16	97	3
1919–20	93	7

Source: Data compiled from *Department of Public Instruction Office of the State Superinten-*
dent High School Inspection Reports [Wisconsin], boxes 1-4, Wisconsin State Historical Society.

Why did young women choose biology over physics? After all, the rise
of natural history in nineteenth-century female schools did not accompany
a general decline in the number of schools offering natural philosophy, or
physics, during the same period. For example, during the period from
1830 to 1889, seventy-seven percent of Pennsylvania schools offered
botany, a marked increase over the earlier period (from 1750 to 1829),
when only fourteen percent offered the subject. Nevertheless, still more
schools (eighty-eight percent) continued to offer natural philosophy during the later period.[107] It is possible that although girls may have continued
to enroll in high school physics in order to meet graduation or teacher certification requirements, a cultural shift in perceptions of gender and science influenced self-selection after they left secondary school. At first
appreciated for its ability to promote mental discipline and natural theology, by the early twentieth century, physics conjured up images of factories and machines, harsh rationality, and cold, inanimate nature. Some
women writers contributed to this portrayal. For example, an article published in *Good Housekeeping* informed readers that the intellectual woman
made a poor mother. Instead, she should work in "the laboratories, where
matter has no feeling, and feeling is not needed to penetrate the mysteries of matter."[108] Girls with an interest in science could consider themselves engaged in a suitably feminine pursuit by studying animate, organic
nature.

In contrast to natural history, nineteenth-century physics had offered few
means by which amateurs could participate in the development of scientific
knowledge, and as a result, physics did not have a historically developed
context of shared interests and informal collaborative relationships between
men and women. Because there were relatively few practicing physicists in
America before 1900, there were far fewer employment opportunities for
women in this area of science. The relatively small group of women who
went on to become professional scientists more often chose to specialize in
the subjects of natural history than in such subjects as physics, astronomy,
or chemistry. A study of the baccalaureate origins of female scientists before 1920 reveals that more women received degrees in botany and zool-

ogy than in other scientific fields, including the nascent field of home economics. According to Margaret Rossiter, who based her study on the first three editions of *American Men of Science*, eighteen percent of female scientists received degrees in botany, and eighteen percent received degrees in zoology. In contrast, only eight percent received degrees in chemistry, five percent in physics, and four percent in astronomy.[109]

Gradually, as increasing numbers of women began to take higher degrees in the life sciences in colleges and universities, they began to find positions as lecturers in departments of agriculture in both land-grant and private universities and as assistants in some branches of the federal government. For instance, during Liberty Hyde Bailey's tenure as dean, the department of agriculture at Cornell had more women faculty members during the first decade of the twentieth century than any other department with the exception of the department of home economics. As dean, Bailey served as a mentor to Anna Botsford Comstock, wife of the entomologist Henry Comstock and part-time lecturer in nature study in the department of agriculture. In 1898, he supported her appointment as assistant professor of nature study. Had her appointment been accepted, she would have been Cornell's first woman professor. However, her appointment was quickly withdrawn when Cornell's board of trustees objected to giving a woman professorial status, and she was designated a full-time lecturer in nature study. It was not until 1913 that Comstock achieved assistant professor status, again with Bailey's support.[110]

CONCLUSION

Although the rise of natural history in nineteenth-century female schools did not accompany a general decline in the number of schools offering natural philosophy, or physics, natural history appears to have become the science of choice for females by the end of the century. Girls may have continued to enroll in high school physics classes in order to meet graduation or teacher certification requirements, but a cultural shift in perceptions of gender and science influenced self-selection after women left secondary school, drawing them to the life sciences as high school teachers, museum and laboratory assistants, and scientists.

A number of factors stand out as having been enormously successful in encouraging nineteenth-century females to pursue the study of natural history. First, selected areas of this science afforded women opportunities for meaningful participation. As amateurs, women's involvement in such fields as botany was welcomed by men in the early nineteenth century, not only because amateurs from both sexes enjoyed botanizing as a recreational and intellectually improving opportunity to socialize and picnic outdoors, but because the scientific work of cataloging the flora of North America was so enormous.

A second factor that eased women's entry into the fields of natural history was the support and patronage of some prominent and highly influential men in the field. Such scientists as Asa Gray, Louis Agassiz, and

Liberty Hyde Bailey supported women's participation as collectors, museum and laboratory assistants, and teachers during an era when comparable support for women was virtually absent in such other fields as engineering or physics. This study suggests that the informal friendships and mentoring relationships that developed between men and women during the heyday of natural history may have played an important if overlooked role in facilitating women's entry into this area of science. Finally, during the latter half of the century, the field of natural history provided women with opportunities for gainful employment in nurseries, museums, agricultural experiment stations, horticultural gardens, and in the United States Department of Agriculture.

Third, prominent female educators advanced rhetoric that portrayed the life sciences as eminently suited to the sphere of privileged American women. During a period when natural history afforded women the widest possible arena for participation in science, female nature writers, textbook authors, and educators characterized the biological sciences as socially, intellectually, morally, and spiritually appropriate for girls. Such culturally approved activities as bird-watching, botanizing, or collecting specimens of shells or rocks conveyed an aura of gentlewomanly polish to the daughters of parents seeking to maintain or elevate their children's social status. In spite of the rhetoric of egalitarianism that sometimes appeared in the prescriptive literature, the majority of those engaged in natural history pursuits hailed from the middle and upper classes.

Cultural views of middle-class women's social roles appear to have not only encouraged but also structured the participation of women in natural history. Almira Hart Lincoln Phelps and subsequent authors did not differentiate the scientific content from that commonly offered to boys; rather, they promoted an alternate scientific identity among girls. Their books portrayed girls and women as turning to nature, not in order to advance scientific knowledge, but to develop orderly habits of observation, to seek beauty and spiritual solace, to develop a patina of gentility, and to nurture and protect wildlife. Such authors traditionally cast women as popularizers of science rather than as creators of scientific knowledge.

Some scholars have suggested that by promoting natural history as a field of endeavor compatible with women's sphere, Phelps and others may have sought to assuage doubts the male scientific community might have had about girls' increasing pursuit of science. According to this view, these authors created a noncontroversial arena in which middle- and upper-class women could begin to participate—and even earn a living of sorts—in the scientific community. However, one problem with this argument is that well before the widespread introduction of gender-stereotyped botany texts into higher female schools, women already participated in natural history as amateur collectors. Amos Eaton's claim that "more than half the botanists of New York are ladies" was made nine years before the publication of Phelps's first botany textbook.

Both Almira Phelps and Catharine Beecher—influential reformers in nineteenth-century female education—emphasized gender differences in ways that set limits on women's participation in science. They each attempted to create a curriculum for females based on respect for women's presumed different qualities and appropriate social roles. In Beecher's case, the effort to create a "domestic science" by linking scientific concepts to the topics of hearth and home did not enjoy initial widespread success, for reasons discussed earlier in this volume. On the other hand, American educators apparently devoured Phelps's botany texts, stimulating a demand for multiple editions. Her strategy of characterizing the study of botany as most appropriate for females, while at the same time setting limits on women's involvement in science, clearly struck a chord with the American public.

Although their texts were not equally successful, the writings of Phelps and Beecher stand as an important precedent for later developments in American education: the domestic science—or home economics—movement in the late nineteenth century, and life adjustment education in the twentieth. The seeds of these movements can be seen in the midnineteenth-century reaction against what some contemporaries believed was an overly "intellectual" or "masculine" tendency in female education. Increasingly during those years, female educators began to express doubts that girls should study the sciences in the same way, or to the same extent, as boys. "It is not proper to assume," concluded a committee considering the establishment of a free academy for females, "that the education of a young woman must necessarily be the same, in all respects, as that of a young man, having precisely the same range, stretching over through a scientific course with applications to the arts, or directed to the business of the world, or to the practice of a learned profession."[111]

Apart from other factors, it remains unclear what effect gender-differentiated curricula had on female enrollments in science. It is important to remember that although Phelps's texts were among the very first, not all natural history texts studied by nineteenth-century girls evidenced any gender differentiation. It may be that the production of textbooks at a level of difficulty suitable for adolescents made possible the introduction of natural history into the curriculum of higher schools and that the subject would have attracted increasing enrollments whether there existed overt gender stereotyping or not. After all, the entry of natural history into secondary schools coincided with an enormous rise in popular enthusiasm across the country for all things related to this science, a passion shared by men and women alike. Additionally, gender differentiation of the curriculum was not a factor in girls' growing mathematics enrollment during the same period. Although there existed ongoing contemporary criticism about the mathematics attainments of females, educators in female schools—including Phelps—generally promoted mathematics for its ability to develop mental discipline and self-control, and in their schoolrooms, girls studied mathematics textbooks produced for a general academy audience, male and female. Similarly, when female enrollments in Latin began to increase near the end of the nineteenth century, a trend discussed later in the volume, girls used the same schoolbooks and traditional Latin texts as boys. These developments suggest that the availability of a gender-differentiated curriculum had far less impact on female interest and enrollments than did the overt promotion of the subject as appropriate for girls by influential female leaders.

Although by itself, the production of a gender-differentiated curriculum in natural history may not have actually encouraged more young women to study science, the attempt by leading educators to portray natural history as particularly suited to girls may have steered female interest away from the physical sciences toward the life sciences. Given the unending controversy surrounding the mathematics study of young girls, the existence of a differentiated curriculum in female schools may also have served to assuage doubts parents may have had about the "overintellectualizing" trend in female schools.

Ultimately, efforts to differentiate the curriculum for girls also may have set the stage for an eventual societal backlash against women who inevitably sought to venture beyond what contemporaries believed to be their appropriate limits. In spite of admonitions neither to collect in the field nor dissect, young women with an interest in science began to traduce the boundaries set by midcentury writers such as Phelps. For instance, Lucy Millington tramped alone across the countryside in search of botanical specimens, going as far as fifteen miles from her home. Potentially even more shocking, Millington searched not for pretty flowers, but for samples of parasitic growth on spruce. Encouraged by Louis Agassiz, young women took up the forbidden dissection of dead animal specimens as well. Similar incursions would eventually threaten the limits that had been established by earlier generations of educators, providing fuel for a backlash motivated by larger social concerns, a development discussed in Chapter 8.

Together with the rise of a popular enthusiasm for natural history and the expansion of employment opportunities for women in related fields, the cultural construction of natural history as a subject fully compatible with the nineteenth-century doctrine of women's sphere had an enormous impact on the scientific interests of American girls. The majority of young women who sought to become professional scientists and science teachers selected the subjects of natural history to a far greater degree than the subjects of physics or astronomy. By the late nineteenth century, the passion of Americans for natural history reached such an apex that prominent educators everywhere agreed that nature study should constitute the science learned in the first eight years of common school. As naturalists, nature writers, and teachers, women appeared well positioned to assume leadership in what would become known as the nature-study movement.

6

"Study Nature, Not Books"

"Every child should be encouraged to study not man's system of nature, but nature's." So wrote Henry David Thoreau before the Civil War.[1] By the end of the century, most American educators appeared to agree with this sentiment. During the late nineteenth century, a movement to promote the introduction of science in the nation's public elementary schools prompted a debate over which scientific subjects young children should study. Although a few astronomy, natural philosophy, and natural history textbooks had appeared in the common schools earlier in the century, many educators now argued that the science most suitable for children in the first eight grades of school was a form of natural history known as nature study.[2] The rise of nature study in the nation's common schools was meteoric. Gaining national prominence during the last decade of the nineteenth century, by 1925 the subject had found a place in the curriculum of virtually every school district in the United States.[3]

Although historians of education have commonly depicted the nature-study movement as the creation of a handful of progressive male educators, documentary evidence suggests that women played an important part in the movement. Such evidence exists not only in the written records of women who helped to advance nature study, but also in the assertions of the movement's twentieth-century male critics. Throughout nature study's school history, a number of influential critics and social commentators argued that female teachers in general and nature study in particular exerted a "feminizing" influence on boys. As the movement declined in the twentieth century, male critics habitually characterized nature study as "romantic" or "sentimental." The nature of such allegations strongly suggests that gender issues may have played a role in the evolution of the nature-study movement.

This chapter considers the following questions: What roles did women play in the evolution of nature study as it appeared in American schoolrooms? If women gained positions of leadership in the movement, how was this accomplished? What was the significance of this curricular reform in girls' science education? In order to understand the evolution of this educational reform, the discussion begins with a general survey of nature study's swift rise to prominence near the end of the nineteenth century.

A GRASSROOTS COALITION

With the exception of a few unpublished dissertations, the nature-study movement has received relatively little attention from historians. Most scholars have highlighted one or two facets of nature study, providing a one-dimensional treatment of the movement. Thus, secondary sources have variously characterized nature study as the legacy of amateur botany, a progressive movement in pedagogy; as a feature of the romantic back-to-nature arcadian movement in the late nineteenth century; or as the prototype of environmental education.[4]

One way to reconcile such varying explanations is by conceiving of the movement as a loose coalition of communities composed of individuals, societies, and institutions able to find some common ground in the study and appreciation of the natural world. The swift rise of nature study on the educational scene in the last decade of the nineteenth century would not have been possible without the support of this large and highly diverse coalition.

Viewing nature study as an outgrowth of the late nineteenth-century back-to-nature movement provides an important social and cultural context within which to understand nature study's widespread appeal. The population of the United States doubled in the last four decades of the century, with much of the growth occurring in cities. With the emergence of a rapidly expanding population and industrial economy came an increased nostalgia for a simpler, more rural life.[5] Americans of the late nineteenth century commonly expressed the belief that close ties to rural nature ensured the continuity of traditional values and the development of moral character. According to the well-known psychologist and university president G. Stanley Hall, when parents and educators denied city children the opportunity to hunt, fish, climb, and explore in the great outdoors, they increasingly indulged in "hoodlumism, juvenile crime, and secret vice." Voicing an opinion common during this period, the American writer Sarah Orne Jewett concluded that Flaubert's tale of Madame Bovary was "a lesson to dwellers in country towns, who drift out of relation to their surroundings, not only social, but the very companionships of nature, unknown to them."[6]

Behind the effort to introduce the study of nature into common schools lay a pervasive anxiety that children would not grow up properly in an urban world. The concerns about the destruction of environmental resources expressed earlier in the century by Susan Fenimore Cooper resurfaced with greater urgency in the writings of those who viewed the rise of industrialization as a threat to society. Nature writer John Burroughs popularized the contrast between rural paradise and urban hell, warning, "Even the simple birds understand not to build their nests in a place that is unclean and unhealthy, where their nerves are rattled, where loud noises assault the ear and foul smells [assault] the nose."[7] Fear of the effects of urbanization on children was not limited to the ranks of naturalists and nature writers. An 1883 report by G. Stanley Hall described the impact of urbanization on "The Content of Children's Minds on Entering School" and concluded that city children displayed an alarming ignorance of nature and country life. Fully ninety percent could not identify a field of wheat or explain the origin of cotton or leather, eighty percent could not identify common trees, and seventy-five percent expressed ignorance of the seasons of the year. Hall recommended classroom-based nature study to help city children recover an acquaintance with the rural countryside: "As our methods of teaching grow more natural, we realize that city life is unnatural, and that those who grow up without knowing the country are defrauded of that without which childhood can never be complete or normal."[8]

Nature study gained widespread support among parents and educators during an era when increased concern for the environment prompted government leaders to pass legislation to promote conservation and elevate the status of country life. Americans had decimated the wildlife of the American West during the last four decades of the nineteenth century. The last of the once great buffalo herds were slaughtered in 1882 in North Dakota. When the young Theodore Roosevelt arrived to begin ranching in the Badlands two years later, he guided his horse through the decaying carcasses of thousands of buffalo abandoned on the plains. By 1906, the last band of Arizona elk had met its end in the Chirichuas Mountains, and the bighorn sheep were extinct by 1908.[9] "We have adapted ourselves to our physical environment by stripping our land of its forests, our air of its birds, our waters of their fish, by using up in the most reckless manner our natural resources," wrote one nature-study advocate. Through the study of nature, conservationists believed that boys and girls would "better appreciate what they receive from their environment, and what they owe to it."[10]

The American Nature Study Society was founded in 1908, the same year the federal government forged a political coalition that established thirty-six wildlife refuges and the Grand Canyon National Park. During this period of environmental activism, Theodore Roosevelt called his famous Joint Conference of Governors, a conference that led to the creation of conservation departments in almost all of the states; the president also appointed a Commission on Country Life to investigate the status of rural life and formulate recommendations for improving rural conditions. Led by Cornell University's Liberty Hyde Bailey, the Commission held schoolhouse meetings across the country, asking questions and listening to the expressed needs of local communities. Newspapers and magazines joined in the propaganda campaign to elevate the status of rural life, printing stories about the healthfulness of living in the country, the virtues of agriculture, and the benefits of nature study.[11]

The community of amateur naturalists also played an important role in the development of popular support for nature study. According to Elizabeth Keeney, when professional botanists turned from natural history to laboratory plant biology near the close of the nineteenth century, amateurs found themselves with little room for involvement. As the interaction between professionals and amateurs declined, the latter began to promote botany as a worthwhile hobby among children.[12] The case of Graceanna Lewis appears to support Keeney's thesis. The author of *Natural History of Birds*, Lewis won election to the Academy of Natural Sciences in 1870. When a position in natural history became available at Vassar in 1877, she applied with the support of the astronomer Maria Mitchell, although both women expressed the opinion that Vassar wanted a man for the position. In a letter to her sister, Lewis noted, "I do not hope at all—not because I have not the very best of recommendations, but because of the preference for a masculine representative in that chair." As predicted, Lewis was turned down, and from that time on, appeared to accept a more limited role for herself as a popularizer of natural history, authoring numerous articles in the *Friend's Intelligencer and Journal*.[13] Another early example of a well-known amateur naturalist who turned to writing for children was Mary Treat (1830–1923), a frequent correspondent and collector for Charles Darwin and other scientists during the 1870s. In 1880, she authored a popular book titled *Home Studies in Nature* and also contributed articles on natural history to the nation's most popular children's magazine *St. Nicholas* and to the family magazine *Hearth and Home*. Not content to promote natural history through writing alone, Treat started a young ladies' club in 1893, inviting young women to meet every other week in her New Jersey home to discuss botanical, entomological, and ornithological topics.[14]

Nature study provided a forum within which amateurs from a variety of fields could promote natural history. The same year that Mary Treat published *Home Studies in Nature*, a Massachusetts schoolteacher named Harlan H. Ballard created the Agassiz Association to encourage children in the study of nature. Named in honor of Louis Agassiz, the organization grew rapidly. By the 1890s, it numbered more than 20,000 young members in 1,200 chapters across the country. In the association's first report, Ballard suggested that members assemble collections and keep a record of "whatever new or curious facts with regard to natural history we can find by our own observation." Ballard also promoted the study of physical phenomena. In his monthly reports, Ballard posed questions for children to answer, some of which related to physical science. In his first report, for example, he asked his young readers, "Does air weigh anything? Prove by experiment . . . How hot must water be before it boil?"[15] Association reports in subsequent issues of *St. Nicholas* testified to children's varied natural history interests. For example, children's letters to the association in 1892 describe such observed phenomena as insects, amphibians, rocks and minerals, shells, fossils, and plants.[16] The primary aim of the association's leaders was to promote nature study as an extracurricular interest rather than to introduce it into schools. The association first announced its inception in the November 1880 issue of *St. Nicholas*, and in subsequent years the association published its minutes, correspondence, and small news articles in *St. Nicholas* and in such other popular child and adult magazines as *The Observer, The Swiss Cross, Santa Claus,* and *Popular Science News.* Agassiz Association chapters across the country promoted the firsthand study of nature by organizing collection contests and field trips, arranging scientific talks, and occasionally running correspondence courses.[17]

As nature study began to gain a place in the curricula of school districts across the country during the next two decades, amateur naturalists continued to influence the development of the movement through their publication of nature articles and stories. Teachers with special knowledge of some aspect of natural history contributed regularly to the official organ of the nature-study movement, *The Nature Study Review.* Maurice Bigelow, professor of biology at Teachers College, Columbia University, founded *The Nature Study Review* in 1905 with the goal of providing some direction and focus for the various nature-study groups then forming across the country.[18] In the first volume, Bigelow announced that the *Review* would publish notes, reviews, and articles by "the leaders in science teaching."[19] Although Bigelow did not mention any leaders by name, he probably had in mind such men as himself and others who composed the *Review's* editorial committee: Liberty Hyde Bailey of Cornell's School of Agriculture; H. W. Fairbanks, noted geologist and author; Clifton F. Hodge, professor of biology at Clark University; and J. F. Woodhull, professor of physical science at Teachers College, Columbia University. However, subscribers soon began asking for articles giving more concrete suggestions for lesson plans and activities, and female members often wrote to the editor of the *Review* recommending articles or talks by other women.[20] Amateur naturalists, many of whom were classroom teachers, were quick to meet this demand with relevant articles.

Besides contributing articles to the *Review,* amateur naturalists authored a stream of nature books for children during the heyday of the nature-study movement, from 1891 to 1916.[21] Although educators insisted that children learn about nature from natural phenonema rather than from textbooks, many well-known nature-study leaders recommended integrating nature study and literature by having children read nature stories either preceding or following their nature-study investigations. Nature-study handbooks and courses of study often included lists of recommended literature, bearing such titles as *Dwellers of the Sea and Shore, Our Winter Birds, Glimpses of Nature for Little Folk,* or *Ways of the Six-Footed.*[22]

Naturalists introduced children to nature study through such extracurricular materials as magazines, nature associations, clubs, and nature literature, but the group with the most direct influence on the introduction of nature study into schoolrooms was the community of professional educators. In his history of progressive education, Laurence Cremin depicted nature study as the creation of progressives Colonel Francis Wayland Parker and his associate Wilbur S. Jackman. Parker, whom John Dewey once referred to as "the father of progressive education," gained national recognition through his pedagogical innovations as superintendent of the school district in Quincy, Massachusetts, and later as principal at Cook County Normal School, Illinois.[23] Born in 1837, Parker interrupted a career as a country schoolmaster to serve in the Union Army, where he attained the rank of colonel. On return from service, he began to study the works of such European educational theorists as Johann Pestalozzi, Friedrich Froebel, and Johann Friedrich Herbart, and in 1872 he traveled in Europe for two and a half years to observe the leading pedagogical innovations of the time.[24]

Shortly after his return to the United States, Parker took the opportunity to put into practice the theories he had acquired abroad. In 1875, the school board of Quincy, Massachusetts, hired him as superintendent, and shortly thereafter, under Parker's leadership, Quincy teachers abandoned their traditional textbooks and copybooks in favor of learning through observing, describing, and understanding. Thus was born "the Quincy Method." The Quincy school became the focus of national attention, and a stream of visitors came to observe the new methods at first hand. Lelia E. Patridge disseminated Parker's innovations through publication of *The Quincy Methods Illustrated*, a book that described many of the day-to-day lessons and practices of the school.[25]

The idea of having children study natural phenomena through direct observation was not entirely new to late nineteenth-century American educators when Parker was superintendent in Quincy. The ideas of the Swiss educator Johann Pestalozzi (1746–1827) had appeared in journals, textbooks, and even several school programs after 1805 in the United States. Pestalozzi and his followers stressed the importance of sense perception, verification, and original research through the direct observation and study of nature. At least a decade before Parker began to implement his methods in Quincy, an interpretation of Pestalozzian methods called "object teaching" was already familiar to educators through the work of Edward A. Sheldon of the State Normal School in Oswego, New York. Through object teaching, teachers expected students to learn from the direct study of natural phenomena rather than books. Graduates of Oswego Normal carried the pedagogical techniques of object teaching to schoolrooms across the country. During the same period, the development of kindergarten associations across the country did much to popularize Froebel's idealist philosophy. Additionally, professors at other universities and normal schools taught Herbartian ideas during the last decades of the century as part of an effort to develop a systematic approach to pedagogy.[26] Parker's unique contribution was to introduce and synthesize European methods throughout an entire public school district.

While Parker institutionalized the observational study of nature in Quincy, the formal development of a fully realized philosophy and pedagogy of nature study fell to one of his later associates, Wilbur S. Jackman. Parker left Quincy in 1880, eventually assuming the principalship of Cook County Normal School in Chicago. There, he surrounded himself with a choice faculty, including Jackman of Harvard University, to whom he gave the task of devising a means of teaching science in the common schools.[27] In 1891, Jackman published a course of study titled *Nature Study for the Common Schools*, the first full-length treatment of the subject. As conceived by Parker and Jackman, nature study integrated investigations in all areas of science through firsthand observation and experimentation. The modern educator, they argued, could unify the entire school curriculum through nature study. "Botany, zoology, and mineralogy," claimed Parker, "are among the best possible means for the teaching of reading and language, [and] how to speak and write the English language correctly can be taught incomparably better by teaching physics than by using technical grammar."[28]

Jackman and Parker advocated fieldwork as the most appropriate method of studying the natural environment. Although students might bring specimens to the schoolroom, Parker claimed, "the way to study a tree, a plant, a flower, is to see these objects in their habitat."[29] Under Jackman's leadership, Cook County schoolchildren conducted trips through fields and along the shore of Lake Michigan. They recorded observations, made drawings, and performed calculations, thus correlating their nature-study work with language, mathematics, and art. Outside their schoolrooms, students planned and laid out gardens, learning about the effects of the environment on the growth of vegetables and flowers and the application of scientific principles to agriculture.[30] "The immediate observation of objects in the environment of the school is an indispensable means of nature study," argued Parker. "The pupils, under the leadership of the teachers, should wander thru and observe with care fields and woods, mountains and valleys, in fact, the whole country that may be reached by the pupils."[31] In the 1890s, student teachers at Cook County Normal School regularly undertook outdoor excursions to learn about this new pedagogical and curricular approach. In 1896, the entire senior class in the Normal School, with a membership of more than 500, made numerous excursions to such sites as Stony Island, the Desplaines Valley, Dune Park, the Purington clay pits, and local drainage canals for the purpose of studying nature in the rough. "Hereafter," reported a local newspaper, "[C]ompasses, clinometers, levels, magnets, hammers, trowels, acids, spades, knives, boxes, bottles, jars, railroad tickets and camping utensils will be quite as necessary to the up-to-date student in Colonel Parker's school as were the slates, sponges, pencils and chalks in the days of the Hoosier schoolmaster."[32]

In its early stages, nature study found support among members of the scientific community. Such scientists as John Merle Coulter, botanist at the University of Chicago, applauded nature study as a vehicle for promoting botany among schoolchildren.[33] Others, such as President Eliot of Harvard, supported efforts to move the study of the natural sciences away from textbooks toward the natural world.[34]

Americans concerned with improving the scientific methods of agriculture also supported nature study as a means of interesting children in farming. During the decades following the Civil War, federal and state support for agriculture increased. The 1862 Morrill Act provided for the establishment of land-grant colleges, and by the middle 1870s, states began to establish experiment stations with the purpose of providing the land-grant colleges both indoor and outdoor research facilities. With the passage of the Hatch Act in 1887, the federal Department of Agriculture evolved from a single central agency into the hub of a system of research institutions permanently established in each state. No other scientific activity in the

United States attained such national visibility and influence.[35] In an effort to improve the agricultural knowledge of the farming population, the land-grant colleges and experiment stations developed extension courses and in some cases published materials to promote nature study among children.

The state of agriculture became an intense social concern near the end of the nineteenth century during the agricultural depression of 1891–1893. During these years, the various philanthropic organizations of New York City became overburdened while attempting to assist the many people who flocked to the city from the rural districts. Frustrated and over-whelmed, the Association for Improving the Condition of the Poor asked, "What is the matter with the land in New York that it cannot support its own population?" In response, the state legislature established a Commit-tee for the Promotion of Agriculture in New York State. In 1893, the com-mittee bestowed an endowment on Cornell University to establish a Bureau of Nature Study within the Department of Agriculture based on the belief that "the first step toward agriculture was nature study" and that it was essential to interest "the children of the country in farming as a reme-dial measure."[36] The bureau created extension programs to train teachers, organized Junior Naturalists Clubs for schoolchildren, and supported the development of school gardens across the state. Institutions in other states followed suit, and a flurry of guides, pamphlets, and courses of study en-sued, published and distributed by agricultural experiment stations, land-grant colleges, private colleges and universities, and normal schools.[37]

Within a decade after the publication of Jackman's first course of study, a progressively faster-growing tide of nature-study articles and handbooks appeared on the educational market, along with three other important books: *Nature Study and the Child* (1900) by Charles B. Scott, instructor in nature study at Oswego Normal School; *Nature Study and Life* (1902) by Clifton F. Hodge, a biology professor at Clark University; and *The Nature Study Idea* (1903) by Liberty Hyde Bailey, dean of the school of agriculture at Cornell University.[38] Land-grant colleges such as Purdue University prepared and disseminated their own nature-study leaflets, and both the Chicago Laboratory School at the University of Chicago and the Horace Mann School at Teachers College developed courses of study for the new subject. Eventually, the tide of publications grew into a flood, and the author who boldly opened his preface by stat-ing, "all progressive educators support nature study" could make this claim with some appearance of verisimilitude.[39]

The Committee of Ten also gave impetus to the role of nature study in the curriculum. In 1892, the National Education Association appointed a committee of ten college and school leaders to study ways of smoothing the transition from high school to college by making college entrance re-quirements more uniform. Charles Eliot of Harvard headed this group, which organized nine conferences on different areas of the curriculum, in-cluding three separate conferences in science: one on physics, chemistry, and astronomy; one on natural history; and one on geography. According to Theodore Sizer, the Committee of Ten's Report was an influential docu-ment used by secondary-school educators as they created or modified pro-

Table 6.1 Percentage of 127 School Systems Offering Nature Study in their Public Schools, 1925

In all grades	In at least six grades	In at least four grades	In three grades or fewer	Not offered
49	25	11	15	0

Source: Data compiled from "Preliminary Report of Committee on School Progress," in *First Yearbook of the American Nature Study Society* (Toledo, Ohio: The American Nature Study Society, 1925), 3–7.

grams in schools. For example, astronomy, which the committee recommended no longer be required for entrance to college, experienced a fifty percent decline in high school enrollment over the following decade. Such other courses as geology and meteorology, recommended only as electives, also experienced declines.[40] On the basis of the science conference reports, the committee recommended that one hour per week be devoted to nature study in the elementary grades and that all work be undertaken without using textbooks.[41] At the elementary level, school districts began to add nature-study programs to their schools, and the number of cities offering nature study increased dramatically between 1892 and 1925.

By 1925, to varying degrees almost every city in the country introduced a form of nature study into its schoolrooms. In that year, the American Nature Study Society published its first yearbook, which included a survey of the status of nature-study teaching in the United States. The study reported data from 127 school systems in cities with a population greater than 5,000 and from fifty-five normal schools. Every school system responding to the survey reported that it offered nature study to its students, although only roughly half of the cities offered the subject in each of the first eight grades (Table 6.1). Of the fifty-five normal schools, forty-nine claimed to teach nature-study pedagogy to prospective teachers.[42]

THE NATURE-STUDY CURRICULUM

What was nature study, as it appeared in published courses of study and in schoolrooms?[43] Based on the rhetoric in their prefaces, the authors of nature-study curricula had an enormous agenda for a pedagogical reform movement, spanning three areas: society, culture, and the environment (Table 6.2).[44] According to its various supporters, nature study would accomplish in one stroke the goals of the nature lover, the naturalist, the conservationist, the scientist, the moralist, the promoter of culture, and the agriculturalist. In continuity with the earlier eighteenth- and nineteenth-century natural history tradition, many authors invoked natural theology when extolling the benefits of nature study.[45] Others claimed that nature study created an appreciation of nature and developed a love of beauty. "The aesthetic phases of nature's handiwork," claimed the noted educator Charles McMurry, "furnish limitless and constant opportunities for aesthetic

Table 6.2 Percentage of Selected Authors Stating Various Aims for Nature Study

Aims	Percentage
To develop observation skills	67
To integrate the curriculum	67
To create an appreciation of natural beauty	67
To increase scientific knowledge	60
To improve agricultural skills	53
To build moral character	47
To provide practical preparation for life	40
To encourage conservation	33

Source: Fourteen nature-study handbooks and courses of study (see note 45).

appreciation and culture."[46] Contrasting nature study with the subjects of literature, art, and music, staples of the so-called ornamental studies of an earlier era, some portrayed nature study as a nonelitist and egalitarian vehicle for bringing culture into the lives of working-class children. "Books [the student] may lack the means or disposition to buy; good pictures he may never see," wrote one author. "[B]ut the landscape is ever with him, and if he [has] learned in his early life to . . . care for his surroundings, then he will have a source of possible culture that will stay with him, without undue effort and without cost, for the rest of his life."[47]

The authors of these handbooks rarely followed through on the grandiose rhetoric of their prefaces. The content of the courses of study—the lessons and suggestions for instruction—included ideas for investigations in a variety of subjects, the majority of which were drawn from the broader and more pedestrian tradition of natural history and from relatively recent developments in experimental agriculture (Table 6.3). For example, some lessons required students to compare the structure and habitat of various animal species; others asked students to conduct experiments to discover the effects of varying soils on plant growth. In these respects, nature-study

Table 6.3 Percentage of Nature-Study Handbooks and Courses of Study, 1891–1918

Subject	Percentage of texts in which the subject appeared
Botany	100
Zoology	100
Geology/mineralogy	86
Meteorology	62
Astronomy	54
Physics	54
Agriculture	23
Chemistry	8

Source: Data compiled from an analysis of fourteen nature-study handbooks and courses of study (see note 45).

handbooks bear some resemblance to biological science curriculum materials developed for elementary students during much of the later twentieth century.

In other ways, the materials published for nature study were similar to the natural history texts developed for use in common schools and academies earlier in the century. For example, nature-study authors emphasized the importance of studying living organisms in the field. Agassiz's famous phrase, "Study nature, not books," appeared in the prefaces of many nature-study texts. The first nature-study handbook, Jackman's *Field Work in Nature Study*, consisted almost entirely of questions aimed to direct investigation, as illustrated by these questions from "Field Work on a Swamp": "Study carefully the conditions under which the swamp is formed. What is the degree of slope of the general surface of the swamp and the surrounding country? How is the swamp drained?"[48] Although no nature-study authors after Jackman imitated his use of questions to such an extreme degree, most did use open-ended questions in their texts. For instance, although the handbook written by Anna Comstock of Cornell University (1911) provided some background information about each specimen, it also included questions that students could not answer without firsthand observation. In a lesson on the codling moth, Comstock directed students to the following observations: "Look at a wormy apple. How can you tell it is wormy from the outside? Can you see where the worm entered the apple? Was the burrow large or small at first?"[49] Comstock did not provide the answer to the last question; presumably, when everyone observed the phenomenon, the answer would become evident.

Turn-of-the-century photographs of schoolchildren's nature-study activities show children engaged in the kind of natural history promoted several decades earlier by the Agassiz Association: making collections of such items as leaves, rocks, or shells; raising wildflowers and vegetables in school gardens; observing the life cycles of butterflies; recording the weather; sketching their observations of plants and animals; and so on.[50] Photographs show boys as well as girls undertaking these activities, although the task of gardening was occasionally differentiated by gender. While the boys may have shoveled and hoed, in some schools, girls engaged in the presumably more genteel task of watering (Plate 6.1).[51]

What was the significance of this curricular reform in girls' science education? The nature-study movement allowed greater numbers of young Americans increased access to the sciences. Through nature study, some degree of scientific observation and experimentation—previously accessibly only to elites—became available to the masses attending common schools. At the elementary level, many schools had already begun to include physiology in the curriculum near the end of the century, but the subject consisted generally of a smattering of health and hygiene along with some of the basic body structures and functions. In 1893, the Committee of Ten recommended that elementary physiology should include "the subjects of personal cleanliness," the need for "pure air . . . wholesome foods" and "sufficient sleep," along with "abstinence from narcotics and stimulants, and from drugs generally," but cautioned against teaching

Plate 6.1   Children Posing with Garden Tools and Equipment in a School Garden (date unknown), WHi-2267. (*Courtesy of the Wisconsin Historical Society.*)

young children much anatomy, fearing that such knowledge could lead to "morbid if not prurient curiosity."[52] Although the elementary curriculum also included geography, by the midnineteenth century, as textbook authors and publishers began to produce books devoted to the individual sciences, they greatly reduced the amount of astronomy, physics, chemistry, and natural history contained in geography texts.

Before the advent of the nature-study movement, study of the individual sciences occurred at the higher levels, accessible to the relatively few students who remained in school beyond the ages of twelve or thirteen. Throughout the nineteenth century and into the first decades of the twentieth, American secondary schools served a narrow and privileged segment of the population. In spite of the egalitarian rhetoric advanced by many supporters of the new public high schools established in many communities after the Civil War, access to secondary education was contingent on social and economic standing.[53]

The population attending elementary schools, the group targeted by promoters of nature study, grew more diverse during the latter half of the nineteenth century. By 1918, every state had passed a compulsory attendance law, a process initiated in 1852, when Massachusetts passed the first. Although passage of such laws did not automatically guarantee that all children came to school, by the turn of the century, students from a wider range of socioeconomic backgrounds attended in greater numbers, and as the school-leaving age moved inexorably upward, they remained in school for longer periods. With the entry of nature study into the curriculum, access to some form of scientific knowledge was no longer restricted to the sons and daughters of elites. In contrast to a familiar textbook image published earlier in the century of a mother and daughter conducting scientific experiments in a well-appointed parlor, using a gold coin as a piece of apparatus, photographs of nature-study lessons often depicted children in plain surroundings, conducting experiments using such everyday artifacts as leaves, vegetables, or rocks. Nearly five decades after Louis Agassiz proclaimed that science in America would be studied "by operatives, by fishermen, by farmers,"[54] his proclamation finally appeared to be coming true.

The nature-study movement was also significant in the history of girls' science education because of its continuity with the earlier natural history tradition. Nature study would undoubtedly have appealed to many girls. Many of the activities promoted in schools were quite similar to the extracurricular nature activities girls enjoyed and often described in letters to their favorite magazines. Additionally, the nature literature published for classroom use depicted both girls and boys as capable investigators of nature and often cast girls as nature's heroines, ready to preserve hapless wildlife from the wanton destructiveness of boys.[55] Sociologists have identified a subjective process in which individuals engage in self-selection by qualifying or disqualifying themselves as suited to a particular area of study or occupation. For instance, an individual with a strong affinity for science or mathematics might say, "This fits who I am, so I can do this." The factors that men or women believe are required for success in a given field constitute the subjective filters they associate with the subject—its *subjective warrant*. Because of self-discouragement, individuals may tend to avoid subjects with perceived negative warrants and select those in which, by talent or disposition, they believe they will succeed.[56] Much of the rhetoric in the prefaces of nature-study handbooks included earlier rationales for taking up the study of natural history, many of which were compatible with traditional views of women's sphere. Girls who regarded their gender as more nurturing and protective of the environment could connect nature study with their self-image as females. Those who encountered female role models in their nature stories could presumably begin to consider the fields of natural history as potentially worthwhile areas of interest or future employment. As a form of elementary science, nature study thus represented a curriculum with a positive subjective warrant for girls.

Early nature-study experiences could have a lasting influence on a young woman's interest in science. When asked what factors contributed to her success as a scientist, Ruth Patrick identified early parental encouragement and experiences with nature study. Patrick earned a Ph.D. in botany at the University of Virginia in 1934 and went on to have a distinguished career in science, receiving the National Medal of Science for her work on rivers in 1996. When she was a child, her father, a lawyer with a keen interest in natural history, often took her on outdoor expeditions with her sister: "An expedition was going to the woods, where we would collect the flowers and the ferns and the mushrooms and the worms and the snails and all living things that little girls would be interested in or should be interested in." In high school, she received additional encouragement from a botany teacher, and by the time she graduated, she had decided to become a scientist.[57]

THE ROLE OF WOMEN IN THE NATURE-STUDY MOVEMENT

Although national leadership of nature study was in the hands of such men as Parker and Jackman at the turn of the century, from the outset of the movement, female educators figured prominently in local efforts to implement nature-study programs. Their participation in nature study can be attributed not only to a widespread social enthusiasm for nature, but also to women's growing involvement in the profession of teaching. The industrialization of the northern and eastern states, the construction of railroads, and the migration of pioneers westward created so many employment opportunities for men that the growing numbers of schools could no longer hope to attract male teachers. An increased demand for schooling, a low supply of men, and a high supply of women willing to teach for lower wages—coupled with contemporary rhetoric that depicted teaching as an evangelical calling commensurate with missionary work and portrayed women as particularly suited for working with children—contributed to the shift from a primarily male teaching force in the colonial era to one that was predominantly female by the end of the nineteenth century.[58] During the first half of the century, some advocates of an increased female presence in education argued that women made able teachers because of their propensity for selfless service. Catharine Beecher and other female evangelical reformers drew parallels between the service provided by teachers and the spiritual work of ministers.[59] For example, in a fund-raising letter written in 1836, Zilpah Grant of Ipswich Seminary claimed that few clergymen "are doing so much to promote the cause of education and religion" as these female teachers.[60] Evangelicals referred to women who went west to teach as "faithful laborers" whose "strong missionary spirit" and "conviction of duty" prompted them to perform an important public service.[61] Evangelical Christians of both sexes approved the work of female teachers, believing them to be doing essential work in claiming the West for Protestant Christianity. Citing financial reasons to hire women, Henry Barnard, editor of the *American Journal of Education*, wrote persuasively that "every instance of the employment of a female teacher in place of a male . . . will save one half of the wages paid to the latter."[62] Some state superintendents gave additional reasons for hiring women, perhaps in order to allay the fears of community members who feared that their school systems were sacrificing quality to thrift. For example, in 1856, after citing financial reasons for hiring women, Wisconsin's state superintendent added that women by nature were more qualified to teach the young: "Females, in consequence of their higher moral instincts, their more refined tastes, together with their more patient and sympathizing natures are fitted in a more eminent degree than the male sex for imparting instruction to the young."[63]

The proportion of female teachers increased dramatically during the Civil War years, and their number continued to grow after the end of the war. One Indiana educator recalled that in 1812, "there was no such thing as a woman teacher. It wasn't a woman's job, any more than milking a cow was a man's job."[64] In a striking shift, from 1859 to 1864, the percentage of women common-school teachers in Indiana more than doubled, from twenty to forty-six percent. In discussing this trend, Indiana's state superintendent George W. Hoss concluded that the rise of women teachers in his state was "a cause for congratulation [rather] than alarm." Hoss believed that women were "more likely to engage permanently in the business of teaching than young men" and for this reason would "devote more attention to their preparation for teaching." By talent and by disposition, he argued, women were highly qualified to teach.[65] Additionally, "The extensive employment of young ladies as teachers, tends to lessen the cost of the schools . . . they do not generally ask or expect so high a rate of compensation as young men do."[66] Leading educators from various regions of the country reiterated such views up to the last decade of the nineteenth century.[67] By the 1890s, women composed sixty-five percent of the nation's teachers. The proportion of women teachers steadily increased thereafter, reaching its historically highest point in 1921–22, when women composed eighty-seven percent of elementary and sixty-four percent of secondary teachers.[68]

Whereas such men as Jackman, Bailey, Hodge, and others authored most of the handbooks and courses of study teachers used in planning their lessons, women had an enormous impact on the nature-study curriculum as it actually appeared in schoolrooms. Because nature study involved the direct investigation of the outdoor world, children ideally did not use textbooks in the nature-study program. The books that children read in their nature-study lessons were therefore either nature stories aimed to integrate literature with nature study or such reference works as Mabel O. Wright's *Birdcraft: A Field-book of Two Hundred Song, Game, and Water Birds*. The authors of such stories were frequently women, as were the majority of teachers in elementary classrooms.[69]

Ultimately, the most important—and later controversial—effect of women's participation in nature study was to modify the subject so that it favored the biological sciences. Because women more frequently chose to study the life sciences, they tended to emphasize biological topics in the curricula they developed and in the lessons they published in educational journal articles. As discussed above, the contributions of women amateur naturalists to the *Review* frequently emphasized the traditional topics of natural history. Similarly, one of the few handbooks authored by a woman, Anna Comstock's *Handbook of Nature-Study*, devoted 462 pages to animal life, 351 pages to plant life, and only 100 pages to an eclectic section titled "Earth and Sky." Aware of the imbalance in her text, Comstock explained that she had omitted various topics in physics because her own training and professional work were in biology: "It should also be stated that it is not because the author undervalues physics nature-study that it has been left out of these lessons, but because her own work has been always along biological lines."[70]

As consumers of published curricula, female teachers modified courses of study to favor biological topics. The case of the nature-study program in California's Oakland City School District illustrates this phenomenon. During the 1896–97 school year, a group of 125 Oakland teachers agreed to work under the direction of Professor Oliver Jenkins of Stanford University, who volunteered to assist in the development and implementation of a course of study for students in the first eight grades of school.[71] Initially, the content of Oakland's course of study balanced the life and physical sciences. Students studied a wide range of both living and nonliving things in their immediate surroundings, focusing on the activity of local organisms and their adaptation to the conditions of their environment. For example, fifth-grade students studied the evaporation of various liquids and solids, condensation, distillation, solution, and filtering, as they observed such natural phenomena as fogs, clouds, snow, rain, the formation of soils, and erosion. Within a three-year period, however, Oakland's teachers, the great majority of whom were female, modified the nature-study program to emphasize the biological sciences. According to Oakland's 1900 annual report, teachers preferred to teach topics from the life sciences because they believed their students were more interested in such topics and learned them more successfully.[72] We shall never know whether Oakland's students were indeed more inclined to learn about plants and animals than chemistry or physics, or whether the teachers' success with the life sciences arose primarily from their own greater familiarity with these traditional topics of natural history. Whatever the reason, in 1900, fifth-grade students studied the growth of the pistil in the flower and the earthworm, snail, and slug, and conducted investigations with magnets. The eighth-grade curriculum, which had largely consisted of physical science topics the year before, now included only such biological topics as plant physiology and experiments with plants or animals.[73]

Whereas the curriculum modifications made by women teachers often occurred in the semiprivate world of the schoolroom, women also began to assert a greater influence over the implementation of nature-study programs in local school districts. In many areas of the country, district administrators hired female college and normal-school graduates to fill the new role of nature-study supervisor. Thus, Effie B. McFadden, a graduate in botany from Stanford University, supervised the creation of a nature-study program in Oakland (California) City School District in 1897.[74] When McFadden left Oakland in 1900 to join the faculty at San Francisco State Normal School, Oakland hired Bertha Chapman, who received a master's degree in entomology from Stanford in 1902.[75] In the Los Angeles City School District, almost all of the local supervisors of the nature-study programs were female.[76] Many of the women who were most active in the American Nature Study Society were supervisors, including Jennie Hall of Minneapolis, Minnesota; Fannie Stebbins of Springfield, Massachusetts; Clelia Paroni of Berkeley, California; Elizabeth Peeples, of Washington, D.C.; and Emelie Yunker, of Louisville, Kentucky.[77] By the second decade of the twentieth century, nature-study supervisors had their own national organization, the National Supervisors of Nature Study and Gardening, whose president in 1928 was a woman, Theodosia Hadley.[78] As late as 1946, a handbook, *Occupational Planning for College Women*, compiled by the Occupational Guidance Council, listed "nature-study supervisor" as an occupation for women.[79]

Able women were drawn into seeking such positions in part because the work of a nature-study supervisor was multifaceted. In addition to having the responsibility for implementing, coordinating, and overseeing a district's nature-study program at one or more school sites, many supervisors held split positions in which they combined supervision with teaching. For example, Helen Swett, daughter of California's one-time state superintendent John Swett, held such a position in the Alameda City School District from 1900 to 1902 after receiving a bachelor of arts in zoology from Stanford University.[80] Along with teaching botany and zoology classes in the local high school, Swett provided after-school nature-study training for elementary teachers, led field trips, assembled collections of specimens, built her own scientific apparatus, developed new curriculum, and supervised the teaching of nature study in elementary classrooms. She filled her Saturdays to the brim. "On Saturday morning I started off on my wheel towards Hayward, alone, in search of sunshine, fresh air, and a creek," she wrote to her fiance. "My captures were as follows . . . : four sticklebacks, 2 small toads, one water snake; 2 small lizards; one pair of handsome orb-weaving spiders; 3 other spiders; one back-swimmer; 3 water boatmen; four grasshoppers of a species I had never seen before; watercress seed; a kind of green algae new to me; a new water grass; a dragon fly . . . and several small water forms which I have not yet had a chance to examine under the microscope. How's that for one day's haul?"[81]

For bright, talented women, the role of nature-study supervisor could also serve as a stepping stone to career advancement. Occasionally, supervisors left school districts to join the faculty of normal schools, as did Effie McFadden; others, such as Bertha Chapman, who was president of the American Nature Study Society from 1928 to 1931, went on to assume leadership of national organizations.[82] Some supervisors gained local, state, or even national recognition through the development and publication of nature-study curriculum materials. For instance, Helen Swett developed several curriculum materials, some of which the Alameda School District published and shared with such larger neighboring districts as Oakland. As word of her work spread, educators asked her to give presentations on nature study at meetings of the California State Teachers Association.[83]

The inclusion of nature study in the curricula of normal schools also created a new position for women in at least a few institutions: professor of nature study. According to a 1925 report, of the 143 member institutions of the American Association of Teachers Colleges, all offered instruction in natural science, but only twelve had specific professors of nature study.[84] In contrast to a professor of natural science, who usually emphasized pedagogical methods and content for secondary school, a professor of nature study emphasized methods for students in the first eight grades of school. Because professorships in nature study were rare, most of the instruction about nature study fell either to the resident professor of natural science or to a lower-status instructor or adjunct faculty member.

The most famous professor of nature study in America was Anna Botsford Comstock (1864–1930) of Cornell University, sometimes referred to by contemporaries as the "dean of American nature study." One of the first women to be awarded a professorship at Cornell, she became widely known throughout the country as a nature-study teacher, writer, and naturalist. An artist as well, Comstock created wood engravings to illustrate the insects in the scientific texts of her husband, Cornell entomologist Henry Comstock. As a wife, naturalist, teacher, and scientific illustrator, Anna Comstock embodied many of the ideals of earlier generations of women who had hoped that their sex might find meaningful careers within natural history. Although her *Handbook of Nature Study* was not the first handbook to appear on the scene, at 938 pages it was not only the most comprehensive, but also by far the most popular, eventually achieving a best-seller status among the books published by Cornell University. Teachers called it the "Nature Bible." Within its covers, readers found 232 carefully planned lessons, complete with suggestions for field trips, experiments, and questions to ask students. In 1923, in recognition of her national influence on education, the League of Women Voters proclaimed Anna Comstock one of the twelve greatest women in America.[85]

During the years from 1908 to 1930, women also began to exert a highly visible influence on the nature-study movement at the national level. The expansion of female participation and leadership in nature study occurred within the context of a national debate over increased social and political rights for women. Having originated earlier with the Seneca Falls Convention in 1848, the suffrage movement in the United States gained momentum near the end of the nineteenth century, culminating in the passage of the Nineteenth Amendment in 1919 and its ratification in 1920. The movement reflected the desire of women to move out of a perceived separate domestic sphere, to claim rights under the Constitution equal to those of men, and to secure practical social goals through legislation.[86] The growing support for the movement also reflected an inexorable shift in the nature of middle-class women's work. By 1890, in addition to taking up schoolteaching in record numbers, women were pouring into factories and offices, graduating from secondary schools and colleges in record numbers, and competing with men to fill positions in the learned professions. In 1906, the popular magazine *Public Opinion* carried an article titled, "Industrial Competition of Women with Men," in which the author described the "rate of increase of the number of women in the five greatest groups of occupations: agriculture, professional service, domestic service, trade and transportation, and manufacturing [as being] greater than the rate of increase of the female population." Among those entering the workforce in record numbers were middle-class women, whose employment had increased at an even greater rate than that of working-class women.[87]

During the first three decades of the twentieth century, women gained access to leadership positions not only in the specific niche of science education, but also in the education profession at large. Increasing numbers of women competed with men for administrative positions and offices in professional associations. When Ella Flagg Young became superintendent of the Chicago public schools in 1909, she undoubtedly unnerved male educators when she claimed, "Women are destined to rule the schools of every city. I look for a majority of big cities to follow the lead of Chicago in choosing a woman for superintendent. In the near future we shall have more women than men in executive charge of the vast educational system."[88] By 1911, this prediction seemed to be coming true. The *Journal of Education* reported that educational authorities in Omaha, Nebraska, had promoted Belle Ryan to assistant superintendent and Kate McHugh to the principalship of the high school. Additionally, Nebraska's teachers had elected Edith Lathrop, superintendent of Clay County, as president of the State Teachers' Association.[89] Noting such trends, in a 1912 article titled, "The Feminizing of Culture," writer Earl Barnes warned, "[E]ven in supervisory positions, there are more women than men in the large centers of population." According to Barnes, "[T]hese figures justify us in saying that women have established a monopoly of education in the United States, except in the higher institutions."[90] In an article titled "The Monopolizing Woman Teacher," published the same year, educator Charles W. Bardeen warned male administrators that an army of women stood ready to drive them from their preserve and create completely female educational institutions. "My article," said Bardeen, "is not a protest; it is a recognition of the inevitable."[91]

Gaining confidence in their political power, women also began to press local school authorities for salary increases and actively supported the candidacy of women for leadership positions in education. In 1906, Grace Strachan, district superintendent in Brooklyn, organized New York City's women teachers in a campaign for equal pay; the city's mayor signed the law mandating equal pay on 19 October 1911. In the same year, the elementary teachers of Boston organized against the "'croakers,' the 'not-yeters,' and the 'anti-womeners'" and won legislative approval of a $1,000.00 salary for teachers of either sex.[92] Jackie Blount argues that two developments originating from the women's suffrage movement gave impetus to the emergence of female school administrators. First, the national movement for suffrage involved the creation of organized women's groups, many of which actively supported the candidacy of women for educational leadership positions. Second, as individual states granted suffrage to women, power at the ballot box enabled them to gain a political constituency. In 1896, women held 228 county superintendencies, two state superintendencies, and twelve city superintendencies. By 1913, 495 women held county superintendencies, and women had won state superintendencies in Colorado, Idaho, Washington, and Wyoming.[93]

Increasing numbers of female members in the American Nature Study Society supported the candidacy of women for leadership positions both at the local and national levels. The participation of amateur naturalists in the American Nature Study Society guaranteed women an increasing presence in the membership of that organization. Founded in 1908, with Cornell's Liberty Hyde Bailey as its first president, the society selected *The Nature Study Review* to serve as its official journal and forum for the publication of notices, minutes, and correspondence.[94]

From its inception, the society extended membership to all subscribers of *The Nature Study Review*, as well as to any individual or organization with an interest in nature study.[95] As a result, subscriber-members came from the ranks of educators, librarians, museum staff, and the membership of naturalist clubs—communities that often included large numbers of women. For example, some of the naturalist clubs that had membership in the American Nature Study Society were the St. Louis Nature Club; the Webster Groves Nature Study Society of Webster Groves, Missouri; the Bangor Bird Conservation Club of Bangor, Maine; and Wachung Nature Club; and the Pittsburgh Nature Club. Women composed the majority of members in such organizations. For example, of the 146 members in the Bangor Bird Club, only one was male, and the entire membership of the Pittsburg Nature Club was female; fifty-five percent of the Webster Groves Nature Study Society was female.[96] Gradually, the addition of such groups had an inevitable impact on the gender of the American Nature Study Society membership. In 1909, only thirty-nine percent of the society's membership was female. However, two years later, the majority of individuals who renewed their subscriptions to *The Review* (and thus their membership to the society) were female. By 1927, sixty-three percent of the members were women.[97]

As their membership numbers grew, women gradually began to assume leadership positions in the local chapters of the American Nature Study Society. The society's policy and organizational structure facilitated this trend. Rather than develop a large central organization, the society's officers encouraged the affiliation of local chapters. The goal of the society was to serve as a national clearinghouse for the efforts of these smaller bodies and to coordinate work at the national level.[98] In 1910, the society had three chapters: in Chicago, St. Louis, and Berkeley. By the following year, the society had additional chapters in Milwaukee; Rockford, Illinois; and New York.[99] The formation of chapters required the cooperation of local members, many of whom were women. For example, in 1911, Fred Charles wrote a Miss Carrie N. Jacobs of Hamilton, Ohio, about the possibility of forming a chapter in her community: "As doubtless you are aware, Prof. Davis of Oxford, Ohio, has been chosen to lead the American Nature-Study Society the coming year. We are endeavoring to organize local sections of the Society wherever interest warrants, and have been quite successful in carrying out the plan. It occurs to me that since you are near Mr. Davis, you and he might co-operate in the organization of a section at Hamilton."[100]

Because local chapters could put forward nominations for office and members voted to elect officers of the American Nature Study Society, the growing numbers of female members began to have an impact on the constituency of the society's leadership at the national level. In the first year of the society's existence, its officers were overwhelmingly male. Cornell's Liberty Hyde Bailey was president, Maurice Bigelow of Teachers College was secretary-treasurer, and the five vice presidents included Clifton F. Hodge of Clark University; F. L. Stevens of North Carolina College of Agriculture; Vernon L. Kellog of Stanford University; W. Lockhead of Macdonald College, Quebec; and F. L. Charles of DeKalb Normal School. Among the ten directors was one woman: Ruth Marshall of the University of Nebraska.[101] In 1911, the president, vice presidents, and directors were all men drawn from the faculty of normal schools, land-grant universities, and private colleges. Gradually, however, some of the larger local chapters began to nominate and vote into office women who were prominent in their organizations. In this way, the St. Louis chapter nominated and voted in Nellie Matlock of St. Louis; she served as secretary-treasurer for a number of years. Eventually, women began to assume even the office of president of the society. Anna Comstock of Cornell was elected president in 1913–14; Bertha Chapman Cady of the Coordinating Council on Nature Activities was president from 1928–31. Later presidents included University of Maine entomologist Edith Patch (1937–38) and Ellen Shaddy Shaw (1939–40).[102] In 1926, although the president was male, three of the four vice presidents were female, as were six of the ten directors. This pattern repeated itself throughout the rest of the decade, and by the late 1920s, the national leadership of nature study had shifted from men to women.[103]

CONCLUSION

Although historians have traditionally credited progressive male educators with creating, implementing, and promoting nature study across the country, this study shows that women played a highly significant, if overlooked, role in the expansion of nature study both at the local and national levels. Within an era in which women sought greater social, economic, and political opportunities in the United States, they succeeded in obtaining leadership positions in school districts and institutions of higher learning as nature-study supervisors, lecturers, and occasionally professors. Female naturalists played an important role in the development of national support for nature study through their contributions as nature writers. Female teachers, the majority of those teaching at the elementary level, implemented nature study to varying degrees in their classrooms and occasionally modified the curriculum created by male professionals so that it favored the life sciences.

The nature-study movement was significant in the science education of American girls for two reasons. First, with the entry of nature study into the first eight grades of publicly funded schools, access to some degree of scientific observation and experimentation was no longer largely restricted to the sons and daughters of the middle and upper classes. Second, in continuation with the earlier natural history tradition, nature study offered young women a form of science education with a positive subjective warrant. Taking up the advanced study of science in college or deciding to become a professional scientist are decisions made only at the end of a far longer process, during which individuals subjectively qualify or disqualify themselves as suited to the field in question. Nature study, with its positive female role models and its connection with traditional views of women's sphere, potentially served as an effective vehicle for interesting young girls in science generally and the life sciences in particular.

During the heyday of the nature-study movement, an era that some scholars have called a "golden age" for female leaders in education generally,[104] women appeared poised to build on their gains in the field of science education. There remained much work to be done. Some educators expressed concern that nature study was neither consistently nor uniformly implemented in classrooms across the nation and that teachers required further training in the subject. Others cautioned that an overreliance on nature stories in some classrooms threatened to transform nature study into a literary pursuit.[105] Women turned their attention to these and other pressing matters in the field of elementary education. In so doing, however, they failed to notice another, far greater threat looming to the scientific interests of American girls. During the same years that nature study reached its peak at the elementary level, the numbers of girls enrolling in physical science and advanced mathematics courses at the secondary level steadily began to decline. The cause lay not within the field of science education, but elsewhere.

7

Other Paths, Other Opportunities

By the 1890s, girls outnumbered boys in public high school science courses across the country, but at the turn of the century, this state of affairs began to change. During the same period that educational reformers began to implement nature-study programs in the first eight grades of school, female enrollments in science declined at the secondary level.[1]

Working in different fields, a number of historians interested in understanding the decline of science as a girls' subject in the late nineteenth century have proposed two developments likely to have contributed to this phenomenon. Focusing on England, a recent study of women's scientific interests concludes that middle- and upper-class women abandoned the sciences in favor of the classics near the end of the nineteenth century. According to Patricia Phillips, as English women sought an educational program equal to that of men, "they resigned the scientific identity that had been theirs since the seventeenth century." In part, this was due to the well-meaning attempts of reformers to improve the quality of girls schools by increasing the quota of classics offered there.[2] Concentrating on the United States, several scholars studying American educational history have identified the late nineteenth-century vocational movement as an important factor in girls' declining enrollments in secondary-school science courses.[3]

This recent scholarship is suggestive of a significant relation between social class and girls' interests and opportunities in science education. To what extent did American middle- and upper-class women, like their English sisters, relinquish scientific study in favor of the classics? What effects did changes in curriculum and policy undertaken during the vocational movement have on the science studies of working-class girls and their more affluent and privileged peers? How did this movement affect the course taking of girls from various ethnic groups? In order to understand the degree to which conditions may have occurred in the United States comparable to those in Great Britain, the following discussion begins by analyzing the rise of the classics in early nineteenth-century female secondary schools and colleges.

TAKING UP THE CLASSICS

During the seventeenth and eighteenth centuries, generations of middle- and upper-class American schoolboys in Latin grammar schools studied a curriculum with higher branches that included the study of Latin and Greek. Their schoolmasters and parents supported this educational program because they viewed the classics as the preferred means of providing a rigorous moral and intellectual training. It was a commonly held view that the best minds were those whose faculties had been strengthened through years of classical application. Contemporaries believed the female mind, on the other hand, to be relatively deficient in rational powers. Many seventeenth- and eighteenth-century educators viewed girls as mentally unfit by nature for the expenditure of effort required to study the classics.[4]

Gradually, almost imperceptibly, at the dawn of the nineteenth century, some schools providing a form of secondary education for girls—female seminaries and academies, boarding schools, ladies' select schools, and so on—began to break with this traditional view by including Latin in their curricula. In contrast to other educational reforms, this particular curricular change was unaccompanied by articles published by leading educators urging the addition of a new subject to the traditional course of study. Instead, this shift occurred almost covertly, its traces enclosed within the covers of school catalogs and courses of study.

Near the turn of the century, female schools in both northern and southern states began to include Latin in their published courses of study.[5] In Massachusetts, one of the first schools to offer the classics to girls was Westford Academy, which included Latin and Greek in its curriculum in 1792. A coeducational institution, Westford admitted students of any age or nationality able to "read in the Bible readily without spelling."[6] It is difficult to know how many female students actually enrolled in Latin or Greek classes during the first decades of the nineteenth century. For females, the classics never composed part of the core curriculum during this early period, because in many cases, schools charged students extra tuition to study Latin or Greek.

Documentary sources suggest that before 1840, the numbers of females actually enrolling in Latin classes in higher schools may have been very few. A small sample of three northern coeducational schools suggests that although Latin may have been on the books as a subject for study, female enrollments in Latin classes were negligible. For example, in 1822, thirty-six percent of the males and none of the females enrolled in Latin at Monson Academy, Connecticut. Less than a decade later in Massachusetts, Wesleyan Academy (1828) and the Sheldon English and Classical School (1830) revealed similar enrollment patterns. At both institutions, no more than one percent of females studied Latin, compared with roughly one-third of the males.[7]

Mount Holyoke Female Seminary in Massachusetts delayed placing Latin among its required subjects for a period of ten years because of community resistance. Mary Lyon offered students the option of studying Latin when she established Mount Holyoke in 1837. Initially, the board of trustees had planned to require all students to study the subject, but community opposition made this impossible. Instead, Latin remained an elective until the 1846–47 school year, when it was required of all pupils. One former student recalled that in 1840, when Latin had an elective status, "about one-fourth of the pupils were voluntarily pursuing it."[8] Requiring the subject for the first time in 1846, the board explained that although the seminary had originally planned to require Latin from its inception, "it has been necessary to accommodate to the general views of the community on female education, and to the desire of many parents to finish the education of their daughters just at the age, when they have acquired strength of constitution enough to begin hard study."[9]

In North Carolina, newspaper advertisements placed by female schools increasingly mentioned Latin after 1810 (see Table 7.1). Like their northern counterparts, such schools initially offered Latin as an elective subject. For example, the female department of North Carolina's Raleigh Academy included Latin, French, music, painting, and needlework as electives in its course of study in 1811, as did New Bern Academy in 1823.[10]

It is possible that the study of Latin may have been more prevalent in some areas of the country than in others. As shown in Table 7.2, forty-two percent of a sample of female higher schools in Connecticut, Massachusetts, New York, and Maryland included Latin in their advertised courses of study from 1820 to 1842, in contrast to thirteen percent in Virginia.[11] At first glance, this seems to suggest that northern institutions may have offered the classics earlier than schools in the South. However, based on a small sample of North Carolina schools during the antebellum period, historian Christie Farnham concluded that Latin appeared more frequently in southern female schools than in northern institutions. The data presented here might support the speculation that female institutions may have offered Latin in North

Table 7.1 Percentage of North Carolina Female Higher Schools Advertising Latin, 1800–1830

· Year	Percentage
1800–1809 (6 schools)	0
1810–1819 (12 schools)	17
1820–1830 (24 schools)	21

Source: Kim Tolley, "Mapping the Landscape of Higher Schooling, 1727-1850," in *Chartered Schools: Two Hundred Years of Independent Academies in the United States, 1727–1925*, eds. Nancy Beadie and Kim Tolley (New York: Routledge, 2002), 33.

Table 7.2 Percentage of Female Higher Schools Offering Latin Before 1840 in Selected States

Dates	Sample size	States	Schools offering Latin
1750–1829	36	Pennsylvania	5 (14%)
1820–1830	24	North Carolina	5 (21%)
1835–1838	31	Virginia	4 (13%)
1820–1842	24	Massachusetts; Connecticut; New York; Maryland	10 (42%)

Sources: Kim Tolley, "Mapping the Landscape of Higher Schools, 1727–1850," in *Chartered Schools: Two Hundred Years of Independent Academies in the United States, 1727–1925,* eds. Nancy Beadie and Kim Tolley (New York: Routledge, 2002), 34.

Carolina earlier than did their counterparts in some areas of New England, but the discrepancy in the results for Virginia and North Carolina make it difficult to draw more general conclusions without further study.

Some educators in northern and southern female schools promoted the study of Latin for its presumed ability to develop the mind or to develop habits of patience and perseverance. "How much patience is needed to get one lesson in Latin," asserted educator John Todd in 1854, "or to make a single good recitation in algebra!"[12]

The founders of academies and their boards of trustees also viewed the classics as a vehicle for increasing their schools' status and prestige and as a means of making their institutions more comparable to male academies. For example, in 1838, the well-known educator Almira Hart Lincoln Phelps proclaimed that the object of her school at West Chester, Pennsylvania, was "to furnish females with the means of acquiring a liberal education, coinciding, as far as the varying conditions of the two sexes will admit, with a collegiate course for the other sex."[13] Almost by definition during this era, pursuing a so-called collegiate course involved some study of the classics.

Another important social development fueling the rise of Latin in female higher schools was the opening of new institutions for women bearing the designation of "college." Some scholars have dismissed these early attempts at postsecondary education, viewing them as colleges in name only.[14] Nevertheless, these institutions had an important influence on the curricula of higher schools aiming to prepare students to meet the new collegiate entrance requirements.

The first experiment in women's collegiate education in the United States took place in the South, with the chartering of Georgia Female College in 1836, an institution authorized to "confer all such honors, degrees, and licenses as are usually conferred in colleges or universities."[15] The college opened on 7 January 1839. As a new educational experiment, the college was the subject of some criticism, not only from those who ridiculed the notion of higher education for women, but from others who questioned the rigor and quality of its studies. Traditionally, the presence of the classics in the entrance requirements served as a marker of an institution's relative quality. Because Georgia Female College did not require a demonstration of classical knowledge for admission, contemporaries judged its academic standards to be relatively low. In the context of defending the college's admission policy, the college president admitted that "the standard of admission especially is reduced so low as to present an incongruity between the high character of a college . . . and the requisitions laid down in our plan, as published in the catalog." Low standards were a financial necessity, he argued, because elevating them would potentially "diminish the number of scholars, and consequently, the receipts from tuition."[16]

Despite fears that high admission standards might limit the number of qualified scholars, it was not long before other newly organized institutions designated as women's colleges began adding the classics to their entrance requirements. For example, in 1842, Wesleyan Female College at Cincinnati, Ohio, required Latin grammar, Latin reader, the *Commentaries* of Caesar, and Greek grammar and reader. Established in 1853, the Wesleyan Female College at Delaware, Ohio, offered students the choice of either a scientific or classical four-year course. Entrance requirements for the classical course required some knowledge of Latin and Greek: "first and second books."[17] The admission requirements of Mary Sharp College, which opened in 1851 at Winchester, Tennessee, specified knowledge of Greek grammar, Testament, Latin grammar, Virgil, Cicero, and Horace. When Vassar opened in 1861, its entrance requirements included Latin grammar, syntax, Latin prose, two books of the *Commentaries* of Caesar, two orations of Cicero, French, and several modern subjects. Finally, the opening of Smith College in 1875 represented a landmark of sorts. Its admission standards, heavily weighted with the classics, matched those of Amherst and Harvard.[18]

Reflecting the shift toward the classics in the entrance requirements of women's colleges, the percentage of girls' secondary schools offering Latin visibly increased during the rest of the century.[19] To a lesser extent, girls' schools began to offer Greek as well, although this subject lagged behind Latin in both male and female institutions throughout the century. For example, in Pennsylvania from 1750 to 1829, only three percent of girls' schools offered Greek, whereas fourteen percent offered Latin. In later years, from 1830 to 1889, thirty-seven percent of girls' schools offered Greek, whereas seventy-two percent offered Latin. Conceivably, girls' schools placed a greater emphasis on Latin than on Greek during this period because educators viewed Greek as a prerequisite subject for those preparing to enter the ministry, a field largely closed to women.[20]

Taking up the classics required female students to devote a substantial proportion of their school hours to practicing Latin grammar and reading such authors as Caesar, Virgil, Cicero, and Xenophon. Students could hardly undertake such study without reducing attention to other subjects. In some cases, girls abandoned the study of the sciences to make room for the classics. For instance, when Swedish commentator Per Siljestrom visited Connecticut's Hartford High School in the 1850s, he reported that the school had enacted a provision that girls might omit "etymology, the geography and history of the United States, natural philosophy, chemistry, and philosophy and substitute for them the study of Latin."[21]

The importance of classical studies in American secondary schools surprised Siljestrom, who had expected to find a curricular emphasis on the sciences and other so-called practical subjects when he visited the United States at midcentury. Instead, he discovered that Latin and sometimes Greek were among "the more substantial accomplishments which form part of the higher education of women in America." In Siljestrom's opinion, this trend was unfortunate. Believing that it was not "of the least value either for woman or for man to possess a smattering of Greek or Latin," he recommended that Americans increase their offerings of such subjects as geometry and geometrical drawing, natural history, and manual arts.[22]

Girls had an increased incentive to study the classics after the Civil War, when growing numbers of previously all-male colleges and universities began to open their doors to women. Without knowledge of Latin, young women could not obtain entrance to the prestigious collegiate courses in liberal arts colleges. Statistical data reveal that in liberal arts universities and colleges in 1872, women more often enrolled in scientific departments than in collegiate departments. In that year, the commissioner of education published statistics on 298 universities, colleges, and collegiate departments. Of these institutions, fifty-nine (twenty percent) enrolled students in a scientific as well as a collegiate course. In institutions that offered both a scientific and a collegiate department, more women chose to enroll in the scientific department (Table 7.3).

Several factors may have influenced women to enroll in scientific courses, in which they studied such subjects as botany, physiology, chemistry, scientific illustration, or horticulture. One factor was the length of the course. Students not interested in a full four-year collegiate course often enrolled in the scientific course, in which they might study for shorter periods of time. A second factor was the perceived practicality of the scientific course, which, in the absence of nearby normal schools, served to prepare students to assume teaching positions in secondary schools. But most importantly, the entrance requirements of such institutions undoubtedly weighed heavily on women's enrollment decisions. In many cases, entrance to the collegiate department required knowledge of Latin, Greek, or both, subjects studied by a minority of girls in secondary schools.[23] For example, to gain admission to the College of Letters at the land-grant University of California in 1871, students had to pass an examination on Latin grammar, four books of Caesar, six books of Virgil, six orations of Cicero, Greek grammar, and Xenophon's *Anabasis*. On the other hand, admission to the scientific College of Arts required knowledge of subjects more famil-

Table 7.3 Enrollments of Women in Collegiate and Scientific Departments in Fifty-nine Universities and Colleges, 1872

Collegiate departments	Scientific departments
599 (41%)	878 (59%)

Source: Data compiled from *Report of the Commissioner of Education for the Year 1872* (Washington, D.C.: Government Printing Office, 1873), 762-770.

iar to girls: higher arithmetic, algebra to quadratic equations, geometry, English grammar, geography, and the history of the United States. In 1873, women composed only ten percent of the freshmen students enrolled in the College of Letters, whereas they composed eighteen percent of freshmen enrolled in the College of Arts.[24]

Reformers anxious to elevate the status of female education were not pleased to discover that girls had difficulty meeting the entrance requirements of the traditional collegiate course. The scientific course, which usually substituted a modern language for Latin, was often considered terribly déclassé. Unlike their great-grandmothers, who had aspired to study the sciences as a means of attaining an acceptable form of cultural polish, late nineteenth-century women now set their sights on the culture provided by the classics and the liberal arts. The growing application of science and technology to business enterprises—and the resultant demand for mechanics, engineers, mining experts, and agricultural chemists—had noticeably shifted science's position in society. Although the middle and upper classes still flocked to hear scientific lectures and read articles about the most recent discoveries, they no longer looked so favorably on such study for their daughters. After all, young men from the lower-middle, working, and farming classes eager to train for new jobs in the new agricultural experiment stations and in industry science courses increasingly filled the new land-grant colleges and universities. Another mark of the inferiority of the scientific course was its relatively short duration, often requiring only two or three years of study, in contrast to the traditional four-year collegiate course.[25]

At the annual meeting of the New England Women's Club in 1873, members discussed with great interest recent efforts in certain private preparatory schools to make classical training available to girls. In its report, the club noted with approval that not only were some girls' schools beginning to offer advanced classical training, but a few all-male preparatory schools had begun to admit girls for the purpose of studying the classics: "Chauncey Hall School [has] thrown its doors open to girls as freely as to boys, offering them the opportunity of obtaining the same thorough fitting for college—the Latin School in Roxbury has, we understand, this year taken the same onward step."[26]

Given the historical role of the classics in the education of gentlemen, girls met a surprising lack of resistance when they began to invade this traditionally male domain. Geraldine Jonçich Clifford suggests that men may have welcomed female enrollments in classical courses at the college level during the last decades of the nineteenth century, because female students allowed institutions the opportunity to more than double their enrollments in their classical courses, areas of declining popularity among male students.[27] Another contributing factor was the rising popularity of science among the more literate public during this period. The historian Frank Luther Mott has documented the enormous growth of American interest in science in the 1860s and 1870s as evidenced in general magazines and newspapers. According to Mott, articles on science typically ranked ahead of fiction, travel, and history-biography in popular magazines during these decades. Statistical records kept by the Astor Library in New York reveal that among the Astor's readers in 1872, scientific works had attained a popularity equal to that of general literature.[28]

Americans grew especially concerned to promote the study of science among boys. For example, *Popular Science Monthly*, first published in 1869, often included articles castigating schools for their lack of science courses and facilities. In 1872, the *Monthly* published an editorial critical of the narrow education available to boys, stating, "When a mother is ambitious that her son shall have a liberal education, and commits him to the accredited agencies, the question, is, 'What will become of him?' It is notorious that a pupil can go through a course of so-called liberal study and graduate with honor at the highest institutions, in complete ignorance of science."[29] The establishment of land-grant universities and agricultural experiment stations, and the increased need for engineers during these decades led many Americans to view science from a new perspective. No longer largely the domain of the interested amateur, the sciences now appeared as professional fields in which a young man might actually be able to make a decent living.[30]

During the same period that growing numbers of boys turned to the sciences, increasing numbers of girls began to take up the classics, motivated by the desire to gain entrance to the more socially prestigious collegiate course in universities and colleges. Many late nineteenth-century high schools offered at least two distinct courses of study: the classical or the scientific; others offered such additional courses as the modern languages and English.[31] During the late nineteenth century, the Office of Education collected data on the numbers of students in private and public high schools preparing for either a classical course in college or for a scientific course in a college or scientific school (Table 7.4). The data reveal a distinctly opposite shift in the curricula studied by the two sexes. In 1890, a greater number and proportion of boys than girls studied a classical curriculum, whereas in the scientific curriculum, the number of girls exceeded that of boys, although the proportion of girls was somewhat smaller. However, by 1910, the number and proportion of girls studying the classical curriculum exceeded that of boys, and the number and proportion of boys enrolled in the scientific curriculum was four times greater than that of girls.

In the last decade of the nineteenth century, science assumed a relatively minor role in the curricula of private girls' secondary schools. In 1893, Great Britain's Gilchrist Trustees sent five female teachers to America to study and report on secondary schools for girls and training colleges for women. In her report, Sara Burstall, mistress at the North London Collegiate School for Girls, noted the presence of Latin in girls' private schools: "Perhaps there is a tendency to do less science," wrote Burstall, "and more history and literature."[32] This trend intensified in the twentieth century. By 1914, more girls than boys enrolled in high school Latin courses across the country. A survey conducted in New York found that among seventh- and eighth-grade students, a larger percentage of girls than boys expressed a preference for Latin. Girls composed sixty-four percent of those who selected Latin.[33] Similarly, a 1915 survey of the interests of high school students in Iowa found that of those who stated a preference for Latin over

Table 7.4   Number and Percentage of Public and Private High School Students by Sex in Grades 9–12 Preparing for One of Two Curricula in College or Scientific School, 1890–1910

Classical curriculum		
	Boys	Girls
1890	8,084 (9.4%)	6,844 (5.9%)
1895	12,816 (8.9%)	13,390 (6.5%)
1900	15,120 (7.0%)	16,059 (5.3%)
1905	14,976 (5.2%)	19,941 (5.1%)
1910	11,970 (3.0%)	16,544 (3.2%)

Scientific curriculum		
	Boys	Girls
1890	6,966 (8.1%)	7,308 (6.3%)
1895	11,520 (8.0%)	10,094 (4.9%)
1900	13,824 (6.4%)	11,211 (3.7%)
1905	17,568 (6.1%)	11,730 (3.0%)
1910	22,748 (4.4%)	5,687 (1.1%)

Source: Data compiled from John Francis Latimer, *What's Happened to Our High Schools?* (Washington, D.C.: Public Affairs Press, 1958), 155.

other school subjects, seventy-one percent were girls. In attempting to explain this phenomenon, the author hypothesized that whereas there was "something inherently attractive to boy-nature in the engineering pursuits," perhaps girls' preference for English, Latin, and German was similarly "due to the fact that the intrinsic quality of the subjects makes more of an appeal to the girl-mind than to the boy-mind."[34]

Women visibly dominated the teaching of Latin in public secondary schools by the second decade of the twentieth century. For example, in Wisconsin, the reports of high school inspectors written from 1915 to 1924 reveal that the great majority of Latin teachers in that state were women. During this period, inspectors visited twenty-three Latin teachers, all of whom were female.[35] One commentator explained that girls preferred Latin because women usually taught the subject, presenting it "in ways better suited to arouse the girls' interest than the boys."[36]

Unlike their British sisters, American girls never wholeheartedly embraced the classics. Although Latin appears to have become thoroughly a girls' subject in America by 1914, during the next several decades, the importance of Latin declined in the public high school curriculum. In contrast to England, where the universities of Oxford and Cambridge maintained the classics in their entrance requirements until relatively late in the twentieth century, American colleges and universities abandoned the classics requirement well before midcentury. For instance, the University of California eliminated its classics requirement by 1918.[37] As colleges and universities began to minimize or omit classical subjects from their entrance requirements, Latin assumed a smaller role in the studies of both sexes. In 1890, thirty-four percent of all boys and thirty-six percent of all girls enrolled in high school Latin courses. By 1928, only twenty-one percent of boys and twenty-three percent of girls took the subject, and by 1948, enrollments had fallen to fourteen percent of boys and seventeen percent of girls.[38]

The significance of classical study in the history of women's education lies in the fact that the turn to the classics led girls away from science. The underlying motive of educators and parents for encouraging girls to take up classical study was never solely to prepare them to become Latin teachers, although women were highly successful in assuming this role. Instead, the goal was to enable girls to gain entrance to the full four-year collegiate course in which they might become liberally educated and, in many cases, to prepare for teaching other subjects than science. In short, the path away from science led directly to the liberal arts.

At the turn of the century, some observers of American culture reported that in addition to adolescent girls, older women of leisure were also taking up the study of the liberal arts. "Step by step," bemoaned American commentator Earl Barnes in an article published in *Atlantic Monthly* in 1912, "women are taking over the field of liberal culture. Who, fifty years ago, could have imagined that today women would be steadily monopolizing learning, teaching, literature, the fine arts, music, the church, and the theatre? And yet this is the condition at which we have arrived."[39] In attempting to explain this phenomenon, another writer, Josephine Conger-Kaneko, noted, "girls whose mothers had never advanced much beyond reading, writing, and arithmetic, find themselves studying Greek art and German music." Conger-Kaneko speculated that the new studies of their daughters created in many older women a desire to learn new things, to "broaden out."[40] Across the country, women of leisure established art and literary clubs and civic courses, organized university lectures, and enrolled in correspondence courses, even in the smallest towns. Conger-Kaneko described "one town of some five thousand inhabitants out in Kansas [which boasted] half a dozen such clubs."[41]

After 1910, when institutional barriers formed against the relatively few remaining women who sought to become science educators and professional scientists, the liberal arts provided college-bound girls with a well-established educational alternative. This alternative, made possible by the efforts of earlier generations of women, led to careers as educators in such subjects as English, modern languages, Latin, history, or art. In this direction, once the preserve of young men, young women encountered far less competition from men, who now looked with hope of greater personal and financial reward to careers in business, law, medicine, and science.

TURNING TO HOME ECONOMICS
AND COMMERCIAL COURSES

By the late nineteenth century, girls were turning from science not only to the classics and liberal arts, but also to the new home economics and commercial courses offered in American public and private high schools. A detailed history of the vocational movement is beyond the scope of this study, but an understanding of the underlying issues giving rise to so-called vocational subjects in secondary schools is essential to understanding the eventual impact of this movement on girls' secondary school mathematics and science studies.

Why did parents support the introduction of home economics into the high school curriculum? Earlier in the century, middle- and upper-class parents had not viewed domestic science as a particularly useful subject for their daughters. As discussed in Chapter 3, when Catharine Beecher's text on domestic economy appeared in 1840, many Americans questioned the value of a study that dealt with the common concerns of home and hearth. Critics asked, "What will be the use of this study?"[42] However, by the end of the nineteenth century, the perceptions of many Americans as to the value of domestic science had changed, for reasons related to changing social demographics in secondary schools, women's increased presence in the labor markets, and rhetoric focused on gender differences in the context of debates over suffrage.

As increasing numbers of states passed compulsory education laws and a greater variety and number of students enrolled in tax-supported secondary schools in the nineteenth century, some observers began to question the desirability of schooling working-class boys and girls in the traditional curriculum that had long been the domain of elites. Relatively few secondary school students ever went on to college. In recognition of this fact, even before educators began to consider offering vocational training in American secondary schools, a number of school districts had begun to modify their high school courses of study to allow students greater election of subjects.[43] In response to increased demands to allow greater flexibility in the secondary school course, the National Education Association's Committee of Ten advocated the use of a limited elective system in public and private high schools. In its 1894 report, the committee recommended that students be allowed to explore a variety of subject areas during the first two years of high school before choosing one of four recommended courses of study: the classical, the Latin-scientific, the modern languages, or the English.[44] Some educators advocated the abolition of all set courses in the high school and the creation of two flexible courses designated by the general titles of "college-preparatory" and "non-college-preparatory." For example, by 1917, educators implemented this approach in most of Michigan's secondary schools.[45]

In large measure, such restructuring was due to a growing belief that many subjects in the core academic programs were irrelevant to the future vocations of working-class children. In 1874, Horace Greeley, editor of the New York *Tribune*, expressed a view that a growing number of educators appeared to share: "I go into one of our public schools, and before me are boys who are to work in shops or mills or till the soil all their lives, and there are girls who are to be wives and mothers of farmers and mechanics; to cook, sew, darn, wash, starch, and make butter and cheese; and when I see them studying Algebra and Trigonometry and Logarithms, and making astronomical calculations, I ask, not whether such studies are not useful for some purposes and persons, but whether this does not preclude or take the place of what would be more useful, what they will urgently need to know."[46]

In response to a growing national interest in adapting schools to students' presumed vocational futures, the National Education Association created an Industrial Section to focus on the issue in 1876.[47] Many late nineteenth-century Americans recommended vocational education as a way to make schools more appealing to working-class boys. For instance, Omaha's superintendent, after noting the high attrition rate of boys from the higher grades of high school, hoped that with the addition of vocational courses to the city's schools, "we shall find before long in the graduating classes nearly as many young men as young women."[48] In 1904, the state superintendent of Wisconsin justified the addition of vocational training in high schools as a means of increasing the self-respect of boys "who naturally have very little taste for intellectual pursuits" and who "are frequently made to feel, in our literary courses of study, that they are of inferior ability."[49]

The national debate over how schooling should best fit American youth occurred within the context of wide-ranging discussions over gender differences during the decades after the Civil War. Concerns about women's increased presence in the workforce, coupled with discussion of Charles Darwin's theory of evolution, sparked widespread discussion of the nature, origin, and social implications of gender differences. Magazines such as *Popular Science Monthly* and *Appleton's Journal of Literature, Science, and Art* carried articles on the subject by scientists, philosophers, and social commentators on both sides of the Atlantic. Were women inherently capable of the steady rationality required for certain forms of professional work? Academics debated the extent to which gender differences could be traced to evolutionary or social causes and whether such differences rendered certain social roles, or particular academic subjects, inherently unattainable for women. According to Luke Owen Pike, a fellow of the Anthropological Society of London, the "smallness of the brain-case" rendered women "more prone to the display of emotion than of pure reason." Additionally, "the desire, if not the capacity, for the prolonged study of abstruse subjects is less in the female than in the male."[50] What would be the consequences for society if women gained entry to jobs formerly reserved for men? Granting women access to jobs traditionally reserved for men would result in "a further diminution in the virile force of the nation," warned a professor of medical psychology at the University of Edinburgh in 1869.[51] Such opinions, expressed in the name of science, justified efforts to differentiate some areas of the curriculum along gender lines.

The rhetoric associated with the women's suffrage movement also provided impetus to national debates over gender differences. Discussion of the separation of spheres and of the inherently different qualities of men and women continued throughout the decades leading up to suffrage, the same period in which the vocational movement gained impetus. In demanding the right to vote, women appeared to attack the presumed sanctity of the male public sphere. In counterarguments, men claimed that women were too physically or emotionally frail for the rough-and-tumble world of politics, that women were inherently illogical and emotional and lacked the steady rationality required to make informed political decisions. Some women opposed to suffrage agreed with this depiction. For example, addressing the Illinois legislature in 1897, a group of antisuffragists stated, "We believe that men are ordained to govern in all forceful and material matters, because they are men, physically and intellectually strong, virile, aggressive."[52] Whether particular individuals or groups rejected the notion of inherent gender differences, believed that gender differences were God-given, or accepted that distinct traits developed through evolution, the issue of difference persisted throughout debates over suffrage.[53] In most debates, whether they supported or opposed suffrage, women by and large supported the doctrine of difference.

Both sexes applied the doctrine of separate spheres to politics. The ideology of different realms for men and women conceived of the woman as the embodiment of self-sacrifice. According to this view, women exerted themselves for the best interests of their families, devoting themselves to their children and submitting to the will of their husbands. Because women's social identify was derived from her husband's social standing, she regarded his self-interest as her own. When women pressed for suffrage, men reacted by claiming that giving women the right to vote would destroy the very fabric of society. The right to vote would allow women— by nature pure and delicate—to enter the sordid, fractious world of politics. Worse yet, giving women the vote would upset the domestic sphere, because women could then politically represent their own interests.[54] To counter such arguments, leading women's organizations took steps to assure the nation that women were firmly committed to hearth and home.

Organizations like the National American Woman Suffrage Association (NAWSA), created in 1890 through a merger of the American Woman Suffrage Association and the National Woman Suffrage Association, increasingly stressed women's special qualities by giving prominence to gender differences. In pamphlets, speeches, and in publications like *Women's Journal*, the NAWSA emphasized the unique characteristics that entitled women to vote, including benevolence; women's traditional role in the home; and an inherent female interest in issues related to children, health, and education. In contrast to older feminist arguments that the vote was essential as a recognition of an equal humanity, NAWSA's emphasis on female differences rather than equality attracted hundreds of members from such disparate women's reform groups as the Women's Trade Union League, the Women's Christian Temperance Union, and the settlement house movement. In rhetorical arguments reminiscent of eighteenth-century notions of republican motherhood, suffragists claimed that women needed to be good citizens in order to be successful mothers and homemakers.[55]

Modern-day historians have tended to depict this increased emphasis on gender differences as a calculated political strategy designed to advance women's interests within the context of a hostile opposition. Late nineteenth-century socialists like Charlotte Perkins Gilman rejected traditional views of women's separate sphere and argued for a full equality of the sexes.[56] From the perspective of writers like Gilman, appeals to women's "special differences" and "worthy home membership" as a means of advancing suffrage can be interpreted as a clever—if insincere—rhetorical tactic designed to build a broad coalition among ideologically diverse groups of women. However, the majority of women who supported suffrage at the turn of the century were not feminist socialists. Most expressed views similar to those of the feminist Antoinette Brown Blackwell, who argued that men and women were "true equivalents—equal but not identical." Blackwell believed that the sexes complemented each other in a partnership necessary to the advancement of society.[57] Like Blackwell, the majority of American women, to varying degrees, also believed firmly in essential differences between the sexes, even as they agitated for equal political rights. For example, the women members of the largest conservative Christian groups supporting the suffrage movement were ideologically committed to the notion of separate spheres as a matter of religious faith.

Many of the rhetorical debates women used to advance suffrage reproduced and reinforced not only traditional views of women's separate sphere, but also deeply held beliefs about ethnic and racial inequality. Feminist scholars have documented the ways that northern suffragists often drew on anti-immigrant feelings to argue that one way to avoid "the ignorant foreign vote" would be to "give it to women." For their part, many southern suffragists claimed that giving the vote to women would swell the numbers of white voters in states where the blacks outnumbered whites.[58]

The concerns and attitudes reinforced through debates over competition in the workforce, gender differences, and women's political activism underlay reforms implemented in the nation's secondary schools. Conservative women argued that because women's place was in the home, the most practical life training available to girls was domestic science, a curriculum based on the applications of scientific principles to the routines and chores of the home. So-called pure science, once viewed as highly appropriate for young ladies, now conveyed a masculine aura. Some contemporaries characterized the rejection of scientific study for women as the expression of a societal fear that girls would lose their feminine traits. "It is my object to urge against the prejudice which still largely prevails in reference to scientific study for women," wrote Mary W. Whitney of Vassar College in 1883. "We are afraid it will make our girls rude and ungentle; in a word, will make them masculine."[59]

In response to social concerns, several large school districts began to experiment with ways to differentiate the science offered the two sexes in coeducational public schools. In a highly publicized experiment in limited segregation in Englewood High School in Chicago in 1906, principal J. E. Armstrong tracked boys into science courses that emphasized experimentation and logical reasoning, and girls into courses that focused on the application of scientific principles to the activities of the household. Armstrong reported the experiment to be a success; grouped together and sheltered from academic competition with girls, boys' enrollment increased from thirty-four to thirty-eight percent.[60] Reporting on a similar experiment several years later, Earl Barnes remarked approvingly that in the Girls' Evening High School in Philadelphia, "the only science courses given . . . are those in domestic science."[61]

Not everyone embraced such reforms. Liberals, interested in correcting gender inequalities in the workplace, argued that girls should have equal rights to the trade and vocational education afforded boys. The National Women's Trade Union League expressed the view that "young women should have access to the same training and educational opportunities as young men." The league strongly objected to the growing practice in some high schools of offering domestic science to girls and limiting trade training to boys. In a speech at the league's 1913 biennial meeting, Margaret Dreier Robins described a case at one school in which boys learned elementary physics, mechanics, and electricity in the science course of an industrial education program, whereas in a differentiated science course, girls studied the removal of stains from clothing and the action of alkalies.[62]

In spite of scattered protests against offering domestic science to working-class girls and industrial science to boys, some school districts experimented with sex-segregated science courses in an effort to adapt science content to the presumed life goals of the two sexes. For example, in 1915, a physics teacher in Seattle authored an article advocating the new method of segregating and differentiating science courses, noting that it was now possible to omit "much of the most difficult part for the girls" and present more challenging material to the boys.[63] In the same year, a high school in San Jose, California, offered a physics course for girls, in which students learned about vacuum cleaners, sewing machines, "the illuminating power of wall surfaces, the efficiency of lamps, and a comparison of colors."[64] In 1919, chemistry teacher Will Courson described a course he had designed specifically for girls, claiming, "Eminent educators have practically agreed that the highest training that can be given girls is that which pertains to home life." Reflecting these views, Courson's chemistry course included such topics as "How to make good bread."[65]

Despite the glowing reports as to the ostensible success of such experiments, the practice of providing segregated instruction in science classes never became widespread, largely for reasons of financial and institutional constraint. Offering separate courses to boys and girls was costly, requiring additional faculty and a large student body from which to create multiple courses. Few high schools had sufficiently large enrollments to allow the kind of sex segregation undertaken in Chicago and Seattle. In 1904, more than sixty-six percent of students attended relatively small high schools, with faculty of only one to ten teachers.[66] Instead, high schools began to differentiate their curricula by introducing sex-typed vocational courses, usually offered as electives. For example, in 1904, Wisconsin required its public high schools "to gradually introduce [for the benefit of boys] work in wood, mechanical drawing, forge work, and work with the lathe in metals, together with work for girls in sewing and cooking."[67] By 1920, most public and private secondary schools in the nation offered their students some form of vocational training along these lines, together with commercial or business courses.

The impetus for the home economics movement came largely from women themselves. The General Federation of Women's Clubs (GFWC) took the position that young women's studies should be consistent with their future roles as wives and homemakers. Rather than study algebra, Greek art, and Latin verbs, GFWC members argued that girls should learn about cooking, mending, hygiene, and health. Some leading women's magazines promoted and popularized this view as well.[68] The educator Earl Barnes noted in 1912 that "one of these journals, which boasts a fabulous circulation . . . oppose[s] the larger interests of women in education, industry, and political life." Although a conservative himself, Barnes found it ludicrous that American women would pay "one dollar and a half a year" to read monthly articles telling them "to go back to their kitchens, churches, and children."[69]

Nellie Kedzie Jones, pioneer founder of the first home economics department at Kansas State Agricultural College, recalled that when the subject first appeared in colleges and universities during the 1880s, many male college authorities opposed it on the grounds that "My wife knows how to keep house," and "there is no need to teach girls to cook."[70] Similarly, in 1882, the city superintendent of Omaha questioned the value of introducing a domestic economy course in the city's high schools, noting that girls already "learn every kind of home industry" within the family circle.[71]

At the college and university level, the growing field of home economics offered college-educated women increased employment opportunities as members of university faculties. According to Jones, after the home economics department at Kansas State Agricultural College staged a successful, highly publicized exhibition at the Chicago World's Fair, "it was not long before young women were called on to go to other Land Grant colleges to organize departments for teaching homemaking."[72] Often the first full professorships awarded to women went to faculty members in departments of domestic science. For example, Cornell University elected Martha Van Rensselaer of the College of Home Economics its first female professor in 1911.[73] Nellie Jones was the first woman granted an emeritus professorship at the University of Wisconsin at Madison.[74]

Home economics appealed to members of the middle and upper classes who promoted the subject as a means of solving a growing servant problem. According to historian Jane Barnard Powers, between 1910 and 1920 the number of domestic servants nationwide fell by approximately twenty-five percent as working women sought higher-paying jobs in manufacturing and other growing sectors of the labor market. Federation Club women noted with anxiety the increasing scarcity of servants and the low skills of the few workers available. "It is perplexing," commented one club woman, "because working women are generally unwilling to accept domestic service as a means of gaining a living, and . . . the woman heads of families are doing little to improve the situation."[75]

In contrast to earlier generations of educators who had sought, without much success, to introduce domestic science to middle- and upper-class girls in private secondary schools, middle-class women now targeted lower- and working-class girls, often of immigrant parentage, as the audience most needful of domestic training. "I hail with delight," wrote Wisconsin's state superintendent in 1904, "[A]nd trust it is not a mere passing fad, that many of the wealthiest women and leaders in society are, within the last few years, beginning to give time, money, and the weight of their influence in the direction of training girls in the supervision and care of the home."[76]

Another factor in the increased support for home economics was the desire of many parents and educators to offer girls courses comparable to the new vocational programs available to boys. At the college level, Nellie Jones reported that in spite of initial resistance, "as women began to see how their daughters enjoyed the work, pressure was brought to bear, and many a college . . . [added] Home Economics . . . just to please the women."[77] As the home economics movement gained ground, well-meaning male educators also began to pressure local school authorities to add home economics courses. For example, during a visit to the high school in Bloomer, Wisconsin, inspector R. A. Walker noticed in 1928 that the school "offers no instruction in home economics," although it provided "instruction in agriculture for the boys." Walker wrote to the principal to suggest that, in all fairness, "girls are entitled to as much consideration with respect to home economics . . . you have plenty of room in the building which might be fitted up for domestic science."[78] Matching boys' vocational courses with similar offerings for girls also solved administrative scheduling problems. Historian Geraldine Jonçich Clifford notes that the introduction of home economics and other sex-segregated courses for girls effectively balanced boys' and girls' courses so as to preserve the basic coeducational mix in the remaining areas of the curriculum.[79] Finally, home economics courses, like other sex-typed courses, undoubtedly appealed to female students who enjoyed participating with other girls in activities related to girl culture. According to Jones, shortly after she joined Kansas State Agricultural School to establish its new department of home economics, "a group of girls graduating next commencement came and asked for a sewing class." In response, Jones suggested that each sew her own graduation dress, with the result that at commencement, "the newspapers made great stories of the beautiful dresses, and thereafter sewing was a permanent course for every girl in college."[80]

Although sometimes billed as a form of science—and described under such various names as "home science," "domestic economy," "household science," "science and art," or "home management"—Jones gave her opinion that "what ever name was used, the teaching was homemaking."[81] George Counts of Teachers College, Columbia, corroborated this view in a secondary school survey conducted in the mid-1920s, concluding that the field consisted primarily of cooking and sewing classes rather than science.[82] Contemporary photographs of high school girls in so-called domestic science classes support these characterizations (Plate 7.1).

In spite of fairly widespread support among educators and community members, home economics was never as popular among high school girls

Plate 7.1 Young Girls' Class in Domestic Science, 1909, WHi-3216. (*Courtesy of the Wisconsin Historical Society.*)

as were the newer commercial courses (Table 7.5). College-bound girls, often from wealthier middle- and upper-class families, preferred instead to concentrate on courses that were required for entrance to colleges and universities. Those seeking employment directly after high school sought to learn clerical skills in the hopes of landing office jobs that paid higher wages.

Commercial education afforded girls a greater degree of respectability and status than did home economics. Clerical work was a white-collar oc-

Table 7.5   Percentage of Public High School Students Enrolled in Typewriting, Industrial, and Home Economics Courses, 1910–1949

	1910	1915	1922	1928	1934	1949
Typewriting	—	—	13.1	15.2	16.7	22.5
Industrial		11.2	13.7	13.5	21.0	26.6
Home economics	3.8	12.9	14.3	16.5	16.7	24.2

Source: "Offerings and Enrollments in High-School Subjects," *Biennial Survey of Education in the United States, 1948–1950* (Washington, D.C.: U.S. Government Printing Office, 1951), 107–08.

cupation that offered some degree of economic and social mobility. Some women climbed a ladder of advancement that led, within the restricted sphere of female office work, to the desirable position of private secretary.[83] It was also a respectable way for young women to earn a living before marriage and meet promising young men "on the job," becoming for the first time a significant alternative to teaching. In a study published in 1922, George Counts reported that in Bridgeport, Connecticut, eighty-eight percent of working-class high school girls enrolled in commercial courses. And in New York, whereas first-generation Italian-American families had encouraged their daughters to leave school early to go to work, by the second generation girls stayed longer in school, in part to obtain the training necessary for white-collar jobs in the city's growing clerical labor force.[84]

The first three decades of the twentieth century witnessed a fourfold increase in the percentage of girls enrolled in commercial courses in the last four years of public high school.[85] The growth in commercial course enrollments paralleled the enormous growth in office and sales work during this period. Historian Maurine Weiner Greenwald demonstrates that during the decade from 1900 to 1910, growth in industrial production created an expanding market for support services, telephone communications systems, insurance firms, advertising companies, and mail-order houses. At the same time, the spread of high school commercial training created a growing supply of young women available and qualified for office employment. Greenwald shows that "the shift toward specialization was accompanied by a feminization of the clerical field," as the number of women employed in clerical work more or less doubled each decade from 1870 to 1910 (Table 7.6).[86]

The events of the First World War created an increased number of openings in clerical work, which women quickly filled. For example, tens of thousands of women gained entry to clerical positions in the railroad industry during the national emergency produced by the war. After the war ended, some employers continued to hire women in preference to men for such work, because, in the words of a Women's Service Section inspector, "They are not so damned anxious to get out and rustle around. Women are

Table 7.6 The Ascendancy of Women Office Workers, 1870–1910

Year	Total number of office workers	Number of women office workers	Women as percent of all office workers
1870	68,819	1,823	2.6
1880	139,819	6,610	4.7
1890	380,141	73,603	19.4
1900	614,509	179,345	29.2
1910	1,525,757	575,792	37.7

Source: Maurine Weiner Greenwald, *Women, War, and Work: The Impact of World War I on Women Workers in the United States* (Westport, Conn.: Greenwood Press, 1980), 9.

more content with the detailed monotonous work because they are filling in between school and marriage."[87]

In spite of the rhetoric of their supporters, home economics and commercial courses never succeeded in truly vocationalizing American high schools.[88] The majority of girls continued to enroll in the basic academic courses, in part because such courses already equipped women to be teachers, office workers, or sales clerks. In the basic courses, girls learned to speak, write, calculate simple sums, and take directions. In the twentieth century, it was increasingly the high school diploma itself, rather than a list of completed commercial courses, that helped a young woman land her first job. For example, the telephone companies preferred girls with high school experience; a survey conducted in 1912 found that eighty-seven percent of Boston's telephone operators had been to high school.[89]

Nevertheless, not every student was able to avoid home economics, in spite of its elective status at most secondary schools. One of the first educational institutions of higher learning open to African-Americans offered a vocational education curriculum designed to cultivate students' industry. The Hampton Normal and Agricultural Institute, established in 1868 for the education of freed slaves living near Hampton Roads, Virginia, opened its doors to American Indian students ten years later. Besides taking the required elementary subjects, female students were expected to master the household arts. In 1898 the institute opened a domestic science department, in which female scholars prepared for careers as home economics teachers, seamstresses, cooks, and laundresses.[90] The Hampton Institute served as a model for schools across the state. For instance, in 1910, the supervisor of colored rural elementary schools reported, "Hampton Institute has been our leader in negro education, and has amply demonstrated the wisdom of this policy by training many hundreds of negros to lives of social and industrial efficiency in the various communities into which they have gone and become leaders of their race. The problem it seems to me is to extend and project this ideal and this practical training from Hampton as a center to all the rural schools of the state."[91]

Educators at Tuskegee Institute further elaborated and defined the model of vocational education developed at Hampton Institute. Established in 1880 in Macon County, Alabama, Tuskegee Institute became best known as the site for Booker T. Washington's philosophy of industrial education for African-Americans.[92] The curriculum at Tuskegee emphasized the importance of domestic science for girls. As noted by one advocate, "[T]he girl in the laundry does not make soap by rote but by principle; and the girl in the dressmaking shop does not cut out her pattern by luck or guess or instinct or rule of thumb, but by geometry."[93] The trend toward vocational education for African-Americans appears to have spread during the subsequent three decades. For instance, in 1922, a news article in the *Wilmington Star* in North Carolina provided an enthusiastic description of the town's new high school for African-Americans: "[In 1914] the colored people also came in for their part of the improvements—the board of education erected a handsome school for the higher grades on the land given to the city by the government in 1910. This building, erected at a cost of $20,000, contains nine large recitation rooms above the basement, with two recitation rooms and other rooms in the basement. This is the beginning of a real industrial school in New Hanover county; as classes are taught there in domestic science, including sewing and cooking and in agriculture."[94]

In spite of the apparently widespread approval for vocational education and home economics training on the part of some educational and community leaders, there is documentary evidence to suggest that in some locations, African-American teachers resisted this curricular trend. For example, the supervisor of colored rural elementary schools in Virginia noted in 1910, "The average negro teacher is untrained, and is ambitious to use many books, and to teach the so-called 'higher branches.' The supervising teacher will prevent this mistake by showing the teachers how to connect the school with the child's every day life through simple forms of industrial work, and by planning a course of study and work that will fit them for a useful and happy life in their own community."[95]

Although evidence is sketchy because of the lack of data on special home economics programs, it appears that school authorities in so-called colored schools more frequently required African-American girls to take the subject than did school authorities in institutions serving white students. For example, the subject was required for female African-American high school students in Winston-Salem, North Carolina.[96] Such differential treatment, coupled with discrimination in the workplace, may explain why few African-American women gained access to clerical work, even in large northern cities; in 1920, only one percent of their nonagricultural employment was in clerical and sales jobs. In that year, three-fourths of employed African-American women worked as farm laborers, servants, and laundresses.[97]

Whether by choice or by school mandate, female enrollments in home economics and commercial courses came at a cost to other subjects. Consistent with their greater persistence in high school, in 1890, a preponderance of girls had filled high school science and mathematics courses (Table 7.7).[98] However, the years from 1910 to 1922 witnessed a precipitous drop in girls' mathematics enrollments, accompanied by a commensurate rise in total commercial enrollments. Similarly, the percentage of girls enrolled in chemistry and physics declined by two-thirds (Table 7.8).

Table 7.7 High School Students Enrolled in Selected Subjects in the Last Four Years of Public High Schools, 1890

	Males	Females
Physics	19,125	26,912
Chemistry	8,415	12,064
Algebra	38,505	53,360
Geometry	18,445	24,708
Trigonometry	5,184	4,545

Source: John Francis Latimer, *What's Happened in Our High Schools?* (Washington, D.C.: Public Affairs Press, 1958), 149.

Table 7.8   Percentage of Girls Enrolled in Selected Subjects in the Last Four Years of Public High Schools, 1890–1948

	1890	1900	1910	1922	1928	1948
Chemistry and physics	33.6	26.1	18.5	12.8	10.2	10.2
Algebra and geometry	67.3	83.5	84.2	56.7	49.4	42.6
Commercial	—	11.8	11.1	44.4	47.0	48.5
Home economics	—	—	—	26.4	29.8	30.1

Source: John Francis Latimer, *What's Happened to Our High Schools?* (Washington, D.C.: Public Affairs Press, 1958), 149-150.

In order to enroll in commercial and home economics courses, students had to give up a number of other subjects not required for graduation or for entrance to college. In 1894, the Committee of Ten recommended that two units of mathematics and one of science be required for entrance to college.[99] By 1910, most high schools offered biology in the tenth grade, chemistry in the eleventh grade, and physics in the twelfth. Students desiring to prepare for entrance to college could fulfill the usual requirements by taking biology. Because of the nature of graduation and college entrance requirements, and because of their placement in the higher grades, chemistry and physics assumed the status of elective subjects, a phenomenon resulting in declining enrollments, not just among girls, but among boys as well. "At the present rate of decline," warned an anxious science educator in 1909, "physics will disappear from the high school curriculum about the year 1930."[100] The intellectual challenges of physics and chemistry were simply not worth the effort for young women who did not require the subjects for high school graduation or for entrance to college. As high school student Florence Peck explained in her diary in 1901, "Tried chemistry. And flunked. It is the horridist of hateful things to flunk. I will, I shall 'drop' it . . . I won't need it for the university of R[ochester] and that is where I shall go on account of the 'lonesome dollars' in the E. C. Peck family."[101]

Bucking the trend, biology enrollments actually rose during this period (Table 7.9). Biology served as a preparatory course for the further study of medicine. During the 1880s and 1890s, increasing numbers of medical

Table 7.9   Percentage of Boys and Girls Enrolled in Biology in the Last Four Years of Public High School, 1910–1948

	1910	1922	1928	1948
Males	1.0	8.9	13.2	19.5
Females	1.2	8.7	14.0	19.5

Source: John Francis Latimer, *What's Happened to Our High Schools?* (Washington, D.C.: Public Affairs Press, 1958), 149.

schools began to accept female students training to become doctors. Middle-class parents did not consider nursing a suitable occupation for their daughters until relatively late in the nineteenth century, but between 1900 and 1910, the numbers of trained nurses increased sevenfold; by 1920, nursing had become a respected profession among women.[102] In part, the increase in biology enrollments may also have been due to the subject's grade placement, coupled with a concomitant drop in girls' mathematics enrollments. The lack of a secure foundation of mathematics left many girls ill-prepared to undertake the study of chemistry and physics. Students of both sexes possibly preferred to fulfill their single science requirement by taking biology in the ninth or tenth grade before turning to other subjects in grades eleven and twelve. Finally, the social and cultural construction of the life sciences as particularly suitable for women, an ideology reinforced through the nature-study movement, may have continued to make this subject attractive to girls.

As part of the wider effort to adjust schooling to students' presumed life goals, a growing number of school districts began to reduce or eliminate the high school mathematics course requirement for girls. By the turn of the century, educators from both ends of the ideological spectrum increasingly questioned the value of requiring girls to study advanced mathematics. For example, in 1900, the *Report of the Commissioner of Education* quoted writer Rebecca Harding Davis, who asserted that girls would be far better prepared "for a full, happy life by a course in dressmaking or cookery and arithmetic," than through the study of "trigonometry and art."[103] In a similar vein, Joseph Van Denburg noted the apparent irrelevance of algebra to everyday life when he studied New York City high school students around 1910. Denburg concluded that high school seemed "hard, uninviting, and entirely out of keeping with what appear to be the realities of life. The contrast between the abstractions of algebra and the life of the neighborhood is too great to be bridged, save by an arch of faith which few indeed can construct."[104]

In 1904, Wisconsin's state superintendent noted that many public high schools had adopted a proposal to make Latin and advanced algebra elective subjects.[105] In 1910, the independent high schools of Wisconsin arranged, with the approval of the state university, courses "which do not require algebra in the first year, and which do make physics an elective study for girls."[106] By 1917, some of the public high schools in the state had followed suit, cutting algebra as a required subject to half a year, or even making it "an elective altogether for students in vocational courses, such as agriculture and domestic science."[107]

In 1914, E. R. Breslich of the University of Chicago High School noted a recurring nationwide demand that girls be allowed to graduate from high school without any algebra. According to Breslich, the question had been "discussed throughout the country by parents and teachers, by administrative officers, and professors of education." Breslich felt that the main question was not whether algebra was more difficult for girls than for boys; in his own experience, he had found that girls often excelled boys in algebra.

Rather, the opponents of algebra denied that its study was of value to young women. Dr. J. H. Francis, superintendent of the Los Angeles schools, caused a stir during the National Education Association meeting that year when he reportedly exclaimed, "God bless the girl who refuses to study algebra. It is a study that has caused many a girl to lose her soul." Dr. Francis reportedly recommended replacing algebra with courses in costume designing for girls.[108] According to Breslich, as increasing numbers of American high schools lowered or eliminated their mathematics requirements for high school graduation, "many pupils did not take any mathematics."[109]

The movement to reduce or eliminate the mathematics requirements in high schools stemmed both from efforts to make schooling more "socially useful" and from new developments in the field of psychology. Throughout most of the nineteenth century, educators believed that any form of mental discipline improved the minds of school students in a general way. Since the eighteenth century, this rationale had served as a popular defense for the study of the classics and advanced mathematics. As discussed in Chapter 1, it also served to justify the introduction of the sciences in girls' courses of study before midcentury. At the dawn of the twentieth century, however, the theory of mental discipline came under attack from such scholars as Edward L. Thorndike and Charles Judd, who reported numerous unsuccessful attempts to demonstrate any transfer of learning from one setting to another.[110]

The effort to provide girls with a more "practical" education, one more suited to their supposed future goals, received added impetus from the creation of a new professional field: vocational guidance. The first National Conference on Vocational Guidance took place in Boston in 1910. Three years later, leaders of this new movement founded the National Vocational Guidance Association.[111] In 1910, a National Education Association Committee, asked to make recommendations concerning the vocational education of girls, expressed a common view among professional guidance counselors: "The girls in our schools will be the wives and mothers of the next generation and the courses of study should be so laid out that these girls will lead happier and richer lives and will be more successful as the future homemakers of our cities."[112] Guidance professionals aimed to match the talents of the individual to the job. They believed that based on a scientific study of education and the workplace, appropriate vocational training and guidance could assist pupils to fill their proper roles in society. In 1913, Thorndike wrote optimistically that once trained in the principles of vocational guidance, "the average graduate of Teachers College in 1950 ought to be able to give better advice to a high school boy about the choice of an occupation than Solomon, Socrates, and Benjamin Franklin all together could give."[113]

What sort of counsel did guidance professionals offer girls? In the literature published for an audience of parents and educators, guidance professionals described a far more limited range of career choices for girls than for boys. Most expressed the belief that girls were destined to become homemakers. "In answer to the question, 'What ought women to be?'" wrote Marguerite Stockman Dickson, a leader in the vocational guidance field, "we say boldly, 'A homemaker.'" According to Dickson, one obstacle to women's successful pursuit of her "ultimate vocation" as homemaker was "the instruction of the times [which] has imbued her with too little respect for her calling."[114] For those girls who sought to enter the workforce, Dickson and other authors followed the recommendations of the National Education Association's Committee on the Vocational Education of Females, which had suggested that girls "train for work in distinctly feminine occupations."[115] Thus, guidance books recommended for girls a narrow range of such sex-typed occupations as factory work, dressmaking, food production, salesmanship, teaching, nursing, and social work.[116]

Such recommendations represented a distinct departure from earlier views. During the 1870s and 1880s, middle-class women had expressed confidence in the opportunities available to them in science, particularly as educators. Those women who needed to work for a living, stated a speaker at the New England Women's Association in 1884, could find "an ample field" in "scientific observation . . . as teacher, curator, lecturer in chemical, physical and biological laboratories, principal and superintendent of schools or professor of pedagogy."[117] However, within the span of a single generation, women began to express doubts that more than a talented few would ever earn a decent living through scientific study and research.[118] More importantly, the field of science generally, once perceived as a source of enjoyment and opportunity for women, increasingly appeared inappropriately unfeminine as the twentieth century began to unfold.

CONCLUSION

Declining female enrollments in advanced science and mathematics courses accompanied increasing enrollments in subjects that contemporaries viewed as more useful, worthwhile, or appropriate for girls. When colleges and universities opened their doors to women, many college-bound girls, like their British sisters, abandoned the sciences to take up the study of Latin, an entrance requirement at some institutions just after mid-century. As American institutions of higher learning generally abandoned the classics requirement for admission near the end of the century, young women continued to enroll in liberal arts courses, a territory they had already staked out as their own.

Latin, a subject that underwent a dramatic shift from a traditionally male domain to one that contemporaries viewed as more suitable for girls, represents an interesting case in the gender stereotyping of the curriculum. From the perspective of the eighteenth century, it is difficult to identify a subject more strongly associated with men than Latin, largely because of its historic association with the traditionally male clergy. Nevertheless, young women predominated in Latin classes at the end of the nineteenth century, a move that apparently was not motivated by any attempts to differentiate the curriculum specifically for a female audience. Instead, this transformation occurred because leading female educators strongly supported its inclusion into the curriculum, because knowledge of Latin helped women gain access to higher education, and because there existed virtually no resistance to the presence of females in Latin classes during an era when the subject faced declining male enrollments. In other words, Latin became "feminized" in secondary schools simply because girls came to dominate the subject.

The efforts of progressive educators to make schooling more "practical" for boys and girls also inevitably drew additional enrollments from science and mathematics classes. Young women enrolled in commercial courses in high school to prepare for work in the expanding clerical market. Students interested in working in the home, or those believed destined to become domestic servants, enrolled in domestic science, or home economics courses. High school guidance counselors undoubtedly contributed to changing enrollment patterns by steering young women away from advanced science and mathematics courses into classes deemed more vocationally appropriate, a trend that appears to have been strongest among African-American girls and those from families recently immigrated to the United States.

The introduction of home economics at the secondary level had a long-range negative influence on the enrollment of girls in higher mathematics, chemistry, and physics classes. Some scholars have argued that the nineteenth-century Victorian domesticity championed by Catharine Beecher that ultimately evolved into the twentieth-century home economics movement focused more on professional careers for women than on keeping women in the home. Recent research supports this viewpoint by documenting the ways that women scientists, unable to find academic employment in chemistry or physiology departments, found a niche for their work in home economics in many institutions of higher education.[119] Nevertheless, although home economics departments may have created faculty positions for women scientists in chemistry, nutrition, and health, the documentary sources analyzed for this study indicate that the introduction of home economics at the secondary level contributed to a reduction in the numbers of young women entering institutions of higher education with the necessary background to major in a scientific field. At the high school level, home economics—also known as domestic science—offered little or no scientific content. Instead, classes for adolescents generally focused on cooking, sewing, and life in the home.

Considerations of social class played a large role in the selection of subjects that women viewed as appropriate for study. Secondary course-taking patterns suggest that near the end of the century, middle-and upper-class native-born white girls continued to enroll in the basic liberal arts classes in preparation for college. Noncollege-bound white girls appear to have predominated in the commercial courses. When they recommended home economics as an addition to the high school course of study, many middle- and upper-class white women targeted girls from the working classes and minority ethnic groups, particularly African-Americans and those recently immigrated to the United States. At the high school level, where home economics courses experienced disproportional enrollments of immigrant and African-American girls, the movement served as a mechanism for tracking certain ethnic and racial groups into training focused on domestic service, a trend that reinforced the relative dominance of white middle-class women in higher-paid clerical and professional work.

Although some scholars have speculated that a decline in feminist activity after the suffrage victory contributed to a decline in women's participation in science, at the secondary level it is not clear that late nineteenth- and early twentieth-century feminism served to promote female interest and participation in science. Rhetoric that stressed women's separate sphere and commitment to the home provided support to the creation of home economics classes and science courses that attempted to differentiate content along gender lines. From the standpoint of its contemporary supporteres, home economics offered the opportunity to elevate the status of women's work, create employment opportunities in institutions of higher education, and provide training to young women interested in becoming homemakers or poised to enter domestic service. If women had concerns about the impact of such vocational courses on girls' secondary science enrollments, they rarely—if ever—voiced them.

Discriminatory practices in secondary schooling reflected widely held beliefs about class, race, and ethnicity. Throughout contemporary debates over gender and science, educators rarely questioned the underlying assumption that a student's social class, ethnicity, or gender largely determined what he or she should study. Whereas on the one hand, efforts to track students of particular class or ethnic groups into vocational courses in secondary institutions can be attributed to the contemporary belief that such training constituted the fairest, most equitable form of schooling possible for a child unlikely to have the financial resources to pursue a college degree, institutional policies that discriminated among girls according to class and ethnicity persisted in high schools for decades, serving as an important barrier to the continued study of science and mathematics. Similarly, although the broad acceptance of gender differences that supported the creation of separate arenas of study and professional employment for women created higher-status professional positions in institutions of higher education, middle-class white women predominated in these positions. At the turn of the century, few middle-class white women appear to have questioned the desirability of creating expanded opportunities in institutions of higher education for their social equals while supporting educational programs at the secondary level to track their presumed social inferiors into lower-paying careers such as domestic service.

Although little reliable data exist on the number and distribution of women scientists during these decades, we know that some women persisted in taking up scientific research. Data compiled by Margaret Rossiter suggest that in 1921 women attained twelve percent of the total doctorates awarded in botany, eleven percent in zoology, four percent in medical sciences, three percent in chemistry, and two percent in physics.[120] These proportions appear extremely low by today's standards, but they would decline over subsequent decades. Within the context of a growing backlash against women's entry into the workforce and a national atmosphere supporting the development of segregated, distinct spheres of professional activity for women, women scientists would encounter great difficulty obtaining positions in male-dominated academic departments. The arguments advanced by women to support women's distinct sphere of professional activity would also have the unforeseen negative consequence of strengthening efforts to differentiate the secondary science curriculum offered the two sexes in the core academic program, a development that is explored in the following chapter.

8

Physics for Boys

During the years following the First World War, two related shifts occurred in the direction and leadership of science education. First, the coalition that had bound together the nature-study movement unraveled. As meteoric as was the rise of nature study near the close of the nineteenth century, its decline occurred with even greater rapidity. In the words of one scholar, the movement was "all but dead" by the early 1930s.[1] Second, although women had come to dominate the leadership of the nature-study movement, the new national associations and organizations in science education that came to power after the war were almost entirely composed of men concerned to increase male enrollments in science.

The new leaders in science education urged a greater emphasis on the physical sciences and recommended the use of textbooks at the elementary level. The schoolbooks that came to market as a result of this policy shift tended to depict physics as a masculine field of endeavor. Such representations stood in stark contrast to the physics textbooks females had encountered more than a century earlier, in which refined ladies discoursed on the concepts underlying various experiments in physics and chemistry.

How can we explain the gender stereotyping of science—particularly physics—as a male school subject in the twentieth century? As discussed in the previous chapter, the nineteenth-century movement to improve female access to colleges and universities led to a decreased emphasis on science in favor of an increased focus on the classics and the liberal arts. Coupled with the vocational movement in secondary education, these educational reforms played a significant role in diverting female enrollments away from science and mathematics courses in secondary schools. Nevertheless, these developments alone do not explain the decline of nature study and the gender stereotyping of physics.

Scholars interested in gender and science have given little attention to factors influencing student science enrollments in high schools during the early and midtwentieth century. This era has significance, because the number of women receiving advanced degrees in science declined steadily from 1920 onward, reaching a low in 1960. Although women's representation in science fell more dramatically than in the liberal arts, this was a period of general diminishment in the share of higher degrees attained by women. Between 1920 and 1950, the total proportion of doctorates awarded to women fell from eighteen to ten percent. To date, explanations for this phenomenon include (1) greater restrictions on job opportunities for women during the Depression, (2) continuing job discrimination against women in the 1940s and 1950s, and (3) the sudden rise in births after World War II, a demographic phenomenon that may have led to an overall decline in women taking advanced degrees. Some researchers have also argued that the decline of organized feminism after the suffrage victory in 1919 may have been a factor, although there exists questionable support for this claim.[2] As noted in Chapter 7, female enrollments in high school mathematics and science courses began to decline two decades earlier in response to efforts by female educators to promote study of the classics, liberal arts, and home economics. Additionally, as it played out at the secondary level, the rhetoric advanced by many feminists to advance suffrage effectively strengthened and reinforced existing notions—among students, educators, and guidance counselors—that a woman's proper place was in the home.

Secondary institutions have always been an important part of the so-called pipeline that leads ultimately to careers in the various professions, including science. A decline in the numbers of students entering colleges and universities with sufficient background, aptitude, or interest in science would inevitably affect the pool of students available to enter science majors as freshmen. To understand the full range of social developments that may have affected female enrollments in science at the secondary level, it is necessary to investigate not only shifting attitudes and practices within the science education community, but also changes in the way American society came to view the meaning and purpose of a scientific education, particularly with respect to physics. As demonstrated earlier in this volume, women gained control of the leadership of the American Nature Study Society in the early twentieth century. What was the reaction of male educators to this development? To what extent was a backlash against women in science education related to the professionalization of the field and to other developments in society at large? How did American views of science change through the Great Depression and two world wars, and how did such changes in perception affect contemporary views of women's participation in science?

This chapter considers a number of the social forces influencing the curriculum from the early twentieth century through 1960, a period that ushered in a heyday of sorts for the physical sciences. What is most significant about the rise of physics, in contrast to the rise of geography and natural history in the previous century, is that the growing prominence of this science in American culture occurred within a very different social and political context than the one in which other sciences had flourished earlier. Gone was the popular enthusiasm for natural theology, the conviction that scientific study of the natural world would necessarily increase religious faith. Gone too was the optimistic belief that mental discipline could be acquired in one generation and transmitted to the next through inheritance. In their place was a pervasive perception that schooling should prepare young men and women for their future roles in a precarious and uncertain world.

In order to explore this changing context, the following discussion focuses primarily on the educational environment in which physics came to power. It gives particular attention to four phenomena: expressed concerns about gender and schooling, a backlash against women leaders in the field of education in general, employment discrimination against women in the new profession of science education in particular, and the evolution of the secondary science curriculum in the aftermath of two world wars. The aim of this chapter is to document the motivations and purposes that impelled educators to stereotype the physical sciences as a domain for boys, an endeavor that echoed the efforts undertaken by female educators a century earlier, when women generally had sought to characterize the life sciences as a realm particularly suited to girls. By the advent of World War I, the scales in science education had begun to tip in the other direction.

THE FALL OF NATURE STUDY

A number of factors contributed to a decline in popular enthusiasm for nature study after the First World War. Some of these related to changes in scientific theory or to religious and cultural beliefs. Others stemmed from political, social, and economic transformations that occurred during the period.

Some of the rhetorical justifications for the study of science in general and for nature study in particular had lost their underpinnings by the end of the century. For example, although natural theology was absent from the work of such writers as Anna Comstock, it appeared in the articles and speeches of some advocates. "No one can love nature and not love its author," wrote one handbook author.[3] "It is one of those living pages of God's book," wrote another, referring to the dandelion.[4] However, by the dawn of the twentieth century, the scientific community had grown increasingly secular, and the era when a leading scientist could comfortably talk about how scientific discovery contributed to the development of religious faith had passed. By and large, natural theology disappeared from the rhetoric of most science educators by the end of the war. Additionally, the belief that it was possible to increase an individual's mental discipline, which had served as an important justification for science education in the eighteenth and nineteenth centuries, had been seriously undermined by recent discoveries in psychology. The discrediting of faculty psychology in the early 1900s resulted in the conclusion that general mental abilities could not be developed indirectly.[5] Subject-matter knowledge was no longer generally perceived as worthwhile for its ability to develop one's intellectual skills, but for its direct relevance to everyday life. Science, its proponents argued, was necessary for its social and vocational relevance, rather than for presumed intellectual or spiritual benefits.[6]

In its initial stages, nature study had gained impetus from a national concern with conservation, but the developments of the First World War altered the perception of the American public concerning priorities in environmental policy and practice. The impact of the war influenced in subtle ways the attitude of Americans to the concept of conservation. With greater demands on the supply of both food and minerals, the term came to have a new meaning. During wartime, conserving resources came to signify ensuring maximum efficiency in production and minimum waste, and the concept of conserving material resources for future generations largely dropped out of public discourse as a meaningful goal.[7]

The events of the war also played a large part in bringing the sciences of physics and chemistry to public attention. Whereas the rise of natural history in secondary schools and nature study at the elementary level had coincided with the increased dominance of the life sciences in America during the midnineteenth century, after the First World War science educators initiated a number of reforms to give greater emphasis to the physical sciences as these fields gained greater national prominence. The urgent need for scientific research in physics and engineering during wartime had motivated the creation of new national institutions for their promotion and development. To combat the poison gas and submarines introduced by the Germans, the Navy created a consulting board that divided into committees on scientific and technological problems of interest to the military: internal-combustion engines, electricity, torpedoes, ordnance and explosives, poison gas, wireless and communications, transportation, production, ship construction, steam engineering, and so on. In April 1916, the National Academy of Sciences entered the field. With astronomer George Ellery Hale as chairman, an organizing committee composed solely of relatively young men, including Robert A. Milikan, professor of physics at the University of Chicago, called for the creation of a National Research Council (NRC) to coordinate the work of existing governmental, educational, industrial, and other research organizations in the wartime effort. In July 1916, President Woodrow Wilson gave his consent, and the NRC came into being, an institution that played an important peacetime role after the war. The heyday of natural history had ended.[8]

Additionally, the decades after the war saw a transition to a business era, during which industrial research came into its own. During the 1920s, the corporation that adopted research as an integral part of its business operations became the norm. The great corporations generally limited themselves to the application of science that might possibly yield some profit, ushering in an age of useful labor-saving devices, improved production processes, advances in engineering, aeronautics, broadcasting, and communications.[9]

In contrast to natural history, which rose to prominence during a period when several leading scientists welcomed women's participation, the rise of physics occurred during a period marked by a growing cultural backlash against the visibly increasing numbers of women in the workforce. By 1890, women were pouring into schoolrooms, factories, and offices; graduating from secondary schools and colleges; competing with men for positions in the professions; and agitating for increased marital and property rights and suffrage. A proliferation of warnings by scholars, religious leaders, medical experts, journalists, educators, and social commentators—male and female—claimed that female activism was responsible for creating a "man shortage" in various occupations, promoting an "infertility epidemic" among educated women, causing "female burnout," and destroying the "values of hearth and home."

Historically, the middle-class professions had been male realms, and the occasionally vehement debates over female suffrage had brought to the forefront the issue of the presumed separate spheres of men and women. Men reacted negatively to attempts by women to seek places in the learned professions, thereby invading the so-called masculine public sphere. In reaction, various professional fields began to erect barriers against women during first decades of the twentieth century. For instance, when a small number of women tried to gain membership in the bar during the last third of the nineteenth century, male lawyers opposed their entry to the legal profession, claiming that women lacked the physical stamina, rationality, and sheer nerve required to practice law. When Belva Lockwood, a woman who had successfully obtained a license in the District of Columbia, sought the right to practice law in Virginia, she sought recourse under a Virginia law that granted the right to practice to "any person" licensed in another state. However, the Virginia state court denied her right on the grounds that "any person" meant "any man," an interpretation that the United States Supreme Court upheld in 1894.[10] Medical schools set quotas on female students just after 1910, and hospitals reinforced the practice by refusing to accept female interns.[11] During the 1930s, journalism schools also took measures to combat the "woman peril." The dean of the journalism school of Syracuse University justified the use of quotas by giving the example of Wisconsin, which in his view had been "almost destroyed . . . a few years ago when it allowed itself to be overrun with women."[12]

The scientific community strengthened barriers of its own against women scientists as new sources and mechanisms for funding research became available after the war. For example, the National Research Council became an indispensable foundation of the nation's peacetime science program, and as the dispenser of Rockefeller and Carnegie money for a variety of projects, the NRC appears to have played a role in supporting men and turning down women for funding. In 1918, NRC leaders began to discuss ways to stimulate basic research, coordinate the nation's scientific societies, and represent the United States in international scientific affairs. From these sessions emerged a group of postdoctoral fellowships in physics and chemistry, administered by the NRC with funds supplied by the Rockefeller Foundations. Executive Order created a permanent National Research Council organized as part of the National Academy in May 1918. During the following decades, the NRC, with its wide connections in the American scientific public, became a key source of funding for a variety of projects, fellowships, and grants that became the indispensable foundation of the nation's peacetime science program.[13] Although little data exist on the sex of the applicants for NRC monies, what little exists suggests that male applicants had an advantage over women. According to Margaret Rossiter, although women represented thirteen percent of the United States doctorates in the sciences in this period, they received only 5.4 percent of the fellowships during the years from 1920 to 1938.[14]

Whereas some of the most prominent American scientists in the fields of natural history had supported the participation of women in the nineteenth century, some of the leading men in physics after the First World War took deliberate steps to encourage men and dissuade women from pursuing positions in the physical sciences. A well-known example is the role played by Robert Millikan, a prominent physicist in the NRC and other national science organizations, in encouraging President W. P. Few of Duke University to refrain from hiring women for positions in physics. Echoing views expressed by men in other professions, Millikan wrote Few to express his opinion that the creation of a reputable physics department depended on the recruitment of young men rather than women.[15]

THE BACKLASH AGAINST WOMEN IN SCIENCE EDUCATION

Although women had obtained leadership positions at various levels in the field of education, that profession also evidenced a backlash against the women in its ranks, a reaction that originated in the last decades of the nineteenth century. This backlash has been so well documented by historians of education that it is not necessary to reiterate a detailed account here; nevertheless, the following paragraphs briefly detail its origins and key features, not only because they framed an important context for subsequent developments in science education, but because similar societal concerns have reemerged within the last decade, a trend that is briefly touched on in the conclusion of this book.[16]

Among educators, a key argument advanced against women teachers arose from the relatively poor academic performance of boys in high school classes. Earlier in the century, when the two sexes studied in separate schools or departments, Americans had not concerned themselves to compare the academic performance of boys and girls. However, with the rise of coeducational public high schools, in which boys and girls studied the same curriculum side by side, it became only too easy to compare the relative performance of boys and girls—and to see that greater numbers of boys were failing in their studies. For example, J. E. Armstrong, principal of Englewood High School in Chicago, reported "the boy, during his first two years in high school, finds himself unable to carry his work beside his more mature sisters." According to Armstrong, twenty percent of the girls graduating from his school "attained an average of 90% in all their studies, while only 2% of boys attained similar results."[17] "In all branches," wrote the author Josephine Conger-Kaneko, "the girls frequently excel the boys. Later, in their higher studies, too, the girls carry off the majority of honors and medals."[18] Cognizant of such schoolroom trends, Walter F. Wilcox of Cornell University warned that women were advancing faster educationally than men: "The young women of this country are now more generally able to read and write than men of corresponding age . . . if this trend of change continues for a generation, elementary and higher education will be possessed more generally by women than by men."[19]

Educators noted with increasing anxiety the low enrollments of boys in public high school courses. For example, the city superintendent of Omaha, Nebraska, reported in 1886 that "Quite generally boys drop out of school as they reach the higher grades and graduating classes are frequently entirely composed of young ladies." In 1889, the United States Commissioner of Education William T. Harris estimated that only twenty-five percent of students in the high schools of the ten largest cities were boys.[20] Some educators worried that the male attrition from high school would lead inevitably to "a comparatively ignorant male proletariat opposed to a female aristocracy."[21]

In seeking an explanation for boys' low enrollments and relatively poor academic performance, some educators claimed that the woman teacher's feminizing influence was driving boys away. In 1891, Commissioner Harris reported that many schoolmen believed that "the increasing femininity of the schools" was a principal reason for the "already noticeable decrease in the proportion of boys in the higher grades."[22] Critics identified a variety of means by which female teachers allegedly repelled boys from schools. "Women teachers do not appeal in any way to the virile or feral qualities of [boys]," wrote one educator. "The want of rapport naturally causes the boys to remain indifferent in their lessons."[23] G. Stanley Hall argued that adolescent boys needed the stronger, sterner discipline of a male teacher, because "[the boy] is now living through that state of the world where fear ruled and law was enforced by punishment; and he is liable to be a little spoiled under a regime of sugary benignity."[24]

The charge of feminization began to surface in attacks against the nature-study movement. Throughout the movement's history, nature study had its share of critics. Some educators agreed with the prominent Herbartian Charles De Garmo, who opposed the idea of integrating the school curriculum around nature study. According to De Garmo, such a scheme involved too much emphasis on the natural sciences. He believed that the history of human development indicated that although civilization had been possible without natural science, it could not have appeared without "culture knowledge." If forced to choose between science and culture, he argued, "we should keep the culture and let the science go."[25] Other critics opposed the idea of setting aside the textbook to study nature directly from the field.[26] Some opponents began to target women specifically in their attacks on nature study, blaming them for the so-called feminization of American boys. "[M]any modern nature books suffer from what might be called effeminization," wrote G. Stanley Hall in 1902. Voicing a growing concern among male educators, Hall recommended the use of books written by men, texts that presumably would have a greater appeal to boys.[27] The botanist John Merle Coulter criticized women's supposed style of teaching science, claiming that the "foolish and forced sprightliness of many primary teachers" tended to "repel rather than attract strong children." Coulter also opposed the use of literature in the nature-study program, arguing that its use encouraged a preference for fantasy over facts. Boys in particular, claimed Coulter, wanted factual truth: "This attitude toward truth appears to be general among boys unless it has been unfortunately suppressed."[28]

Although some critics identified women specifically in their attacks on sentimentalism, anthropomorphism, and the teaching style of primary teachers, it is important to bear in mind that during the course of the nature-study movement, such elements and methods were promoted with equal enthusiasm by both sexes. For example, the *Nature-Study Review* published a story by a male educator titled, "Bufo Junior, A Story for the Pupils When Rearing Tadpoles," in which a fairy describes the metamorphosis of a tadpole into a frog.[29] This tale, and others like it, drew ridicule from critics who decried such methods as sentimental and romantic. Similarly, many male nature-study authors anthropomorphized plants or animals in order to render the content more interesting to young readers. For instance, Purdue University's professor of agriculture James Troop authored a nature-study leaflet in which he mingled fantasy with factual information: "[Mr. Mosquito] is a bashful fellow, and is always found hiding in some out-of-the-way place, such as swamps and woods, while his mate amuses herself by trying to sing us to sleep so that she may have a good chance to stab us with her little spear and suck our blood."[30]

The use of fairy tales, anthropomorphism, and an engaging teaching style had some important supporters as well as critics. The most famous was the prominent Herbartian Charles McMurry of Illinois State Normal University. In answering the critics who opposed the teaching style of primary teachers, McMurry explained that many educational theories of the day approved the use of such methods to motivate and interest the youngest children. McMurry was correct. During the late nineteenth century, educators who sought to develop a curriculum suitable for kindergarten and the first grades of elementary school revolted against the traditional methods passed down from universities and secondary schools. In their efforts to adjust schooling to the nature of the young child, many so-called progressive educators touted the benefits of fairy tales and fantasy literature, experiential learning, and stimulating teaching methods.[31]

Throughout the first three decades of the twentieth century, critics persisted in targeting women in their attacks against the presumed sentimentalism of elementary school nature study, and they continued to blame female teachers for the relatively poor academic performance of boys. The debate raged on despite published statistical evidence indicating that the proportion of women teachers had actually little or no impact on the enrollments of boys in high schools. In 1909, the conservative educational psychologist Edward L. Thorndike conducted a study to discover whether "the ratio of boys to girls in high schools . . . can be largely increased by increasing the percentage of men teachers in these schools." Based upon a statistical analysis of data collected by the United States Commissioner of Education, Thorndike concluded that "the addition of men teachers has made very little difference, and very likely none at all, in the proportion of male students."[32] Survey statistics published by the United States Bureau of Education supported Thorndike's conclusions (Table 8.1). The data reveal that the growing percentage of women teachers from 1890 to 1920 did not accompany a growing increase in the percentages of public high school female students and female graduates.

Why did more boys than girls drop out of school? Although critics targeted women as the cause, the most powerful influence on boys' lower enrollments and school performance lay in the social and economic conditions of the period. Almost all boys who left school before graduation did so in order to go to work. The industrialization of the northeastern and north-central states had created new jobs in manufacturing and commerce, many of which paid higher wages than could be earned by schoolteachers. In the West, the University of Colorado experienced difficulty retaining its male students during the late nineteenth century, when cowboys could earn as much as $100 a month, and the goldfields lured away young men hoping to strike it rich.[33]

Girls stayed in school longer because employment opportunities open to them before the First World War were less gainful than those available to boys. Another reason was that many young women had to defer marriage, the most common career for women, until a young man could support a wife. A 1911–12 study of girls' employment opportunities found little or no difference in the occupations open to the girls who graduated from school at fourteen years (after eighth grade) and those who left school before graduating. Apart from positions in domestic service, when they entered the workforce, such girls could expect to find low-paying jobs as bundle girls or salesgirls in department stores, as seamstresses, or as low-level factory workers.[34] Another reason girls remained in school, especially through to high school graduation, was to obtain the education necessary for such occupations as teaching or nursing. Teachers and nurses accounted for three-fourths of the new professional women by 1920.[35] In contrast to domestic service or factory work, school teaching afforded young working-class women the opportunity to increase their social status. In a study of the enrollment patterns of working-class students, John Rury discovered that greater numbers of working-class girls

Table 8.1 Percentages of Teachers and Students in Public High Schools, 1890–1920

	Women teachers (% of total)	Female students (% of total)	Female graduates (% of total)
1890	58	57	65
1900	50	58	63
1910	55	56	61
1920	65	56	61

Source: U.S. Bureau of Education, *Biennial Survey of Education, 1918–20* (Washington, D.C.: Government Printing Office, 1923), 497.

than working-class boys continued in school. David Tyack and Elizabeth Hansot have shown that the profemale disparity in enrollments between the sexes was even greater for African-Americans than for whites. They conclude that more African-American girls than boys attended high school in order to prepare for "what was becoming a chiefly female occupation—teaching."[36]

In spite of Thorndike's study and evidence published elsewhere indicating that the proportion of women teachers had little or no impact on the school enrollments of boys, opponents of women teachers found a ready audience for their views in educational journals and popular magazines. In addition to the expressed concern over boys' low enrollments, another important factor in the evident campaign against female teachers was the fact that increasing numbers of women competed with men for administrative positions and offices in professional associations.

Concerned male educators sought to counteract the newly named "woman peril" by creating new professional organizations that focused not only on increasing male enrollments in schools but also on enhancing the proportion of men in the education profession. New professional associations, study groups, and clubs abounded at the turn of the century, for both sexes.[37] Among male educators, one of the most influential segregated organizations was Phi Delta Kappa, founded in 1910 as a national professional fraternity committed to the scientific study of education. The fraternity was an outgrowth of what contemporaries commonly called the "scientific movement in education," a scholarly trend, originating with the development of mental tests around 1890, to apply experimental methods to the solution of educational problems.[38] The bylaws of Phi Delta Kappa limited membership to white male graduate and undergraduate students. In the words of the fraternity's national constitution, "Only white males of good character shall be eligible to membership in this fraternity." Phi Delta Kappans chose new members from the ranks of students at the more prestigious universities; graduates of two-year normal schools were barred unless they had later matriculated at a school of education associated with a university. Women were not eligible for membership until after the Second World War.[39]

In their quest to secure support and career advancement for white males, the various chapters of Phi Delta Kappa were not above admitting members whose scholarship was minimal. That some members of the fraternity were becoming concerned about the low scholarship requirements of the organization is evident from a letter written by Dean M. E. Haggerty of the University of Minnesota's College of Education to William S. Gray, dean of the School of Education at the University of Chicago. In his letter, Haggerty urged the development of scholarly standards for fraternity members. He also noted that the race requirements of Phi Delta Kappa had prevented his chapter from electing "a very capable and personally agreeable Filipino last year." Haggerty suggested, "[W]ith adequate scholastic requirements and a conservative method of election . . . the interests of the fraternity will be adequately safe-guarded against the intrusion of undesirable members of other races."[40]

In spite of Haggerty's concern over academic standards, Phi Delta Kappa members maintained the barriers imposed against women with equal force against African-American men and men from other minority groups. According to historian Woodie T. White, Charles H. Judd of the University of Chicago endeavored to discourage nonwhites from matriculating at his institution by trying to deny them financial aid, even in cases in which they appeared qualified.[41] Segregated male groups were not alone in discriminating on the basis of race during this period. The racism evident in the admission procedures of Phi Delta Kappa also existed among women's groups. For example, the General Federation of Women's Clubs (G.F.W.C.), the largest national club organization, generally attracted white, conservative middle-class women. When Josephine St. Pierre Ruffin, a black clubwoman from Massachusetts, attempted to gain delegate status at the 1900 national convention, the G.F.W.C. denied her a seat. Although the G.F.W.C. never included a "whites only" clause in its constitution, clubwomen did gain the right to veto the admission of any club on the basis of race.[42]

Increasing numbers of male educators joined Phi Delta Kappa, drawn to the organization either because of its exclusive nature or for the professional prestige that membership in the fraternity conferred. By 1922, the fraternity boasted a membership of more than 4,500 in twenty-six of the leading universities of the country. Only eight years later, the organization included eighty-two presidents of universities and colleges and seventy-six presidents of teachers colleges and normal schools among its 12,636 members. According to one of the fraternity's leaders, an invitation to join Phi Delta Kappa was "such a distinct honor . . . that no one has ever declined the invitation to join except for religious reasons."[43]

Membership in Phi Delta Kappa conferred important benefits to both established professionals and younger male students. For one, it allowed men to develop important connections with professionals in different organizations and fields. Segregated female clubs operated in similar ways, with one important difference: Women had much less access to powerful sources of patronage and influence. By arranging its meetings in conjunction with several other highly influential organizations, the fraternity increased the likelihood that its members would be able to form important connections with professionals in different organizations and fields. Thus, Phi Delta Kappa arranged for its members to meet on the occasion of the annual meeting of the National Education Association, its Department of Superintendence, and the American Association for the Advancement of Science. In 1915, the fraternity's national council created the *National News Letter of Phi Delta Kappa*, renamed as *The Phi Delta Kappan* in 1916.[44]

Phi Delta Kappa also encouraged the mentorship and support of young male scholars by reputable colleagues. A stated goal of the fraternity was to boost male enrollments in departments, schools, and colleges of education at both the undergraduate and graduate levels. At Phi Delta Kappa national council meetings, it was apparently usual for representatives from various universities to present their institutions' enrollment data for the purpose of demonstrating that their fraternal activities had boosted male enrollments. In 1923, George L. B. Fraser of the University of Chicago wrote to William S. Gray, assuring him that Chicago's enrollment data would make "a substantial showing" at the next council meeting: "I am proud to quote to you the figures . . . the increase is great. Similar increase was shown in the men graduating a year ago and this past spring—jumping from 14 to 30."[45] In their efforts to increase male enrollments and graduation rates, fraternity members who held faculty positions wrote to each other on behalf of male students, asking for assistance and mentorship. For instance, W. H. Burton, director of the training school of Winona State Teachers College, wrote such a letter to William S. Gray: "This will introduce to you Mr. John W. Goddard, the young man of whom I wrote you some time ago. . . . Both Mr. Goddard and myself will appreciate very much anything you can do in assisting him to find his way about [at Chicago] and in planning his work."[46]

One critical way the fraternity worked to ensure an increase in male enrollment was to help young men find the most attractive and career-promising employment after graduation. Men had long been the preferred candidates well before the fraternity was founded; the deans of various universities and normal schools frequently wrote to each other asking for qualified male candidates to fill vacant positions among their faculty. However, before the founding of the fraternity, faculty members often also recommended women when no qualified male candidates were available. For instance, in 1907, R. H. Jesse of the University of Missouri, Columbia, wrote to Nathaniel Butler, then director of the School of Education at the University of Chicago. Jesse expressed his desire to hire for the position of dean "the right kind of man . . . one of little or no experience because we cannot pay enough to attract an older and more experienced teacher."[47] In response, Butler wrote that the only candidates he and others on the faculty deemed qualified were women: "None of us seem to have been able to make any pertinent suggestion to you in regard to a successor for Professor Hill . . . if you have any positions that could be filled by women, I should like to recommend Miss Grace Lyman, who is a very strong woman, well known to the Graduate Department of this University, and also Miss Lola Maria Harmon, who is now at Alexandria, Missouri, and who has considerable ability in pedagogical subjects."[48]

After 1910, members of Phi Delta Kappa exerted an increased effort to find and place men, rather than women, on the faculties of universities, normal schools, and secondary schools. Women could successfully apply for such sex-typed positions as instructors of home economics or as instructors in primary departments, but men were the preferred candidates for all other faculty positions. A letter from Charles H. Judd, director of the School of Education, to William S. Gray, the dean, illustrates this: "I suggest that you go up to Teachers College [Columbia University] if you have time and see whether they have any promising young men. If you find anybody that you want, go ahead with the appointment . . . We have an item of $3,500 in the budget for Home Economics and I will recommend Miss Coon as soon as I get the data from you or from her."[49]

Several influential members of Phi Delta Kappa played key roles in guaranteeing increased male participation in science education during the decades after the war. They accomplished this by avoiding the democratic process of voting in candidates for positions and relying instead almost solely on procedures of nomination and appointment. This method underlay the formation of the National Association of Research in Science Teaching (NARST). William L. Eikenberry, a well-known science educator at the State Teachers College in Trenton, New Jersey, helped to establish NARST in 1928 as a professional organization to promote the scientific study of science pedagogy. The founding executive committee consisted of Eikenberry and four other men: S. Ralph Powers, Francis D. Curtis, Elliot R. Downing, and Harry A. Carpenter. As NARST's first president, Eikenberry determined the initial membership of this organization by simply presenting his colleagues with a list of thirty-two individuals whose scholarly attainments (or potential for scholarship) he deemed sufficiently distinguished for membership. No women appeared on this list. The prestige of NARST and its influence on science education in subsequent decades is apparent in the names of those who published in its official journal: men (and more rarely, women) from such institutions as Teachers College, Columbia; the University of Chicago; and other leading colleges and universities. Initially, the *General Science Quarterly* functioned as the designated journal of NARST; the name of the journal changed to *Science Education* in 1929. *Science Education* continues to this day as one of the most important and widest-circulating journals in its field.[50]

Similarly, the Association for the Education of Teachers in Science (AETS) was established by a self-appointed group of four Phi Delta Kappa men, of whom two were founding members of NARST. AETS grew out of the visits of S. Ralph Powers, of Teachers College, Columbia University, to various science teacher-training institutions in the 1920s. Powers conceived of the idea of forming an association to bring together the work of these science-education institutions. The initial leadership of the association was in the hands of Powers, William L. Eikenberry, Earl R. Glenn, and John C. Johnson. The association held its first meeting in 1932. AETS endures today as an organization that sponsors educational conferences focusing on current issues in science education.[51]

The professionalization of science education proceeded apace during the 1930s and 1940s with the creation of new associations, academic journals, and a new position in some teacher-training institutions: the professional science educator. During the late nineteenth century, those faculty members responsible for teaching science pedagogy and content had held undergraduate or graduate degrees in a scientific field. However, the proliferation of new professional organizations and journals, along with the development of specialized departments of science education in teacher-training institutions, created a demand for a new kind of doctorate: the Ed.D. (doctorate in education) in science education. Teachers College, Columbia, instituted its first science education seminar for doctoral students in 1925; in 1934, the college inaugurated a doctor of education program in a newly formed department of science education.[52]

The development of departments of science education created new faculty positions in some institutions—positions to which women were not always welcome to apply. William Eikenberry made his views known in this regard, as evidenced by a letter from Victor Crowell Jr. of State Teachers' College, Trenton, New Jersey, to E. Laurence Palmer of Cornell University: "We are adding a new member to our department for next year as you undoubtedly know. A Mr. Harp, a graduate student at Teachers College has been appointed. I was rather sorry that Miss Compton did not get a chance at it but Mr. Eikenberry preferred a man."[53]

During the 1930s, the economic depression in the United States made the job competition between men and women even more acute. Constraints on financial resources severely reduced the number of available positions in schools of education across the country. For example, in 1933, Phi Delta Kappan Clarence Pruitt, a graduate student from Teachers College, wrote to his college mentor and fellow fraternity member Gerald S. Craig that the dean of the School of Education at the University of Alabama had informed him that it was "financially impossible to continue my department next year." Pruitt asked Craig to let him know of any job opportunities in science education. He stated that he was also willing to consider a high school position, because "I am more than interested . . . jobs are more than scarce."[54] Given the economic climate of the Depression period, it is reasonable to assume that established men in financially pressed schools of education, particularly those who were members of Phi Delta Kappa, would have done all they could to find positions for their male students and fraternal brothers.

The scarcity of jobs during the Depression magnified the idea that a fair distribution of work should sustain families, and it intensified the debate over who should work. In society at large, it fortified cultural assumptions about the secondary status of women in the workplace. Although a few considered employment as an individual right, the vast majority of Americans did not. Single women questioned the right of married women to work. In the words of one female Western Electric employee, "[T]he company ought to . . . lay off all the married women first. They should keep them when there is plenty of work but I don't think they should lay off a single girl and keep the married women." According to Alice Kessler-Harris, a public opinion poll conducted in the early 1930s revealed that eighty-nine percent of the public believed married women should remain at home and stay out of the workplace. In 1932, Congress passed the Economy Act, which required that in any reduction of civil service personnel, married persons with a spouse employed by the federal government should be laid off first. Policymakers justified this clause as a means of limiting one job per family during a period when many families had no members employed.[55]

An effort to replace departing female faculty with men continued throughout the decade of the 1930s. For example, in 1934, A. W. Miller, a New York school superintendent, wrote to Craig at Teachers College, Columbia, asking for male candidates to replace a departing female teacher. The teacher, Rose Wyler, had accepted a position on the faculty of Plattsburg Normal School in New York. Wyler had recommended five candidates as successors, of whom four were female. Miller wanted a man, however, and he wrote to Craig in the hopes of broadening the list of qualified men: "If we could secure a man of the right caliber, we would look upon such a recommendation with favor."[56] A month later, Miller again wrote Craig reiterating his desire to replace Wyler with a man. Apparently Wyler had given it as her opinion that no qualified men existed to succeed her. Miller's letter to Craig indicates that he would even have preferred a man of limited experience to an outstanding female candidate: "I take it from Miss Wyler that there does not seem to be an outstanding man lying loose at the present time. If you know of a young man with a couple of years experience, who gives promise of developing into an outstanding person, I should be glad to hear of him."[57]

In 1935, the nation faced a twenty-five percent unemployment rate, and efforts to find jobs for young men continued apace. In education, to a far greater extent than in other fields, men rarely pretended to each other that they were raising academic standards by excluding women. Those seeking to fill new positions often had to choose between less qualified male candidates and more experienced women. For instance, in a letter to Superintendent Miller recommending a very inexperienced male candidate for the position of arithmetic and science instructor, Craig justified his action as follows: "You may be adverse to employing a young man with so little experience. Personally, I feel that at the present time some of our best possibilities are in this group."[58] A survey of public high school science teachers conducted in 1916 concluded that the women teachers had more college preparation in their subjects than did the men.[59] Nevertheless, for women, as for members of ethnic minority groups during this period, a greater amount of professional preparation did not necessarily translate into commensurate employment opportunities.

The emerging professional network of science educators developed a new agenda for science education in American schools. Journal and educational yearbook articles published in the 1920s and early 1930s often promoted such goals as conducting scientific research to determine the most effective pedagogy and content in science education, systematizing science curriculum through the development of textbooks to be used in elementary and intermediate schools, and making school science more relevant to students' presumed social needs and interests. The science committee of the Commission on the Reorganization of Secondary Education in 1920 recommended the inclusion of a general science course in grades seven to nine. The stated purpose of this course was to provide a practical orientation to science by taking into consideration the special interests of adolescent boys and girls. Using language similar to that of proponents of the vocational education movement, the committee recommended that science courses prepare students for specific vocations, such as engineering, or "worthy home membership." Schools, reformers claimed, must be relevant, and science in particular should be made more practical. Science course content should be reformed to highlight the relationships of science to technology, industrial processes, and economic development.

In suggesting content for the general science course, the National Society for the Study of Education's (N.S.S.E.) *Thirty-First Yearbook* recommended including topics related to the concerns of everyday life, such as food, water, air, clothing materials, plant and animal life, heat, light, electricity, sound, machines, the weather, climate, sky, crust of the earth, and the soil. Recommendations proposed for the reformation of secondary science during these years retained the life sciences in their traditional position as foundational to the subsequent study of the physical sciences. Many school districts across the country placed biology—a synthesis of zoology, botany, and physiology—in the tenth grade, where it followed general science and preceded chemistry and physics.[60]

In contrast to earlier generations of educators who had promoted nature study as the science most suitable for young children, after the close of the First World War, educators argued that teachers should give equal weight in the elementary school curriculum to both the physical and life sciences. Questioning the value of learning scientific principles directly from nature, they recommended the introduction of textbooks at the elementary level and the addition of the teacher-centered demonstration method in higher schools to replace ostensibly cumbersome individual student laboratory work. Much of their criticism of nature study centered on the overblown rhetoric of some of its advocates, expressions S. Ralph Powers described as "a blend of science and Romanticism."[61]

In some cases, the rejection of women for positions in departments of science education appears to have been due to the belief that female candidates were unduly sympathetic toward nature study. The repudiation of nature study in the 1930s by the new leaders in science education must have made it difficult for the female students of nature study's supporters to find employment. In one case, school superintendent A. W. Miller wrote to Craig in 1939 to ask his opinion of a female job candidate known for her association with nature-study methods. In his response, Craig supported her candidacy but expressed reservations, explaining, "She has been under the tutelage of nature study enthusiasts for many years. She has come under the influence of the museums, and as you probably know, the museums of the country foster a type of teaching all their own."[62]

The association of women with nature study, coupled with the more general desire to hire men for new faculty positions, had an undoubtedly

Table 8.2 Percentage of Male and Female Faculty in Teachers Colleges and Normal Schools, 1919–1948

	1919–1920	1929–1930	1937–1938	1947–1948
Male faculty	37	41	43	52
Female faculty	63	59	57	48

Source: Data compiled from "Statistics of Higher Education," *Biennial Survey of Education in the United States, 1936–1938* (Washington. D.C.: Government Printing Office, 1942), 45.

Table 8.3   Percentage of Male and Female Teachers in Public High Schools, 1919–1940

	1919–20	1929–30	1939–40
Males	32	35	42
Females	68	65	58

Source: Data compiled from "Statistical Summary of Education, 1939–40," *Biennial Survey of Education in the United States,* vol. 2 (Washington, D.C.: Government Printing Office, 1943), 35.

deleterious effect on women's career opportunities as science educators in teacher training institutions. Although scholars have not collected statistical data on departments of science education specifically, the available data on faculties of teachers colleges and normal schools from 1919 to 1948 reveal that the numbers of female faculty in such institutions indeed dropped after the First World War (Table 8.2). The School of Education at the University of Chicago provides a case in point. When Colonel Francis Wayland Parker joined the newly organized School of Education in 1901, he brought with him thirty of the thirty-six teachers from Cook County Normal School, of whom a substantial number were women.[63] However, in later years, as these women retired, their positions often went to men. According to Geraldine Jonçich Clifford and James W. Guthrie, the proportion of women on the Chicago faculty declined from a high of 22.5 percent in 1910 to 10.3 percent in 1940.[64]

The effort to replace retiring female faculty with men also had a visible impact on the proportion of the sexes in secondary school teaching positions. Here again, researchers have not compiled statistical data on teachers of science specifically, but the data collected on the general population of public high school teachers reveal a distinct increase in the proportion of men from 1920 to 1940 (Table 8.3). In that period, there occurred a thirty-one percent increase in the proportion of male teachers in secondary schools.

REORGANIZATION AND REFORM

The official repudiation of nature study occurred in 1932 with the publication of the *Thirty-First Yearbook of the National Society for the Study of Education.* NSSE's Committee on the Teaching of Science, chaired by S. Ralph Powers, prepared a report entitled, "Some Criticisms of Current Practices." In this report, the committee recommended reorganizing elementary school science on a basis fundamentally different than nature study. "On account of the traditions associated with the name," explained Powers in the *Yearbook,* the committee dropped the term *nature study* in its references to courses in science for the elementary school and instead endorsed a new name: "Science for the Elementary School." According to Powers, the committee "sees a more adequate recognition of its point of view in some of the newly organized courses, which are commonly designated as 'Science for the Elementary School.'"[65]

One immediate and far-reaching effect of the *Thirty-First Yearbook* was to arouse the commercial interest of educational publishers. In his section of the report, Craig argued that the science-education specialist could render assistance to the classroom teacher not only by developing new courses of study but also by authoring textbooks. This was a significant departure from earlier pedagogical views. One of nature study's central tenants had been the importance of studying nature directly from the field; virtually every nature-study handbook published during the heyday of the movement exhorted teachers to refrain from using textbooks to teach scientific principles and to rely on books solely as supplementary resources to an instructional program based on direct observation.[66] Craig, however, soundly rejected this view, claiming "Great emphasis upon Agassiz's advice to study nature, not books, as the essential method of nature study has been at times unfortunate."[67]

Many educators welcomed the systematization of science instruction through textbook study. "At last teachers of elementary science have a basic text," wrote a supervisor of science in the Austin Public Schools, Texas.[68] Certainly the most visible result in American schoolrooms of the influence of Craig and other reformers was to replace the direct, if perhaps incidental, study of natural phenomena with a systematized program of textbook study. Craig himself authored many series of science texts, all of which sold well. When he retired, the annual income produced by his textbook royalties was more than four times his salary as a full professor at Teachers College, Columbia.[69]

Nevertheless, there remained a steady core of opposition among some scientists and science educators to the idea of teaching scientific concepts primarily through books. On one side of this debate stood Gerald Craig at Teachers College, Columbia, and others in the new science education associations; on the other side ranged scientists and teacher educators in departments of agriculture at land-grant universities, biology departments at state colleges, and in some teacher-training departments and private institutions such as Cornell University.

Throughout the following years, Craig apparently taught his Teachers College students to oppose nature study wherever they found it. Years later, in 1949, Robert Stollberg, one of Craig's former students who became a professor of science education at San Francisco State College, wrote Craig to describe his institution as a hotbed of nature study. It is evident from Stollberg's letter that he remembered Craig as having been quite critical of the pedagogy and curriculum of nature study: "Of course you know that this particular region is a very hot spot for Nature Study. Yes, we have courses which are brazenly called by that name and further more they are required of elementary teachers. In them the students learn about classification, preservation, nomenclature, and all those *wicked wicked things* you used to warn us about in class."[70]

Craig's persistent opposition to nature study owed much to the fact that despite its rejection by leading science education organizations, supporters of nature study continued to promote their methods among a more general audience. Nature-study methods found expression in courses for teachers at places like Cornell and in the educational activities sponsored by various museums of natural history, institutions that retained their membership in the American Nature Study Society. Critics of the new textbooks viewed science educators as reviving an antiquated schoolbook-driven form of pedagogy under the guise of progressive methods. Referring to Craig by name in a letter sent to the County Superintendent of Schools in Modesto, California, one nature-study supporter wrote in 1950: "The things he proposed killed nature study, school gardens, and science in the elementary schools. His attempt to revive old methods under new dictums is not likely to result in anything but disaster."[71]

Advocates of nature study held fast to the position that students should learn through direct observation and experimentation. Although they did not preclude the use of books to obtain information, they emphasized the active doing of science rather than the textbook study of scientific concepts. Letters written to E. Laurence Palmer on the occasion of his retirement as professor of nature study in Cornell's Department of Agriculture provide glimpses into this method of pedagogy. Dorothy M. Compton, an elementary school science consultant, remembered nature study as "fishing for four-eyed whirligigs in the pond, or identifying trees by sky-lit leaf silhouettes at night." Another former student recalled an initial encounter with Palmer at Cornell: "I had come up for an interview, to find out if I could do my graduate work under you. I found you in the yard back of Fernow, photographing burning paper to illustrate how forest fires spread under different conditions. You soon had me interested, and helping."[72] According to Leo F. Hadsall, a former student of Craig's who eventually became a professor of biology, Craig issued a stern warning against graduate study at Cornell: "When I left Teachers College, Columbia University, Dr. Gerald Craig's parting words were 'If you go to Cornell, you'll regret it.'" In spite of the admonition, Hadsall did attend Cornell, a decision, he later confided to Palmer, "I never felt the slightest regret over."[73]

In addition to producing a new emphasis on textbooks in classroom instruction, the reorganization in science education contributed to the cultural construction of physics as a school subject with a strongly positive subjective warrant for boys. In a sharp break with the older nature-study tradition, science educators after the war applauded the efforts of local school districts to align science instruction with the specific interests and activities of boys. Nationally, reformers in science education sought to revise the curriculum to place a greater emphasis on the kinds of activities that had long formed a traditional part of contemporary boy culture, such as the building of toy cars and ships, or the electrical wiring of model buildings.[74]

This represented a sea change from the first decades of the nineteenth century, when young women could open their physics schoolbooks and encounter portrayals of refined young ladies discoursing on the underlying concepts of various science experiments. For example, in 1924, the New

York *Herald Tribune* carried a full-page article by Gerald S. Craig, describing the science program of a local elementary school. The entire article concentrated almost exclusively on the activities of boys. Following the recommendations of such leaders as Craig, educators at the school had devised lessons that highlighted the applications of physics to such gender-typed male vocations as engineering, believed to be inherently attractive to boy-nature.[75] First-grade boys, "with the help of the teacher, had wired up doll houses with electric lights and door bells;" in fourth grade, "some boys . . . had been chosen as chief electricians." According to Craig, "It is not uncommon to have forty boys assemble voluntarily to report results of [a] study. One has been collecting fossils, another reports on reptiles . . ."[76] Craig's article made only one specific mention of a girl: a fifth-grade student who wanted to study ants. To assist her in her studies, he explained, "the school sees that she is provided with books that she can read and understand."[77] This solitary girl, pursuing a form of nature study in an environment of boy-oriented physics and encouraged to read rather than experiment, must have felt rather out of place, as undoubtedly did a growing number of girls with scientific interests during this era.

THE AFTERMATH OF THE SECOND WORLD WAR

From 1930 onward, the proportion of women earning advanced academic degrees in the sciences steadily declined.[78] The events of the Second World War did not so much significantly alter as strengthen and extend preexisting trends in American education. The tendency to replace departing female faculty with men gained even greater currency after the Second World War as veterans returned home seeking civilian employment. For related reasons, the curricular emphasis on women's domestic role in the home grew even more pronounced.

At the end of World War II, returning veterans found themselves suddenly in competition with millions of other servicemen for jobs and housing. In response, many women relinquished the work they had undertaken during wartime. One female electrical worker, when asked how she felt about giving up her job, answered: "How're you going to feel? You gotta give him a *chance*, right? The fellow that you took his job and [he] went to the service to protect you and your country, the least you can do is give him back his job or there's going to be a war."[79] Many Americans agreed with this sentiment. According to Alice Kessler-Harris, large numbers of women voluntarily gave up their jobs at a rate that was at least double—and in some cases triple—the rate at which they were discharged. In cases in which women appeared inclined to keep their positions, employers laid off women, particularly in the industrial sectors, when returning veterans sought to regain their former jobs. The federal government also instituted Veterans Preference Programs to give preferential consideration to veterans seeking government jobs.[80]

In an attempt to reduce the sheer numbers of men seeking immediate employment, the government subsidized higher education for veterans.

The Servicemen's Readjustment Act of 1944, known as the G.I. Bill of Rights, provided grants of up to $500 per year to cover the costs of a college or university education and a monthly allowance of $50. With this level of support from the federal government, increased numbers of men flocked to institutions of higher education, swelling enrollments and altering the student demographics in many academic departments, including the sciences.[81]

Many school systems encouraged men to become teachers. College and university faculty members, school administrators, and leaders of government and private funding agencies concerned to find useful employment for returning veterans, promoted school teaching and administration among thousands of unemployed war veterans returning home to civilian work. Such efforts had the full support of the American public, male and female. To entice men to enter a profession viewed as "woman's work" and relatively poorly paid, school districts emphasized the possibility of promotion to higher-paid administrative positions.[82] As a result, the numbers of male teachers and other instructional staff in public schools more than doubled from 1950 to 1960, resulting in a thirty percent increase in the proportion of male teachers (Table 8.4).

Although Ella Flagg Young optimistically had proclaimed women "destined to rule the schools" in 1909, the social demographics of school administrators underwent a particularly dramatic change after the war. Whereas women had composed fifty-six percent of elementary school principals in 1950, by 1960 their number had declined to only four percent. The number of women superintendents declined to the lowest level of the century by 1970. According to Jackie M. Blount, the number of women serving as county or intermediate superintendents dropped by half during the period from 1950 to 1970.[83]

The war also reinforced preexisting notions that schooling should provide a functional benefit to society by helping students adjust to their presumed future vocations. Historians have given the term *life adjustment education* to a movement that originated after the presentation in 1945 of a study titled "Vocational Education in the Years Ahead." The report had been commissioned a year earlier by the United States Office of Education. The study's authors argued that the nation's high school students were

Table 8.4 Teachers, Librarians, and Other Nonsupervisory Instructional Staff, in Thousands, 1949–50 and 1959–60

	1949–50	1959–60
Total	920	1,393
Men	196	404
Women	724	989
% Men	21.3	29

Source: Adapted from "Historical Summary of Public Elementary and Secondary School Statistics: 1869-70 to 1997-98," National Center for Education Statistics, http://nces.ed.gov/pubs/2001/digest/dt038.html, 12 January 2002.

inadequately served by the curriculum offered in public secondary schools, and they recommended that the U.S. commissioner of education and the assistant commissioner for vocational education call a conference to consider the issue of vocational education for secondary students. The ideas presented in this study received the endorsement of the United States Office of Education and its official publication, *School Life*.[84]

What was life adjustment education? One of the movement's supporters defined it as "an adequate program of secondary education for fairly complete preparation for all the areas of living in which life adjustment must be made, particularly home living, vocational life, civic life, leisure life, and physical and mental health."[85] Anxieties about whether working women would make way for returning veterans undoubtedly played a part in life adjustment education, but other, older concerns surfaced as well, pertaining to the kind of schooling most appropriate for the noncollege-bound student.

By the 1940s, state and federal legislation had changed the social demographics of high school attendance across the country. Every state had passed compulsory attendance laws by 1918. Although the existence of such laws did not guarantee that students would attend school, during the years of the Great Depression, as adolescents found it more difficult to find employment, their numbers at public secondary schools increased. From 1918 to 1932, student enrollments in grades ten through twelve in public schools grew more than 200 percent.[86] With passage of the Fair Labor Standards Act in 1938, a new law set a minimum age of sixteen for general employment. Fourteen- and fifteen-year-olds could work outside school hours in nonhazardous, nonmanufacturing, and nonmining jobs, but only for limited hours and under specific conditions.[87] Passage of this act largely eliminated the possibility of employment as an alternative to schooling for students younger than sixteen in secondary schools, and the shortage of jobs after the Second World War restricted employment opportunities for older students as well.

Compulsory attendance laws, coupled with federal restrictions on child labor, altered the boundaries between school, work, and home. During the early nineteenth century, students had enrolled in academies sporadically, punctuating periods of attendance with work or with independent study at home. Additionally, academies had offered a range of subjects at varying rates of tuition, so that students could study only what they or their parents felt they needed to know at any given time. For example, a girl might study privately at home before enrolling in an academy for several terms, leave at age fourteen to teach in a district school, and return to the academy when she had sufficient funds for additional schooling. Academy structure had allowed a great deal of flexibility throughout the earlier nineteenth century, similar in some ways to the structure of modern-day community colleges.[88] Compulsory attendance changed the experiences of adolescent students and altered the perceptions of educators and community members about the nature and purpose of schooling. For the first time, schools expected to accommodate a wide range of youth, a situation that summoned new questions for educators. What should students learn?

Was it appropriate for a future ditch digger to learn chemistry? Should a boy destined to become a carpenter learn about medieval art? Why would a future homemaker—or domestic servant—ever need to know mathematical physics?

Proponents of life adjustment sought to make schooling more practical and useful, and to this end, they evaluated school subjects on the basis of their social or vocational utility. As a result, schools began to offer business English or business arithmetic as alternatives to traditional English and mathematics courses. Historians have documented the long-term decline of student enrollment in traditional academic subjects that occurred during the course of this educational reform.[89]

Some scholars have questioned whether life adjustment education had much impact on the public school curriculum apart from the creation of distinctly "practical" courses.[90] Despite a proliferation of electives at many high schools, most students continued to enroll in many of the basic academic courses, including the general science course commonly offered in the ninth grade. However, an examination of secondary school trends from the perspective of science education reveals that reforms undertaken in the name of "life adjustment" had a very definite effect, not only on the access of high school students to advanced mathematics and science courses, but on the curricula available to those who continued to enroll in the basic general science classes.

As one outcome of the life adjustment movement, physics and chemistry lost their status as core academic subjects required for high school graduation. The Harvard Committee on General Education, commissioned by Harvard President James B. Conant, recommended in 1945 that physics and chemistry be treated as specialized, college preparatory courses and suggested that biology, following a course on general science, be "the last formal science instruction that many students not going on to college will obtain."[91] Contesting the recommendation to give an elective status to chemistry and physics, some science educators argued that all high school students should study the physical and not just the biological sciences. Nevertheless, the principles of life adjustment education had the strong support of the U.S. Office of Education. In 1947, the U.S. Commissioner of Education appointed a National Commission on Life Adjustment Education for Youth and a second national commission in 1950 to promote the concept. Following the recommendations issued by these agents of the federal government, school counselors, when considering the futures of boys or girls not deemed interested or capable of gaining admission to college, directed many students away from traditional academic courses—including chemistry, physics, and advanced mathematics—toward classes of a functional nature.[92]

Life adjustment influenced the content of the general science offered in the core secondary program. Curricula published during the 1950s for the general science classes in American high schools evidenced a distinct trend toward the practical applications of science in preference to in-depth exploration and discussion of scientific concepts. Because a key objective was to socialize individuals for their future experiences as homemakers, workers, or citizens, the curriculum that appeared in general science courses evidenced a fairly high degree of gender differentiation.

Textbooks published for the secondary science market during the 1950s reflected the contemporary viewpoint that many of the topics covered in a general scientific course had little relevance to a girl's future life as a homemaker. Females still appeared in such texts, but their presence was often significantly reduced when compared with the texts used in nineteenth-century schools. Additionally, reflecting the national movement to reform science curriculum along the lines of life adjustment education, schoolbook writers almost always explicitly linked references to women with their presumed vocation in the home or with such gender-typed professions as nursing or clerical work. In those cases in which textbook authors could not easily make such connections, they either referred only minimally to females or omitted them altogether. For example, one introductory physical science text published in 1952 used the traditional conversational format as a means of introducing each section. The authors explained that "Each preview is in the form of a conversation between two brothers and, when possible, with the girl next door." Mary, the girl next door, appeared in six of the sixteen preview sections. The authors included her in brief conversations about health, light, air, fuels, plastics, and electronic devices, including television. She did not participate with the boys in conversations about motion and force, atomic energy, chemicals, metals, or electricity.[93] Similarly, in a section devoted to "scientific hobbies," another popular textbook published in 1955 presented pictures in which boys built models of machines and made a collection of minerals, whereas the girls raised house plants and applied first aid.[94] Among its numerous photographs of scientific men, another well-known physics textbook contained a small sample of women, including such images as a homemaker in her kitchen, a nurse, a medical technician, and a woman using an electron microscope.[95]

Although the gender stereotyping in the curriculum might be presumed to have encouraged more boys to enroll in high school physics courses during the decades after the Second World War, this did not happen. Instead, enrollments in physics and chemistry continued to decline from 1930 to 1955. From 1922 to 1955, physics enrollments fell among both sexes, whereas the percentage of boys and girls in biology courses increased slightly (see Table 8.5).

The drop in science enrollments in secondary schools became a source of anxiety to members of the scientific community, many of whom also expressed concern about the perceived watered-down content of science textbooks and an overemphasis on textbook learning and lecture-based instruction. In 1951, *Scientific Monthly* published an address by Harry J. Fuller, professor of botany at the University of Illinois, in which Fuller attacked professors of education for the deterioration of education in high schools. According to Fuller, the thinking of education professionals was confused, inconsistent, and anti-intellectual, and the practice of substituting so-called societally significant subjects for sound education was to be deplored.[96] During the 1950s, other commentators criticized the anti-

Table 8.5 Percentage of Each Sex Enrolled in Physics, Chemistry, and Biology in the Last Four Years of Public High Schools in Certain Years between 1890 and 1955

	Male students						
	1890	*1900*	*1910*	*1922*	*1928*	*1948*	*1955*
Biology	—	—	—	—	18.5	18.8	19.0
Chemistry	9.9	8.2	8.9	9.1	8.0	10.3	8.5
Physics	22.5	19.5	16.5	11.3	9.4	8.4	7.5

	Female Students						
	1890	*1900*	*1910*	*1922*	*1928*	*1948*	*1955*
Biology	—	—	—	—	16.6	17.9	18.5
Chemistry	10.4	7.4	5.3	5.9	5.7	7.2	6.2
Physics	23.2	18.7	13.2	6.9	4.5	3.0	1.8

Source: Adapted from John Francis Latimer, *What's Happened to Our High Schools?* (Washington, D.C.: Public Affairs Press, 1958), 28. *Note:* Because many high schools consolidated courses in natural history topics under "biology" during the early 1920s, data before 1928 may not be reliable and has been omitted.

intellectualism of the life adjustment movement, including the historian Arthur E. Bestor Jr., who set forth his views in a book, *Educational Wastelands*. According to Bestor, life adjustment education was not only anti-intellectual but also undemocratic. It "enthrones once again the ancient doctrine that the majority of people are destined from birth to be hewers of wood and drawers of water to a select few who, by right of superior fitness, are to occupy the privileged places in society."[97] Spurred to action, in the mid-1950s, the National Academy of Sciences–National Research Council began funding committees to discuss ways to improve instruction in secondary physics, chemistry, and biology. In 1956 the National Science Foundation (NSF) provided funds for the Physical Science Study Committee, a group led by Jerrold Zacharias, a physicist from Massachusetts Institute of Technology.

In 1957, when the Soviet Union launched Sputnik, its earth-orbiting satellite, the opponents of life adjustment education expressed a sense of vindication. For nearly a decade, they had warned about the anti-intellectualism of American education and declining enrollments in science. Here, they argued, was the inevitable result: The Soviets had accomplished a technological coup that effectively trumped the United States on a global stage. Vice Admiral Hyman G. Rickover called for a thorough reform of the nation's schools. Rickover's chief concern was to "put our educational system in the forefront—at least ahead of the Russians."[98] With the launch of Sputnik, the status of American education became a matter of national concern, and the condition of science education moved to center stage.

Rickover argued that schools should focus on the education of the intellectually "gifted and talented" students who might contribute most effectively to strengthening the nation's scientific programs.[99] Quick to respond, textbook publishers developed new books targeting the mathematically gifted and talented. One advertisement for a new math book trumpeted: *"The Race is on!* and high schools are eager to develop the mathematical abilities of superior students in grades 11 and 12 to meet the challenge of the age."[100]

When asked to identify the children who would become the scientists of the future, contemporaries focused on boys. For example, the educational researcher William W. Cooley defined "the Potential Scientist Pool" in such a way as to virtually exclude girls. Based on preliminary research, he concluded that "IQ, scholastic average, interest (time spent in science hobby work), abstract reasoning, and sex were among the more frequently found discriminators." Because it was "safe to begin by assuming that not every high school boy could or would become a scientist," Cooley proposed to refine the identification process by "undertaking a 5-year study of over 700 boys in Eastern Massachusetts . . ."[101] Presumably, the chance that a girl might become a scientist was so slim that it was not worth the effort to investigate a comparable population of girls. The association of boys with science was widespread, not only in academic circles, but in public secondary schools. After conducting a study of the attitudes of high school students toward science in 1957, Margaret Mead and Rhoda Métraux found that the students most commonly identified as future scientists by their fellow students and teachers were almost always male.[102]

Congress reacted to the presumed national crisis by passing the National Defense Education Act on 2 September 1958. "The defense of this nation," declared the opening paragraph "depends upon the mastery of modern techniques developed from complex scientific principles." The Act recommended reforming the precollege school curriculum in mathematics, science, and foreign language; strengthening school guidance services; and improving methods of identifying and educating gifted and talented students. Congress channeled money earmarked for curriculum reform through the NSF. The Biological Sciences Curriculum Study formed in 1959 under the leadership of Arnold Grobman at the University of Colorado. At the urging of the American Chemical Society, a group composed of high school chemistry teachers and chemists, under the directorship of Arthur F. Scott of Reed College, received funding to develop a new course in secondary chemistry, one of several projects funded during the late 1950s and early 1960s. Other projects in secondary earth science and elementary science also received similar monetary support in the 1960s. In a swift reaction against the presumed blunders of the professional education community, control and direction of curriculum change shifted to scientists in the academic departments of major universities. Curriculum developers of the late 1950s and early 1960s focused their efforts on developing a deeper understanding of scientific concepts and bringing scientific inquiry back into coursework. For example, to encourage original investigations in biology, the Biological Sciences Curriculum Study included a series of "Invitations to Enquiry," activities to develop a greater understanding of scientific problem solving. Similarly, the Chemical Bond Approach Project sought to produce a course that would acquaint students "with science as a process of inquiry that interrelates the mental and the experimental." Social relevance remained a theme in these new programs, but with a new twist. Rather than seeking relevance by aligning content with students' presumed future roles in life, curriculum authors included content relating advances in science to contemporary social issues.[103]

The reforms initiated by the federal government in science education during this period ushered in a new era in education, one in which the federal government and specialists in the academic disciplines sought to play an increasing role. The national scope of the federally funded projects and the widespread use of the resulting courses across the country made this, in the words of one scholar, an "effort unmatched in the history of American education."[104] Nevertheless, although large in scope, the reforms remained narrow in focus. The curriculum, rather than the institutional structure of the high school, monopolized the attention of reformers. Among a variety of initiatives funded at the federal or state level, none seriously considered revising high school graduation requirements to bring chemistry or physics back into the core academic program. Instead, in most high schools across the country, these two subjects continued to function as elective, college-preparatory courses. Even as electives, enrollments in chemistry remained higher than in physics, because in cases in which a college-bound student wished to prepare for admission to an institution that required two years of specialized secondary science, the requirement could be met by taking biology and chemistry. Few students persevered and took physics in the senior year. Physics thus remained a science for the few, a course that most educators, counselors, and students viewed as best suited to those students exhibiting special talents in science or mathematics.

Although the federal government threw its support behind curriculum initiatives in 1958, not everyone was convinced that reforming the curriculum would solve existing problems in science education. Some contemporary observers suggested that other factors besides school curriculum and pedagogy might be causing declining science enrollments in the nation's high schools. Studies conducted in the 1970s to evaluate the impact of the NSF-sponsored curriculum reforms initiated in the late 1950s and early 1960s gave belated support to this point of view. The new curriculum reforms implemented in American public high schools during the late 1950s apparently had little impact on secondary enrollments in the physical sciences. Students did not flock to the new courses. In fact, enrollments in physics continued to remain persistently low well into the 1960s.[105]

Some scholars identified negative attitudes toward science as a cause of the subject's problematic status in education. By the 1950s, American views had shifted dramatically, from an optimistic faith that science could solve society's problems to the pessimistic belief that science itself was the ultimate source of society's ills. That the very word *science* was becoming an anathema in some circles was becoming evident, not only to the man and woman on the street, but to scholars in a wide variety of fields. In a Rede lecture given at the University of Cambridge in 1959, the British physicist and author Charles Percy Snow drew attention to a rift in communication and a chasm of misunderstanding between scientists and nonscientists. Snow's lecture quickly came into publication as a book titled *The Two Cultures,* a volume that subsequently prompted debate in academic circles on both sides of the Atlantic. In the same year, the journal of the American Academy of Arts and Sciences produced a special issue devoted to the topic of "Education in the Age of Science." This volume brought together thinkers from a broad range of fields, including anthropologist Margaret Mead, historian Arthur Bestor, philosophers Ernest Nagel and Sidney Hook, and theologian Reinhold Niebuhr.

American scholars expressed the opinion that the ordinary citizen had become thoroughly disenchanted with science. "Science," wrote the philosopher Ernest Nagel, "is . . . often condemned as the ultimate source of many of our major evils. The invention of the terrifying instruments of mass destruction, made possible by advances in theoretical atomic physics . . . has evoked vigorous expressions of widespread distrust of science."[106] The theologian Reinhold Niebuhr echoed this perspective, noting that advances in weapons technology developed during the cold war by the United States and the Soviet Union had brought humanity to the very brink of destruction: "[T]he nuclear weapons that each side has at its disposal are sufficient to spell destruction for both victors and vanquished."[107]

In contrast to the nineteenth-century belief that the study of science could be morally and spiritually improving, Nagel argued that twentieth-century Americans no longer trusted the practitioners of science. Science had come to be seen as "inherently amoral," a discipline capable of furthering "inhuman as well as generous ends."[108] The secularization of science had created an unbreachable gulf between science and religion. The philosopher Sidney Hook characterized religion as having "withdrawn from conflict with science by renouncing any pretensions to speak about matters of fact in the dimensions of nature."[109] Some expressed the opinion that exposure to scientific investigation could potentially be morally corrupting. As Nagel noted, "[A] prolonged exposure to the discipline of science is often believed to develop a trained incapacity for distinguishing between good and evil and a callous indifference to humane values." In contrast to the liberal arts, "[T]he study of science is commonly not regarded as contributing significantly to the development of mind sensitive to qualities that ennoble and enrich human life."[110]

Nagel identified three obstacles preventing science from occupying a prominent place in a "humanistically oriented program of education." First, there existed a general climate of negative public opinion toward science. Second, Nagel believed that a considerable proportion of professional scientists simply did not concern themselves with efforts to promote the status of science among liberal arts educators or the general public. Third, many humanistic thinkers were strongly opposed to the idea of placing any increased curricular emphasis on science.[111]

The anthropologist Margaret Mead also noted a cultural gap between scientists and nonscientists. In her opinion, this division had arisen not

only because of the increasing complexity of scientific knowledge
also because of educational policies that separated students into scie
or liberal arts tracks in precollege schools. "By World War II," claimed
Mead, "the future young scientist was well separated from his fellows, and
at the college level the engineering student was expected to have difficulty
in writing English and to abhor the humanities, just as students of the humanities were expected not to understand and to abhor mathematics." This
perceived opposition of the sciences and humanities appeared, not only at
the college and university level, but in secondary and elementary schools
where educators attempted to identify and track into separate, special
classes those students deemed especially gifted and talented in science
and mathematics. At the college level, Mead claimed, such divisions solidi-
fied, with the result that "students of the humanities, as they lost their hold
on contemporary developments in science, began to stress their monopoly
of eternal values."[112]

The negative attitudes toward science noted by academics and other social commentators prevailed as well among high school students. In 1957
Margaret Mead conducted a study to determine the attitudes among high
school students toward scientists. Her findings confirmed the perception of
a cultural gap between scientists and nonscientists, similar to that described by C. P. Snow. "Increasingly," wrote Mead "school children and
those adults in our society who are not directly concerned with science
have come to feel that science is something different and alien, a discipline
they neither can nor care to understand."[113]

Educational policies aiming to identify and provide advanced math and
science training to gifted and talented students had resulted in at least one
unintended negative outcome: Such policies apparently increased the general perception of the scientist as a pariah. "The scientist is set apart by the
very nature of his interests," explained Mead, "and is regarded by nonscientists as . . . unsuitable, both as a marriage partner and as a friend."[114]

Well-meaning attempts to elevate the status of science among the nation's youth by portraying scientists as self-sacrificing and highly dedicated
to their work had backfired. High school students interpreted such portrayals in negative ways, characterizing the scientist as an isolated "brain"
or a kind of "sorcerer's apprentice." Both boys and girls perceived such
images as repellent. Mead speculated that "In part this repulsion may be
attributed to the shift of young Americans' values away from areas of work
that require long-time commitment and toward their present preference for
home life over careers." Nevertheless, she also noted that the students in
her study generally pictured scientific work as "uninteresting," "boring,"
and "concerned mainly with dead things."[115]

Self-selection, Mead believed, played a large role in sorting students
into scientific or nonscientific academic tracks. Only those students who
excelled at or particularly enjoyed mathematics or physics elected those
subjects. The opinions of vocational guidance counselors and parents,
coupled with college and university entrance requirements, played a part
in forming a student's vision of an appropriate and desirable course of

Plate 8.1   "Four High School Pupils with High Interest and Ability in Science," West Bend High School, Wisconsin, 1967, WHi-3217. (*Courtesy of the Wisconsin Historical Society.*)

study. Additionally, the perceived amount of dedication required to excel in advanced mathematics or science courses led students to believe that a choice for science precluded time for sports, social activities, literary pursuits, art, or music. Mead concluded, "They choose against science unless they have the specific type of mind believed to be 'good at' it and the kind of single-minded devotion to the smell of a laboratory that leads them to prefer working there, not only to going to the ball field or the corner drugstore but also to working in a library or studio."[116] Who, in the opinion of American high school students, was destined to become a scientist? "It is almost always a boy," observed Mead in 1959.[117]

CONCLUSION

From the perspective of the twenty-first century, the toll taken by declining science enrollments in the nation's high schools is painfully apparent. In 1920, women had earned fourteen percent of doctorates awarded in the physical and biological sciences. By the end of the 1950s, when Margaret Mead reported highly negative attitudes toward science among high school students, the proportion of women earning advanced academic degrees in scientific fields reached a nadir. In 1960, women composed only five percent of new doctorates in the sciences.[118]

The documentary evidence presented in this chapter suggests additional factors previously not considered in explanations for women's declining presence in scientific fields during the years from 1920 to 1960. To date, scholars have identified the economic downturn during the Great Depression and the marked rise in births following World War II as important causes underlying this trend. However, although the severe unemployment of the Great Depression and the years immediately following the Second World War clearly heightened discriminatory policies regarding the employment of women, developments in the education community indicate that a backlash against hiring and promoting women had already begun decades earlier, motivated by concerns about women's increasing economic and political power and the so-called feminization of boys. Declining enrollments in the physical sciences at the secondary level occurred well before the Second World War, and although the sharp rise in the birth rate following the war undoubtedly influenced the work patterns of married women and single women no longer in school, it remains unclear what influence this phenomenon had on school attendance or course taking at the high school level. This study suggests that institutional changes in secondary schools, coupled with negative attitudes toward the physical sciences after the Second World War, contributed to a *pre-existing decline* in science enrollments among females, a development that negatively affected the pool of potential science majors entering institutions of higher education during that era.

Institutional changes at the high school level, implemented during the vocational and life adjustment movements, resulted in the removal of chemistry and physics from the core academic program, changes that negatively affected the enrollments of both sexes. As noted in Chapter 7, the rise of home economics at the secondary level occurred in the context of rhetoric advanced by female educators that a woman's proper place was in the domestic arena. The curriculum differentiation that occurred in the science textbooks published during the life adjustment movement simply extended and reinforced this point of view. Nevertheless, in spite of a curriculum that presumably would have had a strongly positive subjective warrant for boys, male enrollments in the physical sciences also fell during this period, suggesting that structural changes at the institutional level—in the form of graduation requirements or changes in admission policy at institutions of higher education—may be far more influential on enrollment trends than attempts to reform the curriculum. The fact that female enrollments in biology held steady during this period lends some support to this interpretation, although other factors may also have contributed to female persistence in the life sciences, a countertrend that is explored in the conclusion of this book.

After the Second World War, cultural attitudes toward science appear to have dramatically altered the way that students, teachers, and parents viewed physics, not only as a vocation, but also as a suitable subject for study. Not only did contemporaries view physics as best suited for boys, but science in general had shifted from a study once perceived as desirable for both sexes to a highly demanding, potentially unrewarding, and possibly even morally corrupting pursuit. Female enrollments in high school physics classes, once proportionally higher than those of males, were virtually extinguished by 1955. There remained few girls to fill the pool of potential female physicists entering institutions of higher education from public high schools during this period.

By 1960, nearly two centuries had passed since Americans enthusiastically had recommended study of "the illuminating rays of science" for both girls and boys. In the midnineteenth century, Almira Phelps observed that young women "have been encouraged to approach even to [science's] portals." Some educators of that earlier era fervently believed there would be no limits to women's progress. "Into what profound mystery of science shall man be permitted to enter where woman may not follow?" This question was posed to an audience of young ladies in 1845.[119] If a girl had been asked, in 1845, what progress women might make in science over the subsequent hundred years, she might have predicted that women would achieve full equity with men in scientific endeavors. If so, she would have been wrong. By 1960, it appeared that many young women in secondary schools had little interest in pursuing the study of science beyond the basic general science and biology courses required for graduation. By and large, those girls who persisted in science congregated in the life and social sciences. As for physics, most girls appeared ready and willing to abandon it to the relatively few boys interested in taking it up.

If a girl had been asked, in 1960, what progress women might make in science over the subsequent forty years, she might have predicted that women would remain a marginal presence in scientific fields or abandon scientific study altogether. If so, she would have been badly mistaken. Three years later, Betty Friedan's *The Feminine Mystique* would launch the late twentieth-century women's movement, and in 1968, President Lyndon B. Johnson would sign an executive order requiring that affirmative action be taken to increase the presence of women in the labor market and the professions. During the subsequent thirty years, the proportion of bachelor's degrees awarded to women in the physical sciences would more than triple.[120] In certain fields and at the highest levels of scientific activity, gender equity today remains elusive; nevertheless, the current picture is not what it was a half century ago. The year 1960 was a nadir of sorts for young women in science education, but like all nadirs, it marked the conclusion of a downward trend and the beginning of change.

Conclusion

By the midtwentieth century, the territory of science belonged to boys. In particular, the physical sciences, once perceived as eminently worthwhile and suitable for females, had become culturally constructed as predominantly male subjects in secondary schools. This gendered transformation mirrored another 180-degree shift in the curriculum, from the colonial perception of the classics as the natural and appropriate domain of males to the twentieth-century opinion that the study of Latin was inherently more appealing to girls than boys.

Societies, like individuals, live with the consequences of decisions made in the past. To a great extent, this study portrays women as active agents in their own educational destiny. In part, the decline of science as a girls' subject was the result of discrimination against women by men in the science education community. This depiction casts women as victims and follows a story line now familiar in feminist accounts of women's experience in the broader history of science. However, a historical investigation of schooling at the secondary level reveals another dimension to this narrative. The decline of young women's interest in science was also an unintended result of broader strategic efforts by women to elevate the status of female education and raise the social standing of women's work in the home. The latter interpretation casts women as active negotiators in their own educational fortune. Earlier in the nineteenth century, when secondary school science was a girls' subject, most women turned their attention and efforts from science to the liberal arts. By the dawn of the twentieth century, when a minority of persevering and dedicated women began to enter the scientific professions, they were all but invisible, not only because many of their male colleagues may have preferred to ignore them, but because the vast majority of American women no longer interested themselves in advancing the cause of science among girls.

There has been a long-standing feeling among feminist scholars that those who identify women themselves as contributing in any way to a lack of female participation in fields like science are "blaming the victim." Blaming the victim can take the form of such assertions as "women simply have not worked hard enough," or "females are not sufficiently committed to the profession," or "girls do not have the mental capacity to succeed." By the late nineteenth century, young women graduated from public high schools with generally the same training in advanced mathematics and the physical sciences as young men. Without doubt, those eager to seek careers in science worked extremely hard to gain entry into science-related fields. It is impossible to read of individuals like Eliza Anna Grier, who spent fourteen years working her way through medical school by returning south to pick cotton every other year, without feeling almost overwhelmed by the effort required for girls to succeed solely on their own merits. The discrimination such women faced at almost every step of the way has been well documented by researchers.

Nevertheless, it is important also to address the evidence that some of the very policy decisions made by earlier generations of women to advance female interests had definite long-range negative consequences for women's continued progress in science. In the midnineteenth century, leading female educators chose to add classics to the curriculum to increase the status of female higher schools and help their students gain entry into institutions of higher education. From the perspective of the twenty-first century, it is impossible to fault this decision in light of the context in which it was made. At the time, the sciences conferred far less prestige and afforded women few opportunities for employment. Although today scholars deplore women's lack of participation in science because modern science represents a field of power and prestige, it is important to realize that this popular perception—largely focused on physics—developed in the twentieth century, not the nineteenth. Women's choice for the liberal arts over the sciences facilitated their entry and increasing access to higher education. As a legacy of this choice, today greater numbers of women than men graduate with bachelor's degrees in liberal arts fields. Nonetheless, adding the classics to the curriculum also negatively influenced young women's enrollments and interest in science over subsequent decades. Similarly, the women who supported the later home economic movement, spurred by the desire to increase the status of domestic work, helped to implement programs in public high schools that added to the drain on female enrollments in advanced mathematics and science courses. Together with the earlier movement to embrace the classics, the addition of commercial and home economics courses to the high school curriculum contributed to a decline in the numbers of young women studying science at the secondary level long before a full-fledged backlash arose against women entering the professions and well before the economic crisis of the Great Depression.

The significance of this study lies not only in its findings, but also in its implications for current policy and practice. However, having traversed a period of nearly two centuries in recounting the story of the science education of American girls, it is worth pausing to review the terrain just traveled before turning to a discussion of its larger significance.

A SURVEY OF THE TERRAIN

The introduction of geography into postcolonial schoolrooms marked an important shift in the way Americans began to think about the education of their daughters. A broad coalition of ideologically diverse groups promoted the sciences in private and common schools after the Revolution.

Americans sanctioned the study of the sciences for their ability to promote mental discipline, foster moral virtue, convey pragmatic knowledge, and increase children's knowledge of God. Although contemporaries often emphasized the role of motherhood in advancing the cause of science education for females, they just as frequently used justifications related to the moral, mental, or psychological self-improvement of young women. Above all, the fusion of Enlightenment ideas with evangelical revivalism strongly supported the expansion of higher schooling for women in general and the study of science in particular.

The sciences flourished in the girls' secondary schools established during the first half of the nineteenth century, a period that coincided with the spread of evangelical fervor during the Second Great Awakening. Evangelical reformers from a variety of Protestant denominations collaborated in educational reforms, including the establishment of higher schools for females. The reported courses of study of such institutions show a greater departure from the traditional classical curriculum and a more visible emphasis on scientific subjects than the curricula of similar, contemporary institutions for boys. Initially, girls studied natural philosophy, astronomy, and chemistry not only to improve their mental discipline, but also to attain culture. Many middle- and upper-class parents endorsed their daughters' scientific studies as a means of developing the culture and polish associated with a higher social standing. Throughout a period in which the liberal culture of a classical education was largely forbidden to females, girls took up the sciences in order to become interesting conversationalists, assist in the promotion of science by making scientific activity fashionable, and to engage in what was presumed to be a morally and spiritually uplifting study.

It has been a long-standing paradigm in histories of science education to date the rapid infusion of the sciences into the secondary school curriculum from the publication dates of such writers as Thomas Huxley and Herbert Spencer in the 1850s and 1860s.[1] This paradigm has been fundamentally misleading. Although the writings of such men as Huxley and Spencer were undoubtedly pivotal in efforts to increase the science curriculum, first at the college, and then at the secondary level, this increase represented a marked change for only half of the American student population. Although the decades after the 1860s saw an increase in the sciences in male colleges, boys' academies, and coeducational secondary schools, the data revealed here indicate that the sciences had already long formed a visible part of the schooling of American girls.

Throughout the antebellum period, educators debated whether young women should study subjects related to their vocation in the home or devote themselves to an educational program designed to promote intellectual development. Some contemporaries criticized the practice of teaching so-called pure science to females, because it seemed unrelated to women's presumed domestic sphere. Among the most vociferous opponents were educators in competing female schools, such as Bedford Female Academy in Virginia or Ballston Spa Female Seminary in New York. This early advocacy of a differentiated domestic curriculum for girls foreshadowed the rise of the later home economics movement and an eventual backlash against the practice of encouraging girls to study advanced science and mathematics in higher schools. Nevertheless, despite occasional protests at schools like Ballston Spa and Bedford, the majority of female schools during the early and midnineteenth century continued to add not only the sciences, but also mathematics to their courses of study.

Although some scholars have surmised that girls turned to the nonmathematical science of natural history because they did not receive advanced training in mathematics, evidence suggests that other factors motivated this shift. As the prohibition against studying higher mathematics diminished near midcentury, growing numbers of girls' secondary schools introduced algebra, geometry, and trigonometry into their curricula. Natural philosophy and astronomy textbooks available to girls included increasing amounts of mathematics after the 1840s, and after midcentury, the mathematical complexity of the most advanced texts used in girls' schools did not differ from those used in boys' schools. Although natural history assumed a larger role in girls' schools from 1840 through 1880, this increase did not accompany a corresponding decline in natural philosophy or physics. The turn to natural history occurred precisely at the time that the level of mathematics offered girls in their secondary schools compared favorably with that offered boys.

A number of variables influenced young women to take up the study of natural history and the life sciences after midcentury. Females took up this science because its study provided them the greatest range of opportunities for meaningful participation, initially as amateurs and ultimately as professionals. In contrast to physics or astronomy, natural history afforded a variety of employment opportunities after midcentury. Perhaps most importantly, both leading male and female figures actively promoted this science among young women. The support and patronage of some prominent and highly influential men in the field facilitated women's participation as science teachers, laboratory assistants, and even as scientists. During an era of general widespread enthusiasm for natural history, female authors actively promoted natural history as an arena of endeavor particularly compatible with women's sphere. Although such authors sometimes attempted to set limits on women's potential roles in science, they also created a noncontroversial arena in which middle- and upper-class women could begin to participate and even earn a living of sorts.

The gender stereotyping of natural history—its cultural construction as a subject peculiarly suitable for women—proved to be a two-edged sword. On the one hand, such stereotyping encouraged women's participation in this science by providing a strongly positive subjective warrant. The subjective warrant is defined as a process in which an individual considering an occupation plays an important role in self-selection by qualifying or disqualifying herself, saying in effect, "This fits who I am, so I can do this."[2] Gender stereotyping also may have assuaged anxiety the male scientific community may have had about women's increasing pursuit of science as a vocation, because much of the rhetoric portrayed women as involved in natural history for reasons of culture, gentility, or aesthetics. On the other hand, by creating a defined realm within which women could participate in science, educators also established limits beyond which a young woman might be viewed as having traduced the boundaries appropriate to her gender. Some contemporary advocates of science expressed concern that a strong emphasis on women's "especial attributes" would keep them permanently out of science. In 1883, Mary W. Whitney of Vassar College warned, "Grace, gentleness, and refinement are regarded as the especial attributes of woman, and the fear entertained by those who disapprove of the study of science arises from an apprehension that those attributes will not be nurtured by scientific pursuit."[3] In spite of such cautions, the fact that leading educators continued to strongly stress gender differences and the importance of separate realms of activity for the sexes possibly set the stage for an eventual backlash against those women who began to enter the scientific professions at the end of the nineteenth century.

Some historians have characterized the appeals to domesticity by late nineteenth-century feminists as part of a calculated effort to gain broad-based support for suffrage, but there exists another plausible interpretation. Since the early nineteenth century, a conservative minority had argued that female education should center on topics related to women's vocation in the home. That these voices grew in strength and influence near the end of the century can be explained by growing tensions among the Protestant majority concerning women's increasing political and economic power. Although historians have generally attributed such concerns to men only, it is important to recognize that conservative women also strongly supported notions of women's separate sphere because of ideological beliefs, and it is from this group that the early pioneers in women's education hailed. Early female educators like Emma Willard, Catharine Beecher, Almira Phelps, Mary Lyon, Zilpah Grant, and others played a pivotal role in expanding higher schooling for women. Nevertheless, it is unlikely that any of these individuals, or others drawn from the ranks of the Protestant evangelicals, would have thrown her support behind the idea that young women should take the advanced study of science and begin to compete with men for positions in the scientific professions. The majority of female educators in the antebellum period would undoubtedly have agreed wholeheartedly with Almira Phelps, who explained, "The object in all the attempted improvements in female education, should not be to lead a woman from her own proper sphere, but to qualify her for the better discharge of those duties which lie within it."[4]

Within the socially sanctioned profession of teaching, women gradually assumed leadership of the nature-study movement, bringing the life sciences—and a curriculum with a strong positive subjective warrant for girls—to students in the first eight grades of school. With the entry of nature study into publicly funded elementary schools, access to scientific activity was no longer generally restricted to the daughters of the middle and upper classes. Women played a highly significant role in the expansion of nature study at both local and national levels. During the same years that nature study reached its height at the elementary level, female enrollments in physical science classes at the secondary level began to decline.

Although it is difficult to evaluate the long-range impact of the nature-study movement on female interest in science, the fact that girls' enrollments in high school biology courses remained steady throughout the subsequent decades may have been due, in part, to the efforts of teachers at the elementary and intermediate level to interest girls in the direct study of nature.

The steady fall in the percentage of girls enrolled in secondary school mathematics and physical science classes, a trend that began near the turn of the century, constitutes a significant factor in women's declining presence in scientific fields during the years from 1920 to 1960. The decline in secondary enrollments continued into the early 1960s and occurred as the result of four social developments: (1) the turn to the classics and the liberal arts among female schools, (2) the progressive effort to make schooling more "practical," (3) a societal backlash against women in science generally and female leaders in science education in particular, and (4) the development of negative attitudes toward science in the aftermath of the Second World War.

The first development contributing to a decline in female interest in science was the midnineteenth-century movement among girls' private secondary schools to introduce the classics in their curricula in order to elevate the status of their institutions. Early nineteenth-century girls first took up the study of the sciences during a period in which educators commonly restricted the study of the classics to boys. During this era, the sciences provided a source of mental discipline and afforded a degree of cultural polish—a second-rate polish, no doubt, because contemporaries had long viewed the classics as the most fitting vehicle for the transmission of liberal culture—but a polish attainable by females. As the prohibition against studying classical subjects diminished during the nineteenth century, more girls began to study the classics in their secondary schools. Female educators introduced Latin as a means of enhancing the status of girls' schools and in order to prepare their students to fulfill the entrance requirements of the collegiate courses in the postsecondary institutions open to women after the Civil War. Additionally, as the contributions of middle- and upper-class amateurs became more marginalized within the emerging communities of professional science in the later nineteenth century, science itself seemed a less suitable vehicle for the promotion of culture, a role now most admirably filled by classical study. As documented by Patricia Phillips, a similar turn to the classics occurred in Great Britain, where Latin persisted to a greater extent in female secondary studies because of the admission requirements of the most prestigious colleges and universities. Inevitably, taking up the classics resulted in a diminished study of the sciences in female institutions on both sides of the Atlantic.[5]

A second factor in the demise of science as a girls' subject was the late nineteenth-century progressive effort to make schooling more "practical," an effort that gained greater momentum just after the Second World War. At the close of the century, educators across the country allowed students an increased election of studies and offered a greater array of vocational subjects in secondary schools. During the same period, many school districts reduced or eliminated their mathematics requirements for girls, impelled by a rising belief that algebra and geometry were not particularly useful studies for a young girl's future role as homemaker. As a result of their declining enrollments in these subjects, for the first time since the midnineteenth century, a growing percentage of twentieth-century girls were without the educational foundation necessary for the study of mathematical physics. The promotion of home economics and commercial courses by high school vocational guidance counselors provided additional encouragement to girls desirous of enrolling in these newer subjects, viewed by many as eminently more practical than algebra, physics, or chemistry. Additionally, institutional changes at the high school level, implemented as a result of the vocational and later life adjustment movements, resulted in the removal of chemistry and physics from the core academic program. As chemistry and physics became purely elective subjects, enrollments dropped sharply among both sexes.

A third development contributing to the decline of the sciences among girls was the societal backlash against female science teachers at the end of the nineteenth century. Within the context of a broader social backlash against women's increasing entry into the labor markets and growing political power, a negative reaction to the growing influence of female educators in general and to female nature-study teachers in particular prompted a policy of discrimination against women in faculty hiring for secondary and postsecondary positions. The inevitable result was a gradual decrease in the proportion of women in the field of science education. Concerned about the so-called feminization of boys, the male science educators who came to dominate newly formed professional associations and agencies during these decades turned their attention to the development of new textbooks and methods of instruction with the objectives of increasing the presence of the physical sciences in the curriculum, making schooling more practical and socially relevant, and encouraging more boys to take up science as a vocation. After the launch of the Russian satellite Sputnik in 1957, the federal government threw its support behind curriculum initiatives and policies designed to identify and train the gifted and talented students who would become the nation's future scientists. When asked to identify those who would become future scientists, contemporaries almost always identified boys.

The changing attitudes of Americans toward science constituted a fourth factor contributing to the problematic status of science in American schools. The contribution of physics to the development of weapons of mass destruction appalled academic scholars on both sides of the Atlantic, a feeling shared by many students in public high schools. The philosopher Ernest Nagel summed it up in 1959: "[T]he study of science is commonly not regarded as contributing significantly to the development of mind sensitive to qualities that ennoble and enrich human life."[6] According to Margaret Mead, high school students characterized science as something "different and alien" and the scientist "as a mad, godless 'brain' or a sort of 'sorcerer's apprentice.'" As a result, self-selection played a large role in a student's decision to enroll in subjects other than science.[7] Whereas in 1890, twenty-three percent of girls enrolled in public high school physics classes, by 1955 this figure had fallen to just less than two percent.[8]

IMPLICATIONS FOR CURRENT POLICY AND PRACTICE

Today, educators seeking to advance the sciences and mathematics among girls attempt an array of interventions. Among these are curricula and instructional methods believed to address inherent or culturally developed differences between men and women. For instance, some curriculum developers advocate a mathematics curriculum that emphasizes exercises in logic and spatial reasoning, mental skills in which women have been presumed deficient. Other educators, believing that women tend more naturally toward collaborative and cooperative activity, stress the importance of developing science and mathematics courses that emphasize cooperative learning, team research projects, and other forms of noncompetitive learning.[9]

Such efforts may be laudable, but this study suggests that the assumptions on which they are founded are misplaced. Girls' interest and achievement in science and mathematics appear to have been historically mediated by economic, social, and cultural forces rather than determined by inherent biological traits or abilities. After all, during the historical period in which girls appear to have been most interested in science—the early and midnineteenth century—no one conceived of the modern notion of cooperative learning; instead, instruction occurred largely through recitation from texts or through lecture and demonstration. Similarly, twentieth-century girls' relatively lower achievement in spatial reasoning tasks may be attributed to girls' decreasing enrollments in high school geometry and other mathematics courses during the earlier twentieth century or to the gender stereotyping of mathematics as a boys' subject during that era, rather than to any inherent biological deficit in reasoning ability. Today, the gender gap in mathematics course taking and achievement has very nearly closed in the United States, and in Great Britain, girls currently outperform boys in mathematics on the national examinations taken at the age of eighteen.[10] This development is difficult to explain if one accepts the notion of inherent differences in mathematics ability between the sexes, because traits and skills that are genetically determined are resistant to change.

What then is the process by which females begin to view a subject as a worthwhile area of study? The contrasting stories of women's growing involvement in natural history and Latin afford interesting cases from which to draw several conclusions. A number of factors stand out from the historical record as having been enormously successful in encouraging girls to take up both of these subjects, including (1) the strong support and encouragement of leading women, (2) the active or tacit approval of leading men, (3) perceived opportunities for meaningful participation or employment, and (4) institutional structures that gave the subjects a required status, either for graduation or for admission to an institution of higher education.

Leading female educators threw their support behind the study of natural history and Latin. Female schools added Latin to the curriculum near the midnineteenth century and encouraged their students to take the subject to gain entry into the institutions of higher learning beginning to open their doors to women. Women similarly promoted natural history, with one difference: Some authors attempted to differentiate the curriculum by portraying this science as eminently suited to women's sphere. To male critics, both Latin and natural history had become feminized by the early twentieth century. Botany and nature study appeared to have become "romanticized," in part because of the elements female authors sometimes included to better align the subject with the presumed gender differences of girls. As a result, critics claimed that the nature books authored by women appeared to be "feminizing boys." Some contemporaries viewed Latin, on the other hand, as inherently more appealing to girls simply because girls had come to dominate in high school Latin classes, not because the curriculum had altered in any way.

The support and encouragement—or at least the absence of resistance—on the part of leading men constitutes a second factor in encouraging girls to take up natural history and Latin. In natural history, such scientists as Asa Gray, Louis Agassiz, and Liberty Hyde Bailey supported women's participation as amateur collectors, museum and laboratory assistants, and teachers. Although young women may not have received overt encouragement to study Latin from leading male classics scholars, men in classics departments in coeducational high schools and in institutions of higher education did not oppose the enrollments of young women in their courses during an era when the numbers of male students declined. The growing numbers of women studying Latin during the same period that men turned to science served to maintain classics departments in institutions that would otherwise have had to reduce their faculty.

A third important influence was the perceived opportunity for meaningful participation or employment. As discussed above, naturalists encouraged women to pursue careers as science teachers, museum and laboratory assistants, and in some cases as scientists. Some of the first lectureships and professorships awarded to women went to those filling nature-study positions in teacher-training institutions and the departments of agriculture in colleges and universities. Similarly, as the numbers of men interested in teaching fell, women filled positions as Latin teachers in secondary schools, a field in which they predominated by the early twentieth century.

Finally, the institutional structure of the educational institutions serving young women played a significant role in influencing female enrollments in Latin and the life sciences. College and university admission requirements had an enormous influence on the subjects college-bound women chose to study. As women began to enter institutions of higher education, they enrolled in Latin in order to meet the entrance requirements still in effect in some schools during the later nineteenth century. As colleges and universities abandoned their classics requirements for admission, female enrollments in Latin began to decline at the secondary level in response. Similarly, when institutions began to eliminate chemistry and physics from their entrance requirements, enrollments in these subjects experienced declines as well. Women's persistence in the life sciences can be attributed in part to biology's placement in the tenth grade in most high schools across the country at the close of the nineteenth century. Institutional reforms at the secondary level retained the life sciences in their historic position as a foundation to the subsequent study of chemistry and physics. When high schools eliminated chemistry and physics from their graduation requirements in the early twentieth century, many girls continued to enroll in biology to fulfill the graduation requirement for science. One result of placing biology in the tenth grade, when it was often a required rather than an elective subject, was that girls continued to study the subject well into the twentieth century. Additionally, a long history of female participation in natural history ensured that in high school biology courses, girls continued to encounter female teachers who could serve as role models and potentially effective mentors.

More research is needed to understand how these factors may interact to influence the self-selection of secondary school students. First, the case of female enrollments in secondary school physics suggests that simply requiring a subject for graduation does not ensure that students will self-select the field for study at the college level or for future employment. From 1860 to 1900, when relatively high numbers of girls continued to enroll in high school physics, the young women who chose to become science teachers selected to specialize in the life sciences and mathematics in preference to physics after they departed secondary school. Second, consideration of male enrollments in secondary physics classes during the period from 1930 to 1960 indicates that the active promotion of a school subject by leading scientists and educators, even when coupled with overt gender stereotyping of the curriculum, is not enough to increase enrollments when the subject is given an elective status and viewed negatively by society at large. It is possible that the critical attitudes toward science expressed by leading figures in the liberal arts during the 1950s may have contributed to a general atmosphere so hostile to the physical sciences that attempts to promote physics among high school boys simply failed to overcome what amounted to an environment of cultural disapproval.

Why did young women not persist in the study of physics? One answer to this question is that in contrast to natural history, none of the above factors existed to facilitate women's entry into the physical sciences. During the late nineteenth century, the physical sciences, once viewed as highly appropriate subjects of study for young ladies, represented a territory distinct in many ways from the life sciences. During the early nineteenth century, there existed relatively few practicing physicists in the United States.[11] Physics began its rise to predominance in American science during a period when many female educators and women's magazines, promoting home economics and specific career paths for women, tended to characterize the physics laboratory as a cold unfeeling place, in stark contrast to the kitchen, classroom, or nursing station. In short, virtually no leading female educators at the close of the century took it on themselves to portray physics as a science appropriate for girls. In contrast to the fields of natural history, in which some of the leading male scientists of the day actively had supported women's participation, documentary evidence suggests that leading physicists took direct measures to limit and proscribe the extent of women's employment in that science, developments that paralleled steps taken by powerful men in many professional fields at the time. As a result, American women had virtually no patronage in physics at a national level. Finally, although biology retained its position in the core academic program of public high schools, policy makers in the early twentieth century removed physics from college and university admission requirements and from secondary graduation requirements, giving the subject an elective status.

Some historians, tracing the roots of physics as a male domain back to the medieval period, have portrayed this science as a realm virtually impervious to female access because of its historical association with male clericalism.[12] However, physics is not the only subject that has been long associated with the Christian clergy; Latin is another. Even a subject with a long tradition of male dominance can become feminized under certain conditions. In the case of Latin, more than a thousand years of association with medieval clericalism did not prevent girls from predominating in secondary Latin classes within a mere span of seventy-five years.

Even today, physics is so deeply embedded in modern culture as a male preserve that it is difficult to imagine the possibility of a different state of affairs. Nevertheless, in the textbooks they wrote for girls and young women, late eighteenth-century female writers often characterized physics as a science particularly suited to the intellectual, emotional, and spiritual development of young ladies. We know that in response to the active promotion of this science at the beginning of the nineteenth century, girls took up the subject in higher schools, and that they did so in proportionally greater numbers than did boys in comparable institutions. What would have happened if physics, rather than the natural sciences, had become the predominant scientific field in America during the early nineteenth century? How might women's employment opportunities have differed at midcentury if physicists required a large, cheap labor force, and insufficient numbers of men had existed to provide it? What if high schools had retained physics in the core academic program, where it was required for graduation? How would young women have viewed the subject of physics at the dawn of the twentieth century if leading physicists of the day had actively defended women's scientific achievements and encouraged their participation in physics teaching and research? We will never know the answers to these questions. However, they are worth asking.

Today, biology continues to be a science in which women have been relatively successful in terms of their numbers and achievement. We take this state of affairs so much for granted that we overlook the fact that the course of events could have taken a different path. After all, at the dawn of the nineteenth century, social mores dictated that women could neither collect specimens in the field nor dissect. Changes in attitudes toward women's participation in the life sciences arose as the result of the rhetorical efforts of both female and male scientists and educators to open the doors of natural history to women. Women moved out into the field under the cover of a rhetoric that portrayed them both as nurturing conservationists and as frail creatures needful of outdoor exercise. Later in the century, women took up dissection, protected by the argument that America required their labor in the field of secondary school science education.

To a great extent, discussions of gender and science that have lumped the individual fields of science into one general category have led scholars to overlook the fact that in the life sciences, women have been inordinately successful. It is not just historians who have tended to see science through the lenses of physics; contemporaries also failed to notice female persistence in the life sciences. For example, when Margaret Mead characterized high school students as holding strongly negative attitudes toward science, it is not clear whether such views pertained to all areas of science. Mead described high school students as opting, via a process of self-selection, to enroll in courses other than science. However, during the time she came to this conclusion, the percentage of girls enrolling in public high school biology courses was increasing nationally, as were the numbers of young women taking bachelor's degrees in the life sciences. During the period from 1928 to 1955, when the proportion of females enrolling in secondary chemistry and physics classes declined, biology enrollments exhibited a countertrend, increasing from 16.6 percent of girls in 1928 to 18.5 percent in 1955. In the life sciences, women have made significant progress in attaining postsecondary degrees. Since 1960, women's share of the bachelor's degrees awarded in the life sciences has been increasing at a faster rate than men's. At the undergraduate level, women reached parity with men in the 1980s, and in 1998, women earned a majority of the bachelor's degrees in the biological/life sciences, psychology, and communications. By the end of the century, the gender gap at the doctoral level had nearly closed.[13]

Today there remain areas in which women's progress has lagged behind that of men, including the physical sciences, engineering, and computer information sciences. Nevertheless, despite concerns about women's progress in the physical sciences, women have gained a larger share of degrees in these fields since 1970. In fact, from 1960 onward, the numbers and proportion of women receiving bachelor's degrees in the physical sciences have been steadily increasing. During the same period, the numbers and proportion of men have been declining, possibly in response to perceived opportunities in such growing academic fields as engineering and computer sciences.[14]

If a girl were asked, in 2002, what progress women might make in science over the next hundred years, she might predict, based on current trends, that women would gain full equity with men in science. Would she be right? It is impossible to say. Past or current trends do not predict the future. American views of gender and schooling have been historically mediated by cultural and social conditions, including ideological beliefs and competition in the labor markets. Debates over gender differences persist today, in some cases reproducing and reinforcing ideas advanced by earlier generations of educators.

Those who emphasize gender differences within the context of science and mathematics education currently fall into two distinct groups. In one camp are those who argue that females, by virtue of cultural conditioning, are more collaborative, less aggressive, and more moral than males and are thus incapable of fully participating in scientific activity as it is currently practiced in a male-dominated society. Some of these arguments integrate the antiscience of the midtwentieth century with earlier nineteenth-century notions of gender differences, producing a contemporary critique of scientific practice that largely absolves women and lays full blame for the evils of science and technology at the feet of men. Those who ascribe to some aspect of this view have suggested that girls might benefit from a form of science education that de-emphasizes those practices and activities most often associated with males (such as competition and strict attention to procedures and rules) and that emphasizes issues of interest to females within the context of collaborative activities that are presumably more suited to girl-nature. The effort to develop a form of schooling particularly suited to the perceived different needs and strengths of girls has prompted a recent movement to establish single-sex private educational institutions.[15] In another camp are modern-day social commentators concerned about the predicament of unemployed male workers and underperforming schoolboys in an age when women's share of the labor market continues to grow. A growing list of books in this genre bear such titles as *On Men: Masculinity in Crisis; The Myth of Male Power: Why Men Are the Disposable Sex; The War Against Boys;* and *Boys and Girls Learn Differently!* Although scientists today are not in agreement about the existence or nature of innate inherent cognitive differences between the sexes, many of these works reiterate late nineteenth-century claims of innate gender differences. In the words of one author, "Males like abstract arguments, philosophical conundrums, and moral debates about abstract principles," and "[b]oys are dominant in logical-mathematical intelligence," whereas "[g]irls are generally better listeners than boys." Those who agree with this point of view support a form of schooling more suited to the perceived differences of boys.[16]

From the perspective of one camp, schooling has "shortchanged" girls; from the viewpoint of the other, it has "shortchanged" boys; both groups would generally agree that coeducation—as it has been practiced in American public schools—has not served the best interests of the two sexes. Although theorists in both categories sometimes target coeducation in their arguments, controversy over school policy, as regards gender, has waxed and waned in debates over education since the Revolutionary period, well before the advent of coeducation in private or publicly funded institutions. Its persistence can be attributed, in part, to the American penchant for viewing school reform as a vehicle for effecting social and economic change.

It is important to recognize the ways that arguments based on oppositional gender differences, advanced in the name of increasing full equity for either sex, can effectively reproduce and reinforce older cultural stereotypes. Culturally developed images of what it means to be "male" and "female" are not fixed but are highly mutable. When feminists argue that science does not fit women because it promotes presumably masculine qualities of rationality, aggression, and competition, they reinforce the notion that such qualities do not belong to females, culturally developed or not. But are not some females highly rational, aggressive, or competitive? As Sherry Innis and others have noted, popular images of women's appropriate level of aggression and competitiveness have changed over the past thirty years, particularly in the media, where depictions of women have become increasingly tougher.[17]

Before educational policy makers accept oppositional reasoning in regards to gender identity and begin to develop policy based on such assumptions, they must ask themselves several questions: When we characterize men as rational or competitive and women as intuitive and collaborative, what is gained for both sexes, and what is lost? What are we saying about women, when we make claims that they cannot function or succeed in a discipline characterized as requiring competition and careful attention to rules and procedures, and what are we saying about men? Do such claims serve all individuals, or do they hinder and hurt some? And finally, how do we profit over the long term by developing policies based on the gender stereotypes that exist at the present moment if such stereotypes are mutable and subject to change? In consideration of such questions, some scholars have recently urged educators to replace oppositional thinking in terms of gender and schooling with "an alternative, more fluid and situated, approach."[18]

When Elga Wasserman interviewed women members of the National Academy of Sciences, one member commented, "Women contribute to the image of who women are as much as men."[19] After having surveyed the shifting terrain of gender, science, and higher schooling over a period of nearly two hundred years, this study strongly affirms this conclusion. It is important to recognize that both sexes exhibit a full range of shared characteristics and abilities and to be wary of arguments—whether they arise from the ranks of female conservatives, male moderates, or radical feminists—that attempt to portray one set of attributes as "male" and oppose another as "female" with implications for women's potential success in a scientific field. The historical record indicates that both sexes have characterized occupational realms and academic subjects as "male" during times when men predominated in them and "female" during periods when the numbers of women reached a majority. Looking to the future, it is important to develop practices that facilitate the development, to their fullest potential, of all young women in American educational institutions and to implement policies that enhance their progress and success in science.

Today at the secondary level, the gender gap in course taking in advanced mathematics and science classes has very nearly closed. Nevertheless, inequities remain, especially when enrollments at the high school level are viewed from the perspective of class and race. For example, national data collected in 1998 revealed that of high school graduates, a smaller percentage of black, Hispanic, and American Indian students enrolled in advanced mathematics, chemistry, and physics courses than did white and Asian students. Coupled with the educational attainment of a student's family, course taking at the secondary level appears to bear on the probability that a student will attend college. Data indicate that taking advanced mathematics in high school increases the likelihood of college enrollment, particularly for those whose parents never attended college.[20]

Throughout most of the early period covered by this book, the females studying the sciences came largely from the middle and upper classes of American society. Understanding the relation of social class and science education in the United States is central to comprehending not only why girls and women embraced the sciences in the first place after the Revolution, but also why some abandoned it so readily during the later nineteenth century. This study demonstrates that elite females began to relinquish the sciences at midcentury in favor of other subjects of study more likely to afford a greater degree of social status and entrance to the more prestigious collegiate courses in postsecondary institutions.

Relatively few girls of the farming and working classes gained access to the sciences in their schoolrooms until the rise of the public high school movement during the last decades of the century. For newly freed African-Americans, such opportunity came even more slowly. After the 1870s, however, girls from a broader range of socioeconomic and ethnic backgrounds studied science in order to become schoolteachers. It was this group that bore the brunt of the social backlash against women science educators that arose at the dawn of the twentieth century. Those who sought to become science teachers faced discrimination not only at the hands of the newly professionalized science education community, but at the hands of their school administrators, teachers, and guidance counselors as well.

At the secondary level, the effort to make schooling more vocationally appropriate for girls appears to have served the interests of white middle-class women at the expense of those from other ethnic groups. This study contributes to the work of other scholars who have recently begun to document the ways in which some of the educational reforms—instigated to better align schooling with women's presumed vocation in the home—reflected an impulse to differentiate appropriate vocational tracks not only along gender lines, but along racial and social class lines as well. Encouraging or counseling girls to shift from mathematics and science courses to vocational and home economics classes not only had unforeseen consequences for women's continued gains in science, but also served to steer females from minority ethnic groups into courses designed to train students for lower-paid work in domestic service. By the third decade of the twentieth century, course taking at the high school level—which tracked students into home economics, commercial, core academic, or college preparatory courses—effectively reproduced the existing social divisions among women in the labor market, where ethnic minorities held relatively low-paying jobs in domestic service and industry, middle-class whites predominated in clerical work, and those whose families could afford the tuition attended institutions of higher education in preparation for higher-paying professional careers.[21] The life adjustment movement that arose after the Second World War simply strengthened and extended existing trends.

This study suggests several areas for further research. In order to know why African-Americans, Native Americans, Hispanics, and other ethnic groups have been historically underrepresented in the sciences, it is important to learn more about the nature of the science education available to them. At different periods of history, how have individuals from these and other ethnic groups viewed the study of the sciences? How have institutional and organizational structures limited or enhanced their participation in scientific fields? Asian-Americans, a group that some state legislators barred from attending publicly funded schools during the late nineteenth century, have made enormous gains in mathematics and science education over the past decades. What factors have prompted this shift? How have the educational aspirations, perceptions, and experiences of recent immigrant groups compared with those of the native-born?

To fully understand the issues involved in women's increasing participation in nineteenth-century mathematics and science education, we also need to hear the individual voices of those early young women who became secondary school science and mathematics teachers. What were their experiences in undertaking a role that previously had belonged primarily to men? What influenced them to take up this particular career path? To what extent were women science educators aware of the social backlash and job discrimination that eventually thinned their ranks in the twentieth century?

Throughout the past several years, audiences at various research conferences have listened to the papers that gave rise to this book and have asked, "Why have we not known this story until now?" Perhaps it is because few individuals interested in gender and science undertake historical research, and few historians of education interest themselves in science and mathematics. Of the relatively small number of scholars who labor in the intersection of the history of education and the history of science, fewer still have considered the historical experience of adolescents. There is much more to learn. To a very great extent, the story of the science education of American girls has only begun to be told.

Notes on Sources

The following notes include all of the primary sources cited in the preceding chapters. A separate accounting of the manuscripts, rare books, postcolonial newspapers, nineteenth-century journals, school reports, and other contemporary sources consulted for this study would produce far more text than most readers want or require. Where appropriate, I have tried to direct the reader's attention to relevant secondary sources that might be of interest. To researchers interested in finding good archival sources, the following discussion briefly describes the most important sources for the primary material appearing in this book.

Several libraries and archives are worth mention here, particularly for the historian seeking good collections of textbooks and published school reports. City school records and state superintendents' reports reveal something of the extent to which educational theories are implemented in practice. The collection at Cubberley Library, Stanford University served as an important repository for this study. The library's collection, amassed by Ellwood Cubberley during his tenure at that institution, contains reports from every state in the country, dating in some cases from the antebellum period. The American Antiquarian Society in Worcester, Massachusetts, represented an important site for rare books and early nineteenth-century school catalogs and circulars.

Late eighteenth- and nineteenth-century textbooks provide essential information about the content, mathematical complexity, and in some cases the gender differentiation of the scientific subjects studied by nineteenth-century boys and girls. For the most part, the books surveyed here are housed in the Special Collections of the Cubberley and Green Libraries of Stanford University; texts from the Bancroft Library at the University of California at Berkeley and the American Antiquarian Society rounded out my sample. It is far more difficult to locate good collections of late nineteenth- and twentieth-century schoolbooks, because few have yet fallen under the protective designation of "rare book." Fortunately, Cubberlely Library maintains a fairly substantial compilation of schoolbooks representing a full range of subjects well into the twentieth century. Specifically focused on science, the Emanuel Rudolph Children's Science Collection at Ohio State University in Columbus is possibly the most comprehensive such collection in the country, although the collection had not yet been fully processed at the time of my visit there. Sadly, while conducting the research for this book I learned that one major library had recently given away its collection of schoolbooks, and another institution planned to eliminate its collection of nature study handbooks in the near future. Historians can help to preserve these important documents by alerting archivists and librarians to their importance.

The diaries of teachers and students, personal correspondence, and the written observations of school supervisors provide a necessary counterpoint to the educational rhetoric advanced at any period. The Southern Historical Collection at Chapel Hill has a strong collection of personal correspondence and diaries related to teaching in the nineteenth century. Additionally, the Southern Education Board Papers include the visitation reports of supervisors to segregated schools for African-Americans during the early twentieth century, and this collection contains material from a variety of southern states.

Although the extant manuscripts of individual educators are scattered in collections across the country, researchers interested in the history of science education during the nineteenth and twentieth centuries will find a wealth of manuscript material in two collections: The Gerald S. Craig papers at the Wisconsin State Historical Society, Madison, and the American Nature Study Society Records at Cornell University. Craig's papers contain decades of correspondence with the major figures in professional science education during the early and midtwentieth century, and the American Nature Study Society Records include correspondence with some of the same individuals and with scientists interested in educational reform. Because nature-study adherents and professional science educators were often at odds over proposals for reform, the correspondence provides a variety of perspectives on many aspects of science education during this period. Also at Cornell, the papers of nature-study leaders Liberty Hyde Bailey, Anna Comstock, and others include memoranda, correspondence, diaries, lecture notes, and other documents bearing directly on the nature-study movement and on more general developments in nineteenth- and twentieth-century science. Archives at the University of Chicago and at the Wisconsin State Historical Society also furnish a wealth of information about the male network of professional science educators that gained prominence during the 1920s. The Phi Delta Kappa correspondence in the University of Chicago's College of Education records illuminate practices of discrimination against women and minorities among professional educators at that institution.

ARCHIVAL SOURCES AND ABBREVIATIONS

California

Special Collections, University of California, Berkeley (SCUCB)
    Mary Beaman Joraleman Scrapbook/Papers
    Helen Swett Letters
    Albert H. Tuttle Papers
    University of California Registers

Special Collections, Stanford University (SCSU)
    Eighteenth- and Nineteenth-Century Textbook Collection, Cubberley Library
    Postcolonial Newspaper Collection

Illinois

Special Collections, University of Chicago (SCUC)
    College of Education Records
    Francis Wayland Parker Papers

Massachusetts

Massachusetts Historical Society, Boston (MHS)
    New England Freedmen's Aid Society Records

American Antiquarian Society, Worcester (AAS)

New York

Special Collections, Cornell University, Ithaca (SCCU)
    American Nature Study Society Records
    Anna Botsford Comstock Papers
    Burt Green Wilder Papers
    College of Home Economics Records
    Cornell University Press Papers
    E. Laurence Palmer Papers
    Elsa Allen Papers
    Susannah Phelps Gage Papers
    Liberty Hyde Bailey Papers
    Clara Keopka Trump Papers
    Albert Hazen Wright Papers

North Carolina

Southern Historical Collection, University of North Carolina,
    Chapel Hill (SHC)
    William Kennedy Blake Diary
    Martha Schofield Diary
    M.C.S. Noble Papers
    Susan Nye Hutchison Diary
    Margaret Anne Ulmer Diary
    Southern Education Board Papers

Ohio

Special Collections, State University at Columbus (SCSUC)
    Emanuel Rudolph Children's Science Collection

Wisconsin

Wisconsin State Historical Society, Madison (WSHS)
    Gerald S. Craig Papers
    Nellie Kedzie Jones Papers
    Department of Public Instruction Office of the State Superintendent
        High School Inspection Reports

Notes

Introduction

1. Almira Hart Lincoln Phelps, *Familiar Lectures on Botany* (New York: Huntington and Savage, 1846), 200.
2. Margaret Mead, "Closing the Gap between the Scientists and the Others," *Daedalus* (winter 1959), 139.
3. For a general review of research on gender and mathematics, see Lynn Friedman, "The Space Factor in Mathematics: Gender Differences," in *Review of Educational Research* 65 (Spring 1995): 22–50. For a review that also includes discussion of girls' interest and achievement in science, see the National Association for Women in Education, "Special Issue: Gender Equity in Math and Science," *Journal of NAWE* 55 (1993). For a discussion of current research on women scientists, see *The Outer Circle: Women in the Scientific Community,* ed. Harriet Zuckerman, Jonathan R. Cole, and John T. Bruer (New Haven, Conn.: Yale University Press, 1991). For recent discussion of female self-esteem and attitudes toward science, see I. Mullis and L. Jenkins, *The Science Report Card: Elements of Risk and Recovery* (Princeton, N.J.: Educational Testing Service, 1988); J. Kahle and J. Meece, "Research on Girls in Science Lessons and Applications," in *Handbook of Research in Science Teaching and Learning,* ed. Dorothy L. Gabel (Washington, D.C.: National Science Teachers Association, 1994), 542–556; Angela Calabrese Barton, "Liberatory Science Education: Weaving Connections Between Feminist Theory and Science Education," in *Curriculum Inquiry* 27, no. 2 (1997): 141–163.
4. Bridget Murray, "Gender Gap in Math Scores Is Closing," *Monitor of the American Psychological Association* 43 (November 1995); American Association for the Advancement of Science, *Science for All Americans* (New York: Oxford University Press, 1990), xviii.
5. John Francis Latimer, *What's Happened to Our High Schools?* (Washington, D.C.: Public Affairs Press, 1958).
6. See Zuckerman, Cole, and Bruer, eds., *The Outer Circle: Women in the Scientific Community,* 12, Evelyn Fox Keller, "The Wo/Man Scientist," in ibid., 230–231.
7. Helen S. Evelyn Astin and Linda J. Sax, "Developing Scientific Talent in Undergraduate Women," in *The Equity Equation: Fostering the Advancement of Women in the Sciences, Mathematics, and Engineering,* eds. Cinda-Sue Davis, Angela B. Ginorio, et al. (San Francisco: Jossey-Bass, 1996), 106.
8. These categories are based on explanatory models in Gerhard Sonnert and Gerald Holton, *Who Succeeds in Science? The Gender Dimension* (New Brunswick, N.J.: Rutgers University Press, 1995), 1–7.
9. For studies of the historical development of formal structural obstacles restricting American women's participation in science, see Margaret Rossiter, *Women Scientists in America: Struggles and Strategies to 1940* (Baltimore: Johns Hopkins University Press, 1982) and *Women Scientists in America: Before Affirmative Action, 1940–1972* (Baltimore: Johns Hopkins University Press, 1995). For a general discussion of discrimination against women in the professions, see Penina Migdal Glazer and Miriam Slater, *Unequal Colleagues: The Entrance of Women into the Professions, 1890–1940* (New Brunswick, N.J.: Rutgers University Press, 1987).
10. See Zuckerman, Cole, and Bruer, eds., *The Outer Circle: Women in the Scientific Community;* Jonathan Cole, *Fair Science: Women in the Scientific Community* (New York: Free Press, 1979).

11. See D. W. Chambers, "Stereotypic Images of the Scientist: The Draw-a-Scientist Test," *Science Education,* 67 (1983): 255–265; Alison Kelly, ed., *The Missing Half: Girls and Science Education* (Manchester, England: Manchester University Press, 1981), Alison Kelly, "The Construction of Masculine Science," *British Journal of Sociology of Education* 6 (1985): 133–154.

12. The following brief list includes landmark feminist works on women and science: Evelyn Fox Keller, *Reflections on Gender and Science* (New Haven, Conn.: Yale University Press, 1985); Ruth Bleier, ed., *Feminist Approaches to Science* (New York: Pergamon, 1986); Sandra Harding, *The Science Question in Feminism* (Ithaca, N.Y.: Cornell University Press, 1986); Sandra Harding, *Whose Science? Whose Knowledge? Thinking from Women's Lives* (Ithaca, N.Y.: Cornell University Press, 1991); H. Longino, "Can There Be a Feminist Science?" in *Feminism and Science,* ed. Nancy Tuana (Bloomington, Ind.: Indiana University Press, 1989), 45–57.

13. Longino, "Can There Be a Feminist Science?"

14. See David Noble, *A World without Women: The Christian Clerical Culture of Western Science* (New York: Oxford University Press, 1992). A popular version of this argument is found in Margaret Werthein, *Pythagoras' Trousers: God, Physics, and the Gender Wars* (New York: Random House, 1995).

15. A short selection of the literature on this subject includes Sandra Harding and Merrill B. Hintikka, eds., *Discovering Reality: Feminist Perspectives on Epistemology, Metaphysics, Methodology, and Philosophy of Science* (Dordrecht, Holland, and Boston: D. Reidel, 1983); Jan Harding, ed., *Perspectives on Gender and Science* (London: Falmer Press, 1986); Ruth Bleier, ed., *Feminist Approaches to Science;* Sandra Harding and Jean F. O'Barr, eds., *Sex and Scientific Inquiry* (Chicago: University of Chicago Press, 1987); Evelyn Fox Keller, *Secrets of Life, Secrets of Death: Essays on Language, Gender and Science* (New York: Routledge, 1992).

16. Muriel Lederman and Ingrid Bartsch, eds., *The Gender and Science Reader* (London: Routledge, 2001), 1–9.

17. For example, see Camilla Benbow and Julian Stanley, "Sex Differences in Mathematical Ability: Fact or Artifact?" *Science* 12 (December 1980): 1262–1264.

18. See Bridget Murray, "Gender Gap in Math Scores Is Closing," *Monitor of the American Psychological Association* (November 1995); Gerhard Sonnert, *Who Succeeds in Science: The Gender Dimension* (New Brunswick, N.J.: Rutgers University Press, 1995), 3–4; Evelyn Fox Keller, "The Wo/Man Scientist: Issues of Sex and Gender in the Pursuit of Science," 227–238. For examples of recent arguments that boys and girls exhibit cognitive differences that are genetic in origin, see Michael Gurian, *Boys and Girls Learn Differently! A Guide for Teachers and Parents* (San Francisco: Jossey-Bass, 2001); Anne Moir and David Jessel, *Brain Sex* (New York: Dell, 1990).

19. J. S. Eccles, J. E. Jacobs, and R. D. Harold, "Gender Role Stereotypes, Expectancy Effects, and Parents' Socialization of Gender Differences," *Journal of Social Issues* 46 (1990): 183–201; J. Eccles-Parsons, T. F. Adler, and C. M. Kaczala, "Socialization of Achievement Attitudes and Beliefs: Parental Influences," *Child Development* 53, no. 2 (April, 1982): 310–321; A. Huston-Stein and A. Higgins-Trenk, "Development of Females from Childhood through Adulthood: Careers and Feminine Role Orientations," *Life Span Development and Behavior* 1 (1978): 257–296.

20. L. J. Weitzman, "Sex-role Socialization: A Focus on Women," *Women: A Feminist Perspective,* 3rd ed., ed. Jo Freeman (Palo Alto, Calif.: Mayfield, 1979), 153–216; Marsha Lakes Matyas, "Factors Affecting Female Achievement and Interest in Science and in Scientific Careers," in *Women in Science: Report from the Field,* ed. Jane Butler Kahle (London: Falmer Press, 1985), 27–48.

21. Sheila E. Widnall, AAAS Presidential Lecture: "Voices from the Pipeline," *Science* 241 (Sept. 1988): 1740–1745.

22. L. S. Hornig, "Women Graduate Students," in *Women: Their Underrepresentation and Career Differentials in Science and Engineering,* ed. Linda S. Dix (Washington, D.C.: National Academy Press, 1987), 103–122; Widnall, "Voices from the Pipeline";

V. Kistiakowsky, "Women in Physics: Unnecessary, Injurious and Out of Place?" *Physics Today* 33 (February 1980): 32–40; S. M. Dresselhaus, "Women Graduate Students," *Physics Today* 39 (June 1986): 74–75.

23. Kistiakowsky, "Women in Physics?"; Zuckerman, Cole, and Bruer, eds. *The Outer Circle: Women in the Scientific Community.*

24. Researchers have come to varying conclusions. Those who found no negative effects of motherhood and marriage on women's productivity in science include H. S. Astin, "Factors Affecting Women's Scholarly Productivity," *The Higher Education of Women: Essays in Honor of Rosemary Park*, ed. Helen S. Astin and Werner Z. Hirsch (New York: Praeger, 1978), 133–157; Jonathan R. Cole and Harriet Zuckerman, "Marriage, Motherhood, and Research Performance in Science," *Scientific American* 255, no. 2 (1987): 119–125. Scholars who have found negative effects include L. L. Hargens, J. C. McCann, and B. F. Reskin, "Productivity and Reproductivity: Professional Achievement among Research Scientists," *Social Forces* 57 (1978): 154–163; Kistiakowsky, "Women in Physics."

25. A brief list of works in this field includes Marina Benjamin, ed., *Science and Sensibility: Gender and Scientific Enquiry, 1780–1945* (Cambridge, Mass.: B. Blackwell, 1991); Elizabeth B. Keeney, *The Botanizers: Amateur Scientists in Nineteenth-Century America* (Chapel Hill, N.C.: University of North Carolina Press, 1992); Ludmilla Jordanova, ed., *Languages of Nature, Critical Essays on Science and Literature* (London: Free Association Press, 1986); Roger Cooter and Stephen Pumfrey, "Separate Spheres and Public Places: Reflections on the History of Science Popularization and Science in Popular Culture," in *History of Science* 32 (1994): 237–267.

26. Thomas Woody, *A History of Women's Education in the United States*, vol. II (New York: The Science Press, 1929), 164. According to Woody, female seminaries varied as to the age of admission, from twelve to sixteen. After 1835, the specified age was usually given as from fourteen to sixteen. Nevertheless, contemporary accounts indicate that younger scholars were occasionally admitted. For example, in a reminiscence of her mother's school, Elizabeth Palmer Peabody recalled, "The qualification for entrance was to read English intelligibly; and her youngest scholars were eight and ten years of age." Quoted in "Letter from Mrs. Elizabeth Palmer Peabody," *The American Journal of Education* 30 (1880): 584.

27. Geraldine Jonçich Clifford, *"Equally in View," The University of California, Its Women, and the Schools* (Berkeley, Calif.: Center for Studies in Higher Education and Institute of Governmental Studies, University of California, Berkeley, 1995), 6.

28. See John L. Rury, *Education and Women's Work: Female Schooling and the Division of Labor in Urban America, 1870–1930* (Albany, N.Y.: State University of New York Press, 1991); Jane Bernard Powers, *The "Girl Question" in Education: Vocational Education for Young Women in the Progressive Era* (London, England: Falmer, 1992); Karen L. Graves, *Girls' Schooling During the Progressive Era: From Female Scholar to Domesticated Citizen* (New York: Garland, 1998).

29. For example, Scott L. Montgomery, *Minds for the Making: The Role of Science in American Education, 1750–1990* (New York: The Guilford Press, 1994); George DeBoer, *A History of Ideas in Science Education: Implications for Practice* (New York: Teachers College Press, 1991). Both of these books omit any discussion of female education.

Chapter 1

1. Jedidiah Morse, *Geography Made Easy* (Boston: J. T. Buckingham, 1806 [1784]), vi.

2. Ibid., title page.

3. C. Johnson, *Old-time Schools and School-books* (New York: MacMillan, 1917), 319–320, 338; John A. Nietz, *Old Textbooks* (Pittsburgh: University of Pittsburgh Press, 1961), 225.

4. Sally Gregory Kohlstedt, "Parlors, Primers, and Public Schooling: Education for Science in Nineteenth-Century America," *Isis* 81 (1990): 425–445.
5. See the discussion in Chapter 3 of this volume.
6. The term *Enlightenment* designates a historical period, roughly the eighteenth century, in Western society. Its hallmarks are the popularization of the ideas of seventeenth- and eighteenth-century European and British philosophers. See Scott L. Montgomery, *Minds for the Making: The Role of Science in American Education, 1750–1990* (New York: The Guilford Press, 1994); Lawrence A. Cremin, *American Education: The National Experience, 1783–1876* (New York: Harper & Row, 1980). The nature of the relationship between Enlightenment ideas and American social and political experience has long been a question of particular interest to historians. For a review of several ongoing debates, see Bernard Bailyn, "Political Experience and Enlightenment Ideas in Eighteenth-Century America," in *An American Enlightenment: Selected Articles on Colonial Intellectual History*, ed. Peter Charles Hoffer (New York: Garland Publishing, 1988), 339–351.
7. See Rebecca Rogers, "Competing Visions of Girls' Secondary Education in Post-Revolutionary France," *History of Education Quarterly* 34 (summer 1994): 147–170; James C. Albisetti, *Schooling German Girls and Women: Secondary and Higher Education in the Nineteenth Century* (Princeton, N.J.: Princeton University Press, 1988).
8. For an overview of the current state of research on geography, see Rod Gerber and John Lidstone, eds., *Developments & Directions in Geographical Education* (Clevedon, England: Channel View Publications, 1996).
9. The primary sources used in this chapter include twenty-six geography textbooks housed in Cubberley Library, Stanford University.
10. Thomas L. Hankins, *Science and the Enlightenment* (Cambridge, England: Cambridge University Press, 1985), 113.
11. From the preface of John O'Neill's *A New and Easy System of Geography and Popular Astronomy* (Baltimore: G. Dobbie and Murphy, 1808).
12. For a description of the paradigm of "separate spheres," see Nancy Cott, *The Bonds of Womanhood: "Women's Sphere" in New England, 1780–1835* (New Haven, Conn.: Yale University Press, 1977). According to Linda Kerber, "separate spheres" always has been a figure of speech that historians have interpreted too literally. See Linda Kerber et al., "Beyond Roles, Beyond Spheres: Thinking about Gender in the Early Republic," *William and Mary Quarterly* 44 (July 1989): 565–581. For an overview of higher schools, see Kim Tolley, "Mapping the Landscape of Higher Schooling, 1727–1850," in *Chartered Schools: Two Hundred Years of Independent Academies in the United States*, eds. Nancy Beadie and Kim Tolley (New York: Routledge, 2002), 19–43. For an analysis of colonial literacy rates, see Kenneth Lockridge, *Literacy in Colonial New England: An Inquiry into the Social Context of the Early Modern West* (New York: Norton, 1974), 38–44.
13. See Joseph Kett, *The Pursuit of Knowledge under Difficulties: From Self-Improvement to Adult Education in America, 1750–1990* (Stanford, Calif.: Stanford University Press, 1996); Patricia Cline Cohen, *A Calculating People: The Spread of Numeracy in Early America* (Chicago: University of Chicago Press, 1982); Edward W. Stevens Jr., *The Grammar of the Machine: Technical Literacy and Early Industrial Expansion in the United States* (New Haven, Conn.: Yale University Press, 1995).
14. See Ruskin Teeter, *The Opening Up of American Education: A Sampler* (New York: University Press of America, 1983), 23.
15. Marcia Myers Bonta, *Women in the Field: America's Pioneering Women Naturalists* (College Station, Tex.: Texas A & M University Press, 1991), 5.
16. Eileen Mary Brewer, *Nuns and the Education of American Catholic Women, 1860–1920* (Chicago: Loyola University Press, 1987), 7–8. Discussion of the comparative numbers of mathematics and classical subjects available to males and females in the late eighteenth and early nineteenth centuries can be found in Chapters 2 through 4 in this volume.

17. See advertisements in *South Carolina Gazette*, 11 May 1734, 17 May 1770.

18. Horace Mann, *A Few Thoughts on the Powers and Duties of Woman* (Syracuse, N.Y.: Hall, Mills, 1853), 57.

19. Quoted in Thomas Woody, *A History of Women's Education in the United States*, vol. 1 (New York: The Science Press, 1929), 225.

20. For discussion of the history of coeducation, see David Tyack & Elisabeth Hansot, *Learning Together: A History of Coeducation in American Public Schools* (New York: Russell Sage Foundation, 1992).

21. The first quote is from Brooke Hindle, *The Pursuit of Science in Revolutionary America 1735–1789* (Chapel Hill, N.C.: University of North Carolina Press, 1956), 256; The second quote is from Wyndham D. Miles and Harold J. Abrahams, "America's First Chemistry Syllabus-and-Course for Girls," in *School Science and Mathematics* 58 (1958): 112. For a thorough discussion of the educational ideas of such leaders as Jefferson, Webster, and Rush, see Lorraine Smith Pangle and Thomas L. Pangle, *The Learning of Liberty: The Educational Ideas of the American Founders* (Lawrence, Kans.: University Press of Kansas, 1993).

22. Morse, *Geography Made Easy*, v–vi.

23. Quoted in Hindle, *The Pursuit of Science in Revolutionary America*, 222.

24. Ruth Elson, *Guardians of Tradition* (Lincoln, Nebr.: University of Nebraska Press, 1964), 6.

25. Horace Mann, "Oration Delivered before the Authorities of the City of Boston, July 4, 1842," in *Life and Works of Horace Mann*, vol. 4 (Boston: Lee and Shepard Publishers, 1891), 367.

26. Jedidiah Morse, *Elements of Geography* (Boston: Thomas and Andrews, 1795), title page.

27. See Kim Tolley, "Mapping the Landscape of Higher Schooling," in *Chartered Schools*, 19–43; Theodore Sizer, *The Age of the Academies* (New York: Teachers College Press, 1964); C. Johnson, *Old-time Schools and School-books*, 147; Harriet Webster Marr, *The Old New-England Academies* (New York: Comet Press Books, 1956), 203.

28. Marr, *The Old New-England Academies*.

29. Ibid., 3; Tolley, "Mapping the Landscape of Higher Schooling, 1750–1850," in *Chartered Schools*, 19–43.

30. *North Carolina Schools and Academies 1790–1840: A Documentary History*, ed. Charles L. Coon (Raleigh, N.C.: Edwards & Broughton, 1915). See the newspaper advertisements for the following male academies: Pittsborough Academy (1800), 35; Hillsborough Academy (1801), 280; Caswell Academy (1802), 18; Franklin Academy (1804), 84; Edenton Academy (1805), 326; Hyco Academy (1805), 22–23; Salisbury Academy (1807), 346–347; Kilpatrick's School (1809), 382. Several North Carolina female academies or seminaries also offered geography during the first decade of the nineteenth century: Fayetteville Academy, Female Department (1801), 60–61; Raleigh Academy, Female Department (1806), 396; Mordecai's Female Seminary (1808), 595; Mrs. Milligan's School (1807), 229; Mrs. Gregory's Boarding School (1808), 295.

31. Quoted in *North Carolina Schools and Academies*, ed. Charles L. Coon, 61.

32. Jesse Olney, *A Practical System of Modern Geography or a View of the Present State of the World* (Hartford, Conn.: D. F. Robinson, 1833), preface, v. The universality of geography as a subject in common schools was also noted by Lemuel Shattuck in his article, "Improvements in our Common Schools," published in the *American Annals of Education and Instruction* (1831): 138.

33. See Hindle, *The Pursuit of Science in Revolutionary America*; Dirk J. Struik, *Yankee Science in the Making* (Boston: Little, Brown, 1948); "The American Lyceum," in *Old South Leaflets*, vol. 139 (Boston: Directors of the Old South Work, 1904), 293–312; Carl Bode, *The American Lyceum: Town Meeting of the Mind* (New York: Oxford University Press, 1956).

34. Quoted in Frank Luther Mott, *A History of American Magazines, 1850–1865* (Cambridge, Mass.: Harvard University Press, 1938), 263.

35. Kristen Drotner, *English Children and Their Magazines, 1751–1945* (New Haven, Conn.: Yale University Press, 1988), 57.

36. Ibid., 63–64.

37. Ralph S. Bates, *Scientific Societies in the United States* (Cambridge, Mass.: Massachusetts Institute of Technology Press, 1965), 33. For the role of the federal government in sponsoring surveys, see A. Hunter Dupree, *Science in the Federal Government: A History of Policies and Activities* (Baltimore: Johns Hopkins University Press, 1986), 36–61.

38. Anonymous, "American Forest Trees," in *American Annals of Education* (Boston: Allen & Ticknor, 1831), 126.

39. The following texts include varying amounts of astronomy: James G. Carter and William H. Brook, *A Geography of Massachusetts, for Families and Schools* (Boston: Hilliard, Gray, Little, and Wilkins, 1930); Charles A. Goodrich, *Outlines of Modern Geography* (Boston: Richardson & Lord, 1826); Morse, *Elements of Geography* (Boston: Thomas and Andrews, 1795); Morse, *Geography Made Easy* (Troy, N.Y.: Parter and Bliss, 1816); Jesse Olney, *A Practical System of Modern Geography* (Hartford, Conn.: D. F. Robinson, 1833); John O'Neill, *A New and Easy System of Geography and Popular Astronomy* (Baltimore: G. Dobbie and Murphy, 1808); Roswell C. Smith, *Smith's Geography on the Productive System* (New York: Paine and Burgess, 1845); William C. Woodbridge, *Rudiments of Geography* (Hartford, Conn.: Oliver D. Cooke & Co., 1830).

40. Hindle, *The Pursuit of Science*, 166–167, 174.

41. See William C. Woodbridge, *Rudiments of Geography*, 2, 34–46; Nathaniel Dwight, *A Short but Comprehensive System of the Geography of Our World* (Northampton, Mass.: S. & E. Butler, 1807), 8; John O'Neill, *A New and Easy System of Geography and Popular Astronomy*, 27–28; Daniel Adams, *Geography: or, a Description of the World* (Boston: Lincoln & Edmands, 1821), 331–334.

42. See J. E. Worcester, *Elements of Geography* (Boston: Hilliard, Gray, Little, & Wilkins, 1831), 264, 267.

43. John O'Neill, *A New and Easy System of Geography and Popular Astronomy*, 399.

44. Reverend J. Goldsmith, *An Easy Grammar of Geography for the Use of Schools* (Philadelphia: Benjamin Johnson, 1804), 48.

45. Mann, "Annual Report for 1848," in *Life and Works of Horace Mann*, 259.

46. Morse, *Elements of Geography*, 46.

47. Almira Hart Lincoln Phelps, *Lectures to Young Ladies* (Boston: Carter, Hendee and Co., 1833), 218.

48. Quoted in Thomas Woody, *A History of Women's Education in the United States, vol 1*, 98.

49. Herman Mann, *The Material Creation: Being a Compendious System of Universal Geography and Popular Astronomy* (Dedham, Mass.: W. H. Mann, 1818), 63.

50. See Lloyd P. Jorgenson, *The State and the Non-Public School* (Columbia: University of Missouri, 1987), 31–34.

51. Quoted in Elson, *Guardians of Tradition*, 51. For discussion of the role played by anti-Catholicism in the common school movement generally, see Kim Tolley, "'Many Years Before the Mayflower': Catholic Academies and the Development of Parish High Schools in the United States, 1727–1925," in *Chartered Schools*, 304–330.

52. J. A. Cummings, *An Introduction to Ancient and Modern Geography, on the plan of Goldsmith and Guy* (Boston: Cummings and Hilliard, 1817), 42.

53. Daniel Adams, *Geography; or, a Description of the World* (Boston: West and Blake, 1814), 113.

54. Frederick Butler, *Elements of Geography and History Combined* (Wethersfield, Conn.: Deming and Francis, 1825), 32.

55. Thomas Jefferson to Thomas Hartwell Cocke, 14 March 1820. Earl Swem Library, Department of Manuscripts and Rare Books, College of William and Mary. On microfilm as part of the *Southern Women and Their Families in the 19th Century* series.

56. Linda Kerber argued that during the early Republican period the ideology of motherhood provided an ideological framework to those seeking a political purpose for women's role in the home. See Linda K. Kerber, *Women of the Republic: Intellect & Ideology in Revolutionary America* (New York: W. W. Norton & Co., 1986), 285–287. Recently, Margaret Nash has theorized that historians may have overemphasized the role of republican motherhood as an ideological support for female education. See Margaret A. Nash, "Rethinking Republican Motherhood: Benjamin Rush and the Young Ladies' Academy of Philadelphia," *Journal of the Early Republic* 17 (1997), 171–191.

57. In contrast to such terms as *moral* or *mental improvement*, contemporaries did not use the term *psychological improvement*. I have coined this term to cover a range of postcolonial justifications for female education that contemporaries believed would contribute to the emotional well-being of women.

58. Charles Carpenter, *History of American Schoolbooks* (Philadelphia: University of Pennsylvania Press, 1963), 27.

59. Bowler, *Evolution: The History of an Idea* (Berkeley, Calif.: University of California Press, 1989 [1983]), 53; Thomas Hankins, *Science and the Enlightenment* (Cambridge, England: Cambridge University Press, 1985), 115. For examples of newspaper advertisements, see those in "Voice of Nature" in *The Democratic Press* (Philadelphia, 3 July 1807) and in the *Franklin Gazette* (Philadelphia, 7 August 1819).

60. Lynn Barber, *The Heyday of Natural History 1820–1870* (Garden City, N.Y.: Doubleday & Co., 1980), 21–26.

61. Quoted in "John Calvin," by Nicholas Wolterstorff, in *The Encyclopedia of Philosophy, II,* ed. Paul Edwards (New York: Macmillan Publishing, 1967), 8.

62. See Ola Elizabeth Winslow, *Jonathan Edwards, 1703–1758* (New York: Collier, 1961 [1940]); Barbara B. Oberg, *Benjamin Franklin, Jonathan Edwards, and the Representation of American Culture* (New York: Oxford University Press, 1993).

63. For discussion of evangelicalism, see Paul E. Johnson, *A Shopkeeper's Millennium: Society and Revivals in Rochester, New York, 1815–1837* (New York: Hill and Wang, 1978); William G. McLoughlin, *Revivals, Awakenings, and Reform: An Essay on Religion and Social Change in America, 1607–1977* (Chicago: University of Chicago Press, 1978); Carroll Smith-Rosenberg, *Religion and the Rise of the American City: The New York City Mission Movement, 1812–1820* (Ithaca, N.Y.: Cornell University Press, 1971).

64. For a discussion of Jedidiah Morse's role as a Congregational leader of the Second Great Awakening, see Joseph W. Phillips, *Jedidiah Morse and New England Congregationalism* (New Brunswick, N.J.: Rutgers University Press, 1983).

65. Anne M. Boylan, *Sunday School: The Formation of an American Institution 1790–1880* (New Haven, Conn.: Yale University Press, 1988), 55.

66. John Ludlow, *Address Delivered at the Opening of the New Female Academy in Albany, May 12, 1834* (Albany, N.Y.: Packard and Van Benthuysen, 1834), 7.

67. Morse, *Elements of Geography,* (1795), preface, v.

68. Quoted in Elson, *Guardians of Tradition*, 18.

69. For a discussion of the character of the Enlightenment with regard to science, see Hankins, *Science and the Enlightenment*, 1–16.

70. See Samuel G. Goodrich, *Peter Parley's Universal History, on the Basis of Geography* (New York: Ivison, Blakeman, Taylor, & Co., 1875 [1837]), 30. See also J. L. Blake, *A Geography for Children* (Boston: Richardson, Lord and Holbrook, 1831), 10.

71. For a discussion of the debates raging in the geological community during the 1830s, see Bowler, *Evolution: The History of an Idea,* 134–141; David Lindberg and Ronald L. Numbers, "Beyond War and Peace: A Reappraisal of the Encounter between Christianity and Science," in *Church History* 55 (September 1986): 338–354.

72. See Morse, *Geography Made Easy* (Boston: J.T. Buckingham, 1806), 74; C. Johnson, *Old-time Schools and School-books*, 322. According to Johnson, Morse included this information in his 1800 edition as well.

73. See Goodrich, *A System of School Geography, Chiefly Derived from Malte-brun*, 101. Goodrich derived the content of this book from the large work by the famous French geographer, whose name gives the book its title.

74. Quoted in Frank Luther Mott, *A History of American Magazines 1850–1865*, vol. 2 (Cambridge, Mass.: Harvard University Press, 1938), 78.

75. James G. Carter and William H. Brook, *A Geography of Massachusetts; for Families and Schools*, preface, v.

76. T. Vinson and H. Mann, *Universal Geography* (Dedham, Mass.: 1818), preface, x.

77. See Rebecca Rogers, "Competing Visions of Girls' Secondary Education in Post-Revolutionary France," *History of Education Quarterly* 34 (summer 1994): 147–170.

78. Jean Baptiste Pierre Antoine de Monet, Chevalier de Lamarck, *Zoological Philosophy*, trans. Hugh Elliot (New York: Hafner, 1963). For a brief overview of Lamarckian ideas in America, see Bowler, *Evolution: The History of an Idea*.

79. Bowler, *Evolution: The History of an Idea*.

80. Mann, "Report for 1847," in *Life and Works of Horace Mann*, vol. 4, 179–180.

81. Mann, "Report for 1848," in ibid., 263.

82. Fredrika Bremer, *The Homes of the New World: Impressions of America* (London: Arthur Hall, Virtue, & Co., 1853), 79–80.

83. See Nancy Beadie, "Internal Improvement: The Structure and Culture of Academy Expansion in New York State in the Antebellum Era, 1820–1860," in *Chartered Schools*, 89–115. The quote is on page 107. For a discussion of the ideology of self-improvement among students in southern antebellum academies, see Kathryn Walbert, "Endeavor to Improve Yourself," in ibid., 116–136.

84. Quoted in Walbert, "Endeavor to Improve Yourself," 126.

85. Margaret Nash, "A Triumph of Reason": Female Education in Academies in the New Republic," in *Chartered Schools*, 64–88. The quote is on page 70.

86. Morse, *Elements of Geography* (1795), 67.

87. Samuel G. Goodrich, *Malte-brun* (1832), 282.

88. "Waterton, the Naturalist," in *The Youth's Companion*, vol. 65, no. 4 (January, 1892), 48. The author goes on to explain that the rider was Charles Waterton, a well-known English naturalist, and follows this opening with a biographical sketch.

89. The most extreme examples in the sample examined for this study are those by Dwight, Olney, and Peter Parley, aka Samuel G. Goodrich.

90. Roswell Smith, *Smith's Geography on the Productive System for Schools, Academies, and Families* (N.Y.: Paine and Burgess, 1845), 11. The following texts are those written in the catechismal format: Dwight, *A Short but Comprehensive System of the Geography of Our World; by Way of Question and Answer* (1813); Goodrich, *Peter Parley's Method of Telling about Geography to Children* (Philadelphia: Thomas, Cowperthwait and Co., 1838); S. Augustus Mitchell, *A System of Modern Geography* (Philadelphia: E. H. Butler & Co. 1860); Jesse Olney, *A Practical System of Modern Geography* (1833); and Roswell Smith, *Smith's Geography on the Productive System* (1845).

91. William C. Woodbridge, *Rudiments of Geography*, vi-vii.

92. A teacher, *American Annals of Education and Instruction* 1 (October 1831): 472.

93. The biographical information about Woodbridge was provided by an anonymous author described as "a veteran in female education" in the *American Annals of Education and Instruction* 1 (September 1830): 421–422.

94. William C. Woodbridge, *Rudiments of Geography*, viii.

95. Quoted in Nietz, *Old Textbooks*, 223.

96. Jesse Olney, *A Practical System of Modern Geography, or a View of the Present State of the World* (Hartford, Conn.: D. F. Robinson, 1832), preface, vi.

97. The quote is from Samuel G. Goodrich, *Peter Parley's Method of Telling About Geography to Children* (Philadelphia: Thomas, Cowperthwait and Co., 1838), 1. In the prefaces to the texts they coauthored, Woodbridge and Willard claim to have developed the inductive method independently. See William C. Woodbridge, *Rudiments of*

Geography (Hartford, Conn.: Oliver D. Cooke & Co., 1829), x; Emma Willard, *A System of Universal Geography* (Hartford, Conn.: Oliver D. Cooke & Co., 1829), xii.

98. The quote is from Will S. Monroe, *History of the Pestalozzian Movement in the United States* (Syracuse, N.Y.: C. W. Bardeen, 1907), 100. For information about the spread of Pestalozzi's ideas in the United States, see Thomas A. Barlow, *Pestalozzi and American Education* (Boulder, Colo.: Este Es Press, 1977).

99. For discussion of the importance of Willard's work at Troy Female Seminary, see Anne Firor Scott, "The Ever-Widening Circle: The Diffusion of Feminist Values from the Troy Female Seminary, 1822–72," *History of Education Quarterly* 19 (spring 1979): 3–25; Thalia M. Mulvihill, "Community in Emma Hart Willard's Educational Thought, 1787–1870" (Ph.D. diss., Syracuse University, 1995).

100. For example, see Andrew Phillip Hollis, *The Contribution of the Oswego Normal School* (Boston: D.C. Heath & Co., 1898), 26–38.

Chapter 2

1. "Classes and Subjects Taught," *Raleigh Star,* 25 June 1813.

2. The academy conducted public examinations in June and November. My description of the school examinations in Raleigh Academy is based on an entry in which Susan Nye recorded her impressions of the June 1815 examinations. See Susan Nye Hutchison Diary, 9 June 1815, in Southern Historical Collection, University of North Carolina, Chapel Hill. A reporter from the *Raleigh Register* described the chemistry experiments conducted in November (see following note). For discussion of Nye's teaching career, see Kim Tolley and Margaret A. Nash, "Leaving Home to Teach: The Diary of Susan Nye Hutchison, 1815–1841," in *Chartered Schools: Two Hundred Years of Independent Academies in the United States, 1727–1925,* ed. Nancy Beadie and Kim Tolley (New York: Routledge 2002), 161–185.

3. "Chemistry Experiments Praised," *Raleigh Register,* 10 November 1815.

4. See Thomas Woody, *A History of Women's Education in the United States,* vol. I (New York: Octagon Books, 1980 [1929]), 563–565. Woody included an appendix listing the subjects offered in 162 female seminaries between 1742 and 1871. Natural philosophy, astronomy, chemistry, and botany were among the ten subjects most frequently listed by the seminaries in his sample, which included catalogs from twenty states. For a more recent survey of the science in antebellum female institutions, see Deborah Jean Warner, "Science Education for Women in Ante-bellum America," *Isis* 69, no. 246 (1978): 58–67.

5. Almira Hart Lincoln Phelps, *Familiar Lectures on Botany* (New York: Huntington and Savage, 1846), 14.

6. J. L. Comstock, *Elements of Chemistry* (New York: Robinson, Pratt and Co., 1839), 4.

7. James Mulhern, *A History of Secondary Education in Pennsylvania* (Philadelphia: The Science Press, 1933), 394; Lorraine Smith Pangle and Thomas L. Pangle, *The Learning of Liberty: The Educational Ideas of the American Founders* (Lawrence, Kan.: University Press of Kansas, 1993), 102–103.

8. Elizabeth Keeney, *The Botanizers* (Chapel Hill, N.C.: University of North Carolina Press, 1992), 58ff. According to Keeney, Amos Eaton and Almira Hart Lincoln Phelps (sister of Emma Willard) were highly influential in promoting this view of the sciences among educators. For an example of similar views in a southern state, see "A Syllabus of a Course of Vacation Reading Is Provided for the Students at South Carolina Female Collegiate Institute," in *A Documentary History of Education in the South Before 1860,* vol. V (Chapel Hill, N.C.: University of North Carolina Press, 1950), ed. Knight, 412–413.

9. See "Jefferson to J. Bannister Jr., October 15, 1785," in *A Documentary History of Education in the South,* vol. II, ed. Knight, 4–5. For a general overview of women's ed-

ucation in the early nineteenth century, see Joan N. Burstyn and Thalia M. Mulvihill, "The History of Women's Education: North America," in *The International Encyclopedia of Education*, eds. Torsten Husén and T. Neville Postlewaite, 2nd ed. (Oxford, England: Pergamon, 1994), 6761–6765.

10. Woody, *A History of Women's Education*, vol. I, 413. Woody noted that Latin was offered in the more prestigious female seminaries after 1810. His sample of 162 school catalogs reveals that more than fifty percent of the schools listed Latin between 1810 and 1870, and approximately twenty-five percent listed Greek grammar (563–565). However, Woody's sample should be interpreted with caution, because only the larger and wealthier schools would have published catalogs during this period.

11. For a discussion on the influence of these female educators, see Anne Firor Scott, "The Ever Widening Circle: The Diffusion of Feminist Values from the Troy Female Seminary 1822–1872," *History of Education Quarterly* (Spring 1979): 3–25; Deborah Jean Warner, "Science Education for Women in Ante-bellum America," 58–67.

12. Emma Willard and her sister, Almira Hart Lincoln Phelps, actively promoted the idea that a woman's education should include solid subjects. See Mulhern, *A History of Secondary Education in Pennsylvania*, 394; Woody, *A History of Women's Education in the United States*, vol. I, 108ff; Thalia M. Mulvihill, "Community in Emma Hart Willard's Educational Thought, 1787–1870" (Ph.D. diss., Syracuse University, 1995).

13. The samples of newspaper advertisements used in this study were selected on the basis of the specificity of their content. In many cases, it was not possible to tell from the advertisement whether the school served males or females, or both. Nor, in all cases, was the entire course of study provided. Some advertisers claimed to offer "the usual branches of education" in their schools, and such advertisements were too vague to be included in the samples. The samples included here are drawn from advertisements that clearly specified the gender served in the school and provided a detailed course of study.

14. See Woody, *A History of Women's Education in the United States*, vol. I, 415.

15. *Raleigh Register* (7 July 1831), in *North Carolina Schools and Academies 1790–1840: A Documentary History*, ed. Charles L. Coon (Raleigh, N.C.: 1915), 533.

16. See Chapter 7 of this volume for a discussion of the rise of classics in female institutions during the nineteenth century.

17. Quoted in *North Carolina Schools and Academies*, ed. Coon, 79.

18. Quoted in Vera M. Butler, *Education as Revealed by New England Newspapers Prior to 1850* (Ph.D. diss., Temple University, 1935), 188.

19. Alexis de Toqueville, *Democracy in America* (New York: HarperPerennial, 1969), 591.

20. Frances Trollope, *Domestic Manners of the Americans* (New York: Alfred A. Knopf, 1949 [1832]), 82, 340ff.

21. Fredrika Bremer, *America of the Fifties: Letters of Fredrika Bremer*, ed. Adolph B. Benson (N.Y.: The American-Scandinavian Foundation, 1924), 285.

22. Richard G. Parker, *Juvenile Philosophy: or, Philosophy in Familiar Conversations* (New York, 1857 [1850]), 15.

23. See "Carmelite Sisters' Academy" in the *Baltimore Sun*, 12 August 1842.

24. Nikola Baumgarten, "Education and Democracy in Frontier St. Louis: The Society of the Sacred Heart," *History of Education Quarterly* 34 (summer 1994): 171–192.

25. Devon A. Mihesuah, *Cultivating the Rosebuds: The Education of Women at the Cherokee Female Seminary, 1851–1909* (Urbana, Ill.: University of Illinois Press, 1993), 21.

26. Ibid., 27.

27. Ibid.

28. Brenda Stevenson, ed. *The Journals of Charlotte Forten Grimké* (New York: Oxford University Press, 1988), 1–31, 62, 82, 89, 105, 107–108, 122. The quote is from her entry of 28 May 1854.

29. Linda M. Perkins, *Fanny Jackson Coppin and the Institute for Colored Youth, 1865–1902* (New York: Garland, 1987); Brenda Galloway-Wright, "Cole, Rebecca J.

(1846–1922)," *Black Women in America: An Historical Encyclopedia* (Brooklyn, N.Y.: Carlson Publishing, 1993): 261–262.

30.   This conclusion is based on an analysis of the newspaper advertisements mentioned in the above tables. Out of a sample of twenty-four girls' schools in New England states from 1820 to 1842, forty-two percent advertised Latin, usually offered on an elective basis, in contrast to forty-seven percent of a sample of fifteen boys' schools.

31.   New Bern Academy in Craven County, Fayetteville Academy in Cumberland County, Tarborough Academy in Edgecome County, Greensborough Academy in Guilford County, Vine Hill Academy in Halifax County, Salisbury Academy in Rowan County, and Raleigh Academy in Wake County.

32.   Beadie, "Emma Willard's Idea Put to the Test: The Consequences of State Support of Female Education in New York, 1819–67," *History of Education Quarterly* 33 (Winter, 1993): 560 n.

33.   Quoted in Harriet Webster Marr, *The Old New-England Academies Founded Before 1826* (N.Y.: Comet Press Books, 1956), 247.

34.   See *Western Carolinian* (19 September 1820) in *North Carolina Schools*, ed. Coon, 360.

35.   Ibid., 399.

36.   This was a common practice of the Classical School in Charlottesville, Virginia, from 1835 to 1836. See the *Richmond Enquirer* (10 November 1835), which advertises its course of study, and the issue for 29 December 1835, which reports its examinations.

37.   *The Catawba Journal* (5 December 1826), in *North Carolina Schools*, ed. Coon, 235–236; see also the *Raleigh Star* (10 January 1812) in ibid., 601. The examiners report discusses the students' extensive knowledge of astronomy in Mordecai's Female Academy in Warrenton, North Carolina.

38.   "Boston Grammar and Writing Schools," *The Common School Journal* 7 (15 October 1845): 311–317. Lengthy extracts from the report of the Boston School Committee were published in numbers 19–23 of the *Journal* in 1845; Otis W. Caldwell and Stuart A. Courtis, *Then and Now in Education: 1845–1923* (Yonkers-on-Hudson, N.Y.: World Book Co., 1925), 11, 14.

39.   According to the school committee report, one of the nine coeducational schools was set apart "for colored children." See Caldwell and Courtis, *Then and Now*, 11.

40.   Caldwell and Courtis, *Then and Now*. It is possible to distinguish girls' schools from boys' schools from information given in extracts of the Boston School Committee Report (222–226). Copies of the original tests are reproduced both in Caldwell and Courtis's text and in *The Common School Journal* 7 (1 December 1845): 361–363.

41.   Caldwell and Courtis, *Then and Now*, 168–169.

42.   Ibid., 342–344.

43.   Ibid., 182, 229.

44.   Ibid., 342–344. In fact, the girls' schools Bowdoin and Wells ranked within the top three schools on each of the remaining examinations as well, a phenomenon that must be interpreted with caution. Generally, girls stayed in school longer than boys. In Boston, boys were required to leave school at the end of the term after their fourteenth birthday, whereas girls could remain until the end of the term after their sixteenth birthday. The average age of the girls examined at Bowdoin was fourteen years, eight months, whereas the average age of the boys at Brimmer was thirteen years. Of course, age alone does not account for all the differences in scores. On the history examination, for example, boys from Adams School, whose average age was only twelve years and eleven months, outscored the girls from Wells, whose average age was thirteen years and three months (see pages 14, 330).

45.   Ibid., 184.

46.   Mulhern, *A History of Secondary Education in Pennsylvania*, 323–324; Woody, *A History of Women's Education in the United States*, vol. II, 163ff.

47.   Daniel J. Kevles, *The Physicists: The History of a Scientific Community in Modern America* (Cambridge, Mass.: Harvard University Press, 1987), 12.

48. Quoted in Ruth Arline Wray, *The History of Secondary Education in Cumberland and Sagadahoc Counties in Maine* (Orono, Me.: University of Maine Press, 1940), 47.

49. As late as 1864, the state superintendent of Pennsylvania reported that "It is not probable that more than one-eighth of the students in the academies and seminaries pass on through a college course." Quoted in Rev. J. Fraser, *Report on the Common School System of the United States and of the Provinces of Upper and Lower Canada* (1867), mf 73.216–220, 106, Jonsson Library of Government Documents, Stanford University.

50. Quoted in Patricia Phillips, *The Scientific Lady: A Social History of Women's Scientific Interests, 1520–1918* (London: Weidenfeld and Nicolson, 1990), 240.

51. Edward W. Stevens Jr., *The Grammar of the Machine: Technical Literacy and Early Industrial Expansion in the United States* (New Haven, Conn.: Yale University Press, 1995): 118–123.

52. Linda M. Perkins, *Fanny Jackson Coppin and the Institute for Colored Youth, 1865–1902* (New York: Garland, 1987), 68.

53. William Hooper, "Imperfections of Our Primary Schools," in *North Carolina Schools*, ed. Coon, 729–750. Hooper was professor of ancient language at the University of North Carolina.

54. Quoted in Rev. Benjamin F. Farnsworth, A.M., "Female Classical Seminary, At Worcester, Massachusetts, February 8, 1825," 6, in Catalogues, American Antiquarian Society (AAS); Ralph S. Bates, *Scientific Societies in the United States* (Cambridge, Mass.: Massachusetts Institute of Technology Press, 1965 [1945]), 33; A. Hunter Dupree, *Science in the Federal Government: A History of Policies and Activities* (Baltimore: The Johns Hopkins University Press, 1986), 383–386.

55. "Geological Studies," *American Annals of Education* 1 (October/November, 1830): 141.

56. "Lucy Millington," unpublished manuscript by Liberty Hyde Bailey, file 1, box 8, Liberty Hyde Bailey Papers, Special Collections, Cornell University. Bailey, who grew up in South Haven, Michigan, wrote that he had seen only one botanist, a visiting lecturer in the town lyceum, before meeting Lucy Millington in 1876. The relationship of Bailey and Millington is further explored in Chapter 5.

57. Data compiled from Mulhern, *A History of Secondary Education in Pennsylvania*, 328. Mulhern's sample of forty-seven academies (1750–1829) reveals that nine percent offered mensuration, nineteen percent surveying, and thirteen percent navigation. Data compiled from *North Carolina Schools and Academies*, ed. Coon: The advertisements of fifty-six academies from the period 1794 to 1840 reveal that nine percent offered mensuration, twenty-nine percent surveying, and thirteen percent navigation.

58. See "Evening School," *Columbian Centinal* (Boston, Massachusetts, 6 October 1827); "A Night School," *Raleigh Register* (30 September 1828), in *North Carolina Schools and Academies,* ed. Coon, 494; Mulhern, *A History of Secondary Education in Pennsylvania*, 472.

59. "A Night School," *Raleigh Register* (30 September 1828), in *North Carolina Schools and Academies,* ed. Coon, 494.

60. Per Siljestrom, *The Educational Institutions of the United States, Their Character and Organization* (London: John Chapman, 1853), 393.

61. Mulhern, *A History of Secondary Education in Pennsylvania*, 323; Woody, *A History of Women's Education in the United States,* vol. II, 163.

62. Quoted in Mulhern, *A History of Secondary Education in Pennsylvania*, 391.

63. The exchange of ideas between America and Europe is discussed in Bernard Bailyn, "Political Experience and Enlightenment Ideas in Eighteenth-Century America," in *An American Enlightenment*, ed. Peter Charles Hoffer (New York: Garland Publishing, 1988), 339–351. For an overview of women's participation in natural history and their authorship of popular science books for women, see Marcia Myers Bonta, *Women in the Field: America's Pioneering Women Naturalists* (College Station, Tex.: Texas A & M University Press, 1991); Vera Norwood, *Made from This Earth: American Women and Nature* (Chapel Hill, N.C.: University of North Carolina Press, 1993).

64. Writing in 1850, Susan Fenimore Cooper noted the introduction of scientific subjects into the curriculum of common schools in her community. See Susan Fenimore Cooper, *Rural Hours* (New York: George P. Putnam, 1850), 361, 366. Cooper cautioned that the introduction of the sciences into the curriculum came at the cost of a neglect of religious and moral instruction.

65. See Margaret Rossiter, *Women Scientists in America: Struggles and Strategies to 1940* (Baltimore: Johns Hopkins University Press, 1882), 1–28; Lynn Barber, *The Heyday of Natural History, 1820–1870* (Garden City, N.Y.: Doubleday and Co., 1980); Keeney, *The Botanizers.*

66. Almira Hart Lincoln Phelps, *Familiar Lectures on Botany* (N.Y.: Huntington and Savage, 1846), 200. William Johnston, *An Address on Female Education* (Columbus, Ohio: Charles Scott & Co., 1845), 16.

Chapter 3

1. "Bedford Female Academy," *Richmond Enquirer,* 3 November 1837.
2. Ibid.
3. Thomas Cary Johnson Jr., *Scientific Interests in the Old South* (New York: D. Appleton-Century Co., 1936), 106–125. Largely on the basis of subject listings in girls' courses of study, Johnson concluded that southern women were "remarkably well informed" about science (125). Deborah Jean Warner, "Science Education for Women in Ante-bellum America," *Isis* 69 (1978): 58–67. Warner argued that knowing the identity of the faculty members responsible for science instruction in female schools is indicative of what science a student might have learned. However, this argument has two serious drawbacks. First, although some science educators in female seminaries were widely esteemed by contemporaries for their scientific knowledge, they nonetheless may have simplified their science curriculum for a female audience. Second, identifying faculty members in female seminaries is problematic because of the lack of extant records. Christie Anne Farnham, *The Education of the Southern Belle: Higher Education and Student Socialization in the Ante-bellum South* (New York: New York University Press, 1994). From an examination of the courses and apparatus listed in college circulars, Farnham concluded that female colleges compared favorably with male colleges in the number and level of science courses offered. However, Farnham did not discuss the textbooks used by respective institutions.
4. I used the following method to distinguish texts likely to have appeared in girls' schools from those likely to have appeared only in boys' schools. From the newspaper advertisements of educational institutions catering to girls in North Carolina, Virginia, Connecticut, and Massachusetts (1794–1850), I constructed a short list of some science textbooks used in girls' schools. To this list, I added titles identified by Thomas Woody in *A History of Women's Education in the United States,* vol. 2 (New York: Octagon Books, 1974 [1929], 474–480). Woody's list includes the natural philosophy, astronomy, and chemistry textbooks mentioned in the catalogs of more than 162 female seminaries from 1780 to 1870. If a textbook did not appear in the sample thus obtained, and its title page or preface stated that it was designed "for use in academies" rather than specifically "for use in female seminaries," I inferred that it was likely to have been used primarily in boys' schools. With very few exceptions, most of the textbooks used in female seminaries were also used in male academies. Nevertheless, a few texts, being unmentioned in girls' school advertisements or catalogs, appear to have been used almost exclusively in male academies.
5. See Woody, *A History of Women's Education in the United States,* vol. 1, 230–234.
6. Woody, *A History of Women's Education,* vol. I, 327–328. Woody briefly notes Beecher's interest in domestic science for girls. Rush and Phelps are discussed below.
7. Wyndham D. Miles and Harold J. Abrahams, "America's First Chemistry Syllabus-and-Course for Girls," in *School Science and Mathematics* 58 (1958): 111–118.

8. Jane Powers makes this assumption in her book, *The 'Girl Question' in Education* (London: The Falmer Press, 1992), 14–15. Similarly, Alice Kessler-Harris, citing the work of Catharine Beecher, claims that "homemaking . . . was professionalized" in the 1830s. See Alice Kessler-Harris, *Out to Work: A History of Wage-Earning Women in the United States* (New York: Oxford University Press, 1982), 50.

9. Deborah Jean Warner, "Science Education for Women in Ante-bellum America," 64.

10. Quoted in Jerome Murch, *Mrs. Barbauld and her Contemporaries* (London, England: Longmans, Green, 1877), 9.

11. Patricia Phillips, *The Scientific Lady: A Social History of Women's Scientific Interests, 1520–1918* (London, England: Weidenfeld and Nicolson, 1990), 111.

12. Jane Marcet, *Conversations on Chymistry* (Philadelphia: James Humphreys, 1806), 298–429.

13. Almira Hart Lincoln Phelps, *Chemistry for Beginners* (New York: F. J. Huntington, 1838 [1834]), 56, 124, 141–142, 198.

14. Ibid., 10.

15. Richard G. Parker, *Juvenile Philosophy: or, Philosophy in Familiar Conversations* (New York: A. S. Barnes & Co., 1857 [1850]).

16. Miles and Abrahams, "America's First Chemistry Syllabus-and-Course for Girls," 112, 116. The authors state that only one edition is known of Rush's course syllabus. A small pamphlet of eight pages, it is housed in the Library Company of Philadelphia.

17. For instance, see John de la Howe, "Plan for Establishing Schools in a New Country, Where the Inhabitants are Thinly Settled, and Whose Children are to be Educated With a Special Reference to a Country Life (1789)," in *The American Legacy of Learning: Readings in the History of Education*, ed. John Hardin Best and Robert T. Sidwell (Philadelphia: J. B. Lippincott, 1967), 144–148.

18. Phillips, *The Scientific Lady*.

19. Quoted in Daniel J. Kevles, *The Physicists: The History of a Scientific Community in Modern America* (Cambridge, Mass.: Harvard University Press, 1987), 4; For a discussion of experimental lectures in Great Britain, see Phillips, *The Scientific Lady*, 122–133. For a brief overview of popular experimental natural philosophy in eighteenth-century France, see Roger Hahn, *The Anatomy of a Scientific Institution: The Paris Academy of Sciences, 1666–1803* (Berkeley, Calif.: University of California Press, 1971), 91ff.

20. See Margaret Nash, "'A Triumph of Reason': Female Education in Academies in the New Republic," in *Chartered Schools: Two Hundred Years of Independent Academies in the United States* (N.Y.: Routledge, 2002), eds. Nancy Beadie and Kim Tolley, 64–86.

21. Alfred Charles True, *A History of Agricultural Education in the United States, 1785–1925* (New York: Arno Press, 1996), 267–272. For a discussion of the role of women scientists in developing domestic science (later known as home economics) in American colleges and universities, see Margaret Rossiter, *Women Scientists in America: Struggles and Strategies to 1940* (Baltimore, M.D.: Johns Hopkins University Press, 1982), 65–70; Sarah Stage and Virginia B. Vincenti, eds., *Rethinking Home Economics: Women and the History of a Profession* (Ithaca, N.Y.: Cornell University Press, 1997).

22. See "Hartford Female Seminary and Its Founder," *The American Journal of Education* 28 (1878): 85.

23. C. E. Beecher, "The Profession of a Woman," in T. S. Pinneo, ed., *The Hemans Reader for Female Schools* (New York: Clark, Austin, & Smith, 1847), 226–227.

24. Warner, "Science Education for Women in Ante-bellum America," 59.

25. "Boarding School at Lynchburg," *Richmond Enquirer*, 5 September 1837. Similar advertisements include "Seminary for Young Ladies," *Richmond Enquirer*, 14 October 1834; "Miss Mackenzie's Seminary," ibid., 12 September 1828; "Federal Hill Seminary," ibid., 23 September 1836; "Cumberland Female Seminary," ibid., 12 September 1837. For more discussion of the experimental apparatus used in girls' schools, see

Warner, "Science Education for Women in Ante-bellum America," 58–67; Thomas Cary Johnson, "Sweet Southern Girls," in *Scientific Interests in the Old South* (N.Y.: D. Appleton-Century Co., 1836), 106–125.

26. *Outline of the Plan of Education Pursued at the Greenfield High School for Young Ladies, with a Catalogue for the Year 1832–1833* (Greenfield, Mass.: Phelps and Ingersoll, 1833), 6–7.

27. "Chemistry Experiments Praised," *Raleigh Register*, 10 November 1815, quoted in *North Carolina Schools and Academies 1790–1840: A Documentary History*, ed. Charles L. Coon (Raleigh, N.C.: Edwards and Broughton, 1915), 447; "Andrews & Jones' North Carolina Female Academy," *Raleigh Register*, 12 December 1823, quoted in ibid.; "Groton Academy," *Columbian Centinel*, 22 September 1827; "Oxford Female Seminary," *Raleigh Register*, 26 September 1826.

28. Marcet, *Conversations on Chymistry*, i-ii; Murch, *Mrs. Barbauld and Her Contemporaries* (1876); Phillips, *The Scientific Lady*, 110–111.

29. Marcet, *Conversations on Chymistry*, 67.

30. See Marcet, *Conversations on Chymistry*; Rev. J. L. Blake, *Conversations on Natural Philosophy* (Boston: Lincoln and Edmands, 1829). Blake added examination questions to Marcet's original text.

31. J. S. Denman, *The Students' Series Third Reading Book* (New York: Pratt, Woodford & Co., 1852), 61.

32. Mary Townsend, *Life in the Insect World, or, Conversations Upon Insects, Between an Aunt and her Nieces* (Philadelphia, Penn.: Lindsay and Blakiston, 1844); Elizabeth Cady Agassiz, *A First Lesson in Natural History* (Boston: Ginn, Heath & Co., 1884 [1879]).

33. In 1806, James Humphreys issued a text titled *Conversations on Chymistry* that, except for the name of the author, was virtually identical to Marcet's text. The Reverend J. L. Blake authored *Conversations on Natural Philosophy* and *Conversations on Chemistry*, adding examination questions to the two original Marcet texts. Thomas P. Jones published *New Conversations on Chemistry*, a slight adaptation of Marcet's earlier book. J. L. Comstock authored a version of *Conversations on Chemistry*, then wrote his own textbook in a straightforward prose format several years later.

34. This conclusion is based on data compiled from *First Abstract of the Massachusetts School Returns for 1837* (Boston: Dutton and Wentworth, 1838). The data reveal that seventy percent of Massachusetts towns reportedly used Blake's text in their common schools.

35. *Biographical Dictionary of American Educators*, vol. 1, ed. John F. Ohles (Westport, Conn.: Greenwood Press, 1978), 295–296.

36. J. L. Comstock, *A System of Natural Philosophy* (New York: Robinson, Pratt & Co., 1835), preface.

37. James Renwick, *First Principles of Chemistry* (New York: Harper & Brothers, 1845 [1840]).

38. James Mulhern, *A History of Secondary Education in Pennsylvania* (N.Y.: Arno Press, 1969), 328. Mulhern's data are not broken down by decade, but clearly show an increase in chemistry in boys' secondary schools from 1750 to 1889.

39. Almira Hart Lincoln Phelps, *Chemistry for Beginners* (New York: F. J. Huntington, 1838 [1834]).

40. For example, see Elizabeth Cady Agassiz, *A First Lesson in Natural History*; *The Rose Bud or Youth's Gazette* (16 February 1833); ibid. (2 March 1833).

41. A detailed discussion of girls' evolving mathematics education is found in Chapter 4.

42. See Tables 2.2–2.4 in Chapter 2.

43. Lewis C. Beck, *A Manual of Chemistry* (Albany, N.Y.: E. W. & C. Skinner, 1834), title, vi.

44. Ibid., vi.

45. John A. Nietz, *The Evolution of American Secondary School Textbooks* (Pittsburgh, Penn.: University of Pittsburgh Press, 1961), 151.

46.   Comstock, *Elements of Chemistry* (1831), 3.
47.   Ibid., 143.
48.   Because Comstock's chemistry text does not appear in the sample of girls' school newspaper advertisements and catalogs used in this study, I have inferred that it was in all probability predominantly used in male academies. It was a highly popular text, appearing in numerous editions. Had it been used in many girls' schools, it is likely that it would have appeared in my sample.
49.   For example, see Almira Hart Lincoln Phelps, *Chemistry for Beginners* (New York: F. J. Huntington, 1838 [1834]); John W. Webster, *Manual of Chemistry* (Boston: Richardson & Lord, 1829 [1828]).
50.   From excerpts of the academy's catalogs, included in Johnson, *Scientific Interests in the Old South*, 111.
51.   John Johnston, *A Manual of Chemistry on the Basis of Turner's Elements of Chemistry* (Philadelphia: Charles DeSilver, 1861 [1856]). The title page of Johnston's text states that it is intended "for colleges and other seminaries of learning." James Renwick, *First Principles of Chemistry*. Renwick, professor of natural philosophy and chemistry in Columbia College, designed his text "for the use of schools, academies, and the lower classes of colleges" (title, page). John A. Porter, *Principles of Chemistry* (New York: A. S. Barnes, 1860 [1856]). Porter was professor of agricultural and organic chemistry at Yale College.
52.   Alonzo Gray, *Elements of Chemistry* (New York: Newman & Ivison, 1848), preface.
53.   Gray, *Elements of Chemistry*, 134.
54.   Nietz, *The Evolution of American Secondary School Textbooks*, 143.
55.   Thomas L. Hankins, *Science and the Enlightenment* (Cambridge, England: Cambridge University Press, 1985), 17–45.
56.   For example, see Neil Arnott, *Elements of Physics; or Natural Philosophy* (Philadelphia: Lea & Blanchard, 1845 [1827]); Jane Haldinand Marcet, *Conversations on Natural Philosophy* (Boston: Gould, Kendall & Lincoln, 1841); Comstock, *A System of Natural Philosophy*; Rev. J. L. Blake, *First Book in Astronomy* (Boston: Lincoln & Edmands, 1831); Alva Clark, *A New System of Astronomy* (New York: R. Lockwood, 1838 [1820]); Elijah H. Burritt, *The Geography of the Heavens* (New York: F. J. Huntington, 1853 [1849]); Hannah M. Bouvier, *Bouvier's Familiar Astronomy* (Philadelphia: Childs and Peterson, 1857 [1855]).
57.   John S. C. Abbott, *The Young Astronomer* (New York: J. C. Riker, 1847 [1846]), pref.; See also Thomas Dick, *The Geography of the Heavens* (New York: Huntington and Savage, 1833). Dick's text served as an elementary introduction to astronomy and required no knowledge of mathematics on the part of the reader.
58.   See Denison Olmsted, *A Compendium of Astronomy* (New York: Collins and Brother, 1848 [1839]); John William Draper, *Textbook on Natural Philosophy* (New York: Harper and Brothers, 1847); H. N. Robinson, *An Elementary Class Book on Astronomy* (Cincinnati, Ohio: Jacob Ernst, 1857); Hiram Mattison, *Elementary Astronomy* (New York: Huntington and Savage, 1848 [1846]); James Ferguson, *An Easy Introduction to Astronomy for Young Gentlemen and Ladies* (Philadelphia: William F. M'Laughlin, 1805).
59.   "Laws for the Government of New Bern Academy, with the Plan of Education Annexed," in *North Carolina Schools and Academies*, ed. Coon, 52–59. A third textbook available to boys in this institution was James Ferguson, *An Early and Pleasant Introduction to Sir Isaac Newton's Philosophy* (Printed and sold by the author, 1772); William Nicholson, *An Introduction to Natural Philosophy* (London: J. Johnson, 1790); Tiberius Cavallo, *The Elements of Natural or Experimental Philosophy* (Philadelphia: Thomas Dobson, 1813).
60.   William Holms Chambers Bartlett, *Elements of Natural Philosophy: Spherical Astronomy* (New York: A. S. Barnes & Co., 1855); William A. Norton, *An Elementary Treatise on Astronomy* (New York: Wiley & Putnam, 1845), iii.

61. Alonzo Gray, *Elements of Natural Philosophy* (New York: Harper and Brothers, 1850), title, preface, 39.

62. James M'Intire, *New Treatise on Astronomy* (New York: A. S. Barnes & Burr, 1860 [1850]), vi. M'Intire's text appeared in a limited number of editions, so it is possible that it was not widely used. This may explain its absence from the school catalogs of female seminaries.

63. Denison Olmsted, *An Introduction to Astronomy*, ed. E. S. Snell (New York: Collins and Brother, 1868), title.

64. Nietz, *The Evolution of American Secondary School Textbooks*, 121.

65. Martha Schofield, "Valedictory Address delivered at the Village Church, St. Helena Island, by Lydia Schofield, April 12, 1868," in Martha Schofield's Diary, vol. 1, Southern Historical Collection, University of North Carolina, Chapel Hill (hereafter as SHC).

66. Chris Span has demonstrated that by the time the Freedmen's Bureau arrived in Mississippi in late 1865, a small but significant number of virtually independent academies created and sustained by Mississippi's ex-slaves already existed. See Chris Span, "Alternative Pedagogy: The Rise of the Private Black Academy in Early Postbellum Mississippi, 1862–1870," in *Chartered Schools*, 211–227. The quote is on pages 219–220.

67. "State Compulsory School Attendance Laws," *http://In.infoplease.com/ipa/A0112617. html,* 10 January 2002.

68. W. T. B. Williams, "Negro Education: Special Virginia Studies, 1905," in Southern Education Board Papers, #680, Series 2.4, African Americans, 1898–1911, SHC.

69. Ibid., 6.

70. Ibid., 16.

71. Ibid., 25.

72. "Eliza Anna Grier, M.E.," *Bulletin Briefing: African American Women Doctors, http://www.mcphu.edu/institutes/iwh/whe/briefs/brief8.htm.* 22 January 2002.

Chapter 4

1. John Bennett, *Strictures on Female Education* (New York: Source Book Press, 1971 [1795]), 21.

2. James Furbish, *Some Remarks on Education, Textbooks, Etc.* (Portland: Shirley and Hyde, 1828), 20.

3. Stanley Guralnick, *Science and the Ante-Bellum American College* (Philadelphia: The American Philosophical Society, 1975), 54–55.

4. Bridget Murray, "Gender Gap in Math Scores Is Closing," *Monitor of the American Psychological Association* (November 1995): 43; American Association for the Advancement of Science, *Science for All Americans* (New York: Oxford University Press, 1990), xviii.

5. William Woodbridge, "Female Education Prior to 1800," *Barnard's Journal of Education* 27 (1877): 273–276.

6. This conclusion is based on a study of the American Loyalist claims presented in England in the 1770s and 1780s. See Mary Beth Norton, "Eighteenth-Century American Women in Peace and War: The Case of the Loyalists," *William and Mary Quarterly* 3 (1976): 286–409.

7. Benjamin Franklin, *The Autobiography of Benjamin Franklin* (Philadelphia: J. B. Lippincott, 1868), 109; Benjamin Rush, "A Plan for the Establishment of Public Schools," *Essays on Education*, ed. Frederick Rudolph (Cambridge, Mass.: Harvard University Press, 1965), 29; and Noah Webster, "On the Education of Youth," *Essays on Education*, ed. Frederick Rudolph, 70, 40n.

8. Patricia Cline Cohen, *A Calculating People: The Spread of Numeracy in Early America* (Chicago: University of Chicago Press, 1982), 142.

9. Thomas Woody, *A History of Women's Education in the United States,* vol. 1 (N.Y.: Octagon Books, 1980 [1929]), 138, 140.

10. John Hardin Best cites the advertisement of a private schoolmaster named John Miller, who in 1733 taught boys arithmetic, algebra, geometry, trigonometry, surveying, dialing, navigation, astronomy, gauging, fortification, the stenographic and orthographic projection of the sphere, the use of the globe, and the Italian method of bookkeeping. In *American Legacy of Learning: Readings in the History of Education,* ed. John Hardin Best and Robert T. Sidwell (Philadelphia: J. B. Lippincott, 1967), 14.

11. Quoted in Woody, *A History of Women's Education,* vol. 1, 221.

12. Catharine E. Beecher, "Hartford Female Seminary and Its Founder," *The American Journal of Education* 28 (1878): 68; Kathryn Kish Sklar, *Catharine Beecher: A Study in American Domesticity* (New Haven, Conn.: Yale University Press, 1973), 4–7.

13. Woody, *A History of Women's Education,* vol. 1, 339.

14. Quoted in ibid., 284.

15. Almira Hart Lincoln Phelps, *Lectures to Young Ladies* (Boston: Carter, Hendee and Co., 1833), 242–243.

16. Phelps, *Lectures to Young Ladies,* 238; See Hannah More, *Strictures on the Modern System of Female Education* (London: T. Cadell Jr. & W. Davies, 1799).

17. Emma Willard, *Address to the Public, (Particularly) to the Members of the Legislature of New York, Proposing a Plan for Improving Female Education* (Albany, N.Y.: I. W. Clark, 1819), 4ff.

18. James Furbish, *Some Remarks on Education, Textbooks, etc.,* 20.

19. Timothy Dwight of Yale, director of Greenfield Hill Academy in Connecticut, aroused a great deal of public indignation when he allowed girls to study the same mathematics courses that were offered to boys: algebra, geometry, spherics, and calculus. See Cohen, *A Calculating People,* 143.

20. Quoted in Woody, *A History of Women's Education,* vol. 1, 306.

21. Quoted in Henry Fowler, "Educational Services of Mrs. Emma Willard," in *The American Journal of Education* 6 (1859): 147.

22. Ibid., 147n.

23. Ibid.

24. Woody, *A History of Women's Education,* vol. 1, 345.

25. Fowler, "Educational Services of Mrs. Emma Willard," 146.

26. Ibid.

27. Beecher, "Hartford Female Seminary and Its Founder," 69–70.

28. "Misses C. & M. Beecher," *American Mercury,* 20 April 1824.

29. Woody, *A History of Women's Education,* vol. 1, 317–318.

30. Phelps, *Lectures to Young Ladies,* 246–247.

31. See Anne Firor Scott, "The Ever Widening Circle: The Diffusion of Feminist Values from the Troy Female Seminary, 1822–1872," *History of Education Quarterly* 19 (1979): 3–25.

32. "Scotland Neck," *The Raleigh Star,* 21 June 1837, quoted in *North Carolina Schools and Academies, 1790–1840: A Documentary History,* ed. Charles L. Coon (Raleigh, N.C.: Edwards and Broughton, 1915), 183. Other advertisements mentioning the presence of faculty members trained at Troy Female Seminary include "Northampton Academy," *Raleigh Register,* 12 March 1838, quoted in ibid., 277–278; "Wood's Female Academy," *Raleigh Star,* 26 December 1838, in ibid., 279; "Phillips' Female School," *The Register,* 22 November 1836, in ibid., 314–347; "Mrs. Saffery's Female Seminary," *The Register,* 28 April 1835, in ibid., 335–336. For examples of similar advertisements in Virginia, see "Mt. Pleasant," *The Richmond Enquirer,* 1 December 1835; "A Good Country School," *The Richmond Enquirer,* 22 December 1836.

33. See "Northampton Female Academy," *The Raleigh Register* (1838), quoted in *North Carolina Schools and Academies,* 277–278.

34. "Phillips' Female School," *The Register*, 22 November 1836, quoted in *North Carolina Schools and Academies*, 314–315; "Mrs. Phillips's Female Seminary, at Chapel Hill," in ibid., 315–316.
35. Quoted in Woody, *A History of Women's Education*, vol. 1, 372.
36. "Bedford Female Academy," *Richmond Enquirer*, 3 November 1837.
37. Woody, *A History of Women's Education*, vol. 1, 414.
38. None of the forty-two girls' schools included in the North Carolina sample included navigation and surveying in its advertised course of study. Mulhern did not include these subjects in his tables of subjects offered in secondary girls' schools. In the North Carolina sample, the following schools offered geometry to girls before 1825: Raleigh Academy, female department (1820); New Bern Academy, female department (1823); and Hillsborough Female Seminary (1825). Hillsborough Female Seminary, which advertised algebra in its course of study in 1825, was the only institution to offer girls algebra before 1830. See *North Carolina Schools and Academies, 1790–1840*, ed. Coon, 458, 58, 300.
39. Nicholas Pike, *A New and Complete System of Arithmetic* (Worcester, Mass.: Isaiah Thomas, 1797).
40. John Ward, *The Young Mathematician's Guide* (London: A Bettesworth and F. Fayrham, 1724).
41. Woody, *A History of Women's Education*, vol. 1, 414.
42. "Boston Grammar and Writing Schools," *The Common School Journal* (15 November 1845): 338. Two boys' schools, Phillips and New South, are not included in the sample for Table 4.5 because there exists little information about the math instruction offered in these schools. In reference to Phillips School, the Boston school committee stated only that the school had been established the previous year and that the first class in arithmetic had "gone nearly through the third part." As for New South School, the committee stated only that it had been established a short time. Otis W. Caldwell and Stuart A. Courtis, *Then and Now in Education, 1845–1923* (N.Y.: Yonkers-on-Hudson: World Book Co., 1925).
43. Quoted in "Girls in the Public Schools of Boston," *The American Journal of Education* 13 (1863): 248. This article includes lengthy extracts from the Boston school committee reports.
44. Ibid., 248–249.
45. Ibid., 247.
46. *Annual Report of the School Committee of the City of Boston, 1857* (Boston: Geo. C. Rand & Avery, 1858), 108–109, 113, 118, 120. For discussion of the historical phenomenon of boys leaving school, see John L. Rury, "Urban Enrollment at the Turn of the Century: Gender as an Intervening Variable," *Urban Education* 28 (1988): 68–87; George Counts, *The Selective Character of American Secondary Education* (Chicago: University of Chicago Press, 1922), 113; A. Caswell Ellis, "The Percentage of Boys Who Leave the High School, and the Reasons Therefore," *NEA Addresses and Proceedings* (1903), 792–801; Joseph King Van Denburg, *Causes of the Elimination of Students in Public Secondary Schools of New York* (New York: Teachers College, 1911).
47. *Annual Report of the School Committee of the City of Boston, 1857*, 261.
48. Ibid.
49. See *Annual Report of the School Committee of the City of Boston, 1857*, 108, 124. The report mentions the desirability of having female assistants serve under a male master at each of the city's grammar schools. See also *Annual Report of the State Superintendent of Public Instruction of the State of Wisconsin, December 31, 1849* (Wisc.: Wisconsin Legislature, 1850), 35. David Tyack and Elizabeth Hansot describe this as a widespread trend in *Learning Together: A History of Coeducation in American Public Schools* (N.Y.: Russell Sage Foundation, 1992), 129.

50.   Quoted in *Annual Report of the State Superintendent of Public Instruction of the State of Wisconsin* (Madison, Wisc.: Atwood and Rublee, 1858), Wisconsin State Historical Society (hereafter WSHS), 157.

51.   P. A. Siljestrom, *The Educational Institutions of the United States: Their Character and Organization* (London: John Chapman, 1853), 302n.

52.   Rev. J. Fraser, *Report on the Common School System of the United States and of the Provinces of Upper and Lower Canada (1867)*, mf 73.216–220, 11, Jonsson Library of Government Documents, Stanford University.

53.   J. H. Mathers, "Richland County," in *Fourteenth Annual Report of the Superintendent of Public Instruction of the State of Wisconsin, 1862* (Madison, Wisc.: Atwood and Rublee), 52, WSHS.

54.   Susan Nye Hutchison Diary, 15 January 1838, Southern Historical Collection (SHC), University of North Carolina at Chapel Hill.

55.   Ibid., 27 January 1838.

56.   Ibid., 2 February 1838.

57.   Mary A. Dodge to her mother and father, 5 February and 14 February 1854, in Mary A. Dodge, *Gail Hamilton's Life in Letters*, ed. H. Augusta Dodge (Boston: Lee & Shepard, 1901), 51, 53.

58.   Emma Holmes, *The Diary of Miss Emma Holmes, 1861–1866*, ed. John F. Marszalek (Baton Rouge, La.: Louisiana State University Press, 1979), 311–312.

59.   Lucy Larcom, *A New England Girlhood* (Boston: Houghton, Mifflin & Co., 1889), 266–267.

60.   Margaret Anne Ulmer, "May 7, 1858," *Margaret Anne Ulmer Diary, February-June 1858*, SHC.

61.   Quoted in Tyack and Hansot, *Learning Together*, 101.

62.   Ibid., 134.

63.   Joseph J. Bingham, *Thirteenth Report of the Superintendent of Public Instruction for the State of Indiana* (Indianapolis, Ind.: Joseph J. Bingham, 1865): 31–32.

64.   Walter S. Monroe, "Progress and Promotion of Pupils in Certain Indiana City and Rural Schools," in *Indiana University Studies* 5 (1918): 43, 39.

65.   *Report of the Commissioner of Education for the Year Ended June 30, 1910*, vol. 1 (Washington, D.C.: Government Printing Office, 1910), 129. See also William J. Reese, *The Origins of the American High School* (New Haven, Conn.: Yale University Press, 1995), 224–226.

66.   Tyack and Hansot, *Learning Together*, 137–138.

67.   The data are drawn from the reports made by inspectors who visited Wisconsin High Schools. There is no indication that inspectors visited every class at each school, but they gave the subject of those classes they visited, along with teachers' names and brief evaluations of the teaching observed. I collected data at four-year intervals.

68.   For a discussion of the experience of women preparing to become teachers at the University of California at Berkeley, see Geraldine Jonçich Clifford, *"Equally in View," The University of California, Its Women, and the Schools* (Berkeley, Calif.: Center for Studies in Higher Education and Institute of Governmental Studies, 1995).

69.   *The Stanford Alumnus* 1 (June 1899), 3; *Forty-second Annual Register of Stanford University* (Palo Alto, Calif.: University Press, 1932), 11, in Special Collections at Stanford University (SCSU).

70.   *The Leland Stanford Junior University Twenty-first Annual Register, 1911–1912,* (Palo Alto, Calif.: University Press, 1912), SCSU.

71.   Data compiled from the *University of California Register, 1907–8*, 544–545, Special Collections, University of California at Berkeley (SCUCB). Women congregated in the College of Natural Sciences. Of the forty-three bachelor of science degrees awarded in 1908, thirty-two were awarded to women. The College of Letters awarded one bachelor of arts degree in mathematics that year, also to a woman (549–550). Data compiled from the *University of California Register, 1911–12*, 10–13, 18–19, SCUCB.

See also the *Fortieth Commencement of the University of Wisconsin, 1893*, Wisconsin University Archives, through the *Fiftieth Commencement of the University of Wisconsin, 1902*. At Wisconsin, fewer than five bachelor degrees were awarded in mathematics in any one year.

72. Evelyn Boyd Granville, "My Life as a Mathematician," *Sage* 6 (Fall 1989): 44–46; Patricia C. Kenschaft, "Black Women in Mathematics in the United States," *American Mathematics Monthly* 8 (October 1989): 594–595.

73. "Groveland," in *Twentieth Annual Report of the Board of Education of Massachusetts* (Boston: William White, 1857), 11.

74. S. S. Randall, "Report of the City Superintendent," in *Twenty-Third Annual Report of the Board of Education of the City and County of New York* (New York: C. S. Wescott, 1865), 20–21.

75. Quoted in Woody, *A History of Women's Education*, vol. 1, 115–116.

76. See Chapter 2, Table 2.4. During the period from 1830 to 1889, seventy-seven percent of Pennsylvania schools offered botany, a marked increase over the earlier period (from 1750 to 1829), when only fourteen percent offered the subject. Nevertheless, still more schools (eighty-eight percent) continued to offer natural philosophy during the later period.

77. Ralph Waldo Emerson, quoted in Dirk Struik, *Yankee Science in the Making* (Boston: Little, Brown & Co., 1948), 264.

Chapter 5

1. Quoted in Marcia Myers Bonta, *Women in the Field: America's Pioneering Women Naturalists* (College Station, Tex.: Texas A & M University Press, 1991), 71.

2. See Margaret Rossiter, *Women Scientists in America: Struggles and Strategies to 1940* (Baltimore: Johns Hopkins University Press, 1982), 1–28; Elizabeth Keeney, *The Botanizers* (Chapel Hill, N.C.: University of North Carolina Press, 1992); Lynn Barber, *The Heyday of Natural History, 1820–1870* (Garden City, N.Y.: Doubleday and Co., 1980).

3. The constitution of the National Lyceum was published in *American Annals of Education* (June 1831), 277–279. See also Carl Bode, *The American Lyceum: Town Meeting of the Mind* (New York: Oxford University Press, 1956); "The American Lyceum," *Old South Leaflets,* 139 (Boston: Directors of the Old South Work, 1904), 293–312; Dirk Struik, *Yankee Science in the Making* (Boston: Little, Brown, & Co., 1948).

4. See Charlotte Forten, *The Journals of Charlotte Forten Grimké* (New York: Oxford University Press, 1988): 8 November 1854; 3, 6 December 1854; 12, 24, 30 January 1855; 7 February 1855; 7, 28 March 1855; 25 December 1855; 27 January 1856; 11, 12 February 1856. Quoted in Struik, *Yankee Science in the Making*, 215.

5. This conclusion is based on a survey of issues of *The Youth's Companion* published from 1850 to 1905.

6. Quoted in Keeney, *The Botanizers*, 89–90.

7. Keeney, *The Botanizers*.

8. Brooks Atkinson, ed., *Walden and Other Writings of Henry David Thoreau* (New York: Random House, 1937), 167. For correspondence relating to Thoreau's relationship with Agassiz, see Thoreau to James Elliot Cabot, 3 May 1847; Thoreau to Cabot, 8 May 1847; Thoreau to Cabot, 1 June 1847; and Cabot to Thoreau, undated, in Walter Harding and Carl Bode, eds., *The Correspondence of Henry David Thoreau* (New York: New York University Press, 1958), 178–183.

9. Peter A. Fritzell, *Nature Writing and America: Essays upon a Cultural Type* (Ames, Iowa: Iowa State University Press, 1990), 18.

10. See *Popular Science Monthly,* vol. 1 (1872) and subsequent issues through 1884. For a discussion of the popularization of evolution in American newspapers and journals,

see Frank Luther Mott, *A History of American Magazines 1865–1885* (Cambridge, Mass.: Harvard University Press, 1938), 106–107. For a recent study, see Ronald L. Numbers and John Stenhouse, eds., *Disseminating Darwinism: The Role of Place, Race, Religion, and Gender* (New York: Cambridge University Press, 1999).

11. The quote is from an undated, unpublished manuscript in file 18, box 5, Liberty Hyde Bailey Papers (hereafter LHB Papers), Special Collections, Cornell University, Ithaca, New York (hereafter SCCU).

12. Joseph Richardson, A.M., *The Young Ladies' Selection of Elegant Extracts* (Boston: John Eliot, 1811), 138–139.

13. Quoted in Richardson, *The Young Ladies' Selection of Elegant Extracts*, 68–69.

14. Ibid., 56, 138–139.

15. For further discussion of American women and the doctrine of women's sphere, see Linda K. Kerber and Jane DeHart Mathews, eds., *Women's America: Refocusing the Past* (New York: Oxford University Press, 1991 [1982]); Maxine L. Margolis, *Mothers and Such: Views of American Women and Why They Changed* (Berkeley, Calif.: University of California Press, 1984); Anne Firor Scott, *Making the Invisible Woman Visible* (Urbana, Ill.: University of Illinois Press, 1984). A recent popular discussion of these issues is contained in Glenda Riley, *Inventing the American Woman: A Perspective on Women's History* (Arlington Heights, Ill.: Harlan Davidson, 1987).

16. Quoted in Richardson, *The Young Ladies' Selection of Elegant Extracts*, 45.

17. Alexis de Toqueville, *Democracy in America* (New York: HarperPerennial, 1969), 600–603. The quotes are from page 601.

18. Kathryn Kish Sklar, "The Founding of Mount Holyoke College," in *Women of America: A History*, eds. Carol Ruth Berkin and Mary Beth Norton (Boston: Houghton Mifflin Co., 1979), 177–201; Anne Firor Scott, "The Ever-Widening Circle: The Diffusion of Feminist Values from the Troy Female Seminary, 1822–1872," *History of Education Quarterly* 19 (Spring 1979), 3–24; Geraldine Jonçich Clifford, "'Lady Teachers' and Politics in the United States, 1850–1930," in *Teachers: The Culture and Politics of Work*, eds. M. Lawn and G. Grace (London: Falmer Press, 1987), 3–30; Sari Knopp Biklen, *School Work: Gender and the Cultural Construction of Teaching* (New York and London: Teachers College Press, 1995), 49.

19. See Kim Tolley and Margaret A. Nash, "Leaving Home to Teach: The Diary of Susan Nye Hutchison, 1815–1840," in eds. Nancy Beadie and Kim Tolley, *Chartered Schools: Two Hundred Years of Independent Academies in the United States, 1727–1925* (New York: Routledge, 2002).

20. See Linda K. Kerber, et al. "Beyond Roles, Beyond Spheres: Thinking about Gender in the Early Republic," *William and Mary Quarterly* 44 (July 1989): 565–581.

21. Alice Kessler-Harris, *Out to Work: A History of Wage-Earning Women in the United States* (New York: Oxford University Press, 1982), 49ff.

22. See Kim Tolley, "Many Years before the Mayflower: Catholic Academies and the Development of Parish High Schools in the United States, 1727–1925," in *Chartered Schools*, 305–310.

23. Catharine Beecher, *An Essay on the Education of Female Teachers* (New York: Van Nostrand & Dwight, 1835). For a discussion of this essay, see Kathryn Kish Sklar, *Catharine Beecher: A Study in American Domesticity* (New York and London: W. W. Norton & Company, 1976), 113f; Jeanne Boydston, Mary Kelley, and Anne Margolis, *The Limits of Sisterhood: The Beecher Sisters on Women's Rights and Woman's Sphere* (Chapel Hill, N.C.: University of North Carolina Press, 1988), 115f.

24. Zilpah Grant, "Benefits of Female Education," 1836, Ipswich Female Seminary Papers, Mount Holyoke College Archives.

25. Carole B. Shmurak, "Mary Lyon," in *Historical Dictionary of Women's Education in the United States*, ed. Linda Eisenmann (Westport, Conn.: Greenwood Press, 1998): 253–255.

26. Catherine E. Beecher, *The Evils Suffered by American Women and Children: The Causes and the Remedy. Presented in an Address by Miss C. E. Beecher, to Meetings of*

Ladies in New York, and Other Cities. Also, an Address to the Protestant Clergy of the United States (New York: Harper and Brothers, 1846), 18–19.

27. For example, see Reverend John Bennett, *Strictures on Female Education* (Worcester, Mass: Isaiah Thomas, 1795). This book appeared first in England, in some versions under the authorship of Tiny Bennett, "a clergyman of the Church of England." Numerous editions appeared in the United States from 1787 onward. For discussion of the emergence of the ideology of separate spheres in eighteenth-century England, see Robert B. Shoemaker, *Gender in English Society, 1650–1850: The Emergence of Separate Spheres* (New York: Longman, 1998).

28. Almira Hart Lincoln, *Familiar Lectures on Botany* (Hartford, Conn.: F. J. Huntington, 1832 [1829]), 14–15.

29. Ibid., 16. For discussion of Phelps's life and influence, see Emma L. Bolzau, *Almira Hart Lincoln Phelps: Her Life and Work* (Philadelphia: University of Pennsylvania Press, 1936); Vera Norwood, *Made From This Earth: American Women and Nature* (Chapel Hill, N.C.: University of North Carolina Press, 1993).

30. Lincoln, *Familiar Lectures* (1832), 16.

31. Ibid., 30.

32. Ibid.

33. Quoted in Elizabeth Keeney, *The Botanizers*, 75.

34. Laura D. Nichols, *Underfoot, or What Harry and Nelly Learned of the Earth's Treasures* (Boston: D. Lothrop & Company, 1881), 22, Rare Books and Manuscripts, The Ohio State University Libraries, Columbus.

35. Almira Hart Lincoln, *Familiar Lectures* (1832), 321.

36. Lincoln, *Familiar Lectures* (1832), 31.

37. William Kennedy Blake, in *William Kennedy Blake Diary*, 1851, 11. Southern Historical Collection, University of North Carolina at Chapel Hill. Blake taught at Carolina College in Ansonville, North Carolina, in 1851 and later had charge of the Female Seminary in Fayetteville.

38. "Publisher's Advertisement to the First Edition," *Botany for Beginners: An Introduction to Mrs. Lincoln's Lectures on Botany* (New York: F. J. Huntington, 1840), 5.

39. *First Annual Catalogue of the Officers and Members of the Mount Holyoke Female Seminary, South Hadley, Massachusetts, 1837–8* in Mount Holyoke Female Seminary Catalogs, 1837–1875, American Antiquarian Society; Asa Gray, *Botany for Young People and Common Schools* (New York: Ivison, Blakeman, Taylor & Co., 1858).

40. *Official Report of the Nature-Study Exhibition and Conferences* (London: Blackie and Son, 1903), 32; *Annual Report of the Fresno Public Schools for the Year Ending June 30th, 1908* (Fresno, Cal.: Morning Republican Print, 1908), 15.

41. H. G. Adams, *Dialogues on Entomology, in Which the Forms and Habits of Insects are Familiarly Explained* (London: R. Hunter, 1819), 84.

42. Lincoln, *Familiar Lectures* (1846), 200n.

43. Bonta, *Women in the Field: America's Pioneering Women Naturalists*, 145–180.

44. Fredrika Bremer, *Homes of the New World* (London: Arthur Hall, Virtue & Co., 1853), 35.

45. Lincoln, *Familiar Lectures* (1832), 15–16.

46. Quoted in Alice Kessler-Harris, *Out to Work: A History of Wage-Earning Women in the United States* (New York: Oxford University Press, 1982), 57.

47. Margaret Rossiter has noted that in both 1921 and 1938, women congregated in the branches of biology: agricultural sciences, biochemistry, botany, medical sciences, microbiology, nutrition, and zoology. She states that the field of geology remained among the smallest of fields for women. See Margaret Rossiter, *Women Scientists in America*, 137.

48. Lincoln, *Familiar Lectures* (1846), 200.

49. Ibid., 31. Lincoln Phelps exhorted her readers to popularize natural history by making it fashionable. To accomplish this, ladies should "frequently exhibit specimens of their own scientific taste" in their parlors.

50. Charles Darwin, *The Origin of Species by Means of Natural Selection, or the Preservation of Favored Races in the Struggle for Life, and The Descent of Man and Selection in Relation to Sex* (N.Y.: The Modern Library, 1936), 373.

51. Lynn Barber, *The Heyday of Natural History 1820–1870* (London: Jonathan Cape, 1980), 287.

52. Ibid.

53. Olive Thorne Miller, *The Children's Book of Birds* (Boston: Houghton Mifflin Co., 1915), 2.

54. Elizabeth Cady Agassiz, *A First Lesson in Natural History* (Boston: Ginn, Heath & Co., 1884 [1879]).

55. Peter Schmitt, *Back to Nature: The Arcadian Myth in Urban America* (New York: Oxford University Press, 1969), 22ff.

56. Bonta, *Women in the Field: America's Pioneering Women Naturalists*, 3.

57. Susan Fenimore Cooper, *Rural Hours* (New York: George P. Putnam, 1850), 49.

58. Ibid., 214.

59. Anna Botsford Comstock, *Handbook of Nature Study* (Ithaca, N.Y.: Comstock Publishing Company, 1927 [1911]), 11.

60. Mrs. Jeanette D. Ruby, "Spring Birds," in *Nature Study Leaflets* (Lafayette, Ind.: Purdue University Press, 1898), leaflet no. 8, 1; Frances L. Strong, "In the Rabbit's Place," in *All the Year Round: A Nature Reader* (Boston: Ginn & Co., 1896), 86–87; see also "The Boy Who Hated Trees," in Annie Chase, *Friends of the Fields* (Educational Publishing Co., 1898), 58–66.

61. See Chase, *Friends of the Fields*, 14–19.

62. E. S. Phelps, "The Woodchuck Society," in *Swinton's Fourth Reader* (New York: American Book Company, 1883), 33–46. The quote is on pages 44–45.

63. Frances L. Strong, "The Butterfly," in *All the Year Round: A Nature Reader* (Boston: Ginn & Co., 1896), 60–62.

64. Daniel J. Kevles, *The Physicists: The History of a Scientific Community in Modern America* (Cambridge, Mass.: Harvard University Press, 1987), 3–7.

65. Quoted in Bonta, *Women in the Field: America's Pioneering Women Naturalists*, 21. See also Deborah Jean Warner, *Graceanna Lewis, Scientist and Humanitarian* (Washington, D.C.: Smithsonian Institution Press, 1979).

66. Bonta, *Women in the Field: America's Pioneering Women Naturalists*, 42–48.

67. "Minutes and Records, 1925," box 4, the American Nature Study Society Records, SCCU. The minutes describe a paper presented by Anna Comstock of Cornell, tracing the development of the nature-study movement to the "influence of the work of Agassiz." See also David Starr Jordan, *Days of a Man,* 1 (Yonkers-on-Hudson, N.Y.: World Book, 1922), 119. According to Jordan, who later became president of Stanford University, of all the schools in the country, it was the Anderson School of Natural History that had the most extended influence on scientific teaching in America. Other contemporary accounts of the Anderson School include Frank Haak Lattin, *Penikese: A Reminiscence by One of Its Pupils* (Albion, N.Y., 1895); H. B. C. Beedy, "Reminiscences of Penikese," *Education* (February 1893): 340; Henry Blake, "Personal Reminiscences of Professor Louis Agassiz," *Nature Study Review* (March 1923): 97–103. The most often quoted secondary source is still Edward Lurie, *Louis Agassiz: A Life in Science* (Chicago, Ill: University of Chicago Press, 1960). A useful article for understanding the highly influential role of the school among women is Joan N. Burstyn, "Early Women in Education: The Role of the Anderson School of Natural History," *Boston University Journal of Education* 159 (August 1977): 50–64.

68. Mary E. Beaman Scrapbook, Mary E. Beaman Joraleman Papers (hereafter as MBJ Scrapbook), Bancroft Library, Special Collections, University of California, Berkeley (hereafter as SCUCB). Beaman was a student at the Anderson School in 1873. Her scrapbook is composed of clippings from local newspapers, magazines, and journals.

69. Letter to Mary E. Beaman from Elizabeth Cabot Agassiz, 28 April 1873, Mary E. Joraleman Papers (hereafter MEJ Papers), UCB.

70. Elizabeth Cabot Agassiz to Mary E. Beaman, 28 April 1873, MEJ Papers; MBJ Scrapbook, 1–2, UCB. Among the faculty were Arnold Guyot of Princeton, Count Pourtales of the Coast Survey, and Bert G. Wilder of Cornell.

71. Albert H. Tuttle, "The Harvard That I Knew," an address delivered before the Town and Gown Club of Berkeley, California (21 February 1916), 6, Albert H. Tuttle Papers, UCB. Tuttle states that "The story may not be true; it is certainly *ben trovato.*"

72. Richard R. Olmsted, "The Nature-Study Movement in American Education," (Ed.D. diss., Indiana University, 1967), 25.

73. MBJ Scrapbook, 1, SCUCB. There is disagreement in the sources as to how many women were admitted in 1873. According to local newspaper clippings in Joraleman's scrapbook, eighteen of the fifty students were women. However, David Starr Jordan, who was also a student at the time, recalled that fifteen women enrolled the first year. See Jordan's *Days of a Man*, vol. 1, 108.

74. MBJ Scrapbook, 1–10; 21, SCUCB.

75. The incident is described by Jordan in *The Days of a Man*, 111–112.

76. Quoted in Joan N. Burstyn, "Early Women in Education: The Role of the Anderson School of Natural History," 50–64. The source for the quote is Agassiz's opening address in the New York *Tribune,* 9 July 1873.

77. MBJ Scrapbook, 1, SCUCB.

78. Louis Agassiz to Burt Green Wilder, 7 December 1872, box 1, Burt Green Wilder Papers, Special Collections, Cornell University Archives, Ithaca, N.Y.

79. Liberty Hyde Bailey, "Lucy Millington," 1, in Box 8, folder 1. Liberty Hyde Bailey Papers (hereafter LHB Papers), SCCU.

80. Irene Putnam to Bailey, 12 August 1934, Box 8, fol. 1. LHB Papers, SCCU.

81. Bailey, "Lucy Millington," 2, Box 8, fol. 1. LHB Papers, SCCU.

82. Irene Putnam to Liberty Hyde Bailey, 12 August 1934, LHB Papers, SCCU.

83. Millington published in volumes 2, 3, 4, 9, and 10 of the *Bulletin of the Torrey Botanical Club*. She was listed in the "Botanical Directory for North America and the West Indies," *Bulletin of the Torrey Botanical Club*, vol. 4, no. 11 (November 1873).

84. C. C. Parry, "Visit to the Original Locality of the New Species of *Arceuthobium* in Warren County, New York," in *American Naturalist* 6 (July 1872): 404–406.

85. Liberty Hyde Bailey, "Lucy Millington," an unpublished, undated manuscript in the LHB Papers, SCCU. This is a longer draft of an article later published in 1939.

86. *Bulletin of the Torrey Botanical Club* 2 (November 1871): 42–43.

87. Asa Gray, "New Parasitic Plant of the Mistletoe Family," *The American Naturalist* 6 (March 1872): 166–167; *Bulletin of the Torrey Botanical Club* 4 (April 1873): 15–16.

88. *Bulletin of the Torrey Botanical Club* 3 (April 1872): 24. It was no secret among the botanical community that Peck often took credit for the discoveries of amateurs, both male and female. In 1872, a reviewer of Peck's *Report of the Botanist of the New York State Museum of Natural History* noted that although Peck gave credit "to contributors for the plants sent . . . justice would seem to require that the collector should be named as well when [Peck's] name accompanies the label." See *Bulletin of the Torrey Botanical Club* 3 (December 1874): 2.

89. Bailey, "Lucy Millington," 2, in LHB Papers, SCCU.

90. Charles Peck to Liberty Hyde Bailey, 2 October 1911, Box 8, fol. 1, LHB Papers, SCCU.

91. H. D. House to L. H. Bailey, 27 June 1934, Box 8, fol. 1, LHB Papers, SCCU.

92. Bailey, "Lucy Millington," *Torreya* 39 (November-December 1939): 161–163. Interestingly, in the published article, Bailey does not state that Charles Peck obtained his original specimens of *Arceuthobium* from Millington.

93. John Hendley Barnhart, *Biographical Notes upon Botanists*, vol. 2 (Boston: G. K. Hall, 1956): 493.

94. *Historical Statistics of the United States: Colonial Times to 1970*, vol. 1 (Washington, D.C.: United States Department of Commerce Bureau of the Census, 1975), 129; *A Compendium of the Ninth Census* (Washington, D.C.: Government Printing Office, 1872), 604ff.

95. *Report of the Commissioner of Education for the Year 1872* (Washington, D.C.: Government Printing Office, 1873), 515.

96. *Compendium of the Ninth Census,* 604.

97. Quoted in a review of "Agassiz's Natural History," *The Atlantic Monthly* 1 (January, 1858): 323.

98. Evidence of the middle- and upper-class background of children writing to children's magazines can be found in the letters addressed to such magazines as *The Youth's Companion* and *St. Nicholas Magazine.* For example, see the letter from Emma W. Comfort in *St. Nicholas Magazine* (June 1882), 662.

99. "Progress of Education for Women," in *Report of the Commissioner of Education for the Year 1871* (Washington, D.C.: Government Printing Office, 1872), 511–517. The quote is from page 515. The report adds that even in the fields of industry, new opportunities were opening for women: as stenographers, telegraphers, and printers.

100. *Report of the Annual Meeting of the New England Women's Club* (Boston: Rand, Avery & Co., 31 May 1873), 11, 15.

101. *Second Annual Report of the Women's Centennial Executive Committee* (Philadelphia: Thomas S. Dando, 15 March 1875), 9–10.

102. *Report of the Annual Meeting of the New England Women's Club* (Boston: Rand, Avery & Co., 1873), 14–15.

103. Rossiter, *Women Scientists in America,* 60–61.

104. For wages paid to men and women gardeners and nursery workers, see *Compendium of the Eleventh Census: 1890, Part 3* (Washington, D.C.: Government Printing Office, 1897), 597.

105. Vivian O. Sammons, *Blacks in Science and Education* (Washington, D.C.: Hemisphere Publishers, 1989), 65; Rebecca Lee Crumpler, *Book of Medical Discourses, in Two Parts* (Boston: Cushman, Keating & Co., 1883); Alice Kessler-Harris, *Out to Work: A History of Wage-Earning Women in the United States* (New York: Oxford University Press, 1982), 57, 116.

106. First published in 1872, the magazine *Popular Science Monthly* was an important vehicle for advancing the importance of science education. See *Popular Science Monthly* 1 (March 1869): 23, in which the editors state the pedagogical mission of the magazine. The first graded course of study in natural sciences seems to have been that created by Superintendent William T. Harris for the public schools of St. Louis. See the *Report of the Superintendent of St. Louis, 1872–1873,* 181–191, and Harris's course of study in the appendix of the same volume.

107. See Table 2.4 in Chapter 2.

108. Anne Shannon Monroe, "The Woman Who Should Marry," *Good Housekeeping* 73 (August 1921), 129.

109. Data compiled from Table 1.1 in Rossiter, *Women Scientists in America,* 11.

110. "Anna Botsford Comstock," in Bonta, *Women in the Field,* 154–166; See also "Anna Botsford Scrapbook," in Anna Comstock Papers, SCCU.

111. *Report of the Select Committee of the Board of Education in Relation to the Propriety and Expediency of Establishing a Free Academy for Females* (New York: Wm. C. Bryant & Co., 1849), 7–8.

Chapter 6

1. Quoted in Carolyn Merchant, ed., *Major Problems in American Environmental History: Documents and Essays* (Lexington, Mass.: D. C. Heath, 1993), 200.

2. For example, see C. O. Thompson, "The Scope and Method of Physical Science in the Common School," *The Addresses and Journal of Proceedings of the National Educational Association, 1872* (Boston: N. C. Mason, 1873), 149–158; C. C. Mees, "Indi-

ana State Teachers' Association," *School Science* 1 (May 1901): 166; H. S. Pepoon, "Botanical Field Work in Secondary School," *School Science* 1 (January 1902): 414–418.

3.   Orra Underhill, *The Origins and Development of Elementary School Science* (Chicago: Scott, Foresman and Co., 1941); Lawrence A. Cremin, *The Transformation of the School: Progressivism in American Education, 1876–1957* (New York: Vintage, 1961); Peter J. Schmitt, *Back to Nature: The Arcadian Myth in Urban America* (New York: Oxford University Press, 1969); Tyree Goodwin Minton, "The History of the Nature-Study Movement and Its Role in the Development of Environmental Education" (Ph.D. diss., University of Massachusetts, 1980); Elizabeth Keeney, *The Botanizers* (Chapel Hill, N.C.: The University of North Carolina Press, 1992).

4.   Underhill, *The Origins and Development of Elementary School Science*; Cremin, *The Transformation of the School: Progressivism in American Education, 1876–1957*; Schmitt, *Back to Nature: The Arcadian Myth in Urban America*; Tyree Goodwin Minton, "The History of the Nature-Study Movement and Its Role in the Development of Environmental Education"; Keeney, *The Botanizers*.

5.   Schmitt, *Back to Nature: The Arcadian Myth in Urban America*.

6.   G. Stanley Hall, *Adolescence* (New York: Appleton, 1904), vol. 1, xiv-xv; Sarah Jewett to Mrs. Fields, 12 October 1890, in *Letters of Sarah Orne Jewett*, ed. Annie Fields (Boston: Houghton Mifflin, 1911), 81–82.

7.   Edward J. Renehan Jr., *John Burroughs: An American Naturalist* (Post Mills, Vt.: Chelsea Green, 1992), 127.

8.   G. Stanley Hall's original report, "The Contents of Children's Minds on Entering School," appeared in *Princeton Review* 2 (May 1883): 249–272. See also G. Stanley Hall et al., *Aspects of Child Life and Education* (New York: D. Appleton, 1921), 1–52. The quote is from page 25.

9.   Renehan, *John Burroughs*, 240.

10.   Charles B. Scott, *Nature Study and the Child* (Boston: D.C. Heath & Co., 1900), 123, 34.

11.   Liberty Hyde Bailey to R. H. Chittenden, 31 October 1908 in Liberty Hyde Bailey Papers, box 9, unprocessed additions, SCCU; "The Men Who Have Been Selected by President Roosevelt," *The Farmer's Union Sun,* 11 November 1908, in ibid.; "The Session of the Commission on Country Life," *Atlanta Journal,* 14 November 1908, in ibid.; E. L. Palmer, "Fifty Years of Nature Study," in *Nature Magazine* (November 1957), 475.

12.   Keeney, *The Botanizers,* 133–145.

13.   Marcia Myers Bonta, *Women in the Field: America's Pioneering Women Naturalists* (College Station, Tex.: Texas A&M University Press, 1991), 18–29. The quote is from page 24.

14.   Bonta, "Mary Treat," in *Women in the Field,* 42–48.

15.   Harlan H. Ballard, "The Agassiz Association," *St. Nicholas* 8 (November 1880): 28–31. In the association's first report, Ballard described it as a "natural history society."

16.   See letters in "Agassiz Association, Thirteenth Report," in *St. Nicholas* 9 (May 1892): 585–586.

17.   Keeney, *The Botanizers,* 140–141.

18.   See Maurice Bigelow, "Introduction," in *The Nature Study Review* 1 (January 1905): 1–2; E. L. Palmer, "Fifty Years of Nature Study," 474.

19.   Bigelow, "Introduction," 1.

20.   Fred L. Charles to Gentlemen of the Houghton Mifflin Company, 23 January 1911, box 6, American Nature Study Society Records (hereafter as ANSS), SCCU. Charles wrote, "The membership in the American Nature-Study Society has materially increased during the past year. Teachers throughout this country and Canada are finding it very helpful." Women members often wrote to Charles recommending articles or talks by other women. For example, see Charles to Emily Westberg, 17 February

1911, box 6, ibid. Charles replies, "I should be glad indeed to see the paper by Mrs. Ford on 'Lessons from Nature,' which you suggest be published. Could you obtain it for me?"

21. I have chosen 1891 as the starting date for a period I describe as "the heyday" of the movement. In this year appeared the first published course of study, Wilbur Jackman's *Nature Study for Common Schools*. From then until 1916, education journals and popular magazines often published accounts of nature study; after 1916, such references dropped dramatically from the literature. References to nature study increased again from 1922 to 1929, but during this later period, many of the articles were highly critical of the movement. This conclusion is based on an analysis of the publications listed in *Education Literature, 1907–1932*, ed. Malcolm Hamilton (New York: Garland Publishing, 1979), volumes 1–25.

22. These titles are drawn from the list of reference and literature books included in Anna Comstock's *Handbook of Nature Study* (Ithaca, N.Y.: Comstock Publishing Co., 1927 [1911]), 924–932.

23. Lawrence A. Cremin, *The Transformation of the School: Progressivism in American Education, 1876–1957* (New York: Vintage Books, 1964), 128–135; Jack K. Campbell, *Colonel Francis W. Parker, the Children's Crusader* (New York: Teachers College Press, 1967).

24. "Noted Teachers," in Francis Wayland Parker Scrapbook 4, Francis Wayland Parker Scrapbooks, Special Collections University of Chicago (hereafter SCUC); Campbell, *Colonel Francis W. Parker, The Children's Crusader*, 70ff; Edward H. Reisner, *The Evolution of the Common School* (New York: Macmillan, 1930), 507ff.

25. "The Parker Anniversary," (Quincy, Mass., April 1890), file 3, box 1, in Francis Wayland Parker Papers, SCUC; Lelia E. Patridge, *The "Quincy Methods" Illustrated: Pen Photographs from the Quincy Schools* (New York: E. L. Kellogg, 1885); Campbell, *Colonel Francis W. Parker, The Children's Crusader*, 79.

26. Will S. Monroe, *History of the Pestalozzian Movement in the United States*; Nina C. Vandewalker, *The Kindergarten in American Education* (New York.: Macmillan, 1908); Charles De Garmo, *Herbart and the Herbartians* (New York: Charles Scribner's Sons, 1895); Harold B. Dunkel, *Herbart and Herbartianism: An Educational Ghost Story* (Chicago: University of Chicago Press, 1970).

27. Richard R. Olmsted, "The Nature-Study Movement in American Education," (Ed.D. diss., Indiana University, 1967), 29–32; "The Normal" (1889), a news clipping in Parker Scrapbook 7, SCUC. The clipping states that "W. J. [sic] Jackman, a Harvard graduate, takes the position of teacher of science." See also "The Cook County Normal School, 1891" in ibid., which states: "[Jackman] is attempting the solution of that great problem, 'How to teach science in the common schools.'" At Cook County, Jackman replaced Henry Straight, the man Parker had initially chosen to develop a program of science education. Henry and his wife Emma had both been students of Louis Agassiz at the Anderson School of Natural History; afterward, they had assumed positions at Oswego Normal School, from which Parker recruited them. Straight's career at Cook County was cut short when he died unexpectedly of a heart attack at age 40. For a brief discussion of Straight's contribution to the nature-study movement, see Olmsted, "The Nature-Study Movement in American Education," 29ff.

28. Francis W. Parker, "A Sketch of the Work in the Quincy Schools from 1875 to 1880, Part V," *The School Journal* (August 1885), Parker Scrapbook 6, SCUC.

29. Francis W. Parker, "The Value of Field Excursions," *The School Journal* (11 February 1899), Parker Scrapbook 12, SCUC.

30. "Characteristic Normal Schools: Chicago and Cook County Normal School," a clipping in Parker Scrapbook 12, SCUC. A penciled note gives the date as 1896. Anna de Koven, "The Pioneer of the New Education in America," in *The Illustrated American* (no date given), Parker Scrapbook 12, SCUC.

31. "The School Journal, February 11, 1899," in Col. Francis W. Parker Scrapbooks, Scrapbook 12, SCUC.

32. "Fad May Lead to Strife," newsclipping in Parker Scrapbook 12, SCUC. A handwritten note gives the date as 7 October 1896. According to this article, some students opposed the requirement to do fieldwork.

33. Coulter coauthored a nature-study handbook. See John M. Coulter, John G. Coulter, and Alice Jean Patterson, *Practical Nature Study and Elementary Agriculture* (New York: D. Appleton & Co., 1909).

34. Eliot was quoted as stating that "natural science is to be studied not in books but in things . . ." in "Education in 1884," *Journal of Education*, in Parker Scrapbook 6, SCUC.

35. A. Hunter Dupree, *Science in the Federal Government: A History of Politics and Activities* (Baltimore: The Johns Hopkins University Press, 1986), 169–170.

36. Anna Botsford Comstock, *Handbook of Nature Study* (Ithaca, N.Y.: Comstock Publishing Co., 1911), v–ix.

37. Comstock, *Handbook of Nature Study*, preface; Elizabeth Carss, "Course in Nature-Study" in *Teachers College Record* 1 (March 1900).

38. Clifton F. Hodge, *Nature Study and Life* (Boston: Ginn, 1902); Liberty Hyde Bailey, *The Nature-Study Idea* (New York: Doubleday, Page & Co., 1903).

39. D. Lange, *Handbook of Nature Study for Teachers and Pupils in Elementary Schools* (New York: Macmillan, 1898), preface; Carss, "Course in Nature Study"; Wilbur S. Jackman, "Nature Study," *The Third Yearbook of the National Society for the Scientific Study of Education* (Chicago: The University of Chicago Press, 1904).

40. Theodore R. Sizer, *Secondary Schools at the Turn of the Century* (Westport, Conn.: Greenwood Press, 1964), 148–182, 187–190.

41. George E. DeBoer, *A History of Ideas in Science Education* (New York: Teachers College Press, 1992), 40–45.

42. "Preliminary Report of Committee on School Progress," in *First Yearbook of the American Nature Study Society* (Toledo, Ohio: The American Nature Study Society, 1925): 3–7. Cities from twenty-two states and the District of Columbia are represented in the sample. There is no indication in the published report as to whether this was a randomly selected sample or simply a poor rate of response to a questionnaire mailed to every state. Because the author mentions "cities not yet reached by this investigation" (6), it is possible that the survey was never intended to encompass every state.

43. The following discussion is based on an analysis of fourteen nature-study handbooks and courses of study published between the years of 1891 and 1932. The authors of these materials included educators and scientists from normal schools, private universities, land-grant colleges, and public schools. For the purposes of this study, a *handbook* is defined as a text for teachers containing information about the aims, principles, and methods of nature study. A *course of study* is defined as a graded or ungraded sequential curriculum. Many of the texts included in this study are a combination of both handbook and course of study.

44. The texts examined in this sample include Liberty Hyde Bailey, *The Nature-Study Idea* (New York: Doubleday, 1903); Anna Botsford Comstock, *Handbook of Nature-Study* (Ithaca, N.Y.: Comstock Publishing Co., 1911); John M. Coulter, John G. Coulter, and Alice Jean Patterson, *Practical Nature Study and Elementary Agriculture* (New York: D. Appleton and Co., 1909); Horace Hall Cummings, *Nature Study by Grades* (New York: American Book Company, 1908); Elliot R. Downing, *A Field and Laboratory Guide in Biological Nature-Study* (Chicago: The University of Chicago, 1918); Clifton F. Hodge, *Nature Study and Life* (Boston: Ginn, 1902); Frederick L. Holtz, *Nature Study, a Manual for Teachers and Students* (New York: Charles Scribner's Sons, 1908); Wilbur S. Jackman, *Nature Study for the Common Schools* (New York: Henry Holt & Co., 1894); Wilbur S. Jackman, "Nature Study," in *The Third Yearbook of the National Society for the Scientific Study of Education* (Chicago: The University of Chicago Press, 1904); D. Lange, *Handbook of Nature Study for Teachers and Pupils in Elementary Schools* (New York: Macmillan, 1898); Francis E. Lloyd, "Aims of Nature Study," in *Teachers College Record* 1 (March 1900); Charles A.

McMurry, *Special Method in Science for the First Four Grades of the Common School* (Bloomington, Ill.: Public School Publishing Co., 1896); Charles B. Scott, *Nature Study and the Child* (Boston: D. C. Heath & Co., 1900); Samuel Christian Schmucker, *The Study of Nature* (Philadelphia: J. B. Lippincott, 1909). Because many authors stated more than one aim in their prefaces, the total of the percentages exceeds 100. One author, D. Lange, stated no aims in his text, which is therefore not included in this sample.

45. For example, see Scott, *Nature Study and the Child*, 32, 100; Hodge, *Nature Study and Life*, 31; Schmucker, *The Study of Nature*, 9, 41; Cummings, *Nature Study by Grades*, 21; Holtz, *Nature Study, a Manual for Teachers and Students*, 20.

46. McMurry, *Special Method in Science*, 48–49. Similar statements can be found in Jackman, *Nature Study for the Common Schools*, 7ff; Scott, *Nature Study and the Child*, 30, 113; Hodge, *Nature Study and Life*, 20ff; Cornell, *Cornell Nature-Study Leaflets* (Ithaca, N.Y.: Cornell University, 1904), 19; Holtz, *Nature Study, a Manual*, 6; Schmucker, *The Study of Nature*, 9, 39; Coulter, Coulter, and Patterson, *Practical Nature Study*, 16, 26; Comstock, *Handbook of Nature-Study*, 1.

47. Schmucker, *The Study of Nature*, 39.

48. Wilbur S. Jackman, *Field Work in Nature Study* (Chicago, Ill.: Published by the author, 1984 [1891]), 32, Cubberley Library, Stanford University.

49. Comstock, *Handbook of Nature-Study*, 350.

50. For example, see photographs of children's nature-study work included in Jackman, "Nature Study," *The Third Yearbook of the National Society for the Scientific Study of Education* (Chicago: The University of Chicago Press, 1904). Another source of photographs are city school reports. For instance, the 1914 report of the Los Angeles City School District includes photographs of students collecting specimens on a hillside and at a beach. See *Annual Report of the Board of Education of the Los Angeles City School District, 1913–14* (Los Angeles, 1914), 92.

51. The photograph, which depicts a school garden from an unknown school, is from the Wisconsin State Historical Society Archives, WHI (X3) 36788, CF 3774.

52. National Education Association, *Report of the Committee on Secondary School Studies* (Washington, D.C.: U.S. Government Printing Office, 1893), 159.

53. George Counts, *The Selective Character of American Secondary Education* (Chicago: University of Chicago Press, 1922), 148–149. See also William Reese, *The Origins of the American High School* (New Haven, Conn.: Yale University Press, 1995).

54. Quoted in a review of "Agassiz's Natural History," *The Atlantic Monthly* (Boston: Phillips, Samson & Co., 1858), 323.

55. See Chapter 5 of this book.

56. Dan Lortie, *Schoolteacher, a Sociological Study* (Chicago, Ill.: University of Chicago Press, 1975), 39–40.

57. Quoted in Elga Wasserman, *The Door in the Dream: Conversations with Eminent Women in Science* (Washington, D.C.: Joseph Henry Press, 2000), 37–38. The quote is on page 37.

58. See John L. Rury, "Who Became Teachers and Why: The Social Characteristics of Teachers in American History," in *American Teachers: Histories of a Profession at Work* ed. Donald Warren (New York: Macmillan Publishing Company, 1989), 9–48; Geraldine Jonçich Clifford, "Man/Woman/Teacher: Gender, Family and Career in American Educational History," in ibid., 293–343; Michael W. Apple, "Teaching and 'Women's Work': A Comparative Historical and Ideological Analysis," *Teachers College Record* 86 (Spring 1985), 457–473; Kathryn Kish Sklar, *Catharine Beecher: A Study in American Domesticity* (New York and London: W. W. Norton & Co., 1976), 97–98; Barbara Miller Solomon, *In the Company of Educated Women* (New Haven and London: Yale University Press, 1985), 14–26. See also Carl F. Kaestle, *Pillars of the Republic: Common Schools and American Society, 1780–1860* (New York: Hill & Wang, 1983).

59. Catharine Beecher, *An Essay on the Education of Female Teachers* (New York: Van Nostrand & Dwight, 1835). For a discussion of this essay, see Sklar, *Catharine Beecher: A Study in American Domesticity*, 113ff; Jeanne Boydston, Mary Kelley, and Anne Margolis, *The Limits of Sisterhood: The Beecher Sisters on Women's Rights and Woman's Sphere* (Chapel Hill, N.C.: University of North Carolina Press, 1988), 115ff.

60. Zilpah Grant, "Benefits of Female Education," 1836, Ipswich Female Seminary Papers, Mount Holyoke College Archives.

61. *Third Annual Report of the Young Ladies' Association of the New-Hampton Female Seminary, for the Promotion of Literature and Missions; with the Constitution, etc. 1835–36* (Boston: John Putnam, 1837), 20, 23.

62. Quoted in *Annual Report of the State Superintendent of Public Instruction of the State of Wisconsin* (Madison, Wisc.: Atwood & Rublee, 1858), 157.

63. Ibid., 119. The superintendent quoted Barnard on page 157.

64. Quoted in Geraldine Jonçich Clifford, "'Marry, Stitch, Die or Do Worse': Educating Women for Work," in *Work, Youth, and Schooling: Historical Perspectives on Vocationalism in American Education*, ed. Harvey Kantor and David B. Tyack (Stanford, Calif.: Stanford University Press, 1982): 238.

65. *Thirteenth Report of the Superintendent of Public Instruction for the State of Indiana* (Indianapolis, Ind.: Joseph J. Bingham, 1865), 30–31.

66. Ibid., 32.

67. "Women as Teachers," *Educational Review* 2 (1891): 358–362.

68. Patricia Schmuck, "Women School Employees in the United States," in *Women Educators: Employees of Schools in Western Countries,* ed. Patricia Schmuck (Albany, N.Y., 1987), 75–76; John Clinton Maxwell, "Should the Educations of Boys and Girls Differ?" (Ph.D. diss., University of Wisconsin, 1966), 100. For a comparative discussion of the feminization of the teaching force during this period, see James C. Albisetti, "The Feminization of Teaching in the Nineteenth Century: A Comparative Perspective," *The History of Education* 22 (September 1993): 253–263.

69. Of the sample of fourteen nature-study handbooks and courses of study examined here, only one was solely authored by a women: Anna Comstock's *Handbook of Nature Study.* Alice Jean Patterson of Illinois State Normal University coauthored another, *Practical Nature Study and Elementary Agriculture.* On the other hand, of a sample of forty-seven nature-study readers, twenty-three were authored by women, sixteen by men, and eight were coauthored by men and women. This sample of forty-seven readers comprises all of the texts found on one shelf in the textbook collection of Cubberley Library, Stanford University, from number 518.3 J52 to 518.3 T863v.1.

70. Anna Comstock, *Handbook of Nature Study,* vii.

71. *Annual Report of the Public Schools of the City of Oakland for the Year Ending June 30, 1897* (Oakland, Calif.: R. S. Kitchener, 1897). The report states that 120 teachers initially worked with Professor Jenkins. There is some confusion over the exact figure, because Oakland's 1904 report states that seventy teachers initially worked with Jenkins.

72. *Oakland Annual Report,* 1900, 8.

73. Ibid.

74. *Annual Report of the Public Schools of the City of Oakland, 1897–98* (Oakland, Calif.: R. S. Kitchener, 1898), 14c; "Effie Belle McFadden," in *The Leland Stanford Junior University Sixth Annual Register, 1896–97* (Palo Alto, Calif.: University Press, 1897), 155.

75. "Bertha Chapman Cady," *Stanford University Alumni Directory, 1891–1931* 4 (Stanford, Calif.: University Press, 1932), 149; "Bertha Chapman," *The Stanford Alumnus* 2 (October 1900), 13; "Effie McFadden," in ibid., 14.

76. In Los Angeles, Charles Lincoln Edwards served as director of nature study. The direct supervision of nature-study work in schools was undertaken by assistant super-

visors. In 1924, Edwards listed eight "past and present Assistant Supervisors of Nature Study," of whom seven were women. See Charles Lincoln Edwards, *Nature-Study, Part I* (Los Angeles: Hesperian Press, 1924), vii.

77. Jennie Hall's role as supervisor is mentioned by Theodosia Hadley in a letter to E. L. Palmer, 6 July 1928, file 10, box 2, ANSS, SCCU; Fannie Stebbins, Clelia Paroni, and Elizabeth K. Peeples are mentioned in a letter from L. Lenore Conover to Charles L. Pack, 16 November 1925, file 3, box 2, ibid.; Emelie Yunker is mentioned in the manuscript titled "American Nature Study Society," 3 July 1929, file 3, box 3, ibid.

78. Theodosia Hadley to E. L. Palmer, 29 May 1928, file 10, box 2, in ANSS, SCCU.

79. Occupational Guidance Council, *Occupational Planning for College Women* (Columbia, Mo.: Stephens College, 1946), 280–282.

80. "Helen Swett," *The Stanford Alumnus* 12 (March 1911): 216.

81. Helen Swett to Charles E. Schwartz, 2 September 1900, in Helen Swett Papers, Bancroft Library, SCUCB.

82. E. Laurence Palmer to Richard L. Weaver, 29 April 1943, box 3, ANSS, CUA.

83. Helen Swett to Charles E. Schwartz, 10 November 1900, box 2, in Helen Swett Papers, Bancroft Library, UC Berkeley.

84. See William G. Vinal, "Report of the Committee on Preparation of Teachers," *First Yearbook of the American Nature Study Society* (Toledo, Ohio: The American Nature Study Society, 1925), 8–19. Such positions were still relatively rare, however. According to Vinal's report, of the 143 members of the American Association of Teachers Colleges, all were found to be teaching natural science, but only twelve had professors of nature study.

85. "Anna Botsford Comstock," *Ithaca Journal* (Tuesday, 26 August 1930) in Anna Comstock Papers, SCCU; Ruth Sawyer, "What Makes Mrs. Comstock Great," in *The Woman Citizen*, (undated), Anna Comstock Papers. Comstock is discussed in some detail in Bonta, *Women in the Field*, 154–166. See also Anna Comstock, *The Comstocks of Cornell* (Ithaca, N.Y.: Cornell University Press, 1953); Edward H. Smith, "The Comstocks and Cornell: In the People's Service," *Annual Review of Entomology* 21 (1976): 1–25.

86. See Elizabeth Cady Stanton, Susan B. Anthony, Matilda Joslyn Gage, et al., eds., *History of Woman Suffrage*, 6 vols. (New York: Fowler and Wells, 1881–1922); Anne Firor Scott and Andrew M. Scott, *One Half the People: The Fight for Woman Suffrage* (Philadelphia, Penn.: Lippincott, 1975); Marjorie Spruill Wheeler, *One Woman, One Vote: Rediscovering the Woman Suffrage Movement* (Portland, Ore.: New Sage Press, 1995).

87. "Industrial Competition of Women with Men," *Public Opinion* 40 (February 1906): 208.

88. Ella Flagg Young, quoted in anonymous, "The Highest Salaried Woman in the World," *Western Journal of Education* 14 (1909): 10.

89. "Women in Nebraska," *Journal of Education* (7 September 1911): 241.

90. Earl Barnes, "The Feminizing of Culture," *Atlantic Monthly* 109 (June 1912): 773.

91. Charles W. Bardeen, "The Monopolizing Woman Teacher," *Educational Review* 43 (January 1912): 19–20. For a recent history of women administrators in the field of education, see Jackie M. Blount, *Destined to Rule the Schools: Women and the Superintendency, 1873–1995* (New York: State University of New York Press, 1998).

92. "Grace Strachan," *Journal of Education* (16 November 1911): 520; "Triumph of Boston Teachers," ibid. (20 April 1911): 436.

93. Blount, *Destined to Rule the Schools: Women and the Superintendency, 1873–1995*, 61–90.

94. Fred L. Charles to Philip Dawell, 13 January 1911, box 6, ANSS, SCCU. In this letter, Charles explains that the *Review* is the official journal of the American Nature-Study Society.

95. Fred Charles to Frank C. Patten, 16 January 1911, box 6, ANSS, SCCU.

96. The society's records include membership lists of these clubs published in the early 1940s. See Harold O'Byrne to Grace M. Fiske, 16 May 1942, file 34, box 2, ANSS, SCCU; "Bangor Bird Conservation Club," Inc., ibid.; Mildred V. Hinderer to Harold I. O'Byrne, 29 September 1942, file 35, box 2, ibid.; "Nature Club: Pittsburgh, Pennsylvania 1943–1944," ibid.; Richard Weaver to Grace A. Clapsaddle, 22 November 1943, ibid.; Grace Clapsaddle to Richard Weaver, 5 December 1943, ibid.; Edith Long to Richard L. Weaver, 13 May 1943, file 38, box 2, ibid.; "Membership List: Webster Groves Nature Study Society, April 1941," ibid.

97. The 1909 figure is based on a random sample of 273 members listed alphabetically from Albert to Lamont published in *The Nature-Study Review* 5 (March 1909), 3. The information about membership renewals in 1911 is found in Fred L. Charles to Emily C. Westberg, 17 February 1911, box 6, ANSS, SCCU. The figure for 1927 is compiled from a list of members in "Members of the American Nature Study Society Who Sent in Their Dues to the Secretary-Treasurer," file 6, box 3, ibid.

98. Charles to the Assoc. Editorial Service, 30 January 1911, box 6, ANSS, SCCU.

99. Fred L. Charles to B. M. Davis, 19 January 1911, box 6, ANSS, SCCU; Charles to Miss L. L. Wilson, 19 February 1911, ibid.

100. Fred L. Charles to Miss Carrie N. Jacobs, 1 February 1911, box 6, ANSS, SCCU.

101. Maurice Bigelow, "First Meeting of American Nature-Study Society—Report of the Secretary," in *Nature-Study Review* 4 (January 1908).

102. E. Laurence Palmer to Richard L. Weaver, 29 April 1943, box 3, ANSS, SCCU.

103. "Minutes of the Kansas City Meeting," file 3, box 3, ANSS, SCCU; Palmer, "Fifty Years of Nature Study," 475, 477, 478.

104. See Blount, *Destined to Rule the Schools*.

105. Clifton F. Hodge, *Nature Study and Life* (Boston: Ginn, 1902), 2ff.

Chapter 7

1. John Francis Latimer, *What's Happened to Our High Schools?* (Washington, D.C.: Public Affairs Press, 1958), 149; David B. Tyack and Elizabeth Hansot, *Learning Together: A History of Coeducation in American Public Schools* (New York: Russell Sage Foundation, 1992), 182–183.

2. Patricia Phillips, *The Scientific Lady: A Social History of Women's Scientific Interests, 1520–1918* (London, England: Weidenfeld and Nicolson, 1990), 251ff.

3. Margaret Rutherford, "Feminism and the Secondary School Curriculum, 1890–1920: (Ph.D. diss., Stanford University, 1977); Jane Bernard Powers, *The 'Girl Question' in Education: Vocational Education for Young Women in the Progressive Era* (London: The Falmer Press, 1992).

4. For a discussion of seventeenth-century views of female rationality, see Patricia Phillips, *The Scientific Lady*, 11–25.

5. The discussion on pages 151–153 is taken, with little adaptation, from "Mapping the Landscape of Higher Schooling," in *Chartered Schools: Two Hundred Years of Independent Academies in the United States, 1727–1925,* eds. Nancy Beadie and Kim Tolley (New York: Routledge, 2002), 32–35. I would like to thank my coeditor Nancy Beadie and Routledge for granting permission to reproduce the text here.

6. Thomas Woody, *A History of Women's Education in the United States,* vol. 1 (New York: Octagon Books, 1974 [1929]), 341.

7. See Kim Tolley, "Mapping the Landscape of Higher Schooling, 1727–1850," *Chartered Schools,* 32–33.

8. Mary O. Nutting, "Mount Holyoke Female Seminary, South Hadley," *The American Journal of Education* 30 (July 1880): 589–592. The quote is on page 590. For more

information about Mount Holyoke, see Elizabeth Alden Green, *Mary Lyon and Mount Holyoke: Opening the Gates* (Hanover, N.H.: University Press of New England, 1979).

9. *Tenth Annual Catalogue of the Mount Holyoke Female Seminary in South Hadley, Massachusetts, 1846–7* (South Hadley, Mass.), 12, American Antiquarian Society.

10. Thomas Coon, ed., *North Carolina Schools and Academies, 1790–1840: A Documentary History* (Raleigh, N.C.: Edwards & Broughton, 1915), xxx, xxxiv. It is important to note, however, that the mere inclusion of a subject in an institution's advertised course of study is no indication of the numbers of students who may actually have enrolled.

11. See Christie Anne Farnham, *The Education of the Southern Belle: Higher Education and Student Socialization in the Ante-bellum South* (New York: New York University Press, 1994), 28–32.

12. Quoted in Thomas Woody, *A History of Women's Education in the United States*, vol. 1, 408–409.

13. Quoted in James Mulhern, *A History of Secondary Education in Pennsylvania* (New York: Arno Press, 1969), 396.

14. See Farnham, *The Education of the Southern Belle*, 12ff. Farnham argues that current scholarly assessments of these schools reflect not only a northeastern bias, but an unwarranted dependence on the views of earlier scholars, who dismissed women's colleges because they did not offer the classics to the same degree as the leading men's colleges of the period.

15. Quoted in Woody, *A History of Women's Education*, vol. 2, 161.

16. Quoted in ibid., 164.

17. Ibid.

18. Ibid., 167, 169–170.

19. Based on a sample of 162 girls' schools from twenty states, historian Thomas Woody reported that forty-seven percent provided instruction in Latin between 1749 and 1871. However, by including eighteenth-century schools in his sample, Woody's data may not accurately reflect the degree of increase of Latin in the curriculum after 1830. James Mulhern, who discovered that between 1830 and 1889, seventy-two percent of Pennsylvania girls' schools offered Latin, provides a possibly more representative picture of developments in the latter half of the century. See Woody, *Women's Education in the United States*, vol. 1, 418; Mulhern, *A History of Secondary Education in Pennsylvania*, (New York: Arno Press, 1969), 428. Mulhern's data were derived from the catalogs of ninety Pennsylvania girls' schools.

20. Mulhern, *A History of Secondary Education in Pennsylvania*, 428.

21. Per Siljestrom, *The Educational Institutions of the United States, Their Character and Organization* (London: John Chapman, 1853), 308–309.

22. Ibid.

23. See Charles Alfred True, *A History of Agricultural Education in the United States, 1785–1925* (New York: Arno Press, 1969), 215.

24. *Register of the University of California, 1871* (Oakland, California), 30; *Register of the University of California, 1873*, 15–16, Bancroft Library, Special Collections, UC Berkeley. This pattern, in which more women enrolled in the College of Arts than in the College of Letters, changed drastically after 1874, when the College of Letters divided into two categories: a classical course and a literary course. Admission to the literary course did not require knowledge of the classics. See *Register of the University of California, 1874*, 12–14.

25. For a discussion of the relatively low status of the scientific course, see Geraldine Jonçich Clifford, "Scientists and the Schools of the Nineteenth Century: The Case of American Physicists," *American Quarterly* 18 (Winter 1966): 680–681.

26. *Report of the Annual Meeting of the New England Women's Club* (Boston: Rand, Avery & Co., 1873), 19.

27. See Geraldine Jonçich Clifford, *"Equally in View": The University of California, Its Women, and the Schools* (Berkeley, Calif.: Center for Studies in Higher Education and Institute of Governmental Studies, 1995), 98–99.

28. Frank Luther Mott, *A History of American Magazines, 1865–1885* (Cambridge, Mass.: Harvard University Press, 1938), 104–105.

29. "Editor's Table," *Popular Science Monthly* 1 (May-October, 1872): 497.

30. For a discussion of the effect of economic expansion of technological change and work, see Edward W. Stevens Jr., *The Grammar of the Machine: Technical Literacy and Early Industrial Expansion in the United States* (New Haven, Conn.: Yale University Press, 1995), 8–29. For the impact of the land-grant universities and agricultural experiment stations on employment opportunities in science, see A. Hunter Dupree, *Science in the Federal Government: A History of Policies and Activities* (Baltimore, Md.: Johns Hopkins University Press, 1986), 149–183; Daniel J. Kevles, *The Physicists: The History of a Scientific Community in Modern America* (Cambridge, Mass.: Harvard University Press, 1987), 60–74.

31. Ellwood P. Cubberley, *Public Education in the United States* (Boston: Houghton Mifflin Co., 1947), 542–543.

32. Sara Burstall, *The Education of Girls in the United States* (New York: Arno Press, 1971 [1894]), 76.

33. I. E. Goldwasser, "Shall Elective Courses be Established in the Seventh and Eighth Grades of the Elementary School?" in *Readings in Vocational Guidance*, ed. Meyer Bloomfield (Boston: Ginn & Co., 1915), 211.

34. Irving King, "The Vocational Interests, Study Habits, and Amusements of the Pupils in Certain High Schools in Iowa," in *Readings in Vocational Guidance*, 174, 177.

35. *Department of the Office of the State Superintendent High School Inspection Reports [Wisconsin]*, Wisconsin State Historical Society (hereafter WSHS), boxes 1–4. The data are drawn from the reports made by inspectors who visited Wisconsin high schools. There is no indication that inspectors visited every class at each school, but they gave the subject of those classes they visited, along with teachers' names and brief evaluations of the teaching observed. I collected data at four-year intervals.

36. Frank P. Goodwin, "Vocational Guidance in Cincinnati," in *Readings in Vocational Guidance*, 177.

37. Geraldine Jonçich Clifford, *"Equally in View," the University of California, Its Women, and the Schools*, 45.

38. John Francis Latimer, *What's Happened to Our High Schools?* (Washington, D.C.: Public Affairs Press, 1958), 149.

39. Earl Barnes, "The Feminizing of Culture," *Atlantic Monthly* 109 (June 1912): 770.

40. Josephine Conger-Kaneko, "The 'Effeminization' of the United States," *The World's Work* 12 (May 1906): 7523.

41. Ibid.

42. See discussion in Chapter 3.

43. Calvin Olin Davis, *Public Secondary Education* (Chicago: Rand McNally & Co., 1917), 209.

44. *Report of the Committee of Ten on Secondary School Subjects* (New York: American Book Co., 1894), 209.

45. Davis, *Public Secondary Education*, 210.

46. Quoted in Woody, *A History of Women's Education in the United States*, vol. 1, 115–116.

47. Geraldine Clifford, "'Marry, Stitch, Die, or Do Worse': Educating Women for Work," in *Work, Youth, and Schooling: Historical Perspectives on Vocationalism in American Education*, ed. Harvey Kantor and David B. Tyack (Stanford, Calif.: Stanford University Press, 1982): 228.

48. *Omaha City Schools Annual Report of the Board of Education* (Omaha, Nebr.: Rees Printing Co., 1886), 39, 58.

49.   *Eleventh Biennial Report of the Department of Public Instruction [Wisconsin]*, 101, WSHS.

50.   Luke Owen Pike, "Women and Political Power," *Popular Science Monthly* 1 (May–October 1872): 82–94. The quotes are on pages 85 and 83, respectively.

51.   Dr. Thomas Laycock, "Manhood and Womanhood," *Appleton's Journal of Literature, Science, and Art* 1 (12 June 1869), 343.

52.   Quoted in E. Anthony Rotundo, *American Manhood* (New York: Basic Books, 1993), 217.

53.   See E. Anthony Rotundo, *American Manhood*, 217ff; Sally Gregory Kohlstedt and Mark R. Jorgensen, "'The Irrepressible Woman Question': Women's Responses to Evolutionary Ideology," in *Disseminating Darwinism: The Role of Place, Race, Religion, and Gender*, eds. Ronald L. Numbers and John Stenhouse (New York: Cambridge University Press, 1999).

54.   See Aileen Kraditor, *The Ideas of the Woman Suffrage Movement 1890–1920* (New York: Norton, 1981 [1965]); Rotundo, *American Manhood*, 217–221.

55.   See Nancy Cott, *The Grounding of Modern Feminism* (New Haven, Conn.: Yale University Press, 1987); Marjorie Spruill Wheeler, *New Women of the New South: The Leaders of the Woman Suffrage Movement in the Southern States* (New York: Oxford University Press, 1993); Aileen S. Kraditor, *The Ideas of the Woman Suffrage Movement, 1890–1920* (New York: Norton, 1981 [1965]).

56.   For a discussion of Gilman's role in debates concerning the "woman question" and Darwinism at the end of the century, see Sally Gregory Kohlstedt and Mark R. Jorgensen, "'The Irrepressible Woman Question,'" 267–293. See Gilman's autobiography for discussion of the influences that shaped her work: *The Living of Charlotte Perkins Gilman: An Autobiography* (New York: Appleton-Century, 1935). For a recent study of views of women before Darwin, see Nancy Tuana, *The Less Noble Sex: Scientific, Religious, and Philosophical Conceptions of Woman's Nature* (Bloomington: Indiana University Press, 1993). An excellent source for Gilman's publications is Gray Scharnhorst, *Charlotte Perkins Gilman: A Bibliography* (Methchen, N.J.: Scarecrow Press, 1985).

57.   Antoinette Brown Blackwell, *The Sexes Throughout Nature* (New York: Putnam, 1875), 11; For discussion of Blackwell's ideas in the context of debates over Charles Darwin's theories, see Kohlstedt and Jorgensen, "'The Irrepressible Woman Question,'" 274–278.

58.   Carol Hymowitz and Michaele Weissman, *A History of Women in America* (New York: Bantam Books, 1978), 273ff. The quotes are on page 274.

59.   Mary W. Whitney, "Scientific Study and Work for Women," *Education* 3 (September–July 1883), 64.

60.   J. E. Armstrong, "Limited Segregation," *School Review* 14 (December 1906): 729–734. Armstrong's experiment is discussed at some length in Tyack and Hansot, *Learning Together*, 179–180.

61.   Barnes, "The Feminizing of Culture," 773.

62.   Quoted in Powers, *The "Girl Question" in Education*, 52–53.

63.   Thomas R. Cole, "Segregation at the Broadway High School, Seattle," *School Review* 22 (1915): 550–553.

64.   Quoted in Tyack and Hansot, *Learning Together*, 182.

65.   Will Courson, "Sociological Aspect of Chemistry for Girls," *School Science and Mathematics* 19 (December 1919): 823–828.

66.   Tyack and Hansot, *Learning Together*, 181–182.

67.   *Eleventh Biennial Report of the Department of Public Instruction* (Madison, Wisc.: Democrat Printing Co., 1904), 105.

68.   Powers, *The "Girl Question" in Education*, 67.

69.   Barnes, "The Feminizing of Culture," 773.

70.   Nellie Kedzie Jones, typescript of an article "Written for Home Economics Journal," in Nellie Kedzie Jones Papers, WSHS.

71.   *Omaha City Schools Annual Report* (Omaha, Nebr.: Rees Printing Co., 1882), 38.

72.   Jones, "Mrs. Nellie Sawyer Kedzie Jones," typescript in Jones Papers, WSHS.

73.   Margaret Rossiter, *Women Scientists in America: Struggles and Strategies to 1940* (Baltimore: The Johns Hopkins University Press, 1982), 64–65.

74.   "Nellie Kedzie Jones, Teacher is Dead at 97," newsclipping in Jones Papers, WSHS.

75.   Quoted in Powers, *The "Girl Question" in Education*, 66–67.

76.   *Eleventh Biennial Report of the Department of Public Instruction*, 103.

77.   Jones, typescript titled "Written for Home Economics Journal," 3, in Jones Papers, WSHS.

78.   R. A. Walker to R. M. DeWitt, 3 March 1928, box 4, Department of Public Instruction High School Inspection Reports, WSHS.

79.   Clifford, "Marry, Stitch, Die, or Do Worse," 242.

80.   Jones, typescript titled "Mrs. Nellie Sawyer Kedzie Jones," 6, in Jones Papers, WSHS.

81.   Jones, transcript titled, "What Did You Do?–Questions Asked Me," in Jones Papers, WSHS.

82.   George S. Counts, *The Senior High School Curriculum* (Chicago: University of Chicago Press, 1926), 104.

83.   Powers, *The "Girl Question" in Education*, 41.

84.   George Counts, *The Selective Character of American Secondary Education* (Chicago: University of Chicago Press, 1922), 57.

85.   See Table 7.7.

86.   Maurine Weiner Greenwald, *Women, War, and Work: The Impact of World War I on Women Workers in the United States* (Westport, Conn.: Greenwood Press, 1980), 8.

87.   Greenwald, *Women, War, and Work*, 87–138, 97.

88.   See Harvey Kantor and David B. Tyack, "Introduction: Historical Perspectives on Vocationalism in American Education," in *Work, Youth, and Schooling*, ed. Harvey Kantor and David B. Tyack, 1–14.

89.   See Clifford, "Marry, Stitch, Die or Do Worse," 251ff.

90.   For more information on the Hampton Institute, see Mary Lou Hultgren and Paulette F. Molin, *To Lead and to Serve: American Indian Education at Hampton Institute, 1878–1923* (Virginia Foundation for the Humanities and Public Policy in Cooperation with Hampton University, 1989); David Wallace Adams, *Education for Extinction: American Indians and the Boarding School Experience, 1875–1928* (Lawrence, Kans.: University Press of Kansas, 1995).

91.   Jackson Davis, "Report of Supervisor of Colored Rural Elementary Schools from May 15 to September 1, 1910," 1, in Southern Education Board Papers, #680, Series 2.4, African Americans, 1898–1911, fol. 91, in Southern Historical Collection (SHC), University of North Carolina at Chapel Hill.

92.   See Booker T. Washington, *Up from Slavery: An Autobiography* (New York: A. L. Burt, 1901); Tuskegee and its People; Their Ideals and Achievements, ed. Booker T. Washington (New York: Negro Universities Press, 1969).

93.   R. C. Bruce, *Address in New Old South Church*, Boston (1904), 7.

94.   "Clayton Giles Bellamy Writes on Development of Education in County," *The Wilmington Star*, Sunday, 20 March 1922, in Noble Papers, fol. 5, vol. 9, SHC.

95.   Jackson Davis, "Report of Supervisor of Colored Rural Elementary Schools from May 15 to September 1, 1910," 5, in Southern Education Board Papers, fol. 191, SHC.

96.   Powers, *The "Girl Question" in Education*, 88.

97.   Clifford, "Marry, Stitch, Die, or Do Worse," 243, 252.

98.   Enrollment data for trigonometry were not published until 1900. In that year, trigonometry was the only subject in which boys constituted a majority. Still, the subject attracted a pitiful number of students, as fewer than three percent of boys enrolled during the last four years of high school. See Latimer, *What's Happened to Our High Schools?* 149. Lattimer's data are reported as the percentage of each sex enrolled. Using the percentages and overall enrollment figures, I calculated the enrollments in each subject.

99.   Latimer, *What's Happened to Our High Schools?*, 68.

100. C. R. Mann, *Physics Teaching as It is and as It Might Be in Wisconsin*, (Madison, Wisc.: Democrat Printing Co., 1910), 3.

101. Quoted in Clifford, "Marry, Stitch, Die, or Do Worse," 259.

102. Alice Kessler Harris, *Out to Work: A History of Wage-Earning Women in the United States* (Oxford, England: Oxford University Press, 1982), 116.

103. Rebecca Harding Davis, "The Curse in Education," in *Report of the Commissioner of Education for the Year 1898–99*, vol. 2 (Washington, D.C.: Government Printing Office, 1900), 1333–1335.

104. Quoted in Clifford, "Marry, Stitch, Die, or Do Worse," 249.

105. *Eleventh Biennial Report of the Department of Public Instruction [Wisconsin]*, 99, WSHS.

106. *Report of the Special Committee on Education, Wisconsin Legislature* (17 December 1910), 4, WSHS.

107. C. P. Cary, State Superintendent, *Requirements and Suggestions Relating to High Schools of Wisconsin* (August 1917), 9, WSHS.

108. E. R. Breslich, "The Girl and Algebra," *The School Review* 22 (January–December 1914): 562–564.

109. Ernst R. Breslich, "Mathematics," in *A Half Century of Science and Mathematics Teaching* (Oak Park, Ill.: Central Association of Science and Mathematics Teachers, Inc., 1950), 58.

110. Jean Lave, *Cognition in Practice: Mind, Mathematics and Culture in Everyday Life*, (Cambridge, Mass.: Cambridge University Press, 1988), 23–24.

111. Meyer Bloomfield, "Briefs of Papers on Vocational Guidance," in *Readings in Vocational Guidance*, 13–18; Donald E. Super, *The Dynamics of Vocational Adjustment* (New York: Harper & Bros., 1942).

112. "The Vocational Education of Females," in *American Education and Vocationalism: A Documentary History, 1870–1970*, ed. Marvin Lazerson and W. Norton Grubb (New York: Teachers College Press, 1974), 114.

113. Edward L. Thorndike, "The University and Vocational Guidance," in *Readings in Vocational Guidance*, 100.

114. Marguerite Stockman Dickson, *Vocational Guidance for Girls* (Chicago: Rand McNally & Co., 1919), 3; 16. NEA Report of the Committee, "The Vocational Education of Females," in *American Education and Vocationalism: A Documentary History, 1870–1970*, 114–115.

115. "The Vocational Education of Females," in *American Education and Vocationalism: A Documentary History, 1870–1970*, 114–115.

116. For example, see Dickson, *Vocational Guidance for Girls*; Latham Hatcher and Emery N. Ferriss, *Guiding Rural Boys and Girls* (New York: McGraw-Hill, 1930).

117. "History of the Committee on Status of Women," 3, box 5, Elsa Allen Papers, Special Collections, Cornell University.

118. For example, in giving consideration to the question, "What work, what profession does science offer to women?" Mary W. Whitney, a stanch advocate of science for women, nevertheless concluded that, "Scientific investigation is largely without pay, and will always be so." Whitney, "Scientific Study and Work for Women," *Education* (Sept.–July 1883) 61.

119. See Sarah Stage and Virginia B. Vincenti, eds., *Rethinking Home Economics: Women and the History of a Profession* (Ithaca, N.Y.: Cornell University Press, 1997).

120. Derived from Table 6.9 in Rossiter, *Women Scientists in America*, 157.

Chapter 8

1. Tyree Goodwin Minton, "The History of the Nature-Study Movement and Its Role in the Development of Environmental Education" (Ed.D diss., University of Massachusetts, 1980), 139.

2. See Harriet Zuckerman, Jonathan R. Cole, and John T. Bruer, eds., *The Outer Circle: Women in the Scientific Community* (New Haven, Conn.: Yale University Press, 1991), 12; Maxine Schwartz Seller, *Women Educators in the United States, 1820–1993,* ed. Maxine Schwartz Seller (Westport, Conn.: Greenwood Press, 1994), xxi-xxii.

3. Clifton F. Hodge, *Nature Study and Life* (Boston: Ginn, 1902), 30.

4. Charles B. Scott, *Nature Study and the Child* (Boston: D.C. Heath & Co., 1900), 37.

5. See discussion in Herbert M. Kliebard, *The Struggle for the American Curriculum, 1893–1958* (New York: Routledge, 1986), 105ff.

6. For a discussion of these changes, see George DeBoer, *A History of Ideas in Science Education: Implications for Practice* (New York: Teachers College Press, 1991), especially Chapters 4–6.

7. A. Hunter Dupree, *Science in the Federal Government: A History of Policies and Activities* (Baltimore: Johns Hopkins University Press, 1986), 322.

8. Ibid., 302–318.

9. For a discussion of economic and social changes in this period, see A. Hunter Dupree, "Transition to a Business Era," in ibid., 327–343; Glen Porter, *The Rise of Big Business, 1860–1910* (New York: Crowell, 1973); Alfred D. Chandler Jr., *The Visible Hand: The Managerial Revolution in American Business* (Cambridge, Mass.: Belknap Press, 1977).

10. D. Kelly Weisberg, "Barred from the Bar: Women and Legal Education in the United States, 1870–1890," *Journal of Legal Education* 28 (1977).

11. Mary Roth Walsh, *Doctors Wanted, No Women Need Apply: Sexual Barriers in the Medical Profession, 1835–1975* (New Haven, Conn.: Yale University Press, 1977).

12. Quoted in Harvey Strum, "Discrimination at Syracuse University," *History of Higher Education Annual* 4 (1984): 111.

13. A. Hunter Dupree, *Science in the Federal Government,* 326–329.

14. Margaret Rossiter, *Women Scientists in America: Struggles and Strategies to 1940* (Baltimore: The Johns Hopkins University Press, 1982), 269–270.

15. For a discussion of this case, see Margaret Rossiter, *Women Scientists in America,* 190–193.

16. For discussion of the backlash against women teachers in education, see David Tyack and Elizabeth Hansot, *Learning Together: A History of Coeducation in American Public Schools* (N.Y.: Russell Sage Foundation, 1992), especially chapters 6–9; Jane Bernard Powers, *The "Girl Question" in Education: Vocational Education for Young Women in the Progressive Era* (London, England: Falmer, 1992).

17. J. E. Armstrong, "Limited Segregation," *School Review* 14 (December 1906): 729.

18. Josephine Conger-Kaneko, "The 'Effeminization' of the United States," *The World's Work* 12 (May 1906): 7522.

19. Walter F. Wilcox, "More Men Than Women in This Country," *Public Opinion* 40 (June 1906): 692–693.

20. Quoted in the *Omaha City Schools Annual Report of the Board of Education* (Omaha, Nebr.: Rees Printing Co., 1886), 39; *United States Commissioner of Education Report for 1889,* 2 (Washington, D.C.: Government Printing Office, 1890), 775. Tyack and Hansot elaborate on this trend in *Learning Together,* 165–200.

21. F. E. DeFoe and C. N. Thurber, "Where Are All the High School Boys?" *School Review* 8 (April 1900): 234–243. The quote is on page 240.

22. Harris is quoted in Tyack and Hansot, *Learning Together,* 158.

23. William Lee Howard, "The Feminization of the High-School," *Arena* 35 (June 1906): 595.

24. G. Stanley Hall, "Feminization in School and Home," *World's Work* 16 (May 1908): 10237–10240.

25. Charles De Garmo, "Colonel Parker's Theory of Concentration," Parker Scrapbook 10, the University of Chicago Library Department of Special Collections (hereafter SCUC). This newsclipping does not indicate the source or date.

26. A Conservative Progressist [*sic*], "Opposition to the 'New Education,'" *The Journal of Education* (11 February 1886), Parker Scrapbook 6, SCUC.

27. G. Stanley Hall, "Introduction," in Hodge, *Nature Study and Life*, xv.

28. John M. Coulter et al., *Practical Nature Study and Elementary Agriculture* (New York: D. Appleton and Co., 1909), 35–39, 68.

29. B. P. Reed, "Bufo Junior, A Story for the Pupils When Rearing Tadpoles," *Nature-Study Review* 19 (March 1923): 132.

30. James Troop, "A Study of Our Insect Enemies," *Purdue Nature-Study Leaflets* 11 (Lafayette, Ind.: Purdue University, 1898): 3.

31. Charles A. McMurry, *Special Method in Science for the First Four Grades of the Common School* (Bloomington, Ill.: Public School Publishing Co., 1896).

32. E. L. Thorndike, "The Influence of the Number of Men Teachers Upon the Enrollment of Boys in Public High Schools," *Educational Review* 37 (January 1909): 71–75.

33. Patricia Schmuck, "Women School Employees in the United States," in Schmuck, ed., *Women Educators: Employees of Schools in Western Countries* (Albany, N.Y.: State University of New York Press, 1987), 75–76; Michael McGiffert, *The Higher Learning in Colorado: An Historical Study, 1860–1945* (Denver: Sage Books, 1964), 31ff.

34. Eleanor M. Colleton, "From the Viewpoint of Its Application to Girls in Elementary Schools," in *Readings in Vocational Guidance*, ed. Meyer Bloomfield (Boston: Ginn & Co., 1915), 119.

35. Alice Kessler-Harris, *Out to Work: A History of Wage-Earning Women in the United States* (New York: Oxford University Press, 1982), 116.

36. John Rury, "Urban Enrollment at the Turn of the Century: Gender as an Intervening Variable," *Urban Education* 28 (1988): 68–87; Tyack and Hansot, *Learning Together*, 172.

37. Carol Hymowitz and Michaele Weissman, *A History of Women in America* (New York: Bantam Books, 1978), 220ff.

38. Frank N. Freeman, "Introduction," in *The Thirty-Seventh Yearbook of the National Society for the Study of Education, Part II: The Scientific Movement in Education* (Bloomington, Ill.: Public School Publishing Co., 1938), 1.

39. Quoted in *Phi Delta Kappa Directory, 1931* (Fulton, Mo.: Ovid Bell Press, 1931), 84. The directory includes the entire constitution and bylaws of the fraternity; "Guide to the College of Education Records 1900–1926" (hereafter CER), SCUC, 1980, 8; *Phi Delta Kappa Directory, 1931*, 17–73.

40. Dean M. E. Haggerty to Dean W. S. Gray, 6 October 1923, file 10, box 34, CER, SCUC.

41. Woodie T. White, "The Decline of the Classroom and the Chicago Study of Education, 1909–1929," *American Journal of Education* 90 (February 1982): 168.

42. Hymowitz and Weissman, *A History of Women in America*, 222–223.

43. Vernon Bowyer, "A Preliminary Report on the History of Zeta Chapter of Phi Delta Kappa," in Vernon Bowyer to Mr. J. David Houser, 31 October 1923, file 2, box 43, CER, SCUC. The 1930 Phi Delta Kappa directory included the names of such eminent educational leaders as the philosopher John Dewey; psychologist Edward L. Thorndike; Ellwood Cubberley of Stanford; Elmer Ellsworth Brown, chancellor of New York University (formerly of the United States Commissioner of Education); Charles Hubbard Judd of the University of Chicago; and George S. Counts and Otis Caldwell of Teachers College, Columbia. These men are listed as members in the *Phi Delta Kappa Directory* (Fulton, Mo.: The Ovid Bell Press, 1931), 66.

44. William S. Gray, "Phi Delta Kappa," a monograph prepared by Gray in response to a written request from B. T. Baldwin at the State University of Iowa, 2 October 1922, file 2, box 34, CER, SCUC; Paul M. Cook, "The History of the Organization and Development of Phi Delta Kappa," in *Phi Delta Kappa Directory* (Fulton, Mo.: The Ovid Bell Press, 1931), 42–43.

45. George L. B. Fraser to W. S. Gray, 9 December 1923, file 8, box 34, CER, SCUC.

46. W. H. Burton to W. S. Gray, 21 July 1922, file 5, box 34, CER, SCUC.

47. R. H. Jesse to Nathaniel Butler, 28 May 1907, file 9, box 3, CER, SCUC.

48. Nathaniel Butler to R. H. Jesse, 27 July 1907, file 9, box 3, CER, SCUC.

49. Charles H. Judd to William S. Gray, 15 March 1926, file 7, box 32, CER, SCUC.

50. Willard J. Jacobson, "The First Meeting of the National Association for Research in Science Teaching" (paper presented at the meeting of N.A.R.S.T., Cincinnati, Ohio, 23 March 1977), box 1, Gerald S. Craig Papers, unprocessed additions, Wisconsin State Historical Society (hereafter WSHS). I identified members as Phi Delta Kappans if their names were included as such in the *Phi Delta Kappa Directory, 1931*. Not surprisingly, Phi Delta Kappa members composed a majority of the editorial board and associate editors of *Science Education* throughout the 1920s and 1930s. For example, in 1928, the chairman of the editorial board, Charles J. Pieper of New York University's School of Education, was a fraternity member, as were thirteen (sixty-two percent) of the journal's twenty-one associate editors. Only one associate editor was a woman: Florence G. Billig, a graduate of Teachers College, Columbia, who held a position with the State Board of Education in Sacramento, California.

51. Typescript titled "The Early Years of AETS," box 1, Craig Papers, unprocessed additions, WSHS. Glenn and Johnson are listed as members in *Phi Delta Kappa Directory, 1931*, 182, 216.

52. Willard J. Jacobson, "A History of the Department of Science Education, Teachers College, Columbia University" (paper presented as part of the session "Illuminating the Present from the Past: The History of Science Education" at the twenty-sixth National Convention of the National Science Teachers Association, Washington, D.C., 7 April 1978), box 1, Craig Papers, unprocessed additions, WSHS.

53. Victor Crowell Jr. to E. Laurence Palmer, 20 May 1930, file 5, box 2, American Nature Study Society Records, SCCU.

54. Clarence Pruitt to Gerald S. Craig, 10 April 1933, file 1, box 1, Craig Papers, WSHS. Pruitt is listed as a member of Phi Delta Kappa in *Phi Delta Kappa Directory, 1931*, 281.

55. See Alice Kessler-Harris, *In Pursuit of Equity: Women, Men, and the Quest for Economic Citizenship in 20ᵗʰ Century America* (New York: Oxford University Press, 2001), 56–63. The quote is from page 58.

56. A. W. Miller to Gerald S. Craig, 23 March 1934, file 9, box 5, Craig Papers, WSHS.

57. A. W. Miller to Gerald S. Craig, 12 April 1934, file 9, box 5, Craig Papers, WSHS.

58. Gerald S. Craig to A.W. Miller, 19 May 1936, file 9, box 5, Craig Papers, WSHS.

59. Harry A. Greene, "The Status of the Sciences in North Central High Schools in 1916," *School Science and Mathematics* 18 (May 1918): 421–422.

60. Two influential documents published during this period were the National Education Association, *Reorganization of Science in Secondary Schools: A Report of the Commission on the Reorganization of Secondary Education* (Washington, D.C.: U.S. Government Printing Office, 1920), and the National Society for the Study of Education, *A Program for Teaching Science: Thirty-First Yearbook of the National Society for the Study of Education* (Chicago: University of Chicago Press, 1932). For a discussion of the aims and goals of prominent science educators during this period, see George DeBoer, *A History of Ideas in Science Education*.

61. S. Ralph Powers, "Preface," in Orra Underhill, *The Origins and Development of Elementary School Science* (Chicago: Scott, Foresman, 1941). See also Gerald S. Craig, *Tentative Course of Study in Elementary Science for Grades III and IV* (New York: Teachers College Bureau of Publications, 1927); Gerald S. Craig, "The Program of Science in the Elementary School," in *The Thirty-First Yearbook of the National Society for the Study of Education, vol. 1: A Program for Teaching Science* (Bloomington, Ill.: Public School Publishing Co., 1932), 133–162; S. Ralph Powers, "The Plan of the Public Schools and the Program of Science Teaching," in ibid., 1–11; S. Ralph Powers, "Some Criticisms of Current Practices in the Teaching of Science in Elementary and Secondary Schools," in ibid., 13–26; S. Ralph Powers, "What Are Some of the Contributions of Science to Liberal Education?" in ibid., 27–40; S. Ralph Powers, "The Ob-

jectives of Science Teaching in Relation to the Aim of Education," in ibid., 41–57; Francis D. Curtis, "Investigations Relating to the Content of Science Courses," in ibid., 109–119; Francis D. Curtis, "Curricular Developments in the Teaching of Science," in ibid., 121–131.

62. Craig to A. W. Miller, 1939, file 9, box 5, Craig Papers, WSHS.
63. "Will Secede from the Normal School," newsclipping dated 17 June 1899, Scrapbook 12, Francis Wayland Parker Scrapbooks, SCUC.
64. Geraldine Jonçich Clifford and James W. Guthrie, *Ed School: A Brief for Professional Education* (Chicago: The University of Chicago Press, 1988), 160–161.
65. Powers, "Some Criticisms of Current Practices," 17–18.
66. For example, see Anna Comstock, "The Teaching of Nature-Study," in *Handbook of Nature Study* (Ithaca, N.Y.: Comstock Publishing Co., 1927 [1911]), 1–24.
67. Craig, "The Program of Science in the Elementary School," 145.
68. W. W. McSpadden to Gerald Craig, 26 May 1932, box 6, folder 9, Craig Papers, WSHS.
69. "Ginn & Co. Publishers Annual Royalty Statement to Nov. 30, 1961," in Craig Papers, box 2, unprocessed additions, WSHS. As of 1958, the average yearly royalty payment to Craig during the previous five years was $38,689.33. In 1955, Craig's base salary as a full professor at Teachers College was $8.000.00. See letter from the president of Teachers College to Craig, 15 February 1955, file titled "Teaching Appointments," in ibid.
70. Robert Stollberg to Gerald S. Craig, 12 January 1949, file 2, box 3, Craig Papers, WSHS. I have added the italics for emphasis.
71. Dr. Watson L. Johns to E. H. Annear, 31 March 1950, folder 1, box 3, Craig Papers, WSHS.
72. Dorothy M. Compton to E. Laurence Palmer, 21 August 1952; Robert M. McClung to E. Lawrence Palmer, 11 August 1952, in "Letters from Students, Associates, and Friends," box 4177, E. Laurence Palmer Papers, SCCU.
73. Leo F. Hadsall, professor of biology at Fresno State College, to E. Lawrence Palmer, 20 August 1952, box 4177, "Letters from Students, Associates, and Friends" (bound in commemoration of Palmer's retirement), E. Lawrence Palmer Papers, SCCU.
74. See "Boy Culture," in E. Anthony Rotundo, *American Manhood: Transformations in Masculinity from the Revolution to the Modern Era* (New York: Basic Books, 1993), 31–55.
75. For contemporary views concerning subjects inherently interesting to boys, see Irving King, "The Vocational Interests, Study Habits, and Amusements of the Pupils in Certain High Schools in Iowa," in *Readings in Vocational Guidance*, 174.
76. Gerald S. Craig, "Kindergarten Children Learn Science Lessons in Modern City School," *Herald Tribune*, box 1, Gerald S. Craig Papers, unprocessed additions, WSHS. A handwritten note at the top of this news clipping states that it was published in 1924.
77. Ibid.
78. Harriet Zuckerman, Jonathan R. Cole, and John T. Bruer, *The Outer Circle: Women in the Scientific Community*, 12.
79. Quoted in Alice Kessler-Harris, *In Pursuit of Equity: Women, Men, and the Quest for Economic Citizenship in 20th Century America* (New York: Oxford University Press, 2001), 203.
80. Alice Kessler-Harris, *Out to Work: A History of Wage-Earning Women in the United States,* 286–287.
81. See Stephen Peeps, "A B.A. for the G.I. . . . Why?" *History of Education Quarterly* 24 (Winter 1984): 513–525.
82. Jackie M. Blount, *Destined to Rule the Schools; Women and the Superintendency, 1873–1995* (Albany, N.Y.: State University of New York Press, 1998), 113–115.
83. Jackie M. Blount, *Destined to Rule the Schools,* 111–112. The quote is on page 1.

84. See Herbert M. Kliebard, *The Struggle for the American Curriculum, 1893–1958*, 240–270; See also Diane Ravitch, *The Troubled Crusade: American Education, 1945–1980* (New York: Basic Books, 1983).

85. Quoted in Kliebard, *The Struggle for the American Curriculum*, 251.

86. See "Statistics of City School Systems for the Year 1931–32," in *Biennial Survey of Education, 1930–32* (Washington, D.C.: U.S. Government Printing Office, 1935), 2.

87. "History of the Fair Labor Standards Act of 1938," U.S. Department of Labor, *http://www.dol.gov/dol/esa/public/regs/statutes/whd/0001.fair.pdf*, 20 January 2002.

88. See Nancy Beadie and Kim Tolley, eds., *Chartered Schools: Two Hundred Years of Independent Academies, 1727–1925* (New York: Routledge, 2002), especially Chapters 5 and 15.

89. See Kliebard, *The Struggle for the American Curriculum*, 240–270.

90. For instance, Wayne Urban and Jennings Wagoner raise this question in *American Education: A History* (New York: McGraw Hill, 2000), 290–291.

91. Quoted in DeBoer, *A History of Ideas in Science Education*, 141.

92. See David L. Angus and Jeffrey E. Mirel, *The Failed Promise of the American High School, 1890–1995* (New York: Teacher's College Press, 1999); Harvard Committee, *General Education in a Free Society* (Cambridge, Mass.: Harvard University Press, 1945), 159; DeBoer, *A History of Ideas in Science Education*, 140–142.

93. William O. Brooks and George R. Tracey, *Modern Physical Science* (New York: Henry Holt and Co., 1952). The quote is from page vi.

94. Francis D. Curtis and George Greisen Mallinson, *Science in Daily Life* (Boston: Ginn & Co., 1955), 13.

95. Richard Brinckerhoff et al., *The Physical World: A Course in Physical Science* (New York: Harcourt Brace & Co., 1958). The photographs I refer to are on pages 95, 129, 262, and 264.

96. See Kliebard, *The Struggle for the American Curriculum*, 259–260.

97. Arthur E. Bestor Jr., *Educational Wastelands: The Retreat from Learning in Our Public Schools* (Urbana, Ill.: University of Illinois Press, 1953), 12–13.

98. Hyman G. Rickover, *Education and Freedom* (New York: E. P. Dutton, 1959), 154.

99. Ibid.

100. Advertisement by D. C. Heath & Company in the front matter of *School Science and Mathematics* 59 (May 1959).

101. William W. Cooley, "Identifying Potential Scientists: A Multivariate Approach," *School Science and Mathematics* 59 (May 1959): 381–396. The quotes are on pages 394, 381, and 395, respectively.

102. This study is discussed in Margaret Mead, "Closing the Gap Between the Scientists and the Others," *Daedalus* (Winter 1959): 139–145. The original study is Margaret Mead and Rhoda Métraux, "Image of the Scientist among High-School Students," *Science* 126 (30 August 1957): 384–390. Interestingly, the original study evidences a surprising degree of bias, because the researchers differentiated their questions by gender. They asked boys to respond to: "If I were going to be a scientist, I would *not* like to be the kind of scientist who . . ."; whereas they asked girls to respond to: "If I were going to marry a scientist, I would *not* like to marry the kind of scientist who" (385).

103. DeBoer, *A History of Ideas in Science Education*, 147–158. The quote is on page 152.

104. Kliebard, *The Struggle for the American Curriculum*, 268–269; The quote is from George E. DeBoer, *A History of Ideas in Science Education*, 166.

105. See George E. DeBoer, *A History of Ideas in Science Education*, 166–171.

106. Ernest Nagel, "The Place of Science in a Liberal Education," *Daedalus* (Winter 1959), 64.

107. Reinhold Niebuhr, "Education and the World Scene," in ibid., 117.

108. Nagel, "The Place of Science in a Liberal Education," in ibid., 65.

109. Sidney Hook, "The End and Content of Education," in ibid., 22.

110. Nagel, "The Place of Science in a Liberal Education," in ibid., 65.
111. Ibid.
112. Mead, "Closing the Gap Between the Scientists and the Others," in ibid., 141.
113. Ibid., 139.
114. Ibid.
115. Ibid., 139–140.
116. Ibid., 141.
117. Ibid., 139.
118. Harriet Zuckerman, Jonathan R. Cole, and John T. Bruer, *The Outer Circle: Women in the Scientific Community,* 12.
119. Almira Hart Lincoln Phelps, *Familiar Lectures on Botany* (New York: Huntington and Savage, 1846), 200; William Johnston, *An Address on Female Education* (Columbus, Ohio: Charles Scott & Co., 1845), 16.
120. "Earned Degrees in the Biological/Life Sciences Conferred by Degree-Granting Institutions, by Level of Degree and Sex of Student: 1951–52 to 1997–98," Center for Education Statistics, *http://nces.ed.gov/pubs2001/digest/dt279.html,* 22 January 2002; "Earned Degrees in the Physical Sciences Conferred by Degree-Granting Institutions, by Level of Degree and Sex of Student: 1959–60 to 1997–98. *http://nces.ed.gov/pubs2001/digest/dt292.html,* 22 January 2002.

Conclusion

1. This view appears most recently in George DeBoer, *A History of Ideas in Science Education: Implications for Practice* (New York: Teachers College Press, 1991).
2. Dan C. Lortie, *Schoolteacher, a Sociological Study* (Chicago: University of Chicago Press, 1975), 39–40.
3. Mary W. Whitney, "Scientific Study and Work for Women," *Education* 3 (September–July 1883), 59.
4. Almira Hart Lincoln Phelps, *Lectures to Young Ladies* (Boston: Carter, Hendee and Co., 1833), 247.
5. Patricia Phillips, *The Scientific Lady: A Social History of Women's Scientific Interests, 1520–1918* (London: Weidenfeld and Nicolson, 1990).
6. Ernest Nagel, "The Place of Science in a Liberal Education," *Daedalus* (Winter 1959), 65.
7. Margaret Mead, "Closing the Gap Between the Scientists and the Others," in ibid., 139–140.
8. See Table 8.5.
9. For example, see "Successful Teaching Strategies," in *How Schools Shortchange Girls: The AAUW Report* (New York: Marlowe & Co., 1995), 124–127; Muriel Lederman and Ingrid Bartsch, eds., *The Gender and Science Reader* (London: Routledge, 2001), especially the introduction; Joan Skolnick, Carol Langbort, and Lucille Day, *How to Encourage Girls in Math & Science: Strategies for Parents and Educators* (Englewood-Cliffs, N.J.: Prentice-Hall, 1982). A landmark book on women-centered education remains Mary Field Belenky et al., *Women's Ways of Knowing: The Development of Self, Voice, and Mind* (New York: Basic Books, 1986).
10. "Sometimes It's Hard to Be a Man," *The Economist* (22 December 2001–4 January 2002), 33.
11. Edward Pickering, as director of Harvard College Observatory, began to hire female assistants in astronomy near the end of the nineteenth century, but fewer employment opportunities existed in astronomy than in natural history. For a discussion of the women at Harvard College Observatory, see Margaret Rossiter, *Women Scientists in America: Struggles and Strategies to 1940* (Baltimore, Md.: Johns Hopkins University Press, 1982), 53–57.

12. See David Noble, *A World without Women: The Christian Clerical Culture of Western Science* (Oxford: Oxford University Press, 1993); Margaret Wertheim, *Pythagoras' Trousers: God, Physics, and the Gender Wars* (New York: Random House, 1995).

13. See "Degrees Earned by Women," National Center for Education Statistics, *http://nces.ed.gov/programs/coe/2001/section3/indicator30.html,* 22 January 2002.

14. See "Earned Degrees in the Physical Sciences Conferred by Degree-Granting Institutions, by Level of Degree and Sex of Student: 1959–60 to 1997–98," National Center for Education Statistics, *http://nces.ed.gov/pubs2001/digest/dt292.html,* 22 January 2002.

15. For discussions of culturally developed gender differences, see Nel Noddings, *Caring: A Feminine Approach to Ethics and Moral Education* (Berkeley, Calif.: University of California Press, 1984); Carol Gilligan, *In a Different Voice: Psychological Theory and Women's Development* (Cambridge, Mass.: Harvard University Press, 1982); Jane Roland Martin, *Reclaiming a Conversation: The Ideal of the Educated Woman* (New Haven, Conn.: Yale University Press, 1985). For an overview of radical feminist critiques of science, see Hilary Rose, *Love, Power, and Knowledge: Towards a Feminist Transformation of the Sciences* (Bloomington, Ind.: Indiana University Press, 1994). See also Sandra Harding, *The Science Question in Feminism* (Ithaca, N.Y.: Cornell University Press, 1986); Sandra Harding, *Whose Science? Whose Knowledge? Thinking from Women's Lives* (Ithaca, N.Y.: Cornell University Press, 1991); H. Longino, "Can There Be a Feminist Science?" in *Feminism and Science*, ed. Nancy Tuana (Bloomington, Ind.: Indiana University Press, 1989), 45–57; Sandra Harding and Merrill B. Hintikka, eds., *Discovering Reality: Feminist Perspectives on Epistemology, Metaphysics, Methodology, and Philosophy of Science* (Dordrecht, Holland; Boston: D. Reidel, 1983); Jan Harding, ed., *Perspectives on Gender and Science* (London: Falmer Press, 1986). For applications of feminist theory to science education, see Angela Calabrese Barton, "Liberatory Science Education: Weaving Connections between Feminist Theory and Science Education," *Curriculum Inquiry* 27, no. 2 (1997): 141–163. For an overview of the influence of feminist theory on the movement to establish single-sex schools, see David Tyack and Elizabeth Hansot, *Learning Together: A History of Coeducation in American Public Schools* (New York: Russell Sage Foundation, 1992), 279–292.

16. See Anthony W. Clare, *On Men: Masculinity in Crisis* (London: Chatto & Windus, 2000); Warren Farrell, *The Myth of Male Power: Why Men Are the Disposable Sex* (New York: Simon & Schuster, 1993); Christina Hoff Sommers, *The War Against Boys: How Misguided Feminism Is Harming Our Young Men* (New York: Simon & Schuster, 2000); Michael Gurian, *Boys and Girls Learn Differently! A Guide for Teachers and Parents* (San Francisco: Jossey-Bass, 2001). The quotes are from Gurian, *Boys and Girls Learn Differently!,* pages 45, 52, and 46, respectively.

17. For discussion of changing images of the "tough" woman, see Sherrie Inness, *Tough Girls: Women Warriors and Wonder Women in Popular Culture* (New Haven, Conn.: Yale University Press, 1998); Margarita Stocker, *Judith, Sexual Warrior: Women and Power in Western Culture* (Philadelphia: University of Pennsylvania Press, 1998).

18. See Barrie Thorne, "Children and Gender: Constructions of Difference," in Deborah L. Rhode, ed., *Theoretical Perspectives on Sexual Difference* (New Haven, Conn.: Yale University Press, 1990), 100–113.

19. Elga Wasserman, *The Door in the Dream: Conversations with Eminent Women in Science* (Washington, D. C.: Joseph Henry Press, 2000), 206.

20. See "Science Coursetaking: Percentage Distribution of High School Graduates According to the Highest Levels of Science Courses Taken, by Student and School Characteristics, 1998," National Center for Education Statistics, *http://nces.ed.gov/programs/coe//2000/charts/chart39c.html,* 22 January 2002; "Percentage of High School Graduates Taking Selected Mathematics and Science Courses in High School, by Sex and Race/Ethnicity: 1982 to 1998," ibid., *http://nces.ed.gov/pubs2001/digest/dtl40.html,* 22 January 2002.

21.   See John L. Rury, *Education and Women's Work: Female Schooling and the Division of Labor in Urban America, 1870–1930* (Albany, N.Y.: State University of New York Press, 1991); Jane Bernard Powers, *The "Girl Question" in Education: Vocational Education for Young Women in the Progressive Era* (London: The Falmer Press, 1992); Karen L. Graves, *Girls' Schooling during the Progressive Era: From Female Scholar to Domesticated Citizen* (New York: Garland, 1998).

Index